村田雄介

Yusuke Murata

Riichiro Inagaki

"Don't cut corners!"
"Don't cut corners!"
"You're tired, but don't start cutting corners now!" I've heard that George Morikawa, the author of *Fighting Spirit*, repeats such things to himself when he works on a manuscript. They're simple words, but I think that's precisely why they're able to keep my spirits up when I'm buried under work. I like those words, so I've taken it upon myself to start copying him.

I went to America for research. Since I went to the West Coast before, this time I went to the East Coast. I went to so many places in such a short time that I barely had enough time to get from place to place. I felt like I was doing nothing but running around the whole time! Sorta like Sena! (I'm not as fast as he is, though...) I'll tell you more in future volumes.

Eyeshield 21 is the most exciting football manga to hit the scene. A collaborative effort between writer Riichiro Inagaki and artist Yusuke Murata, *Eyeshield 21* was originally serialized in Japan's *Weekly Shonen Jump*. An OAV created for Shueisha's Anime Tour is available in Japan, and the *Eyeshield 21* hit animated TV series debuted in spring 2005!

EYESHIELD 21
Vol. 34: The Last of the Deimon Devil Bats
SHONEN JUMP ADVANCED Manga Edition

STORY BY RIICHIRO INAGAKI
ART BY YUSUKE MURATA

English Adaptation & Translation/John Werry, HC Language Solutions, Inc.
Touch-up Art & Lettering/James Gaubatz
Cover Design/Sean Lee
Interior Design/Matt Hinrichs
Editors/Megan Bates, Kit Fox

Printed in Canada

Published by VIZ Media, LLC
P.O. Box 77010
San Francisco, CA 94107

10 9 8 7 6 5 4 3 2 1
First printing, January 2011

www.viz.com

RATED T+ FOR OLDER TEEN
PARENTAL ADVISORY
EYESHIELD 21 is rated T+ for Older Teen and is recommended for ages 16 and up. It contains graphic fantasy violence and crude humor.
ratings.viz.com

THE WORLD'S MOST CUTTING-EDGE MANGA
SHONEN JUMP ADVANCED
www.shonenjump.com

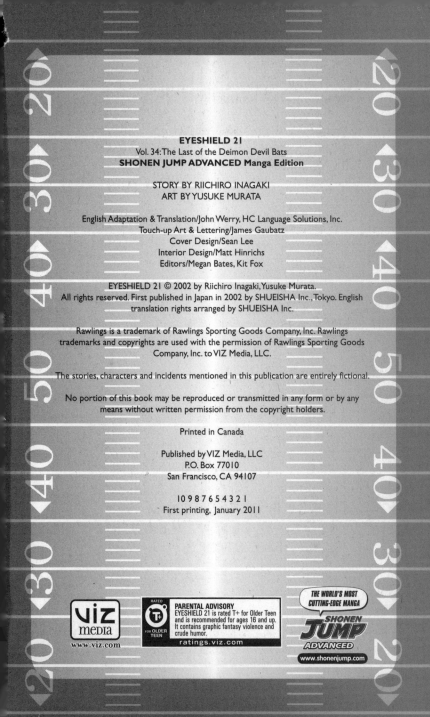

Vol. 34: The Last of the Deimon Devil Bats

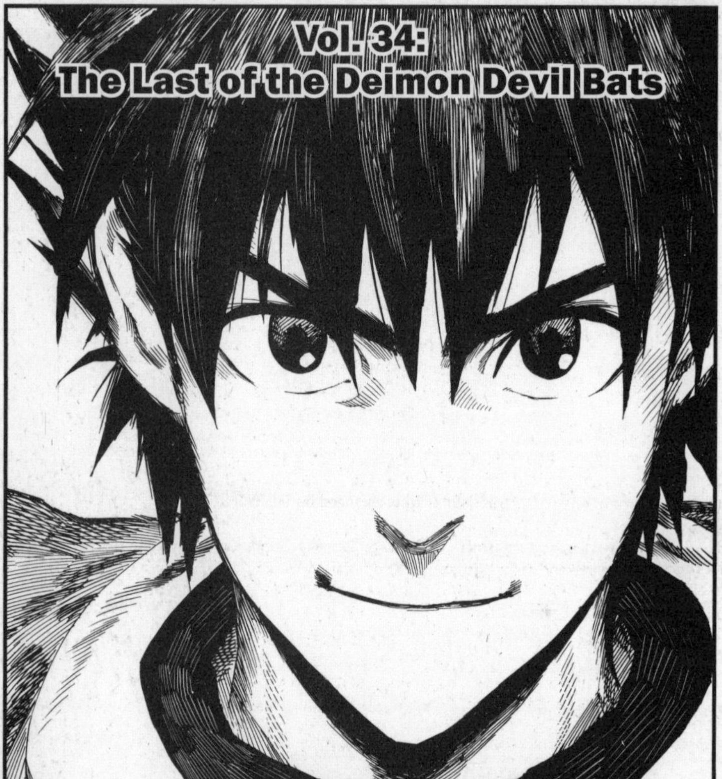

EYESHIELD 21

STORY BY
RIICHIRO INAGAKI

ART BY
YUSUKE MURATA

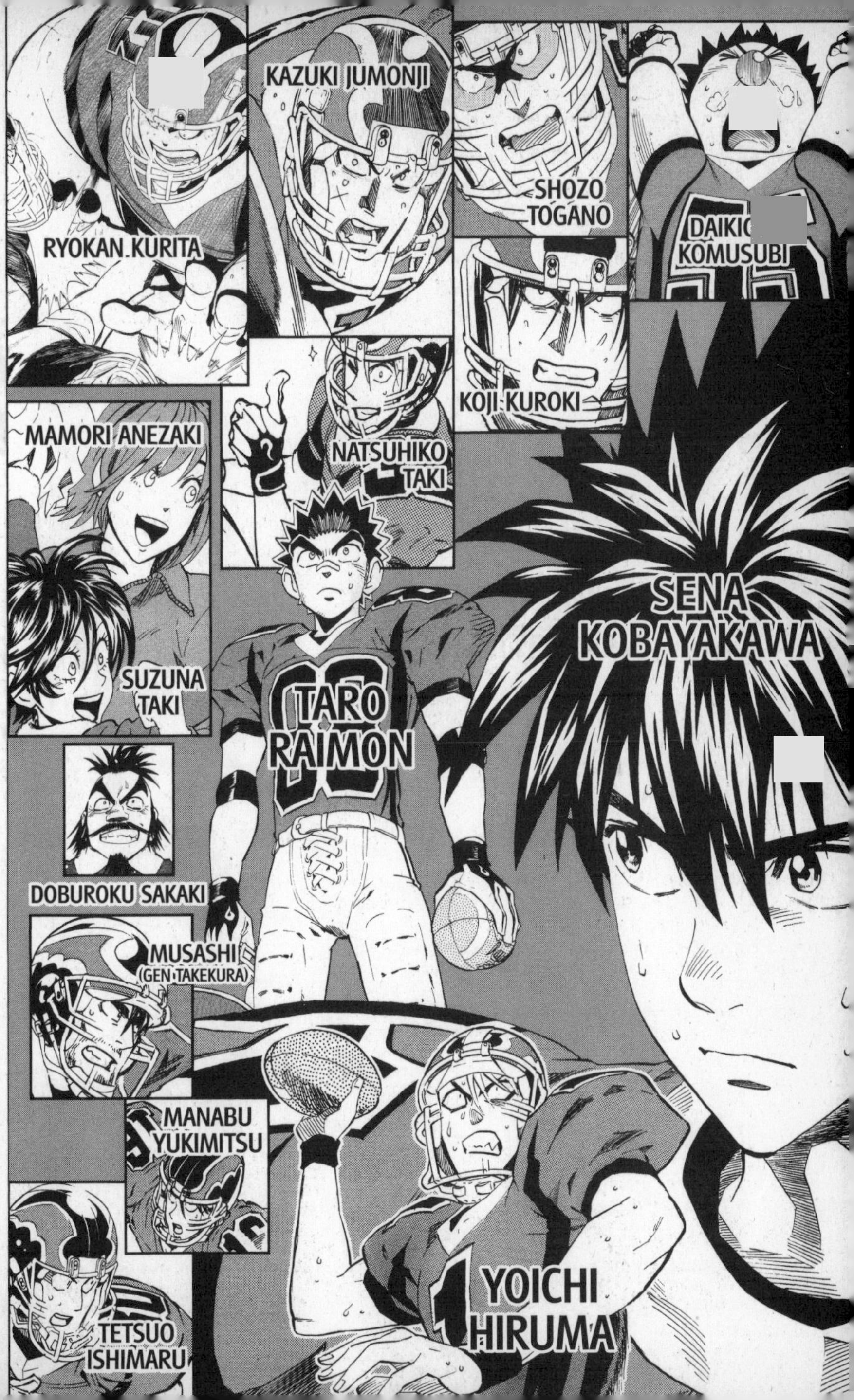
DAIKIC
KOMUSUBI
SHOZO TOGANO
KOJI KUROKI
KAZUKI JUMONJI
RYOKAN KURITA
NATSUHIKO TAKI
MAMORI ANEZAKI
SENA KOBAYAKAWA
TARO RAIMON
SUZUNA TAKI
DOBUROKU SAKAKI
MUSASHI (GEN TAKEKURA)
YOICHI HIRUMA
MANABU YUKIMITSU
TETSUO ISHIMARU

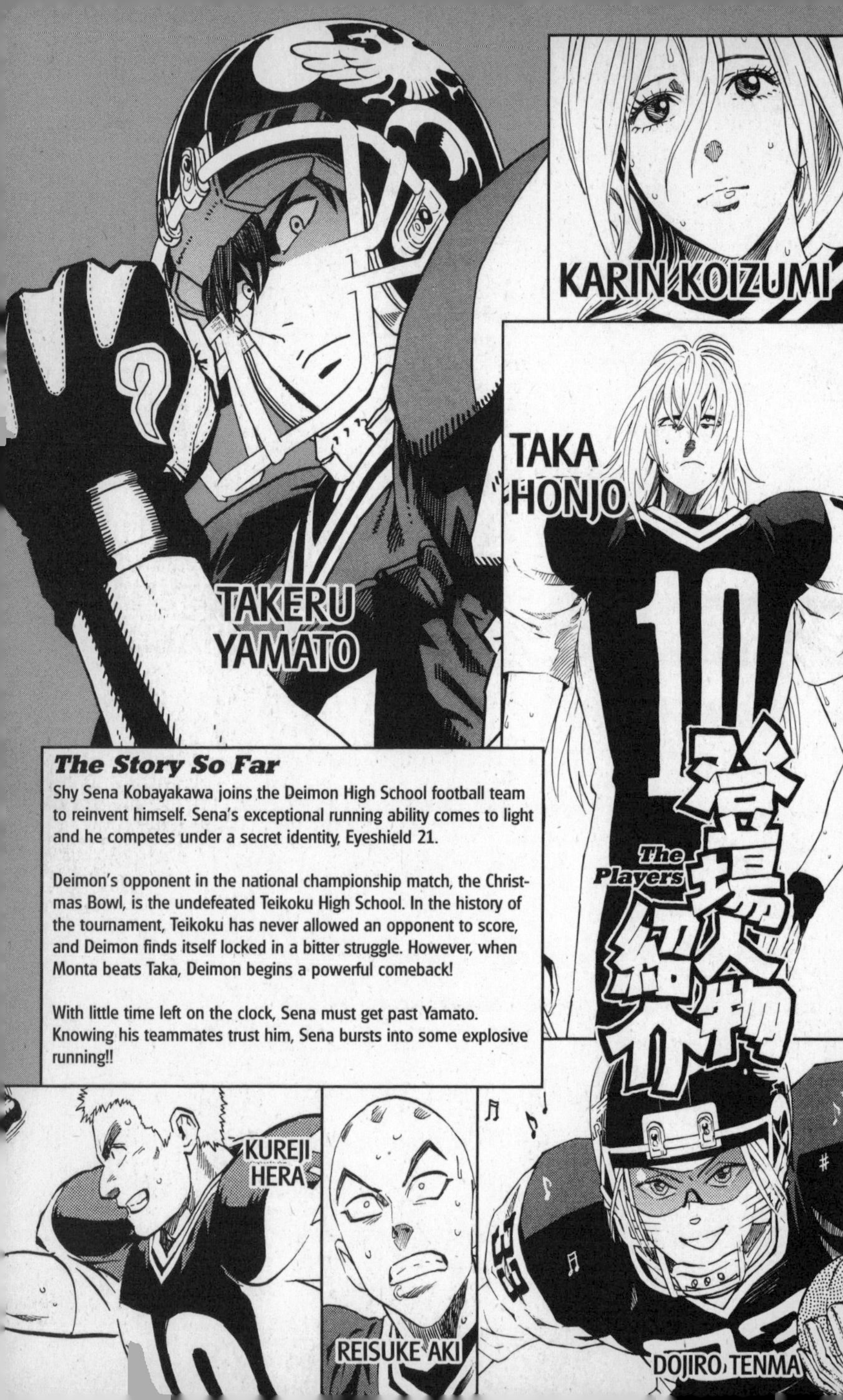
KARIN KOIZUMI
TAKA HONJO
TAKERU YAMATO
The Players
登場人物
DOJIRO TENMA
REISUKE AKI
KUREJI HERA

The Story So Far

Shy Sena Kobayakawa joins the Deimon High School football team to reinvent himself. Sena's exceptional running ability comes to light and he competes under a secret identity, Eyeshield 21.

Deimon's opponent in the national championship match, the Christmas Bowl, is the undefeated Teikoku High School. In the history of the tournament, Teikoku has never allowed an opponent to score, and Deimon finds itself locked in a bitter struggle. However, when Monta beats Taka, Deimon begins a powerful comeback!

With little time left on the clock, Sena must get past Yamato. Knowing his teammates trust him, Sena bursts into some explosive running!!

Vol. 34:
The Last of the Deimon Devil Bats

CONTENTS

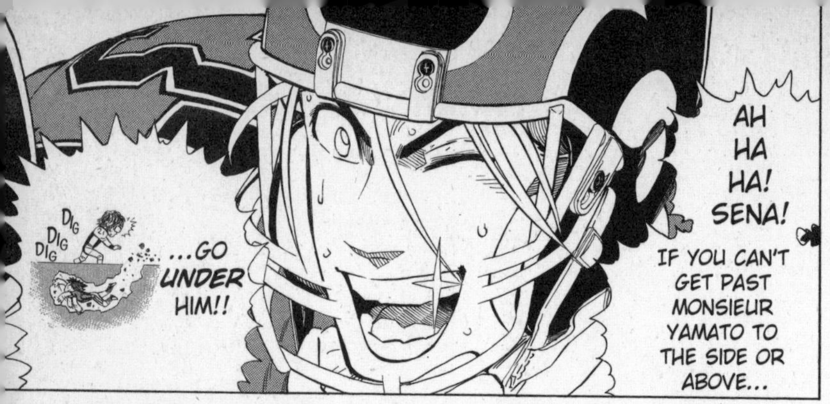
AH HA HA! SENA!
IF YOU CAN'T GET PAST MONSIEUR YAMATO TO THE SIDE OR ABOVE...
...GO UNDER HIM!!
DIG DIG DIG

Chapter 296 The Path Through a New Dimension

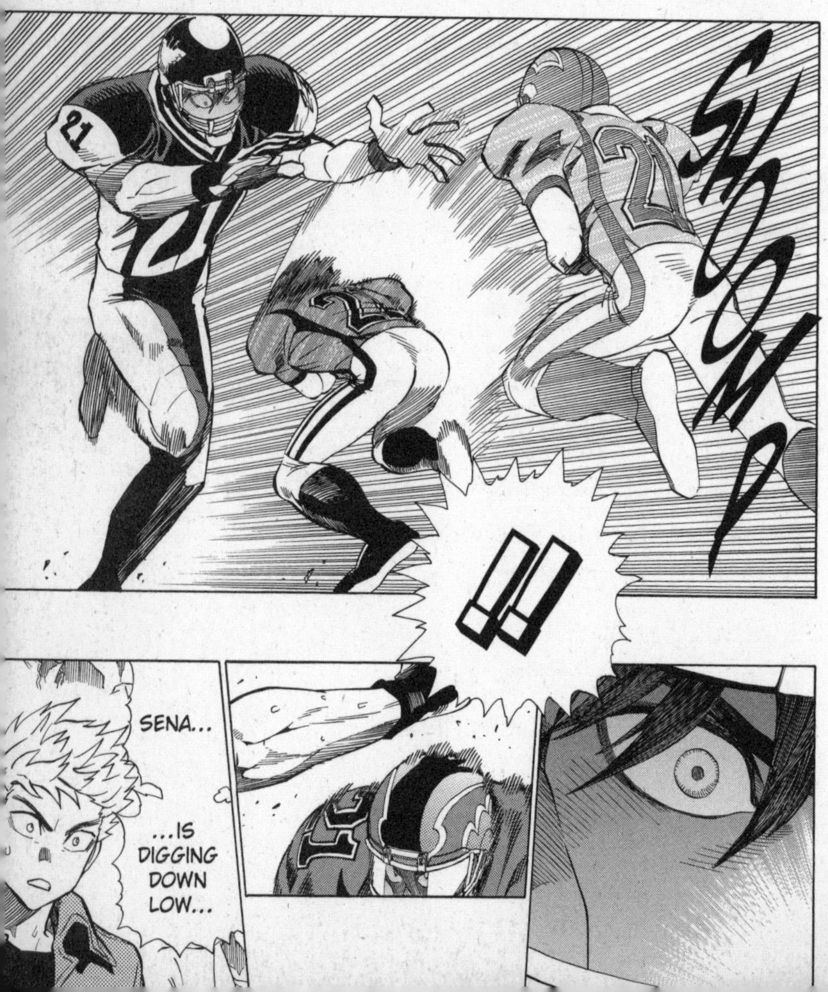
SHOOMP
!!
SENA...
...IS DIGGING DOWN LOW...

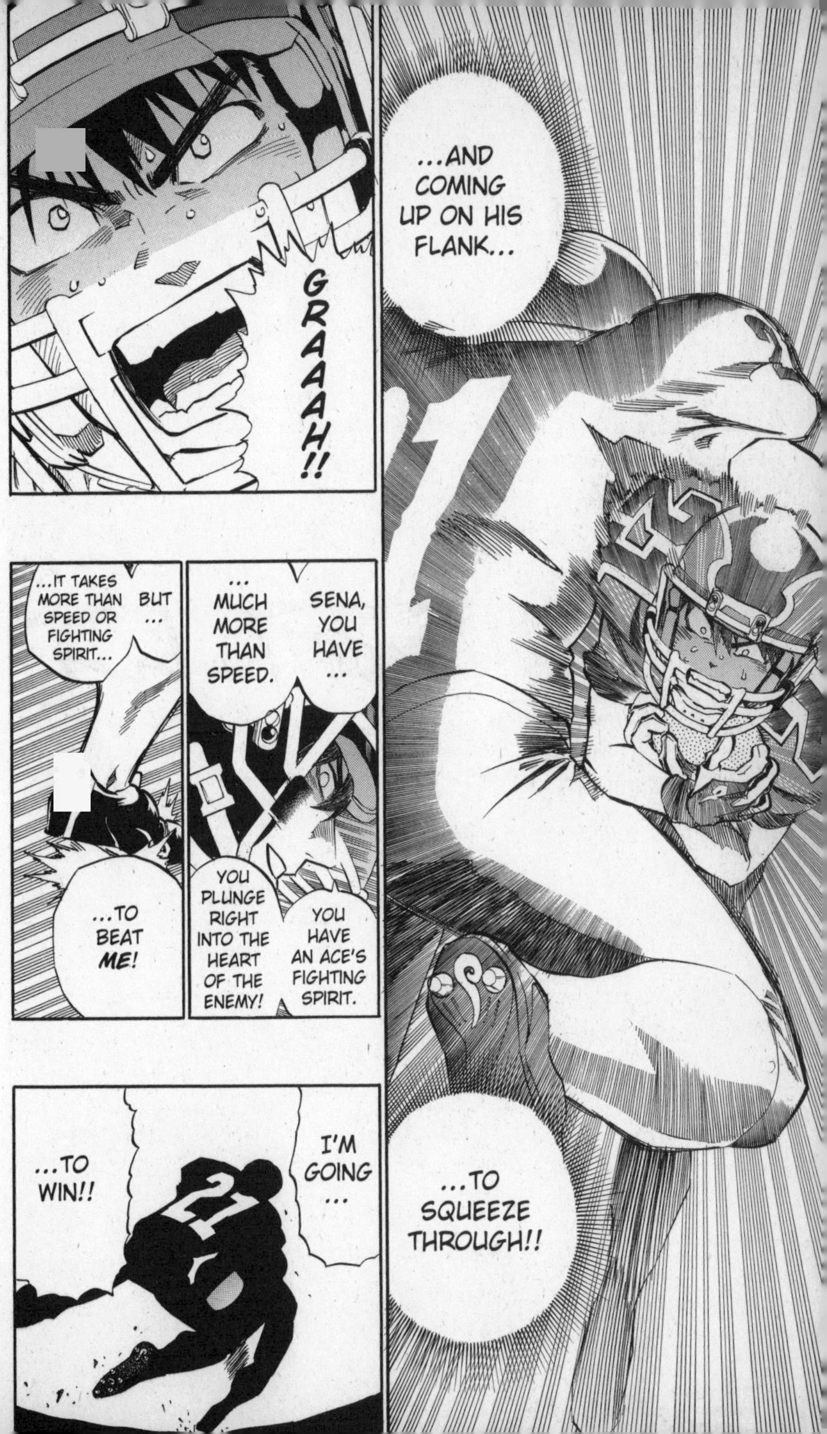
...AND COMING UP ON HIS FLANK...
...TO SQUEEZE THROUGH!!
GRAAAAH!!
SENA, YOU HAVE...
...MUCH MORE THAN SPEED.
YOU HAVE AN ACE'S FIGHTING SPIRIT.
YOU PLUNGE RIGHT INTO THE HEART OF THE ENEMY!
BUT...
...IT TAKES MORE THAN SPEED OR FIGHTING SPIRIT...
...TO BEAT *ME*!
I'M GOING...
...TO WIN!!

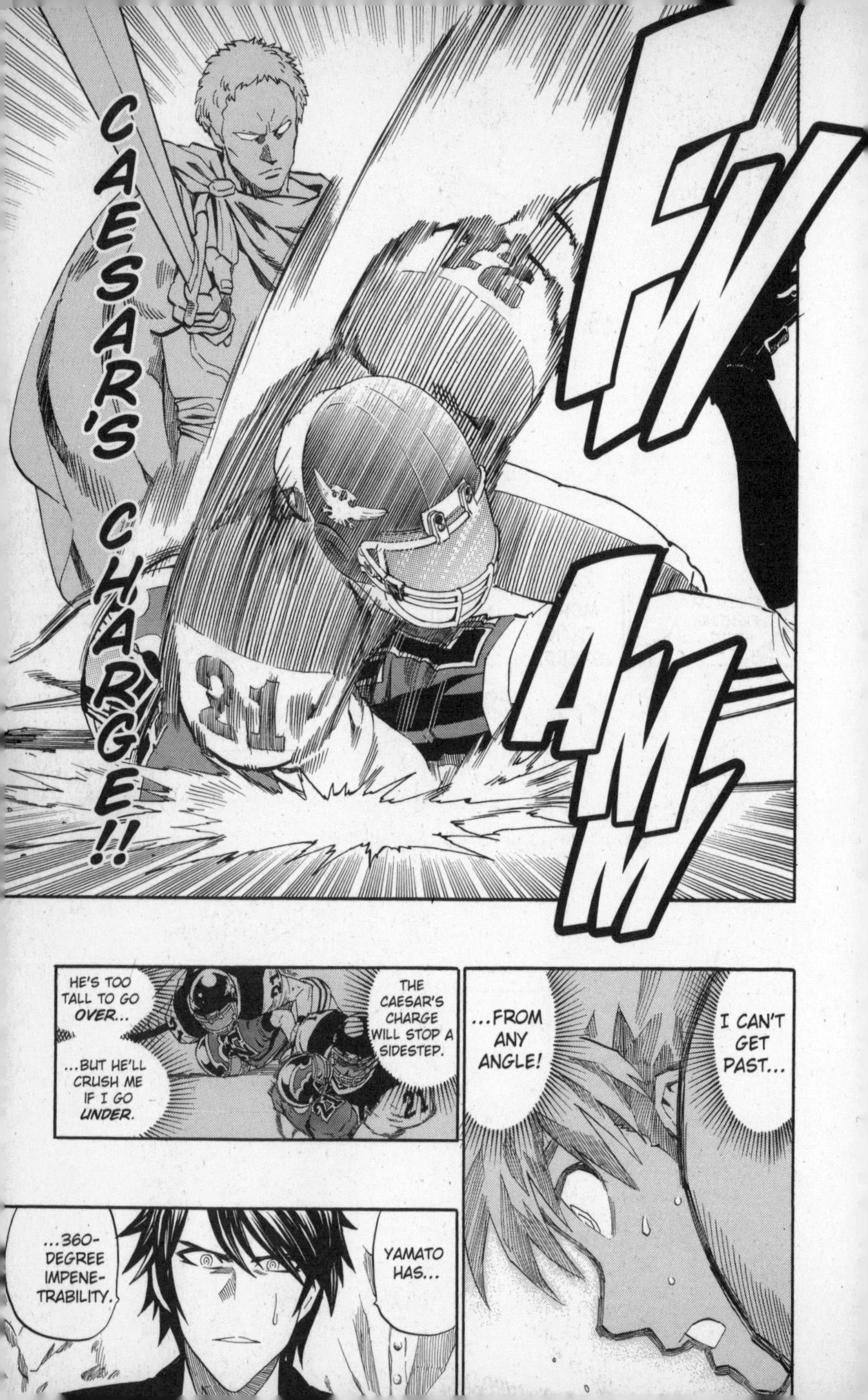
WHAMM
CAESAR'S CHARGE!!
I CAN'T GET PAST...
...FROM ANY ANGLE!
THE CAESAR'S CHARGE WILL STOP A SIDESTEP.
HE'S TOO TALL TO GO *OVER*...
...BUT HE'LL CRUSH ME IF I GO *UNDER*.
YAMATO HAS...
...360-DEGREE IMPENE-TRABILITY.

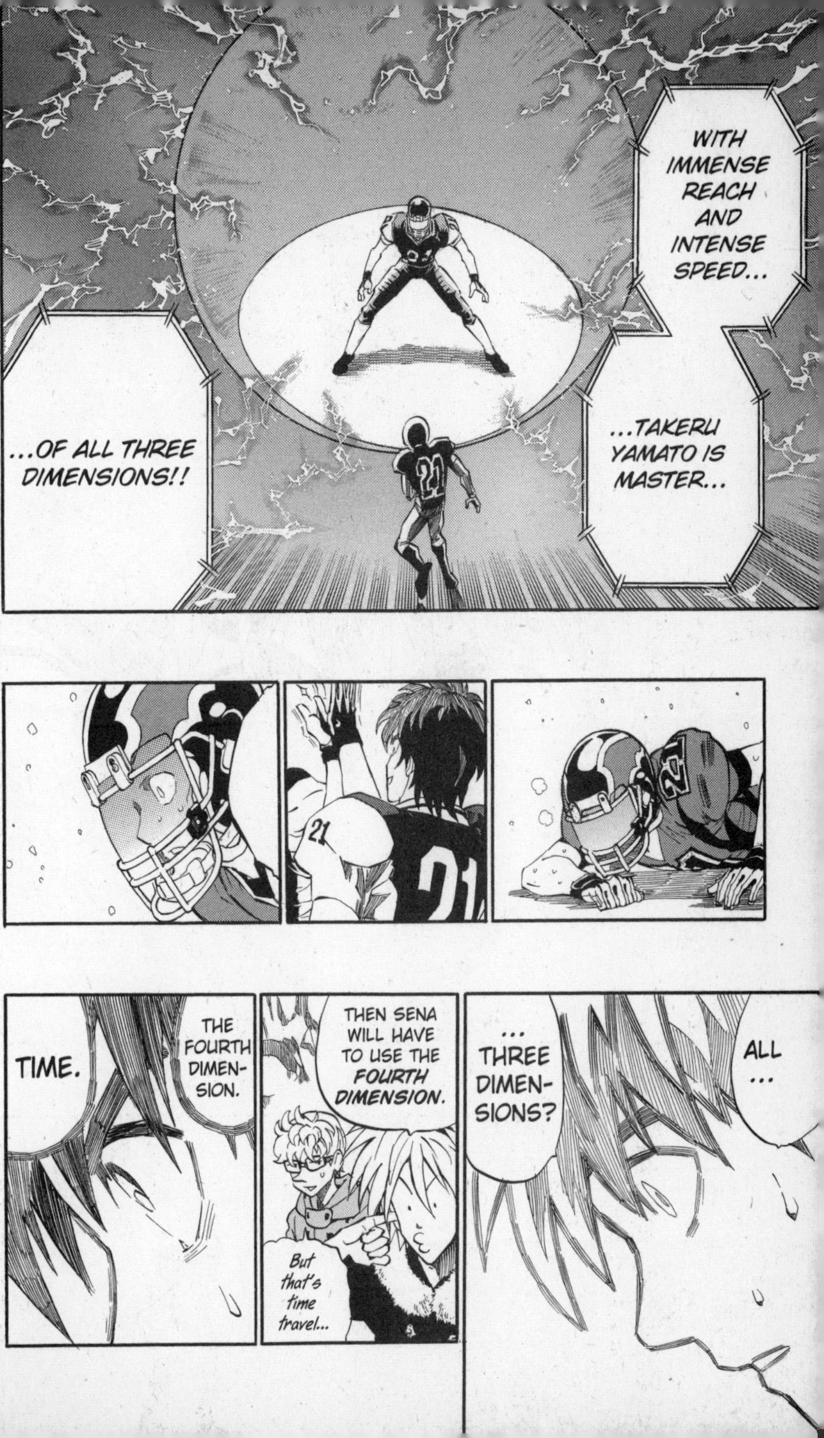
WITH IMMENSE REACH AND INTENSE SPEED...
...TAKERU YAMATO IS MASTER...
...OF ALL THREE DIMENSIONS!!
ALL ...
... THREE DIMENSIONS?
THEN SENA WILL HAVE TO USE THE *FOURTH DIMENSION*.
But that's time travel...
THE FOURTH DIMENSION.
TIME.

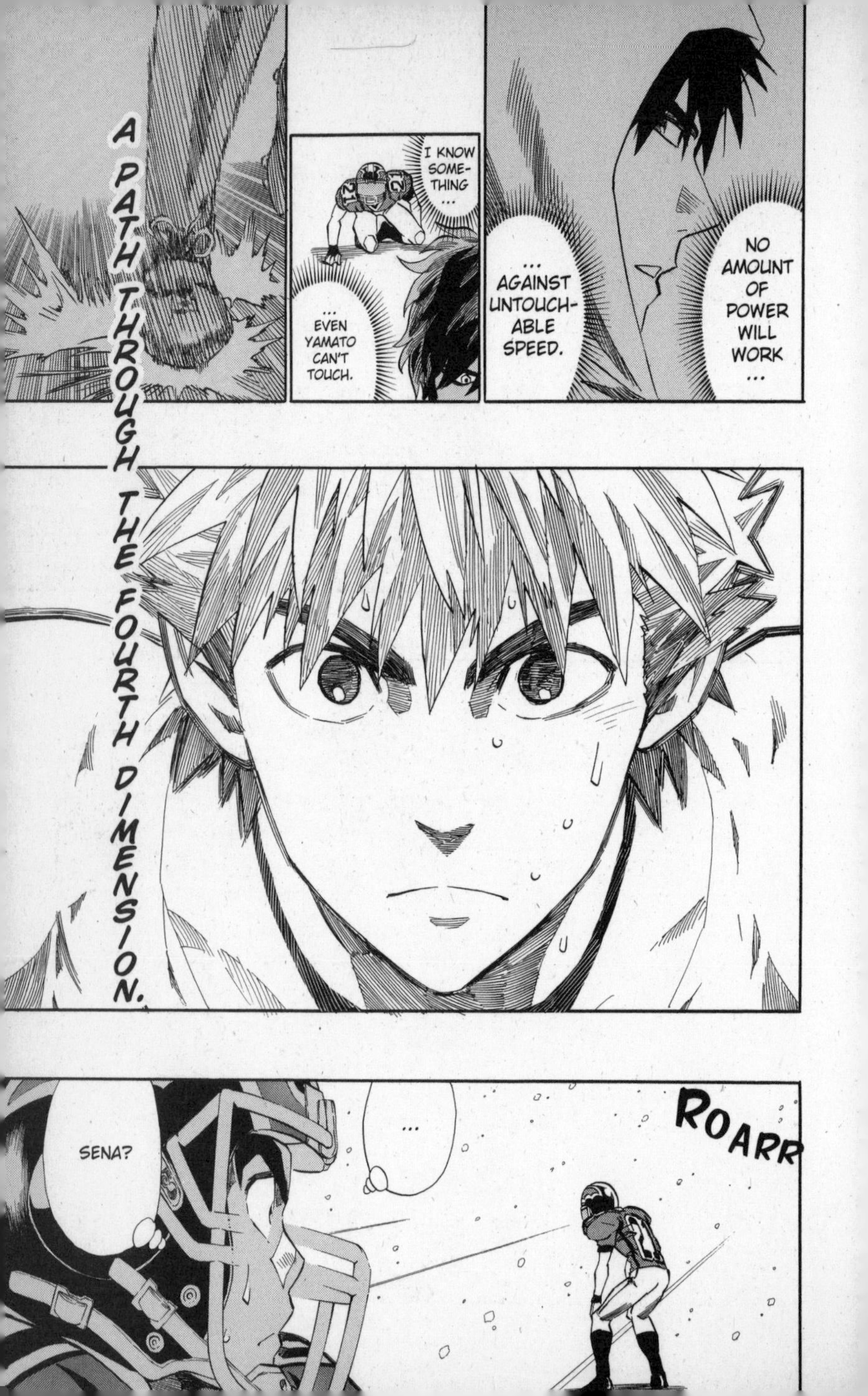
NO AMOUNT OF POWER WILL WORK ...
... AGAINST UNTOUCHABLE SPEED.
I KNOW SOMETHING ...
... EVEN YAMATO CAN'T TOUCH.
A PATH THROUGH THE FOURTH DIMENSION.
ROARR
...
SENA?

Chapter 296 The Path Through a New Dimension

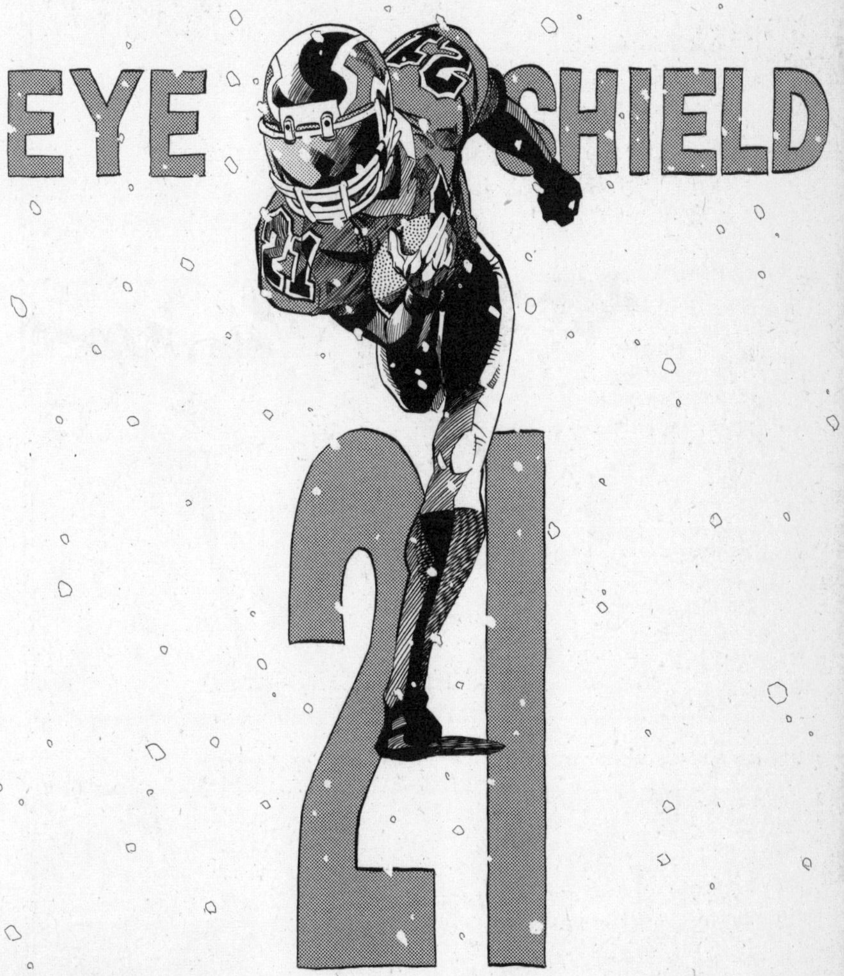
EYESHIELD
21

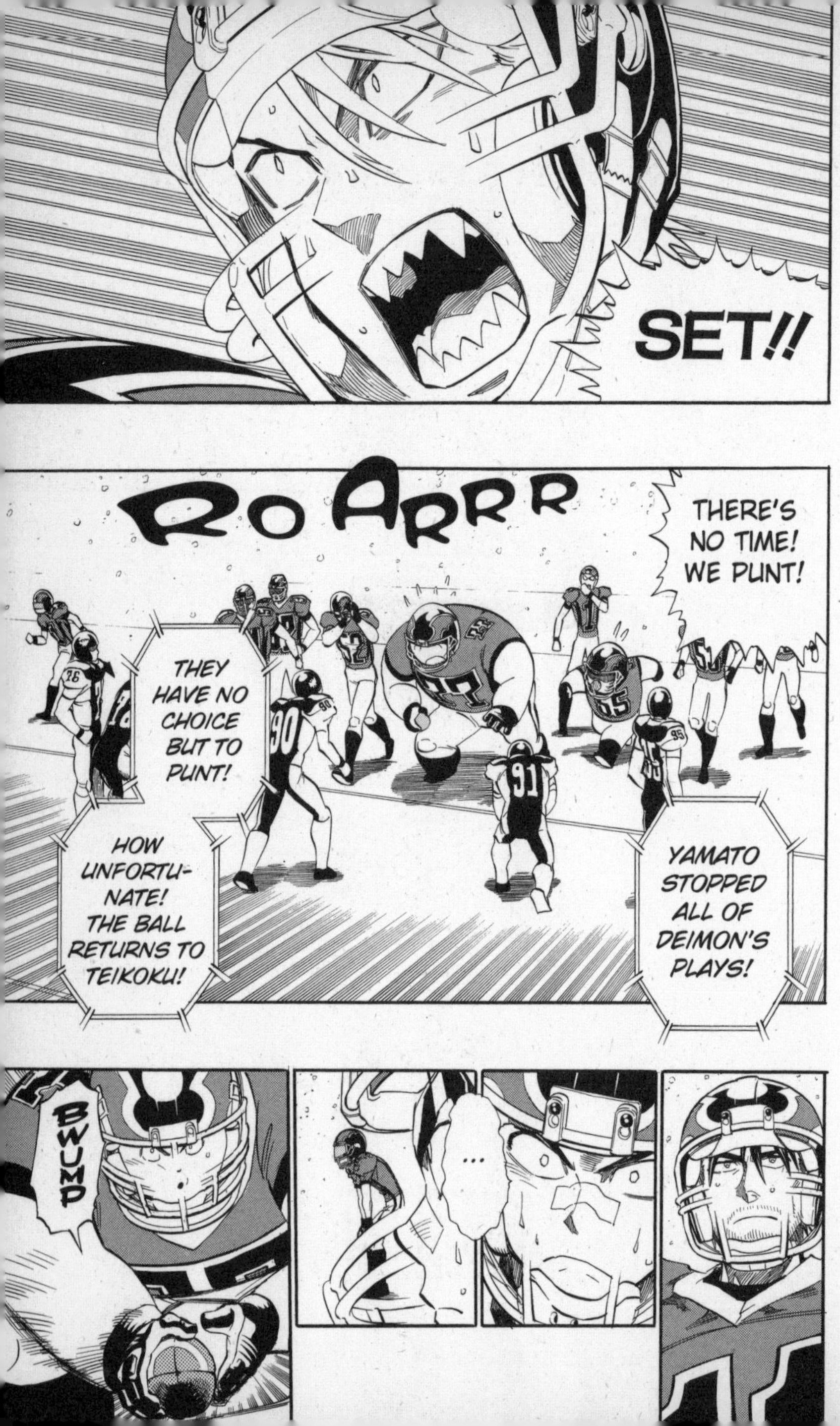
SET!!
THERE'S NO TIME! WE PUNT!
ROARRR
THEY HAVE NO CHOICE BUT TO PUNT!
YAMATO STOPPED ALL OF DEIMON'S PLAYS!
HOW UNFORTUNATE! THE BALL RETURNS TO TEIKOKU!
...
BWUMP

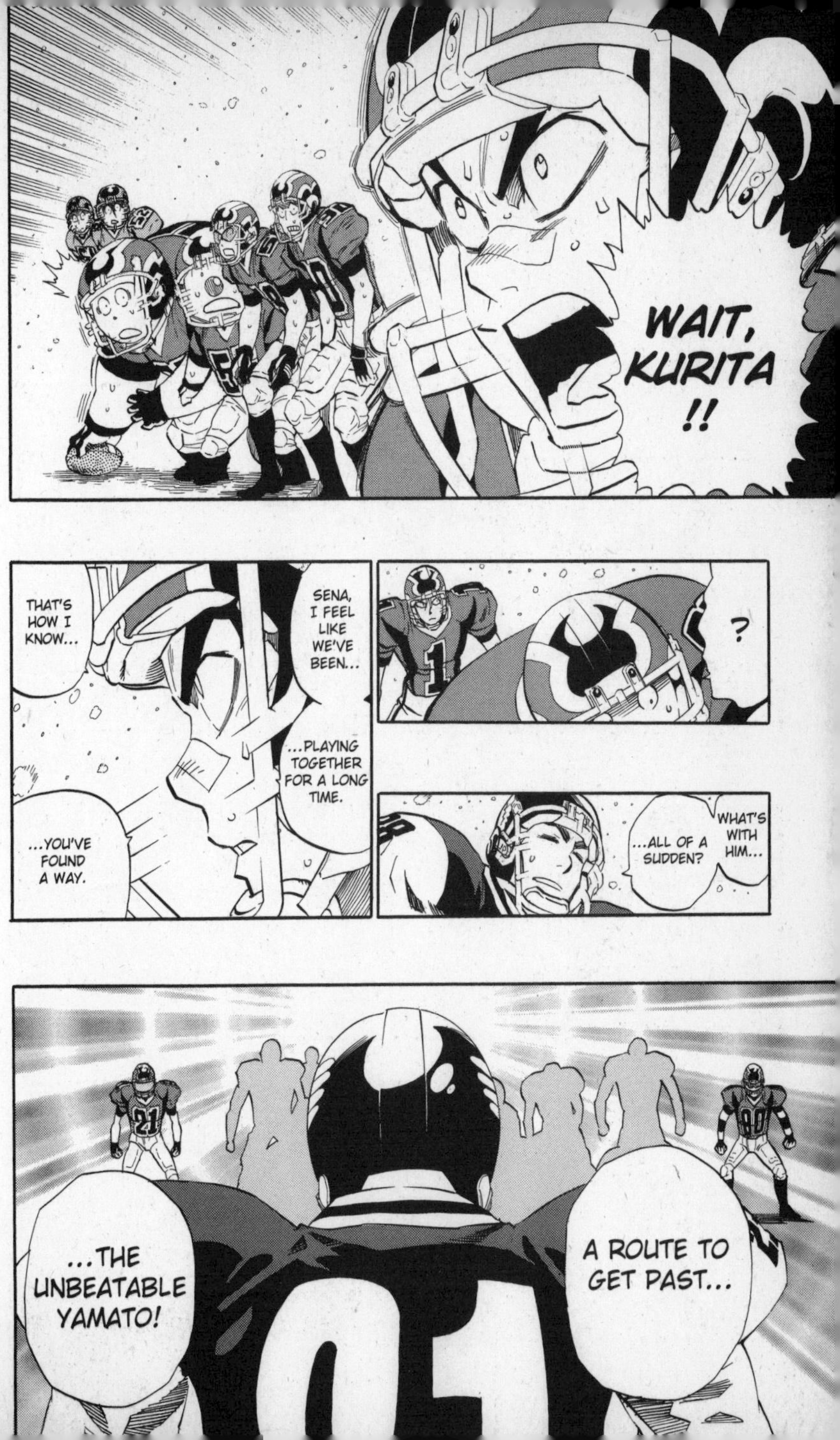
WAIT, KURITA !!
?
WHAT'S WITH HIM...
...ALL OF A SUDDEN?
SENA, I FEEL LIKE WE'VE BEEN...
...PLAYING TOGETHER FOR A LONG TIME.
THAT'S HOW I KNOW...
...YOU'VE FOUND A WAY.
A ROUTE TO GET PAST...
...THE UNBEATABLE YAMATO!

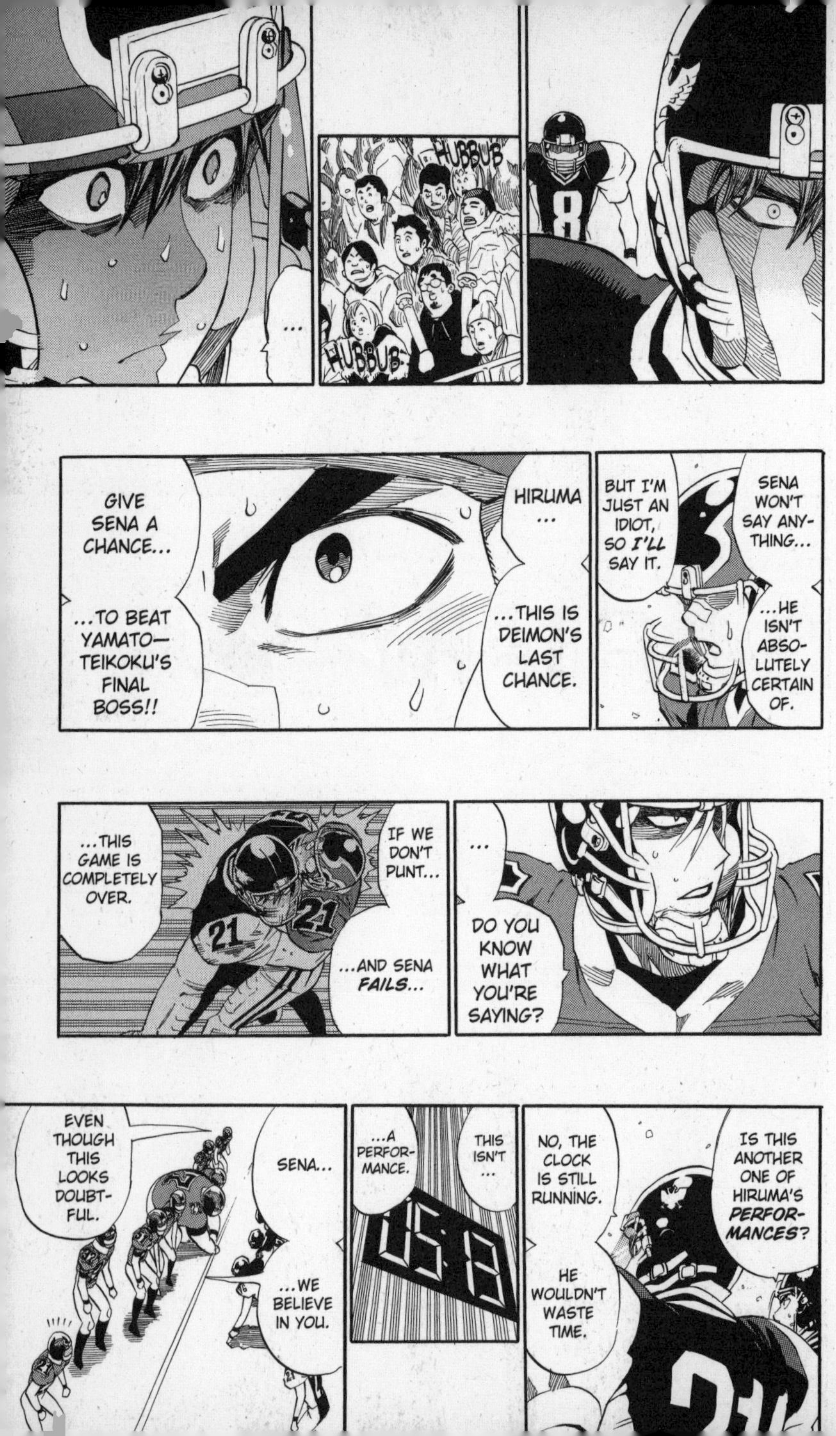
HUBBUB
HUBBUB
...
SENA WON'T SAY ANYTHING...
...HE ISN'T ABSOLUTELY CERTAIN OF.
BUT I'M JUST AN IDIOT, SO *I'LL* SAY IT.
HIRUMA...
...THIS IS DEIMON'S LAST CHANCE.
GIVE SENA A CHANCE...
...TO BEAT YAMATO-TEIKOKU'S FINAL BOSS!!
...
DO YOU KNOW WHAT YOU'RE SAYING?
IF WE DON'T PUNT...
...AND SENA *FAILS*...
...THIS GAME IS COMPLETELY OVER.
IS THIS ANOTHER ONE OF HIRUMA'S *PERFORMANCES*?
NO, THE CLOCK IS STILL RUNNING.
HE WOULDN'T WASTE TIME.
THIS ISN'T...
...A PERFORMANCE.
SENA...
...WE BELIEVE IN YOU.
EVEN THOUGH THIS LOOKS DOUBTFUL.

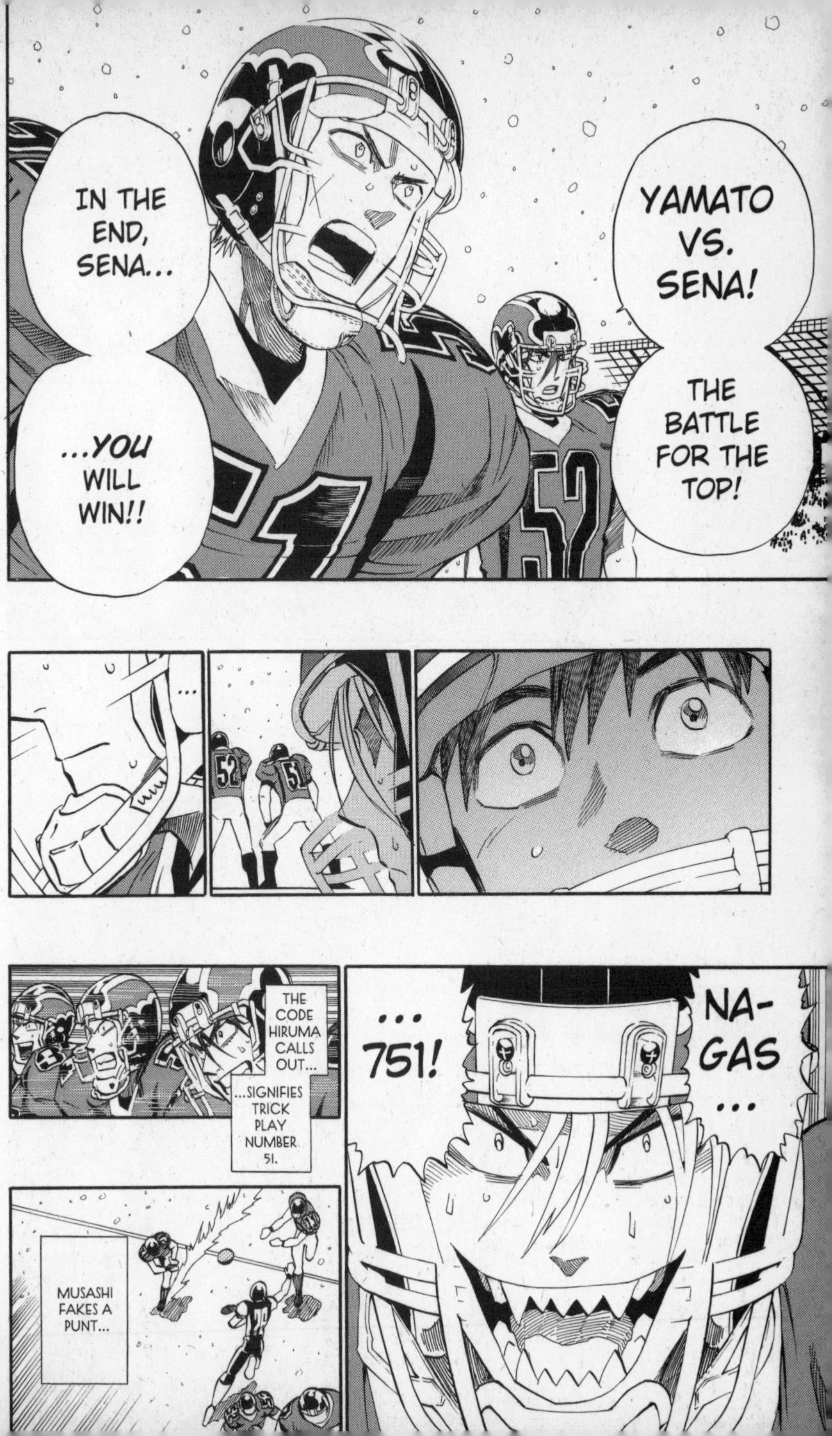
YAMATO VS. SENA!
THE BATTLE FOR THE TOP!
IN THE END, SENA...
...YOU WILL WIN!!
...
NA-GAS...
...751!
THE CODE HIRUMA CALLS OUT...
...SIGNIFIES TRICK PLAY NUMBER 51.
MUSASHI FAKES A PUNT...

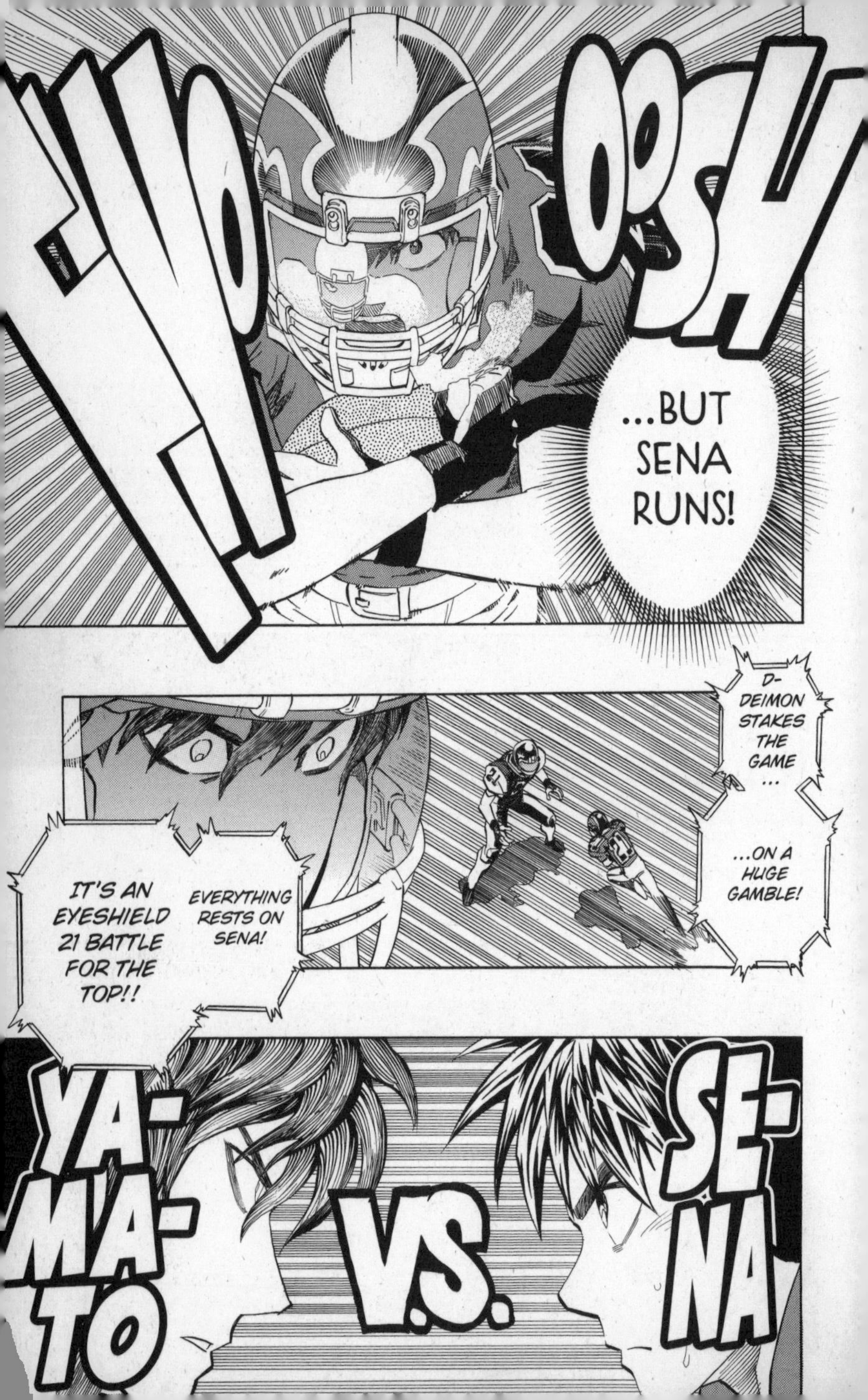
WHOOSH
...BUT SENA RUNS!
D-DEIMON STAKES THE GAME ...
...ON A HUGE GAMBLE!
EVERYTHING RESTS ON SENA!
IT'S AN EYESHIELD 21 BATTLE FOR THE TOP!!
YA-MA-TO
V.S.
SE-NA

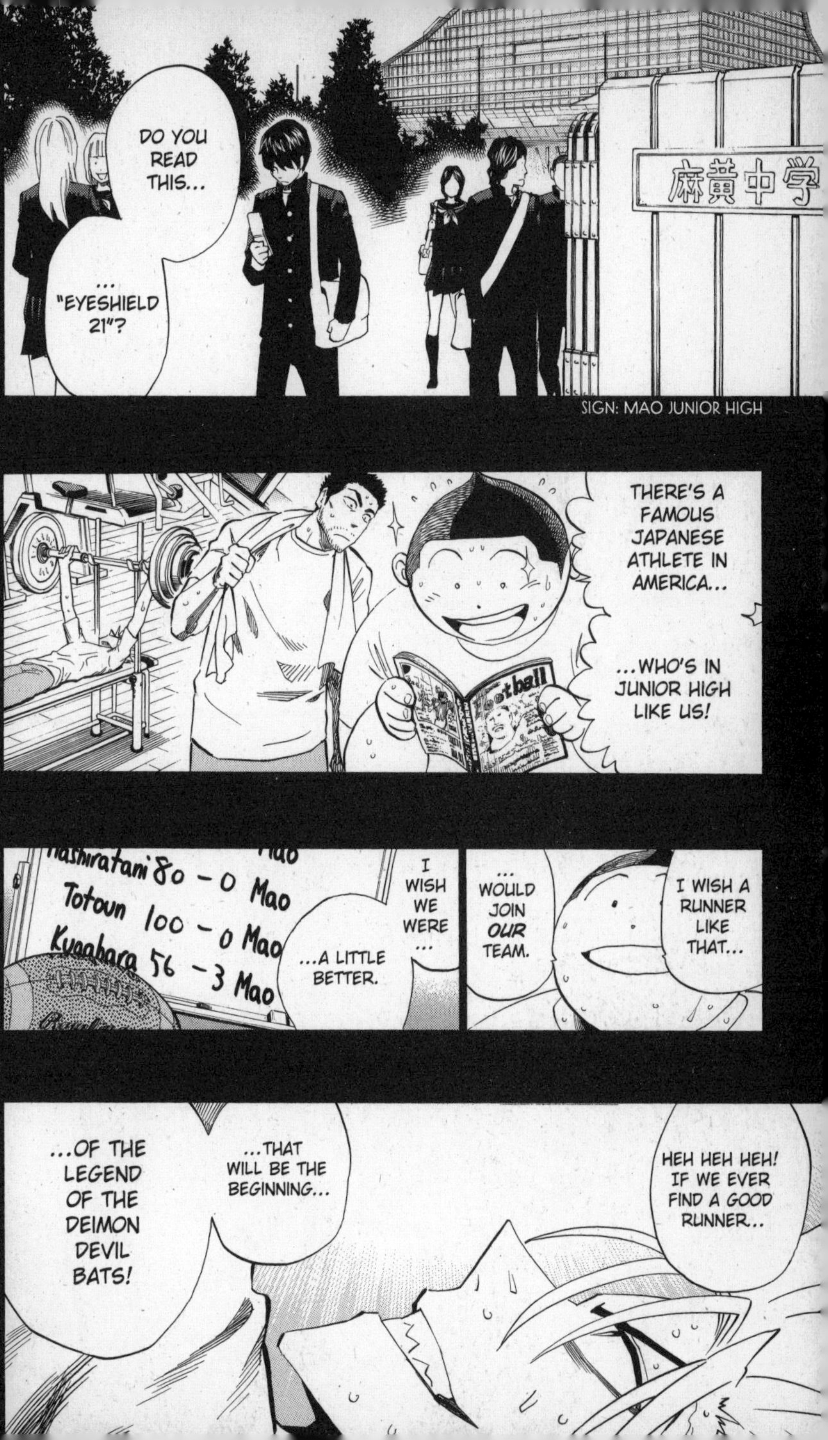
麻黄中学
DO YOU READ THIS...
..."EYESHIELD 21"?
THERE'S A FAMOUS JAPANESE ATHLETE IN AMERICA...
...WHO'S IN JUNIOR HIGH LIKE US!
I WISH A RUNNER LIKE THAT...
...WOULD JOIN *OUR* TEAM.
I WISH WE WERE...
...A LITTLE BETTER.
Totoun 100 - 0 Mao
Kyoabara 56 - 3 Mao
HEH HEH HEH! IF WE EVER FIND A GOOD RUNNER...
...THAT WILL BE THE BEGINNING...
...OF THE LEGEND OF THE DEIMON DEVIL BATS!
SIGN: MAO JUNIOR HIGH

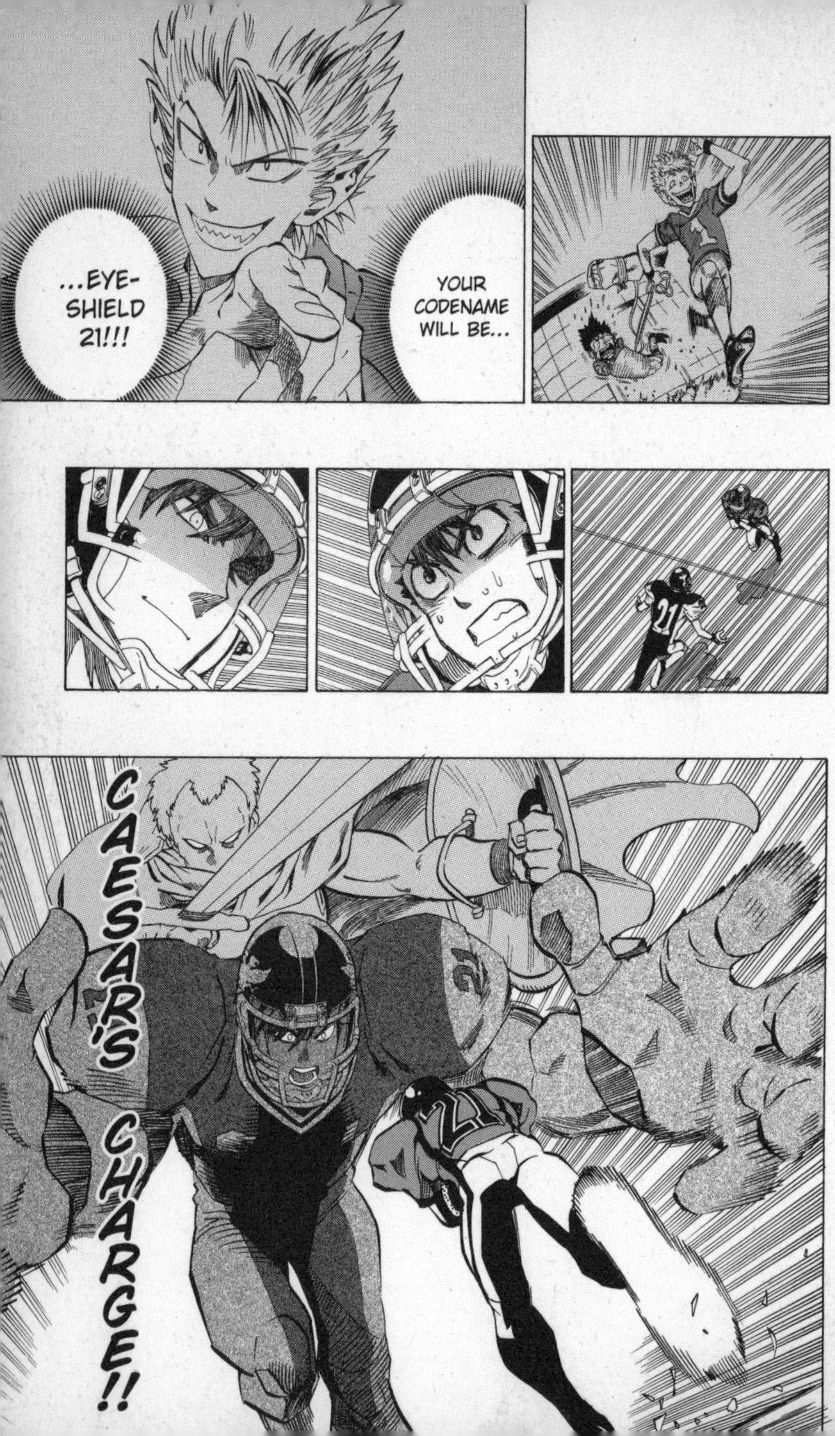
YOUR CODENAME WILL BE...
...EYE-SHIELD 21!!!
CAESAR'S CHARGE!!

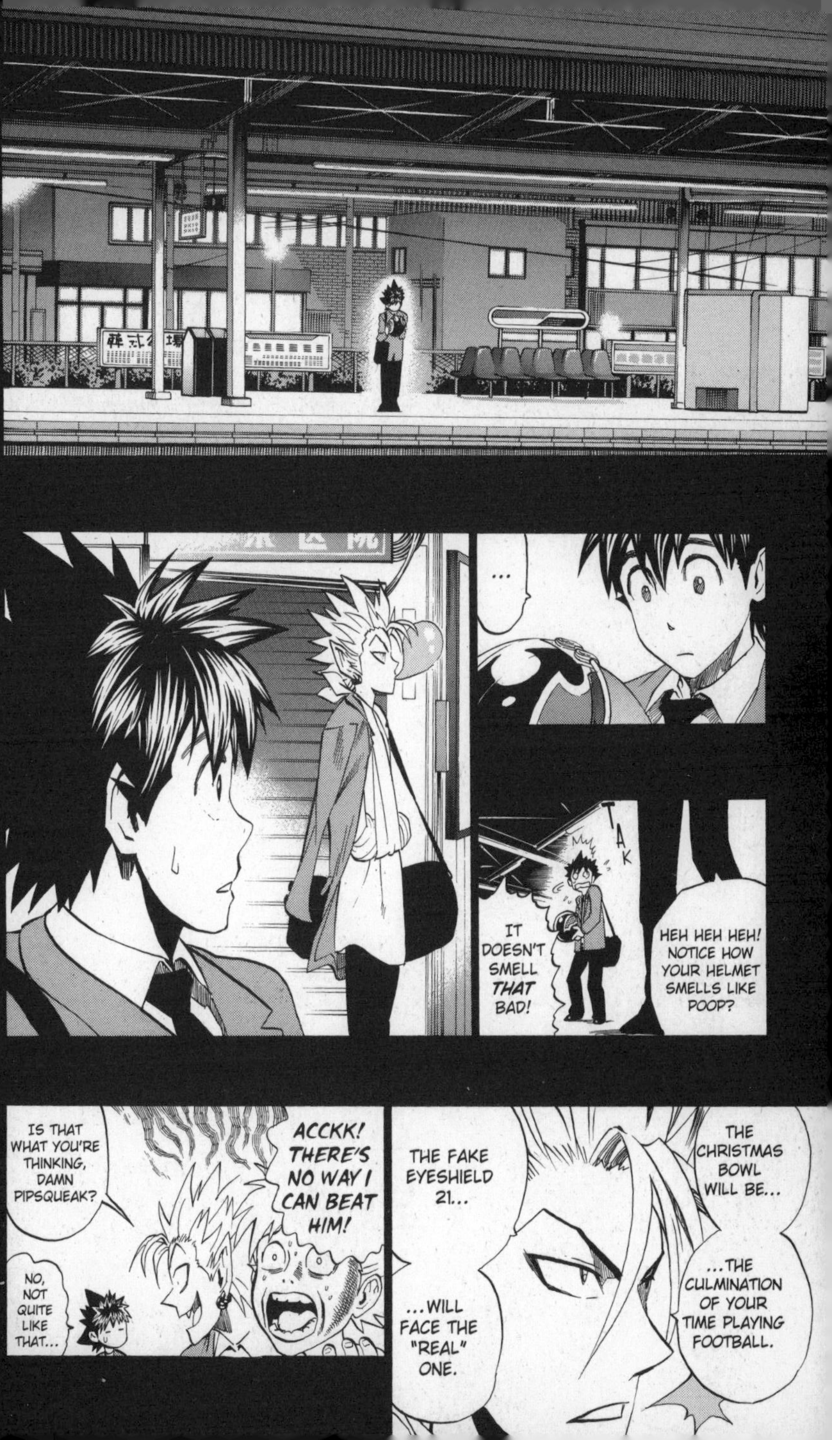
...
TAK
HEH HEH HEH! NOTICE HOW YOUR HELMET SMELLS LIKE POOP?
IT DOESN'T SMELL *THAT* BAD!
THE CHRISTMAS BOWL WILL BE...
...THE CULMINATION OF YOUR TIME PLAYING FOOTBALL.
THE FAKE EYESHIELD 21...
...WILL FACE THE "REAL" ONE.
ACCKK! THERE'S NO WAY I CAN BEAT HIM!
IS THAT WHAT YOU'RE THINKING, DAMN PIPSQUEAK?
NO, NOT QUITE LIKE THAT...

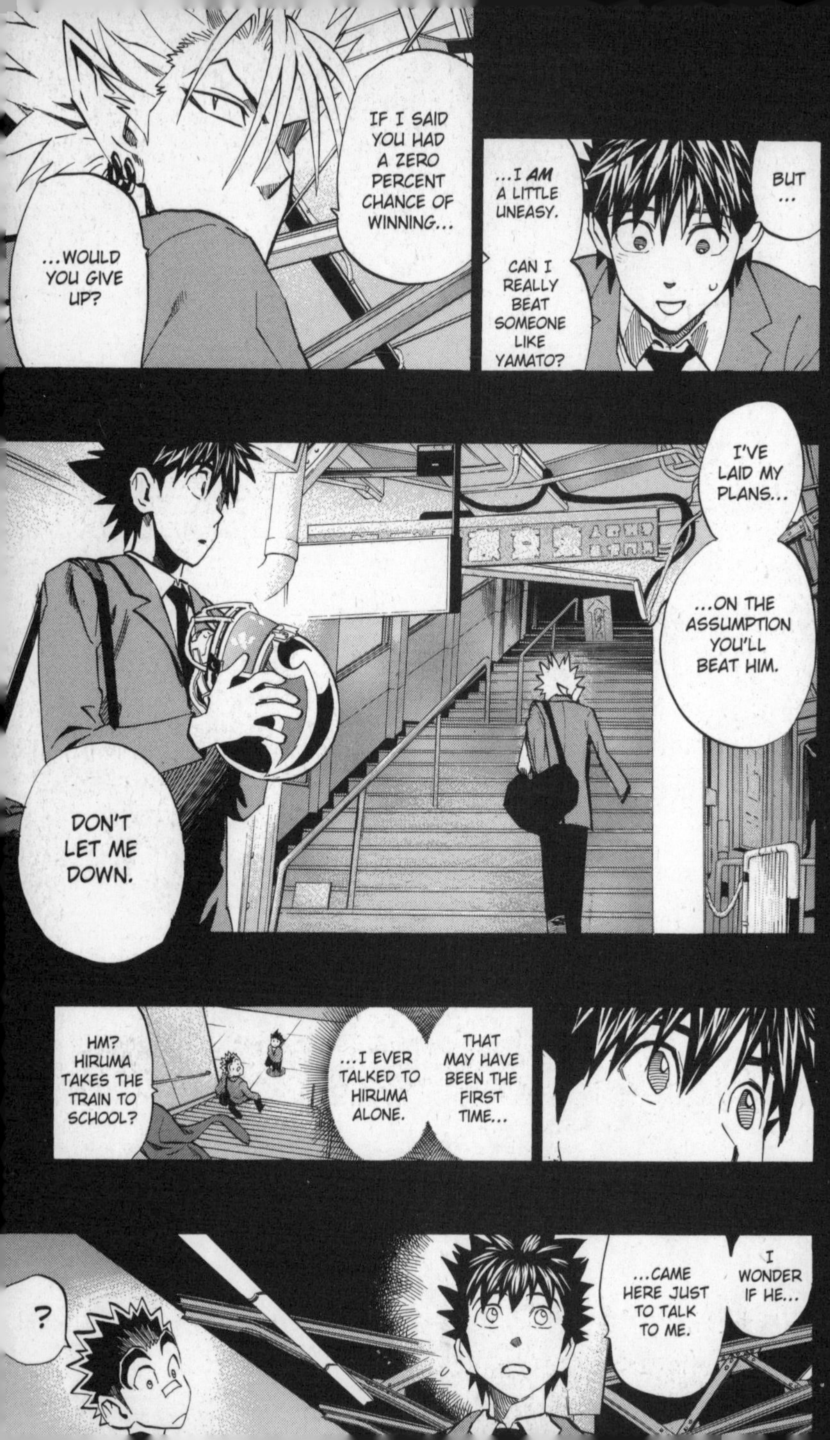
BUT ...
...I AM A LITTLE UNEASY.
CAN I REALLY BEAT SOMEONE LIKE YAMATO?
IF I SAID YOU HAD A ZERO PERCENT CHANCE OF WINNING...
...WOULD YOU GIVE UP?
I'VE LAID MY PLANS...
...ON THE ASSUMPTION YOU'LL BEAT HIM.
DON'T LET ME DOWN.
THAT MAY HAVE BEEN THE FIRST TIME...
...I EVER TALKED TO HIRUMA ALONE.
HM? HIRUMA TAKES THE TRAIN TO SCHOOL?
I WONDER IF HE...
...CAME HERE JUST TO TALK TO ME.
?

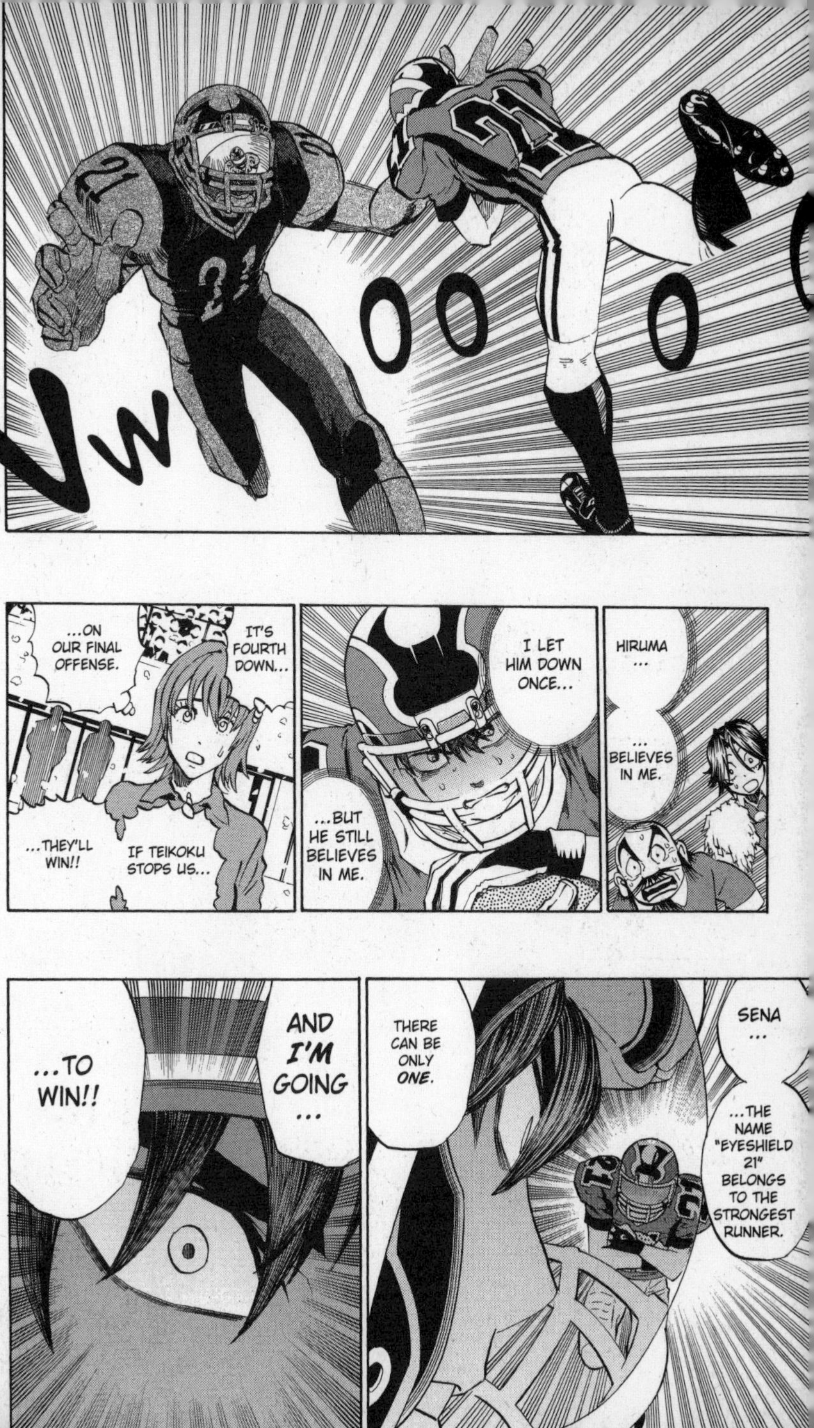
VwOOOO
HIRUMA ...
... BELIEVES IN ME.
I LET HIM DOWN ONCE...
...BUT HE STILL BELIEVES IN ME.
IT'S FOURTH DOWN...
...ON OUR FINAL OFFENSE.
IF TEIKOKU STOPS US...
...THEY'LL WIN!!
SENA ...
...THE NAME "EYESHIELD 21" BELONGS TO THE STRONGEST RUNNER.
THERE CAN BE ONLY *ONE*.
AND *I'M* GOING ...
...TO WIN!!

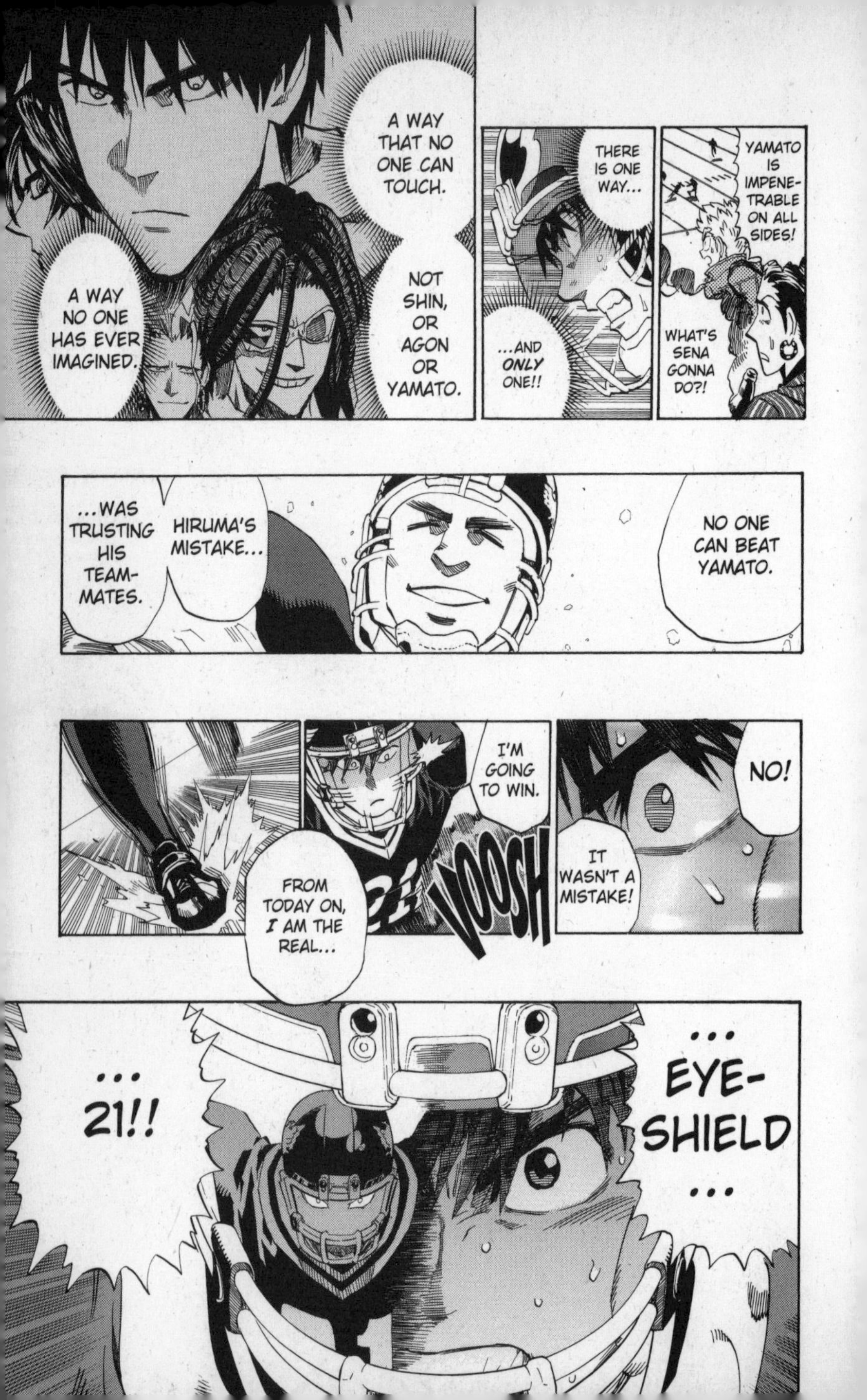
YAMATO IS IMPENETRABLE ON ALL SIDES!
WHAT'S SENA GONNA DO?!
THERE IS ONE WAY...
...AND *ONLY* ONE!!
A WAY THAT NO ONE CAN TOUCH.
NOT SHIN, OR AGON OR YAMATO.
A WAY NO ONE HAS EVER IMAGINED.
NO ONE CAN BEAT YAMATO.
HIRUMA'S MISTAKE...
...WAS TRUSTING HIS TEAMMATES.
NO!
IT WASN'T A MISTAKE!
I'M GOING TO WIN.
FROM TODAY ON, *I* AM THE REAL...
VOOSH
...EYE-SHIELD...
...21!!

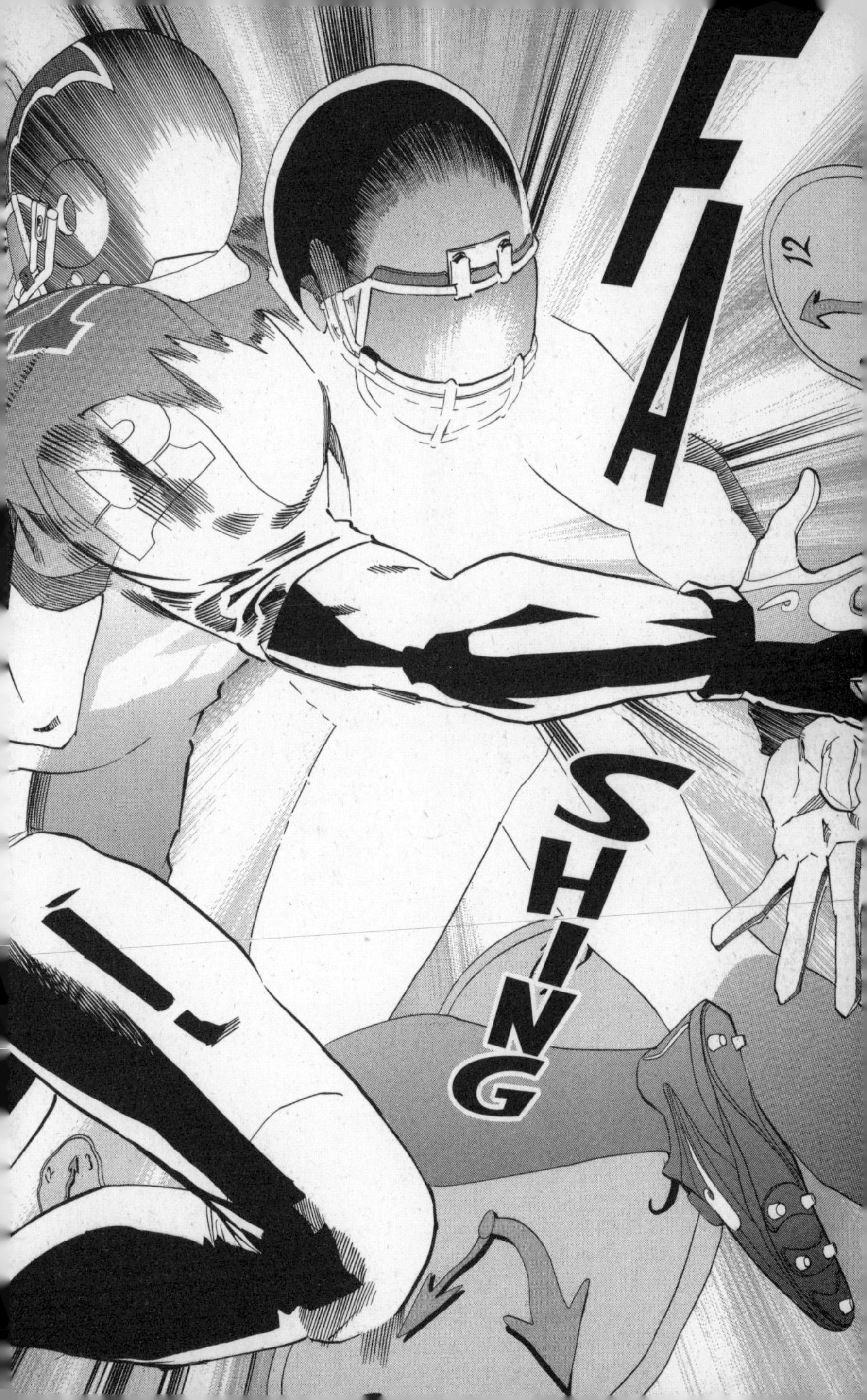
FA
SHING
!!

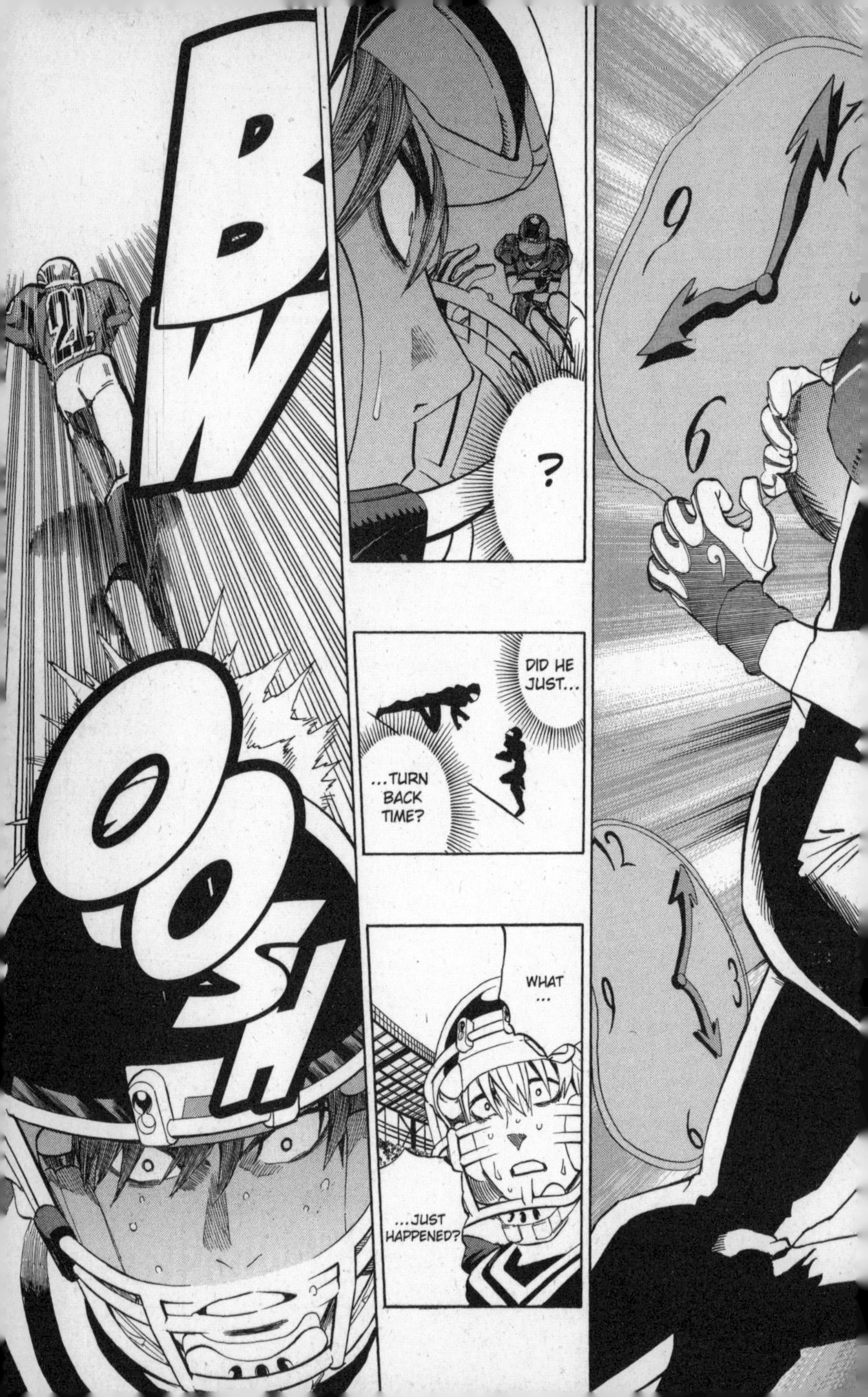
?
DID HE JUST...
...TURN BACK TIME?
WHAT...
...JUST HAPPENED?
BWOOSH

Miracle Ito
President
Jari Productions

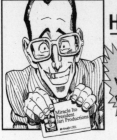

He's still alive! Shrewd Miracle Ito's

New product!!

HIGH SCHOOL FOOTBALL STAR GOODS

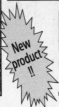

I never fall down!

Yamato Soy Sauce Pointer

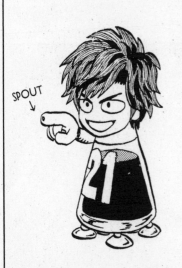

SPOUT

Have you ever accidentally bumped the soy sauce with your elbow during dinner and spilled soy sauce all over the table?

With **five super-strength suction cups**, this Caesar's Charge never falls! This item securely prevents major mishaps!!

※ It's hard to pick up, though, so be careful.

SPECIAL PRICE **¥1,980**※

※$22

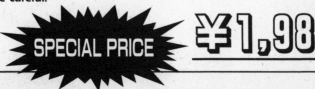

Chapter 297 Devils Back-to-Back

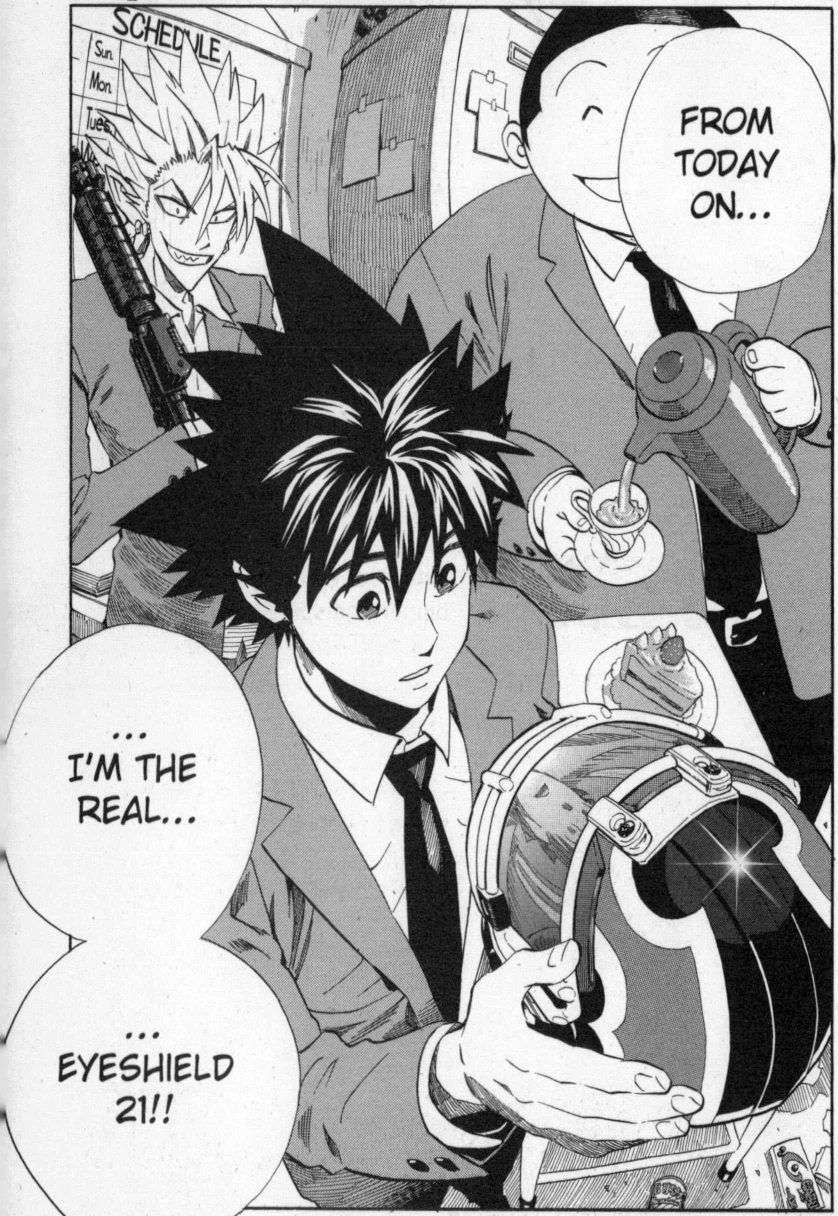
FROM TODAY ON...
SCHEDULE
Sun.
Mon.
Tues.
...I'M THE REAL...
...EYESHIELD 21!!

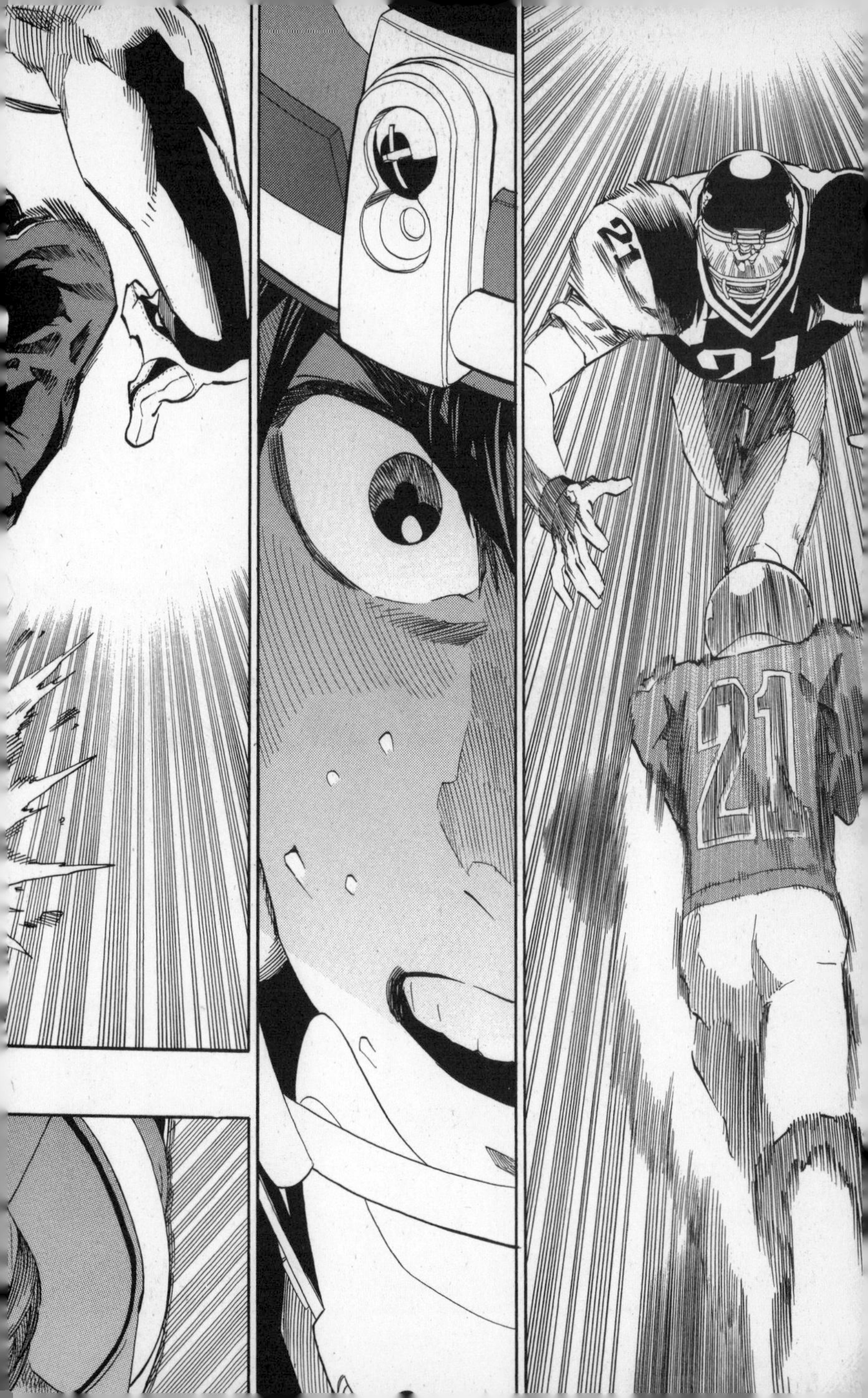

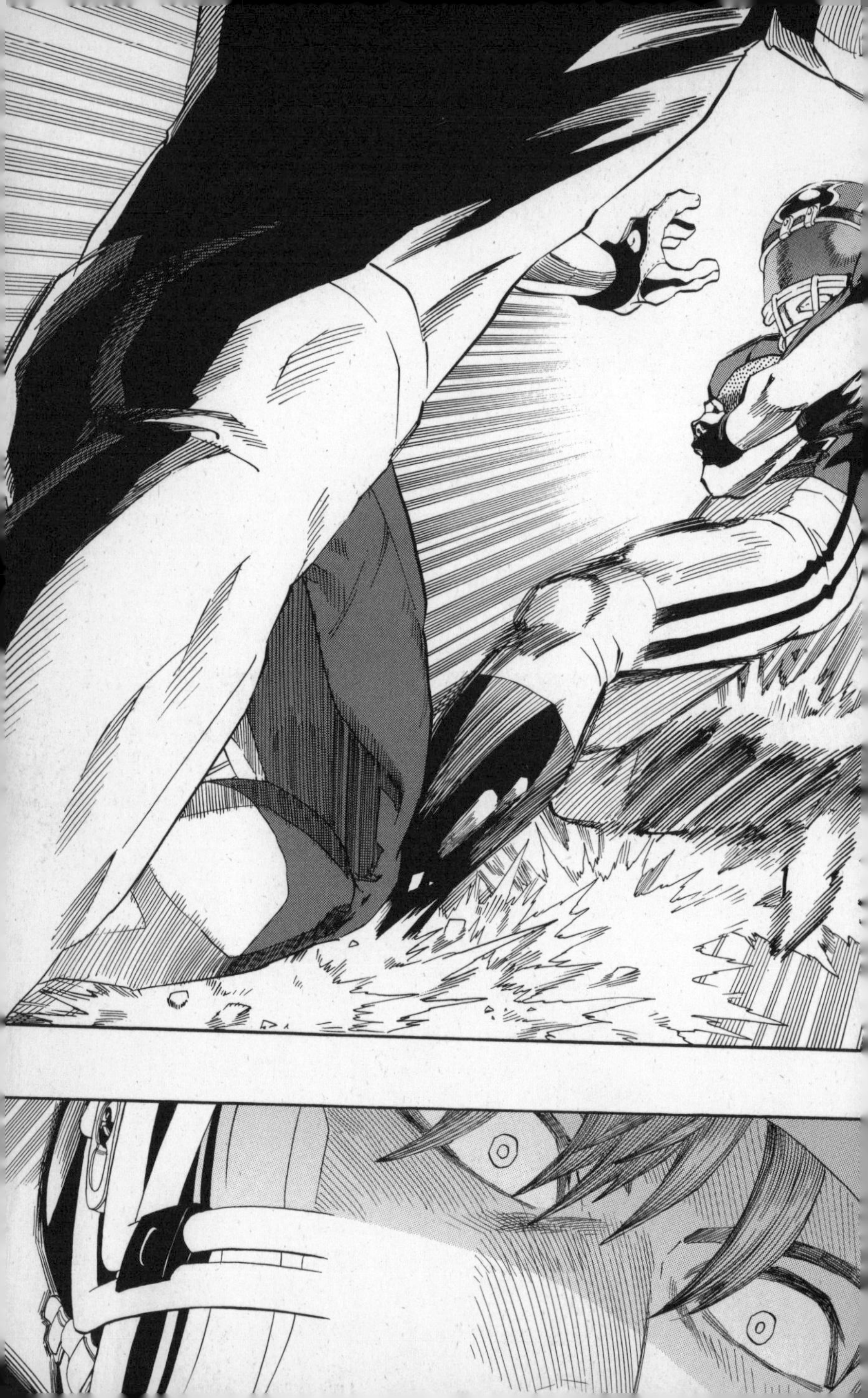

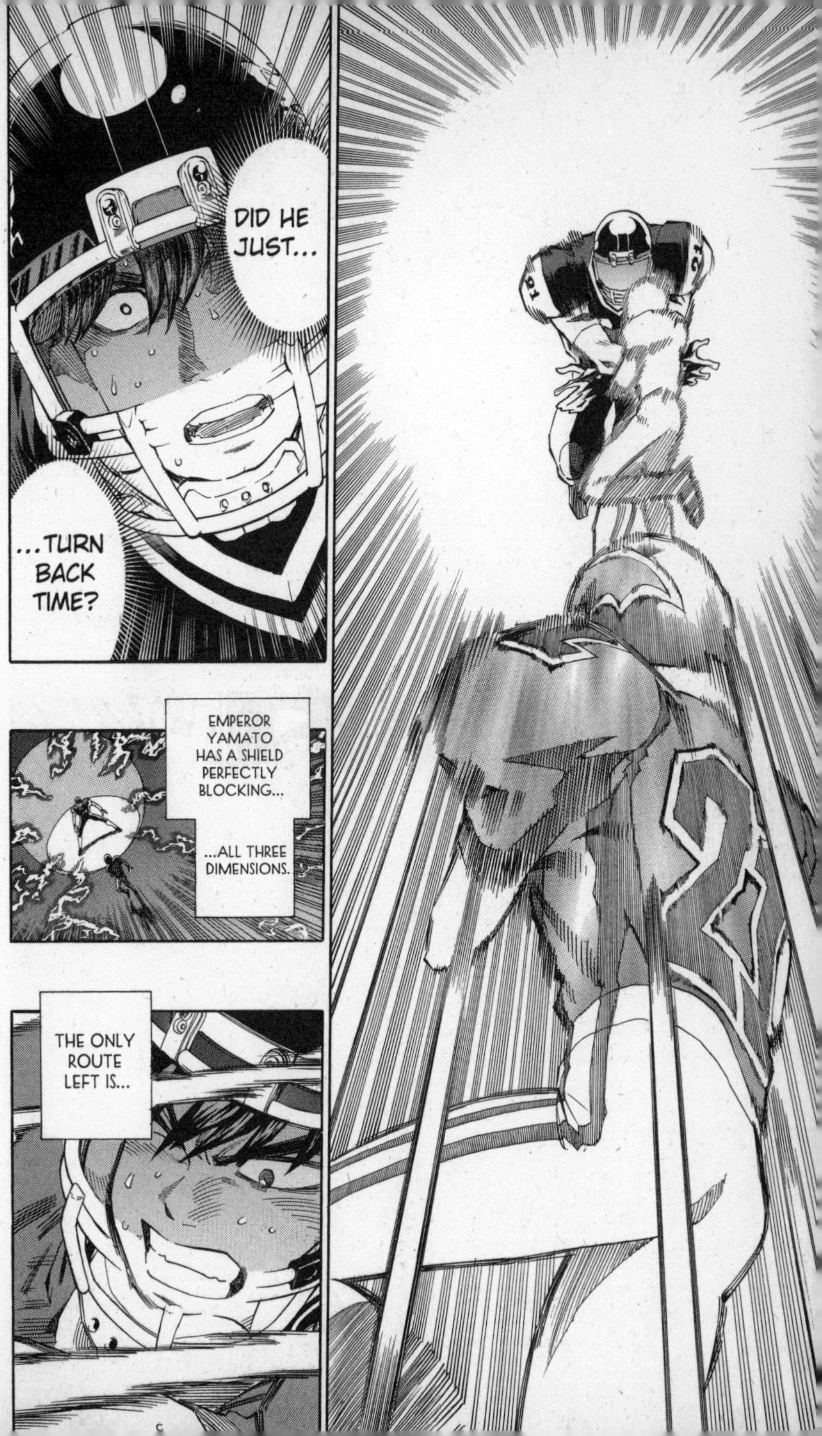
DID HE JUST...
...TURN BACK TIME?
EMPEROR YAMATO HAS A SHIELD PERFECTLY BLOCKING...
...ALL THREE DIMENSIONS.
THE ONLY ROUTE LEFT IS...

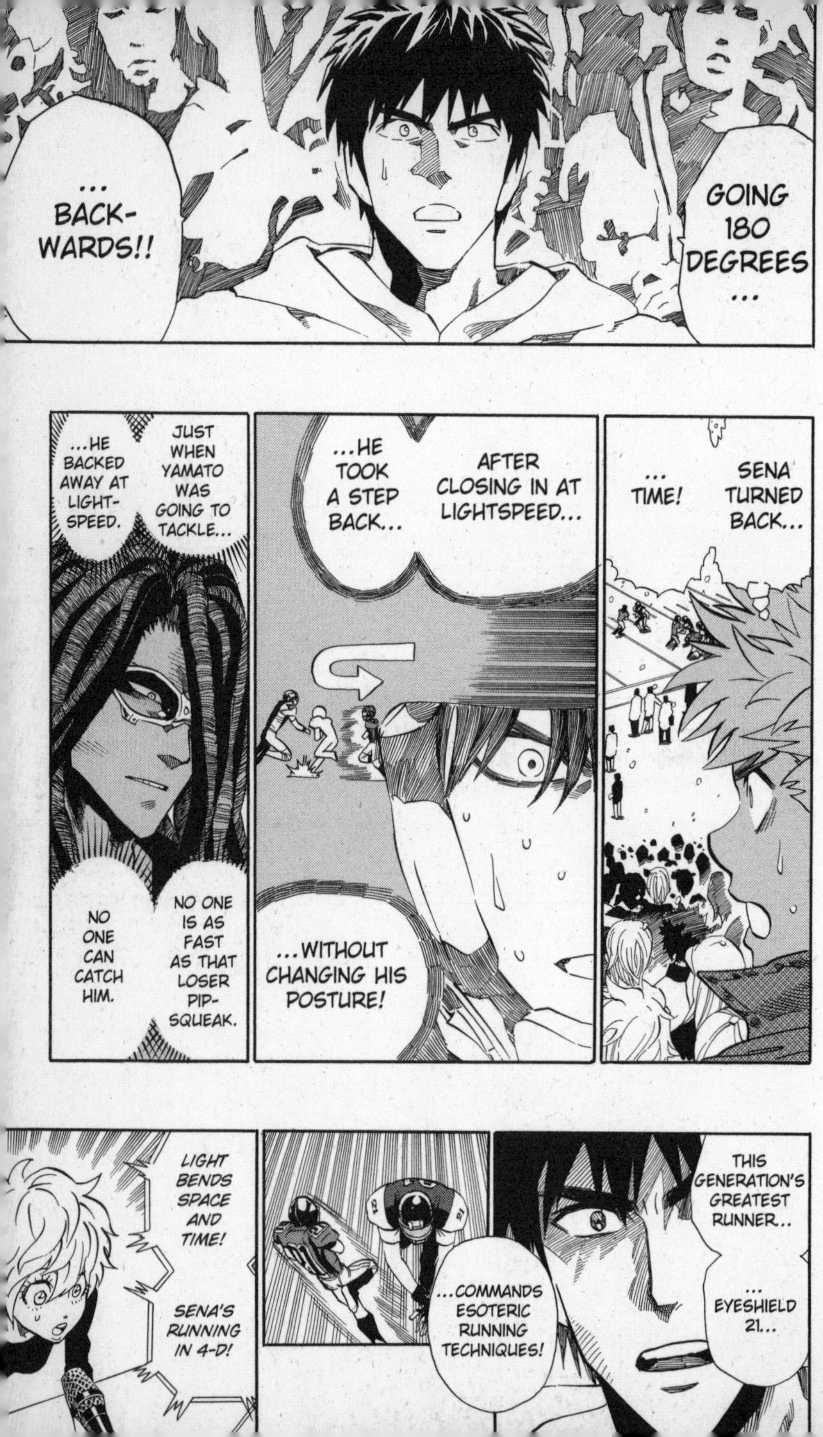
GOING 180 DEGREES ...
... BACKWARDS!!
SENA TURNED BACK...
... TIME!
AFTER CLOSING IN AT LIGHTSPEED...
...HE TOOK A STEP BACK...
...WITHOUT CHANGING HIS POSTURE!
JUST WHEN YAMATO WAS GOING TO TACKLE...
...HE BACKED AWAY AT LIGHT-SPEED.
NO ONE IS AS FAST AS THAT LOSER PIP-SQUEAK.
NO ONE CAN CATCH HIM.
THIS GENERATION'S GREATEST RUNNER..
... EYESHIELD 21...
...COMMANDS ESOTERIC RUNNING TECHNIQUES!
LIGHT BENDS SPACE AND TIME!
SENA'S RUNNING IN 4-D!

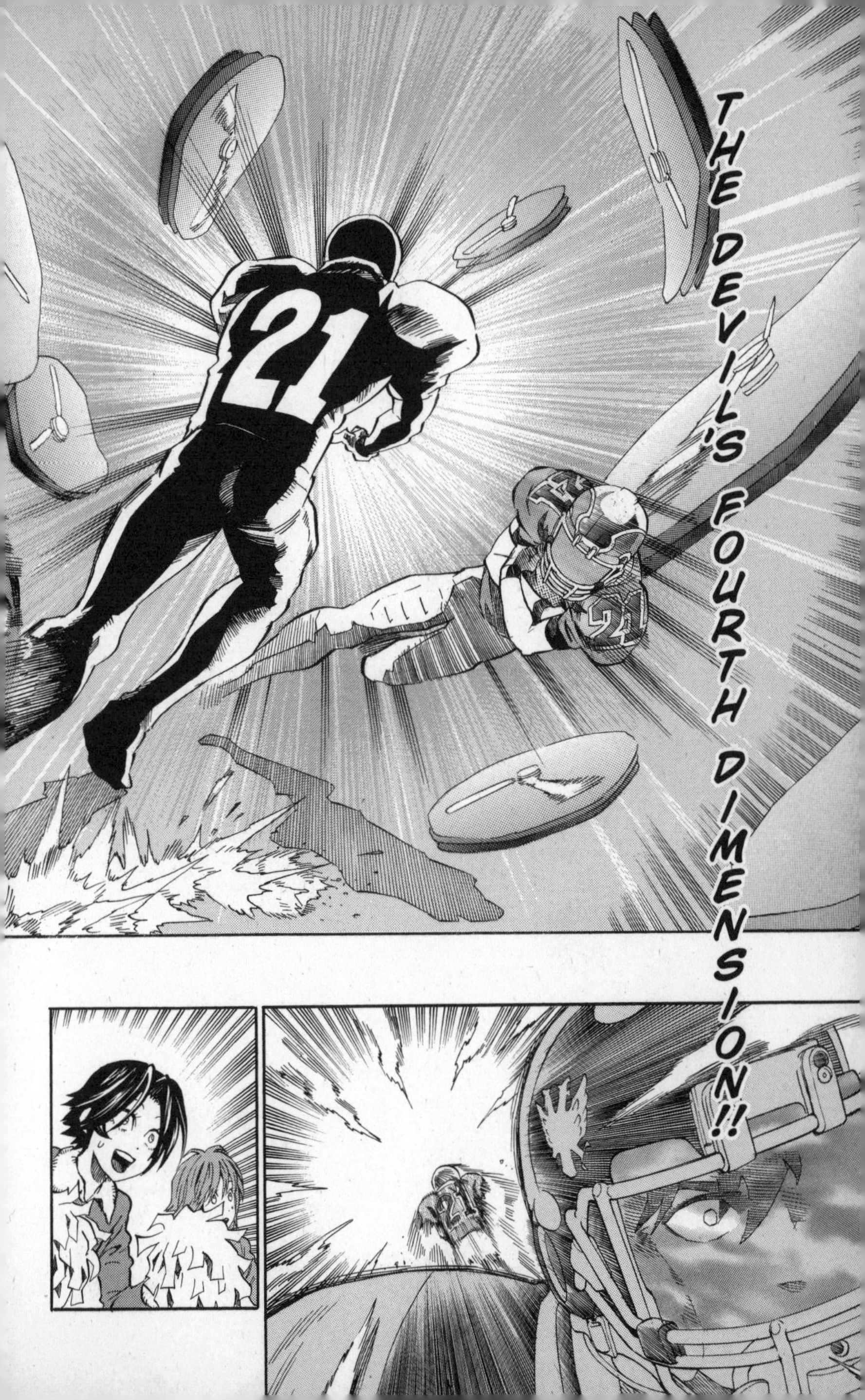
THE DEVIL'S FOURTH DIMENSION!!

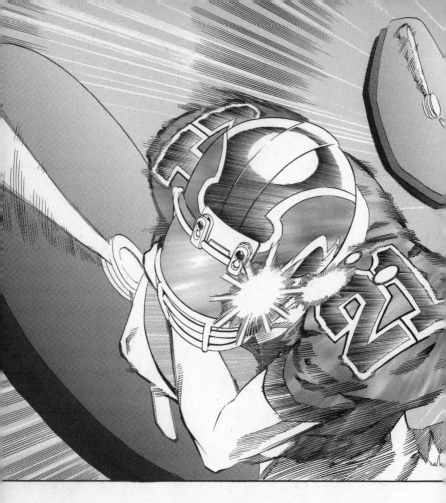

... YAMATO !!

HE GOT PAST ...

EYESHIELD 21

... THE "REAL" ...

... EYESHIELD 21!

HE FINALLY BEAT...

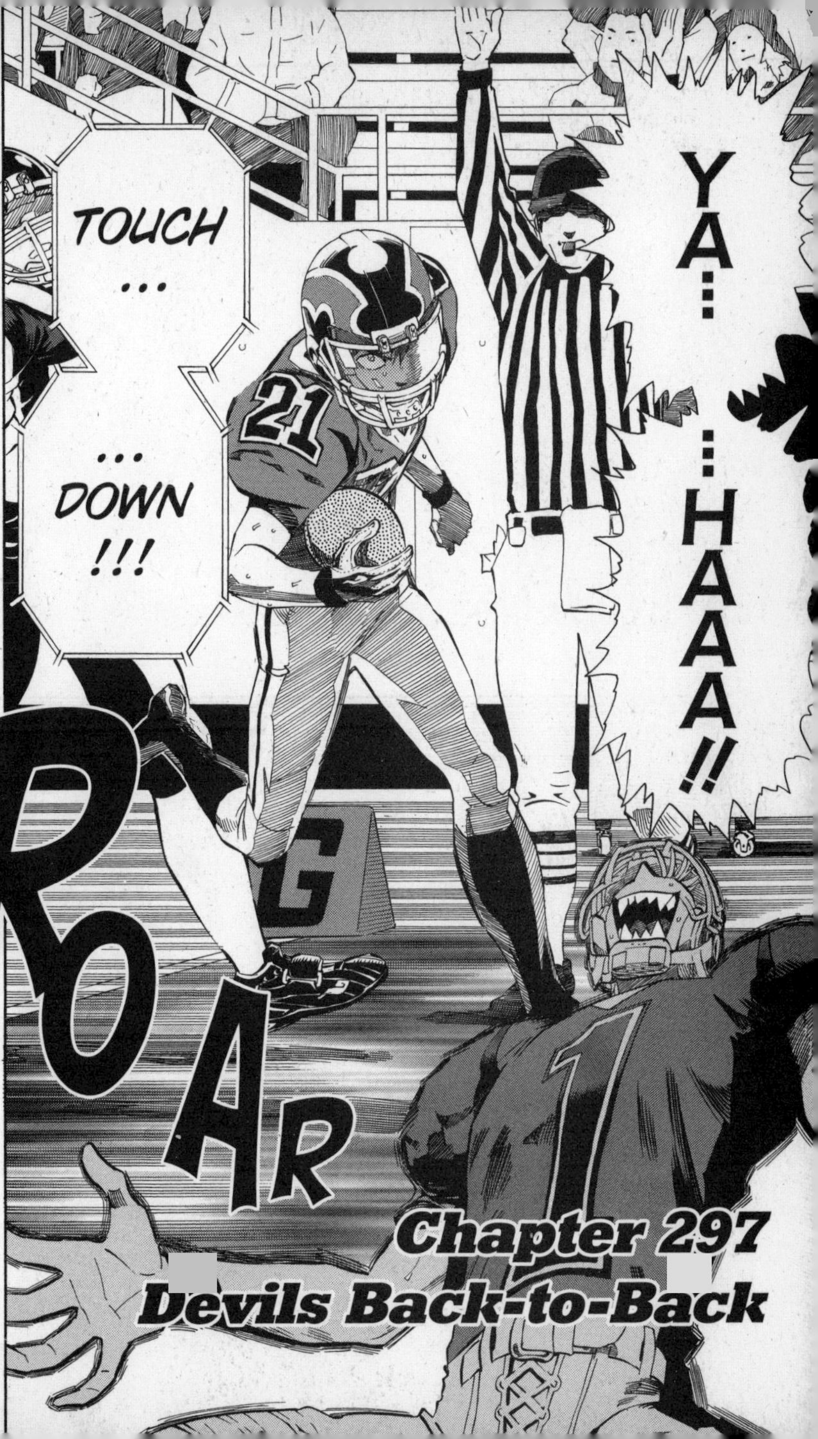
YA...
...HAAAA!!
TOUCH...
...DOWN!!!
ROAR
Chapter 297
Devils Back-to-Back

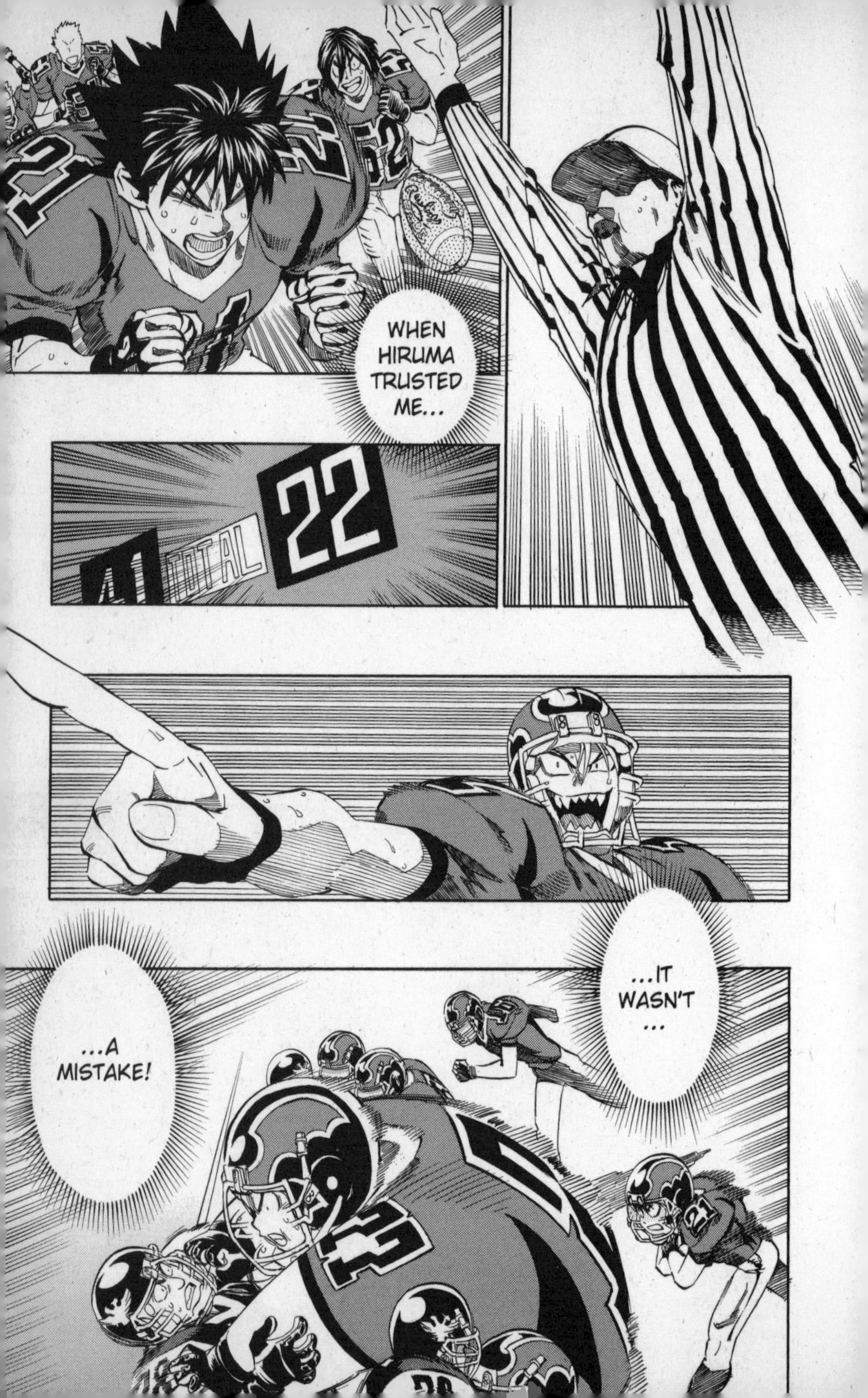
WHEN HIRUMA TRUSTED ME...
TOTAL
22
...IT WASN'T ...
...A MISTAKE!

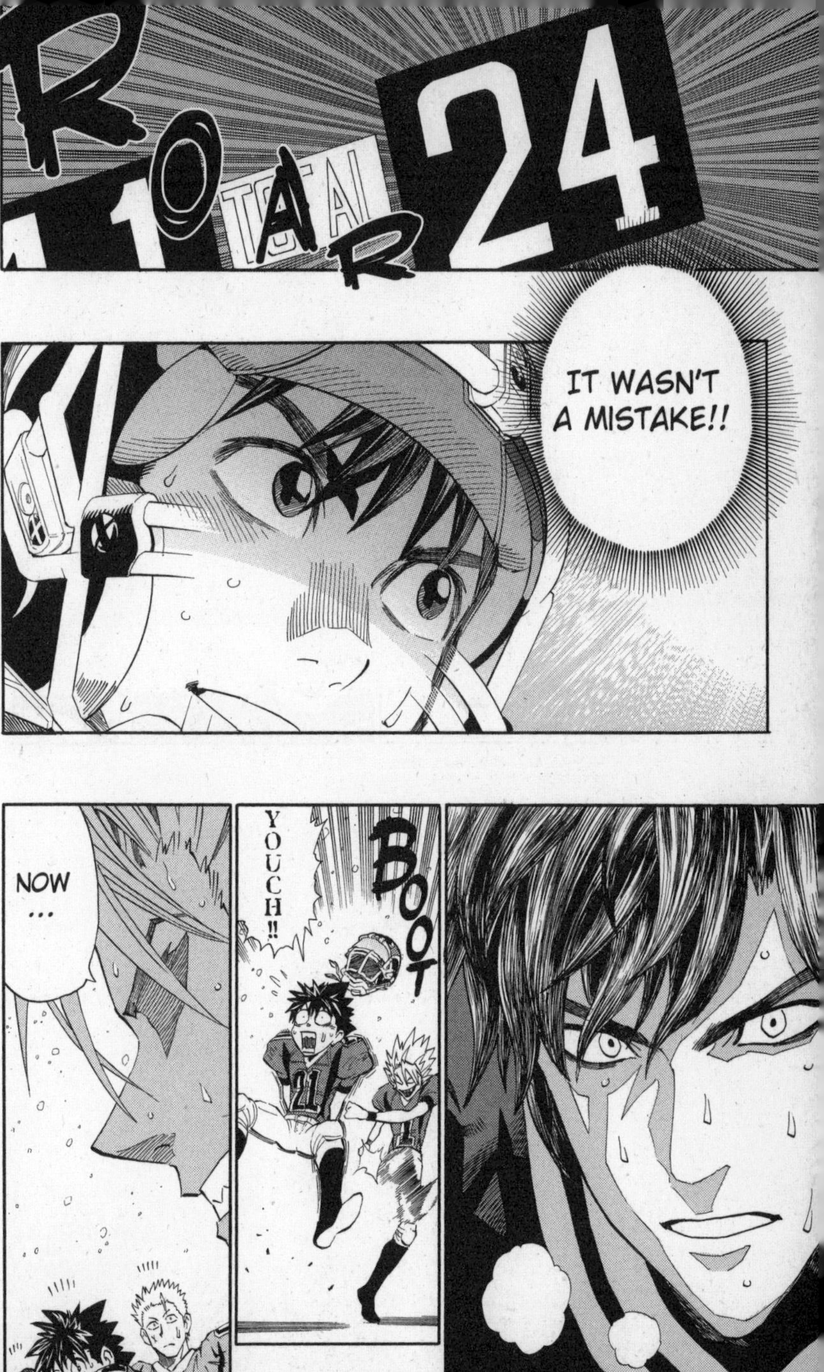
ROAR
TOTAL
24
IT WASN'T A MISTAKE!!
YOUCH!!
BOOT
NOW ...

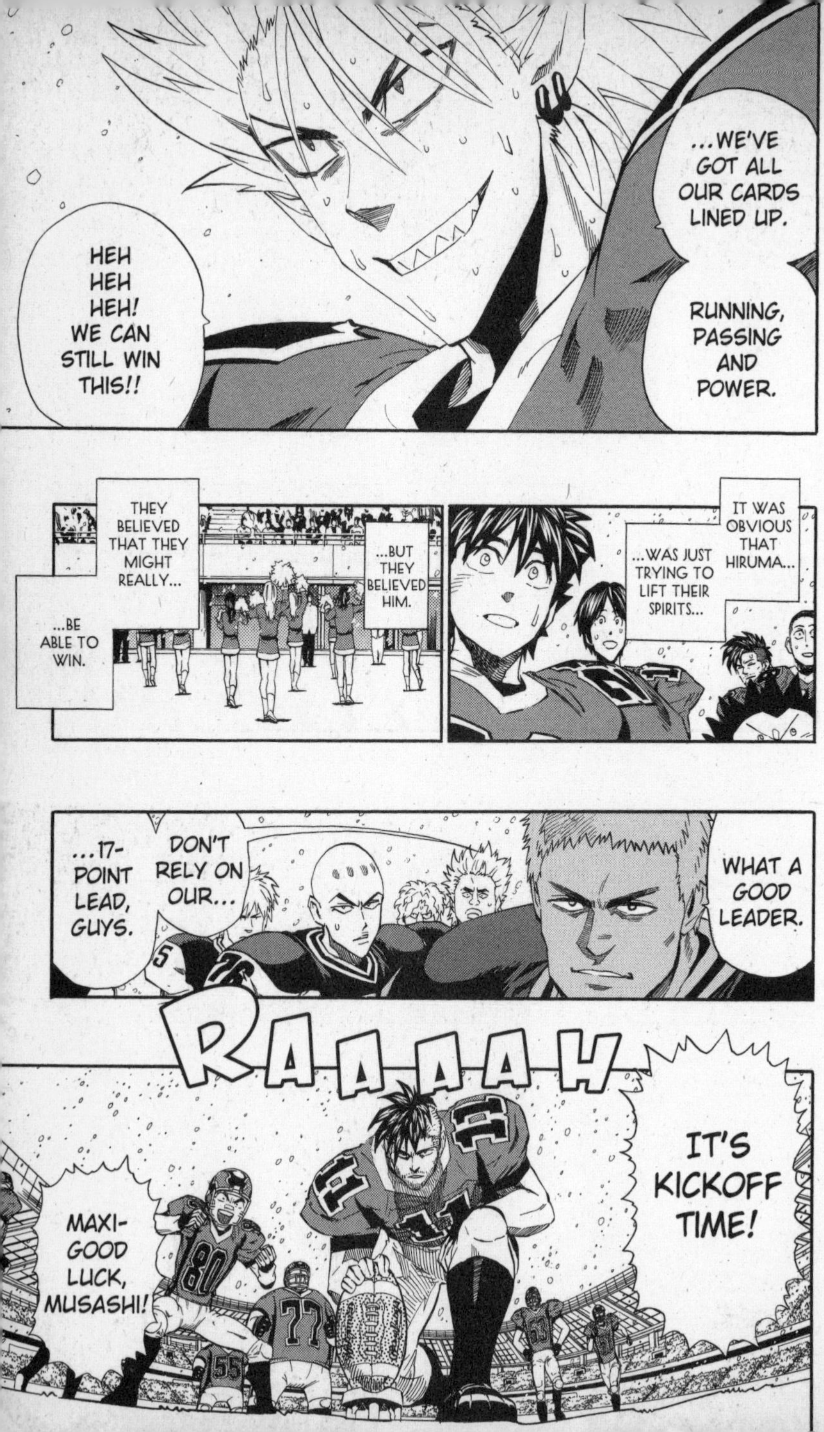
...WE'VE GOT ALL OUR CARDS LINED UP.
RUNNING, PASSING AND POWER.
HEH HEH HEH! WE CAN STILL WIN THIS!!
IT WAS OBVIOUS THAT HIRUMA...
...WAS JUST TRYING TO LIFT THEIR SPIRITS...
...BUT THEY BELIEVED HIM.
THEY BELIEVED THAT THEY MIGHT REALLY...
...BE ABLE TO WIN.
WHAT A GOOD LEADER.
DON'T RELY ON OUR...
...17-POINT LEAD, GUYS.
RAAAAH
IT'S KICKOFF TIME!
MAXI-GOOD LUCK, MUSASHI!

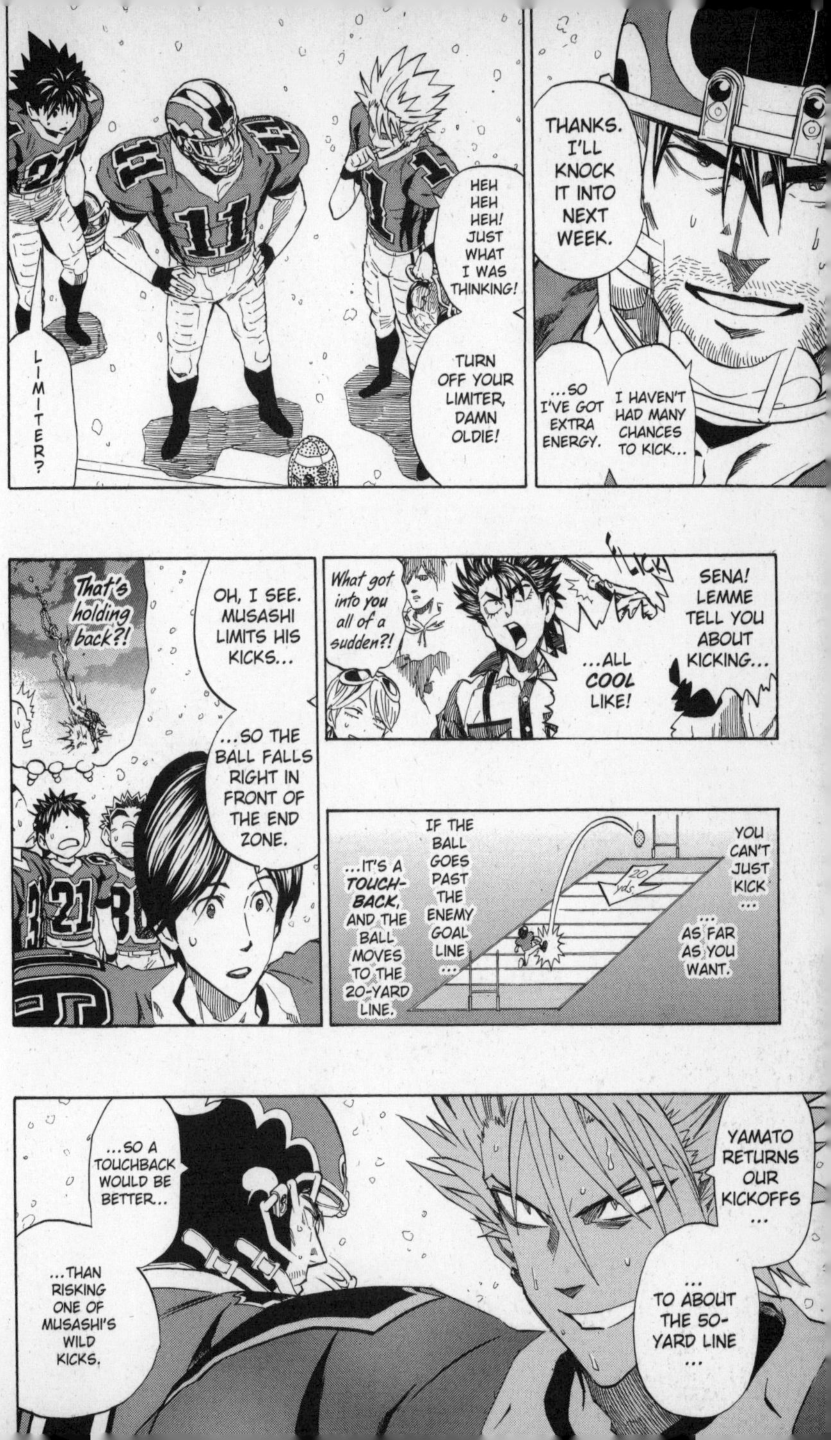
THANKS. I'LL KNOCK IT INTO NEXT WEEK.
I HAVEN'T HAD MANY CHANCES TO KICK...
...SO I'VE GOT EXTRA ENERGY.
HEH HEH HEH! JUST WHAT I WAS THINKING!
TURN OFF YOUR LIMITER, DAMN OLDIE!
LIMITER?
SENA! LEMME TELL YOU ABOUT KICKING...
...ALL COOL LIKE!
What got into you all of a sudden?!
YOU CAN'T JUST KICK ...
... AS FAR AS YOU WANT.
IF THE BALL GOES PAST THE ENEMY GOAL LINE ...
...IT'S A TOUCHBACK, AND THE BALL MOVES TO THE 20-YARD LINE.
20 yds
OH, I SEE. MUSASHI LIMITS HIS KICKS...
...SO THE BALL FALLS RIGHT IN FRONT OF THE END ZONE.
That's holding back?!
YAMATO RETURNS OUR KICKOFFS ...
... TO ABOUT THE 50-YARD LINE ...
...SO A TOUCHBACK WOULD BE BETTER...
...THAN RISKING ONE OF MUSASHI'S WILD KICKS.

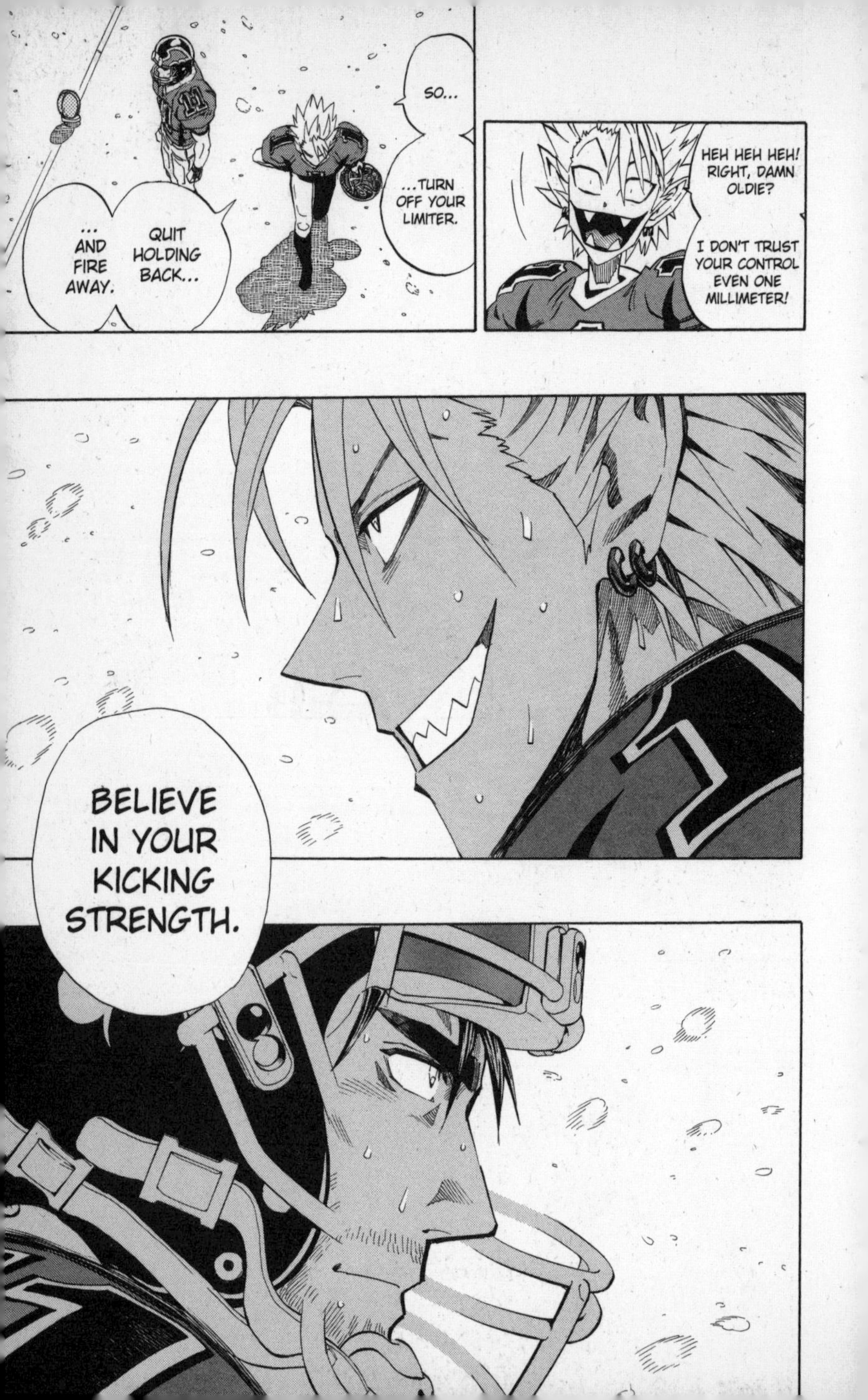
HEH HEH HEH! RIGHT, DAMN OLDIE?
I DON'T TRUST YOUR CONTROL EVEN ONE MILLIMETER!
SO...
...TURN OFF YOUR LIMITER.
QUIT HOLDING BACK...
...AND FIRE AWAY.
BELIEVE IN YOUR KICKING STRENGTH.

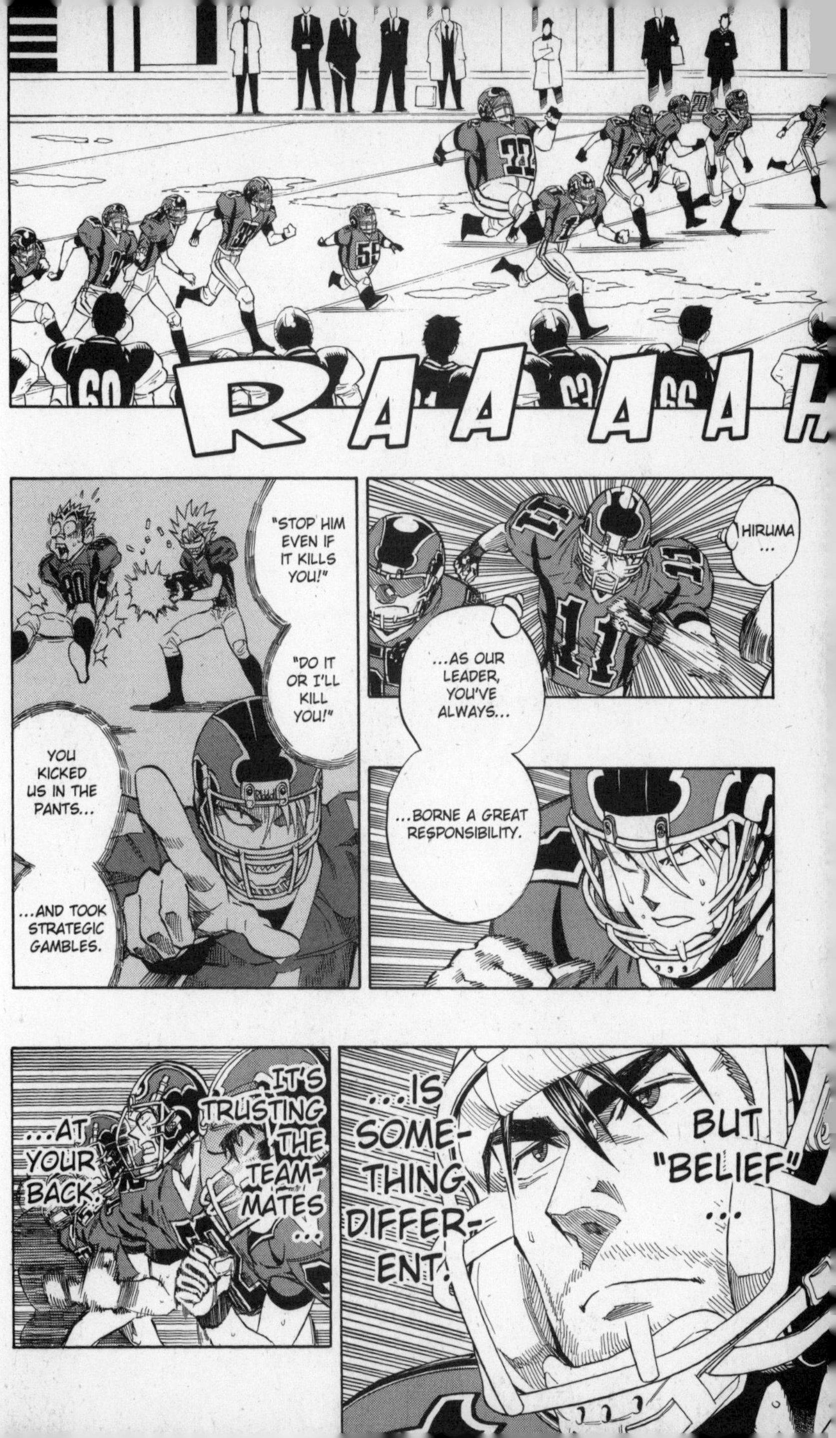
RAAAAH
HIRUMA...
...AS OUR LEADER, YOU'VE ALWAYS...
...BORNE A GREAT RESPONSIBILITY.
"STOP HIM EVEN IF IT KILLS YOU!"
"DO IT OR I'LL KILL YOU!"
YOU KICKED US IN THE PANTS...
...AND TOOK STRATEGIC GAMBLES.
BUT "BELIEF"...
...IS SOME-THING DIFFER-ENT!
IT'S TRUSTING THE TEAM-MATES...
...AT YOUR BACK.

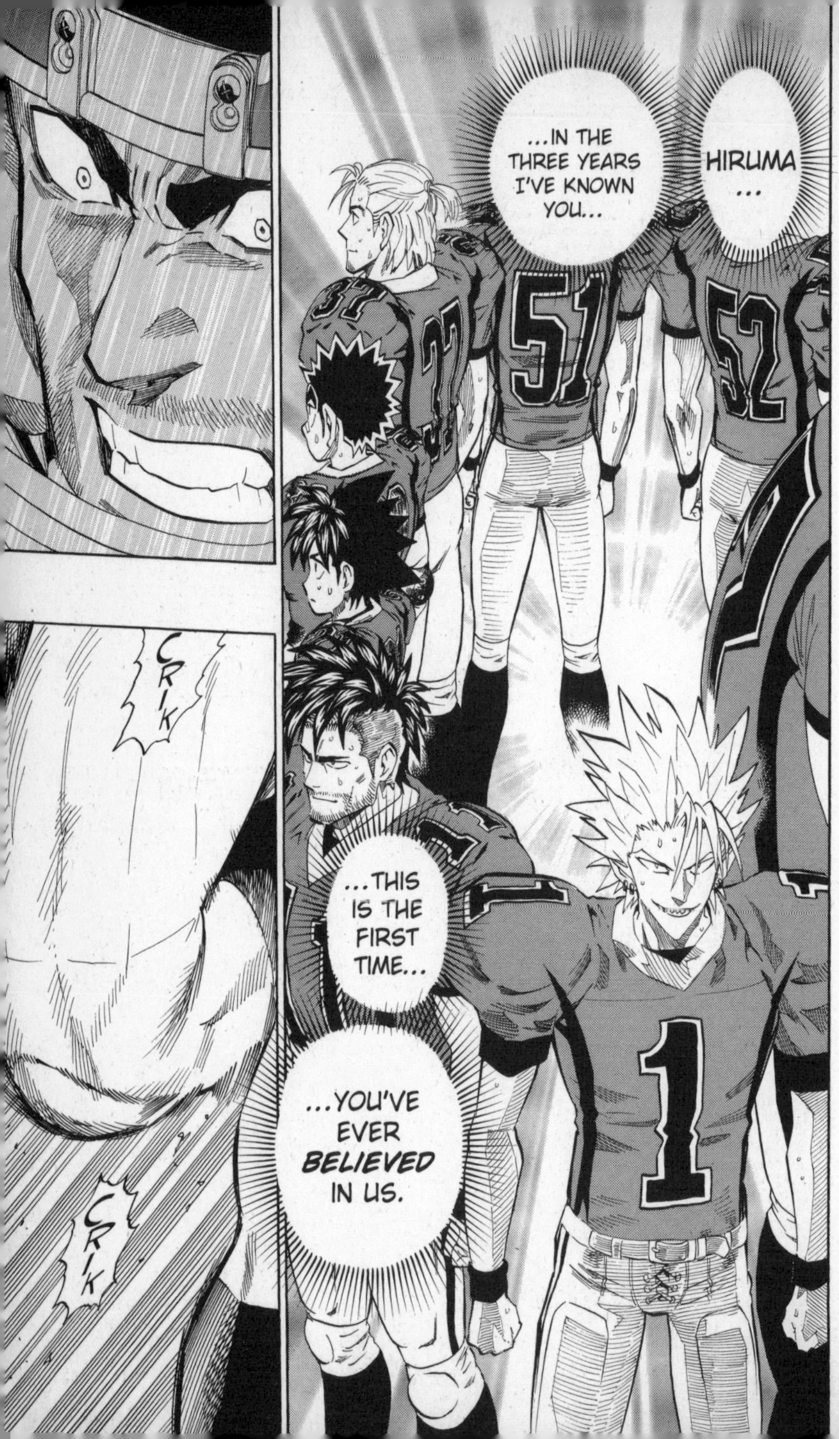
HIRUMA...
...IN THE THREE YEARS I'VE KNOWN YOU...
...THIS IS THE FIRST TIME...
...YOU'VE EVER BELIEVED IN US.
CRIK
CRIK

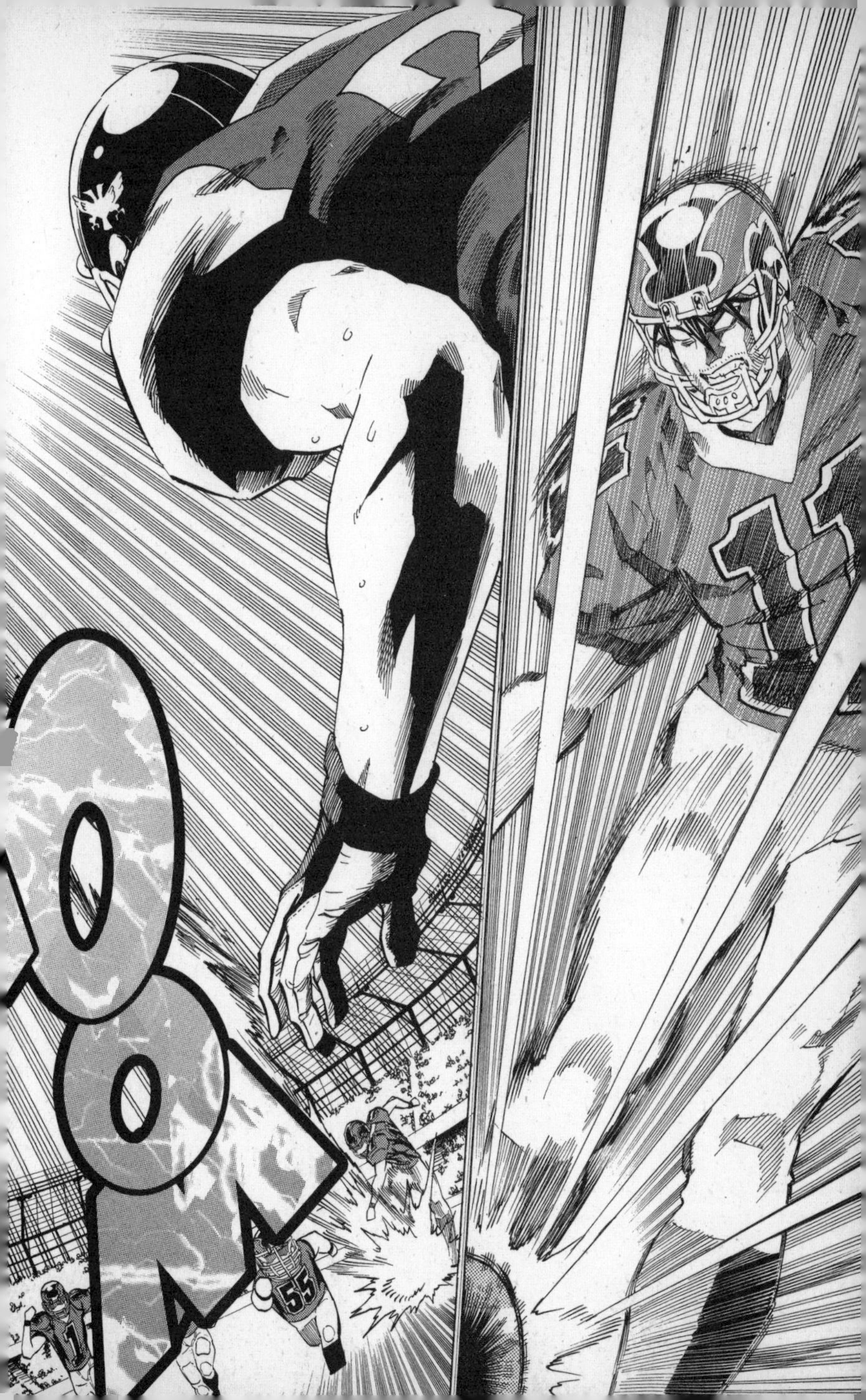

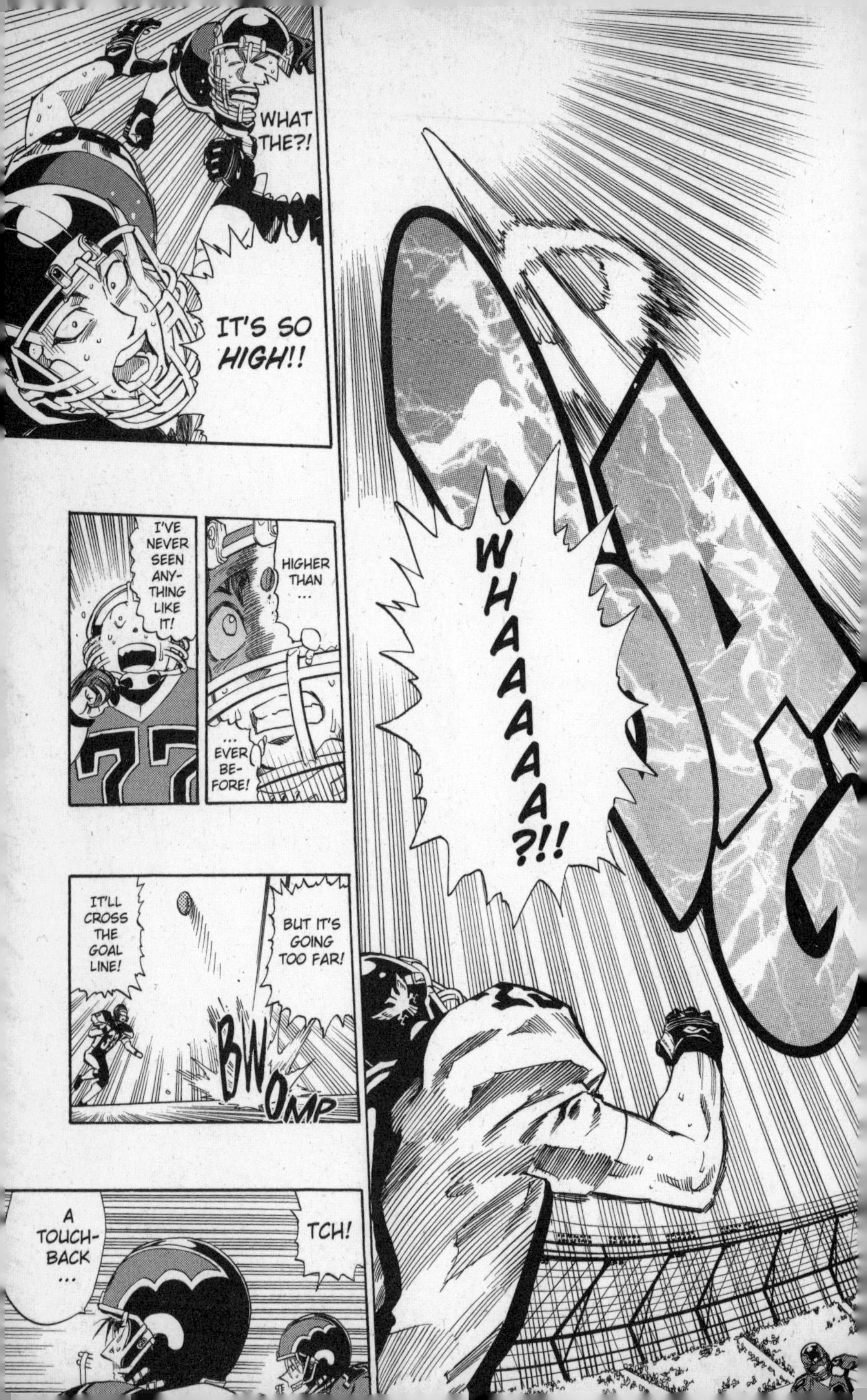
WHAAAAAA?!!
WHAT THE?!
IT'S SO HIGH!!
HIGHER THAN ...
... EVER BE-FORE!
I'VE NEVER SEEN ANY-THING LIKE IT!
BUT IT'S GOING TOO FAR!
IT'LL CROSS THE GOAL LINE!
BWOMP
TCH!
A TOUCH-BACK ...

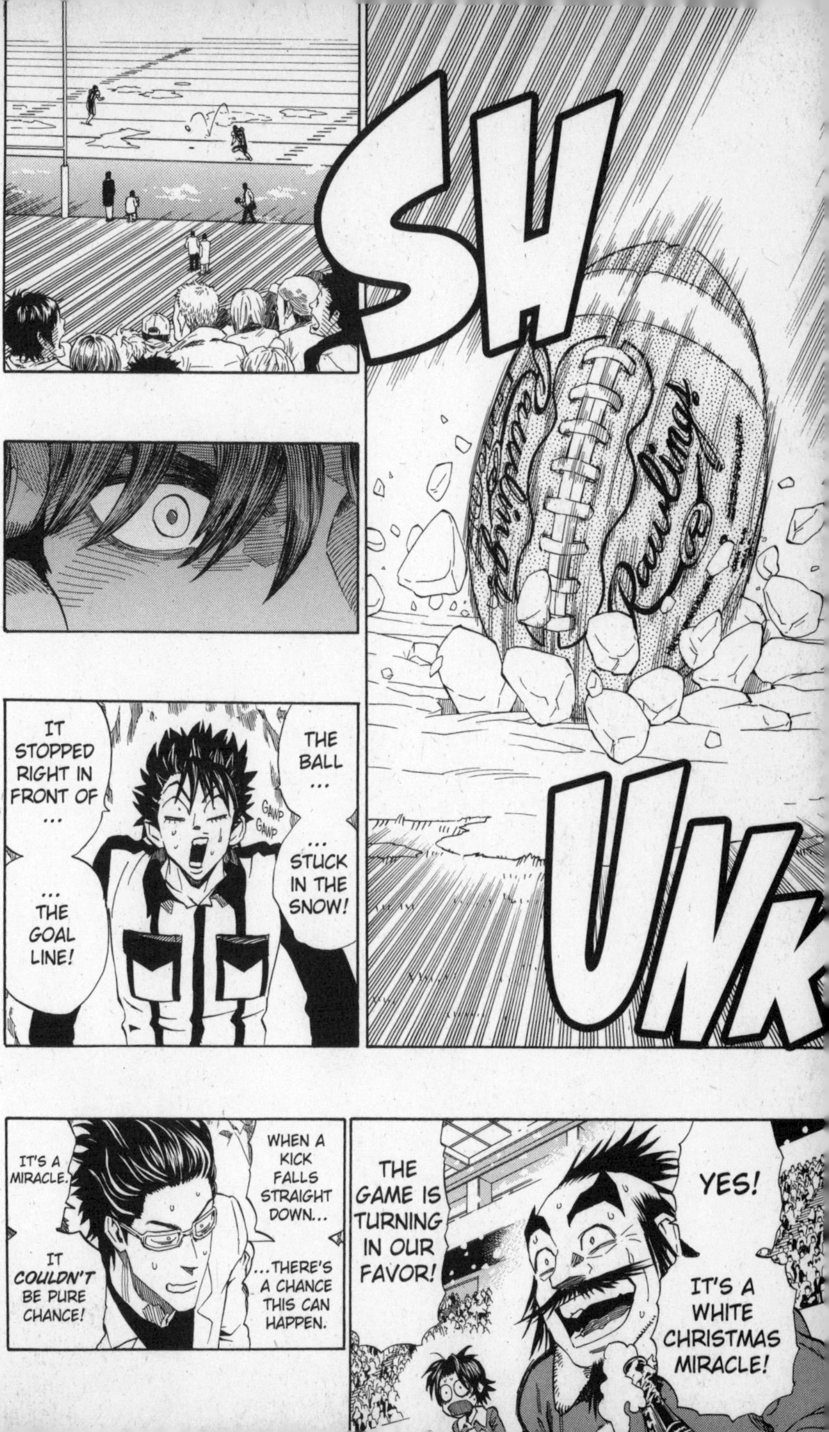
SH
Rawlings
UNK
THE BALL...
... STUCK IN THE SNOW!
IT STOPPED RIGHT IN FRONT OF...
... THE GOAL LINE!
GAWP GAWP
YES!
THE GAME IS TURNING IN OUR FAVOR!
IT'S A WHITE CHRISTMAS MIRACLE!
WHEN A KICK FALLS STRAIGHT DOWN...
...THERE'S A CHANCE THIS CAN HAPPEN.
IT'S A MIRACLE.
IT *COULDN'T* BE PURE CHANCE!

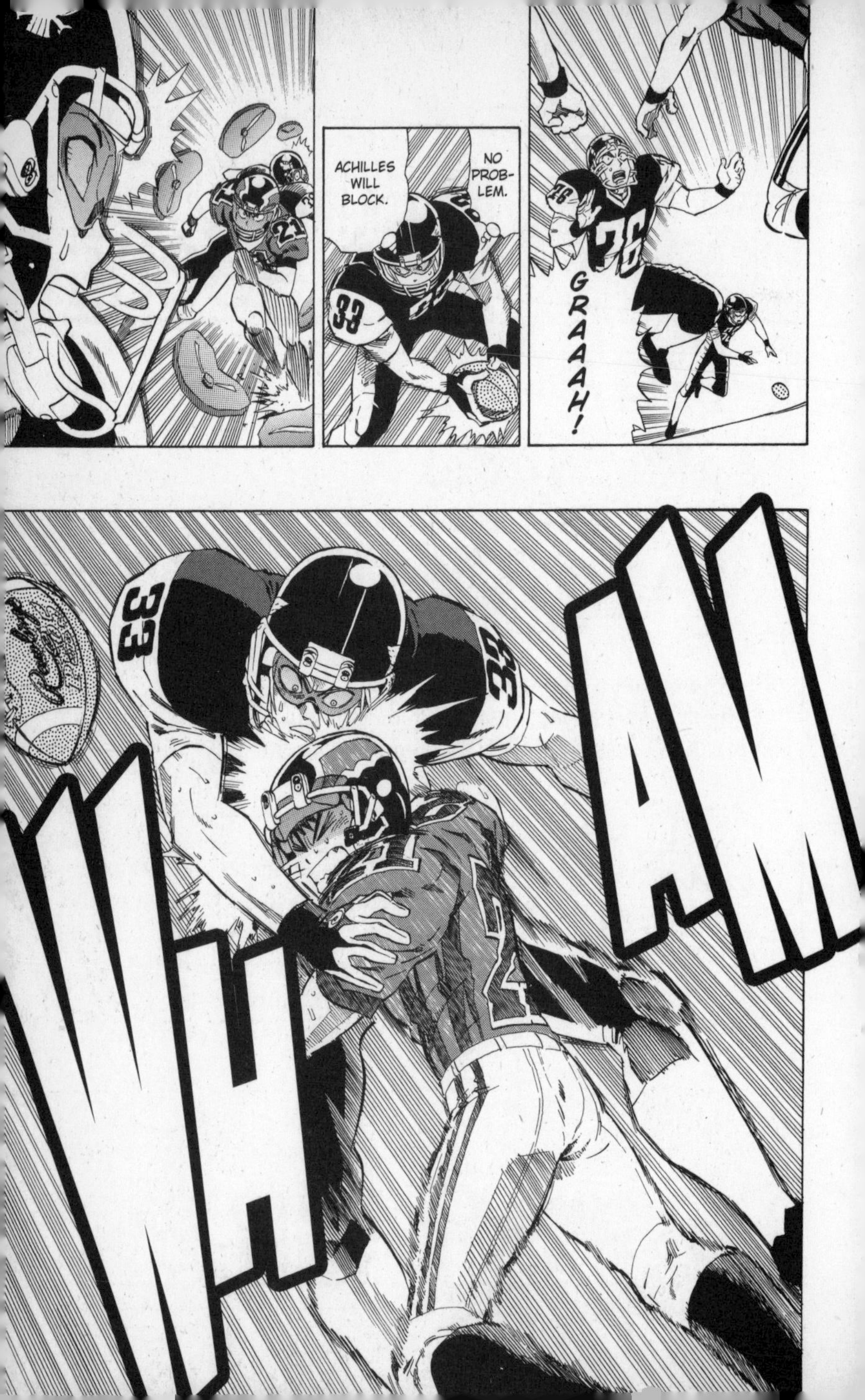
GRAAAH!
NO PROB-LEM.
ACHILLES WILL BLOCK.
WHAM

Miracle Ito
President
Jari Productions

He's still alive! Shrewd Miracle Ito's

New product!!

HIGH SCHOOL FOOTBALL STAR GOODS

Shoes that walk the air!

Taka Model

"Air Walker"

"Thick-soled boots make you taller,
but the design is always bulky and looks awful."
"Ever since I was little, I've wanted to walk the sky."

These shoes are the ultimate response to such statements. The thick soles are made of an acrylic with over 90 percent transparency. You too can be Taka Honjo!

※Floating sensation may vary by person.

SPECIAL PRICE **¥17,800**※

※$197

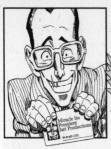

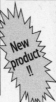

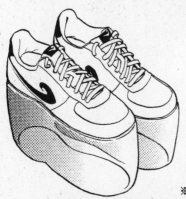

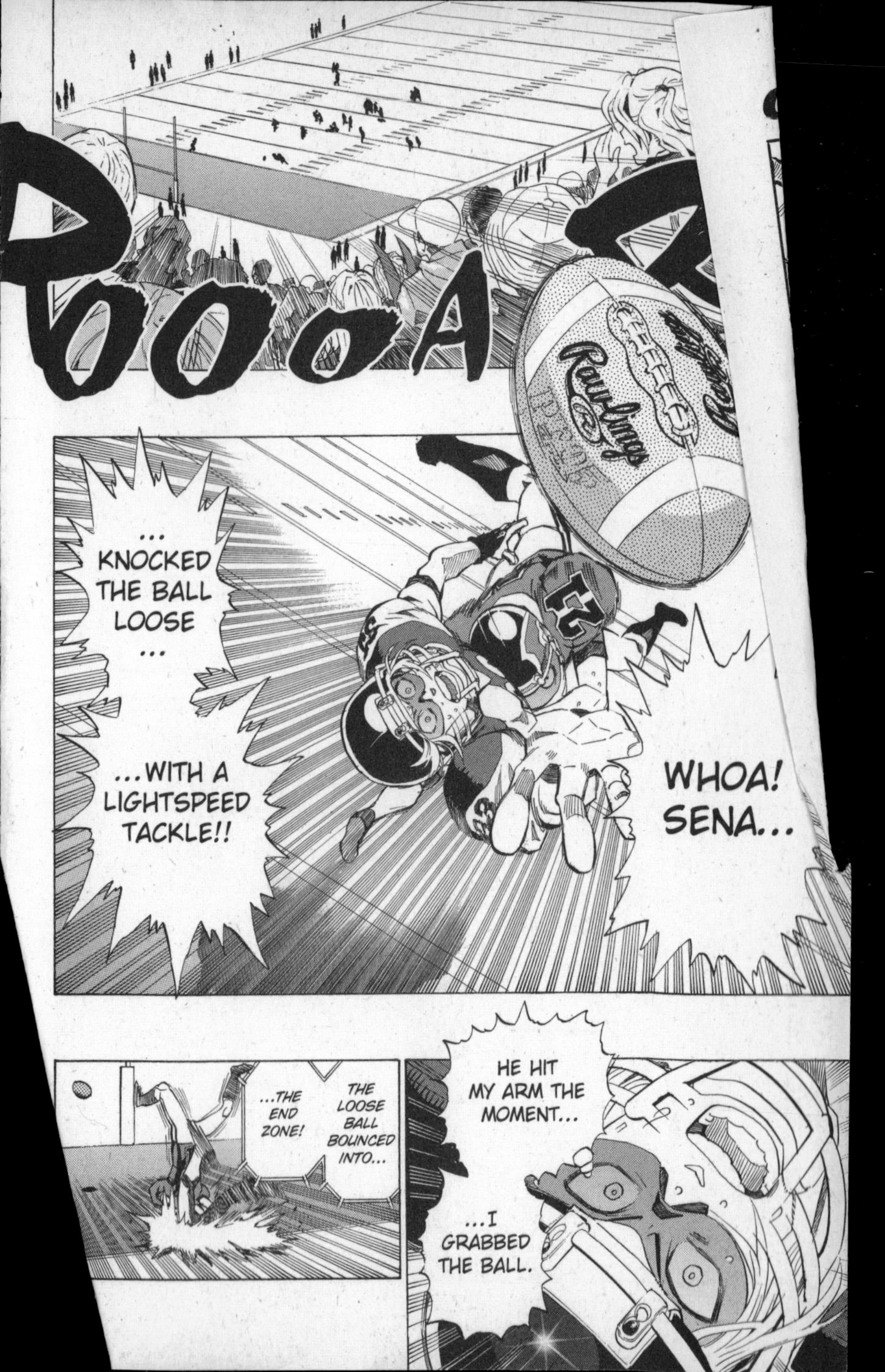
WHOA! SENA...
... KNOCKED THE BALL LOOSE ...
...WITH A LIGHTSPEED TACKLE!!
HE HIT MY ARM THE MOMENT...
...I GRABBED THE BALL.
THE LOOSE BALL BOUNCED INTO...
...THE END ZONE!

Chapter 298 Brains for an Idiot

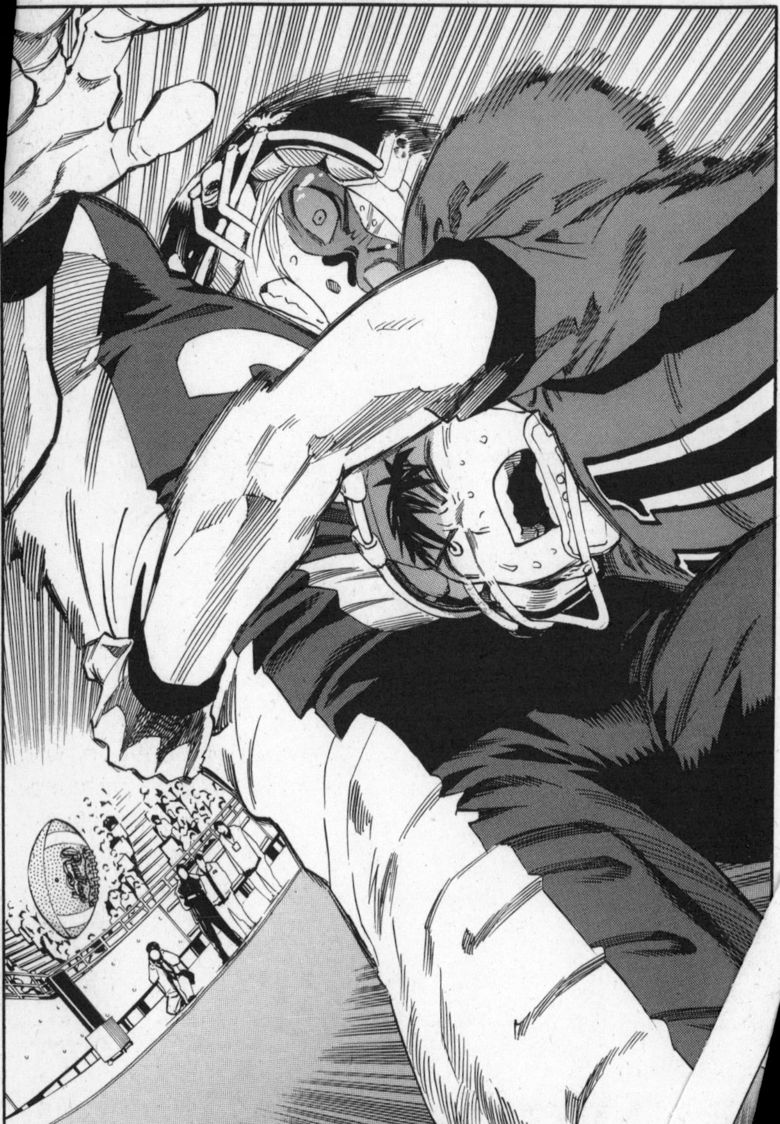

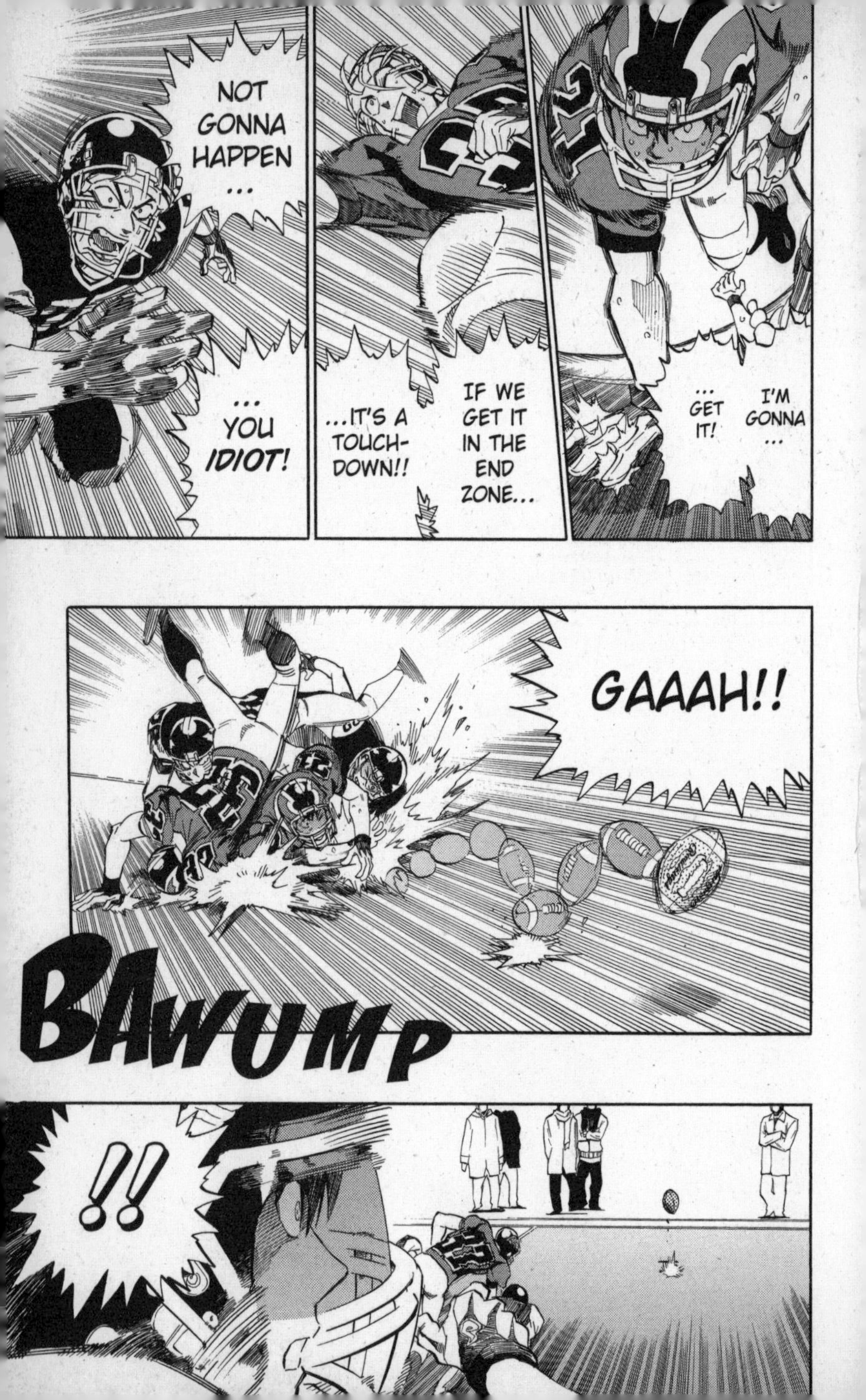
I'M GONNA ...
... GET IT!
IF WE GET IT IN THE END ZONE...
...IT'S A TOUCHDOWN!!
NOT GONNA HAPPEN ...
... YOU IDIOT!
GAAAH!!
BAWUMP
!!

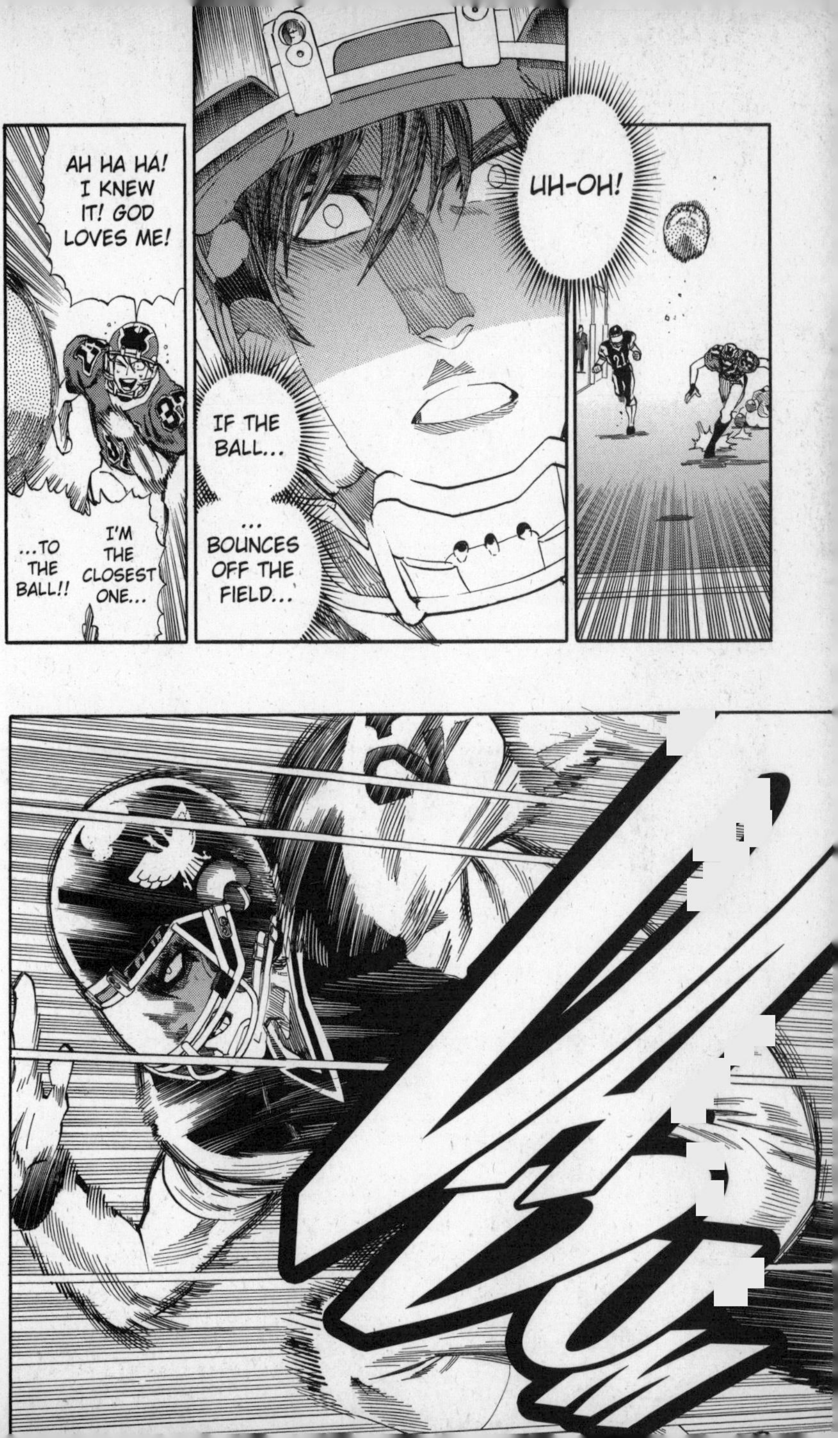
UH-OH!
IF THE BALL...
...BOUNCES OFF THE FIELD...
AH HA HA! I KNEW IT! GOD LOVES ME!
I'M THE CLOSEST ONE...
...TO THE BALL!!

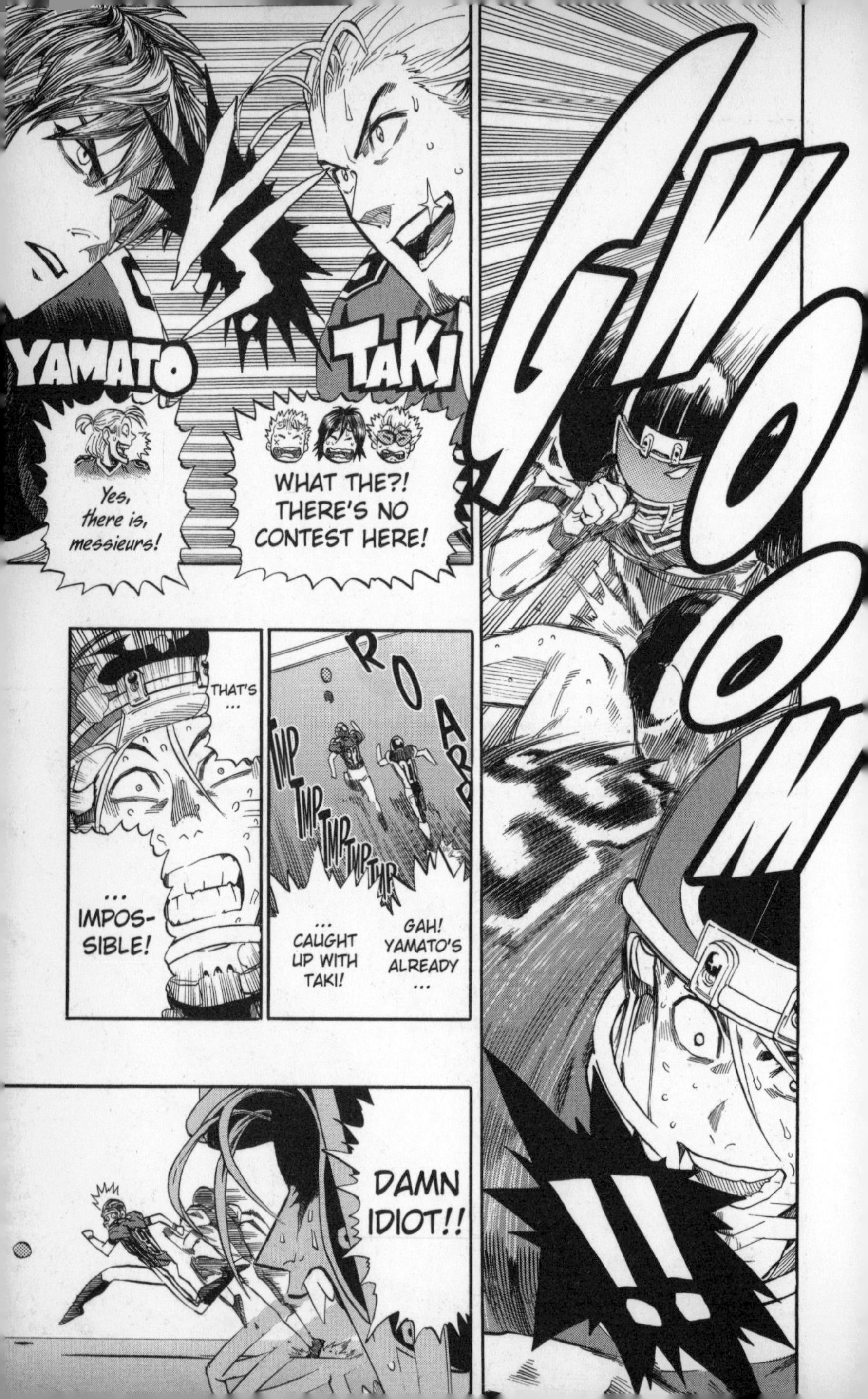
GWOOOM
!!
TAKI
YAMATO
WHAT THE?! THERE'S NO CONTEST HERE!
Yes, there is, messieurs!
ROAR
TMP TMP TMP TMP TMP TMP
GAH! YAMATO'S ALREADY ...
... CAUGHT UP WITH TAKI!
THAT'S ...
... IMPOS-SIBLE!
DAMN IDIOT!!

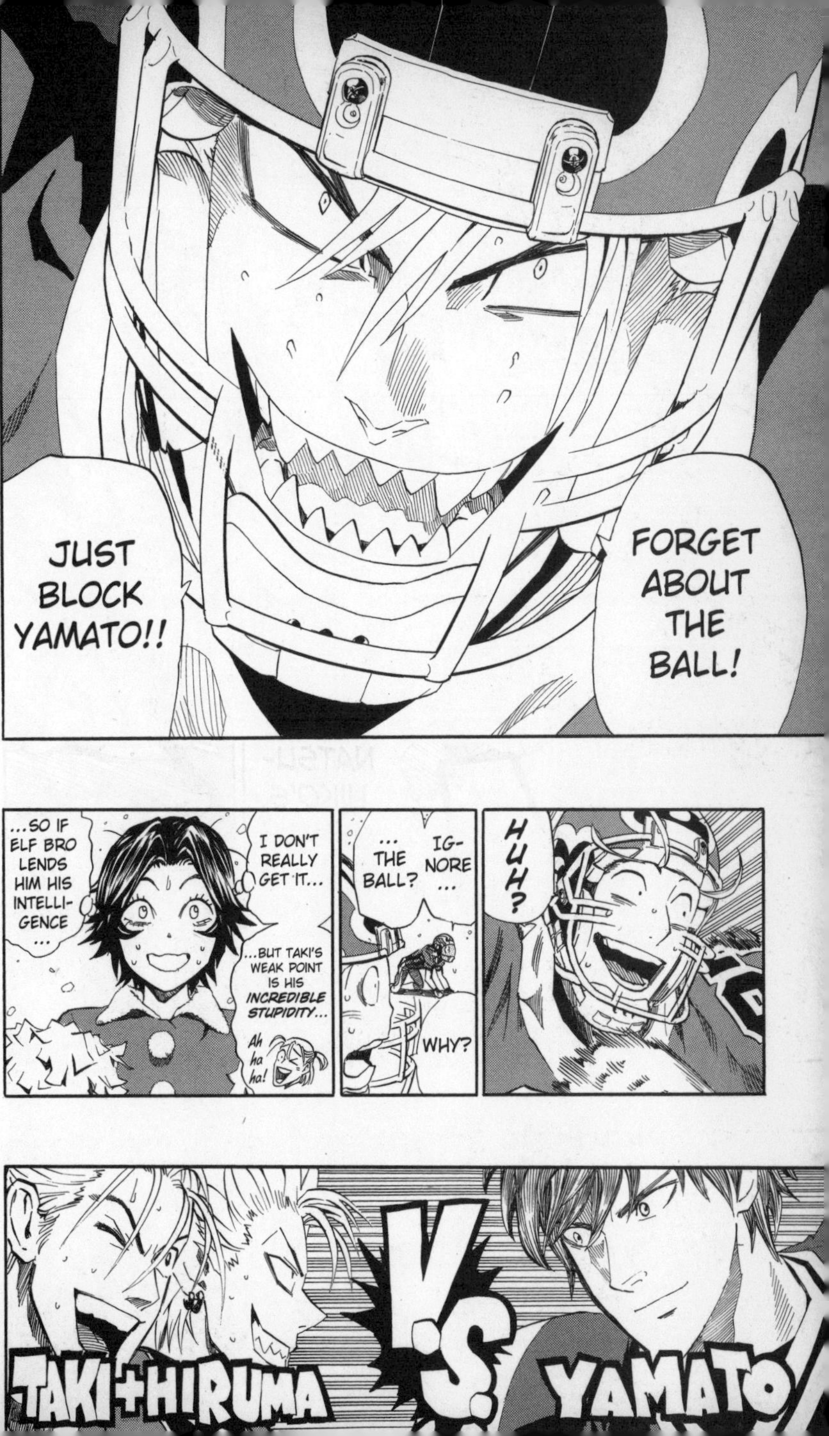
FORGET ABOUT THE BALL!
JUST BLOCK YAMATO!!
HUH?
IG-NORE ...
... THE BALL?
WHY?
I DON'T REALLY GET IT...
...SO IF ELF BRO LENDS HIM HIS INTELLI-GENCE ...
...BUT TAKI'S WEAK POINT IS HIS *INCREDIBLE STUPIDITY*...
Ah ha ha!
TAKI+HIRUMA V.S. YAMATO

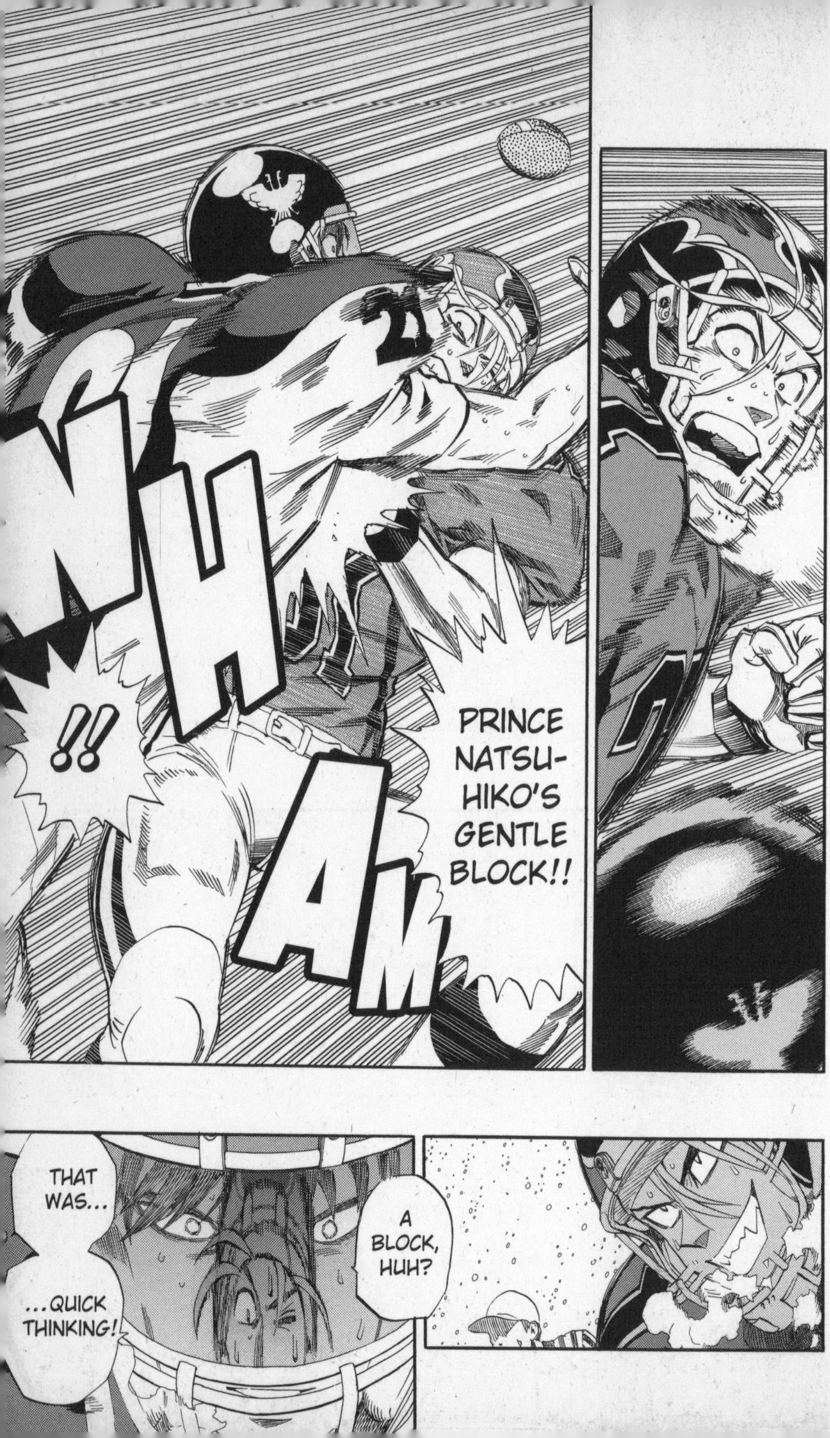
WHAM!!
PRINCE NATSUHIKO'S GENTLE BLOCK!!
A BLOCK, HUH?
THAT WAS...
...QUICK THINKING!

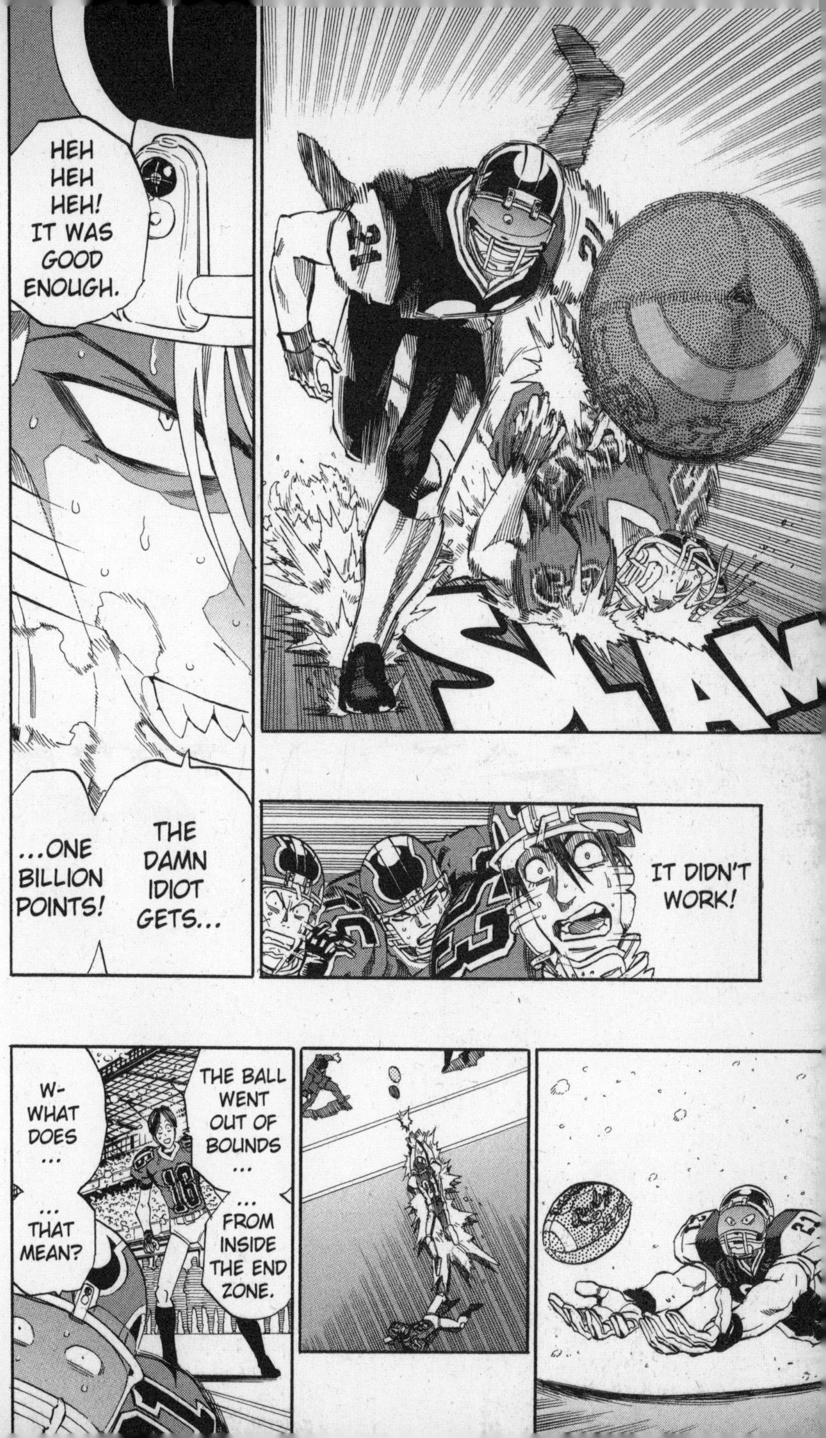
SLAM
IT DIDN'T WORK!
HEH HEH HEH! IT WAS GOOD ENOUGH.
THE DAMN IDIOT GETS...
...ONE BILLION POINTS!
THE BALL WENT OUT OF BOUNDS...
...FROM INSIDE THE END ZONE.
W-WHAT DOES...
...THAT MEAN?

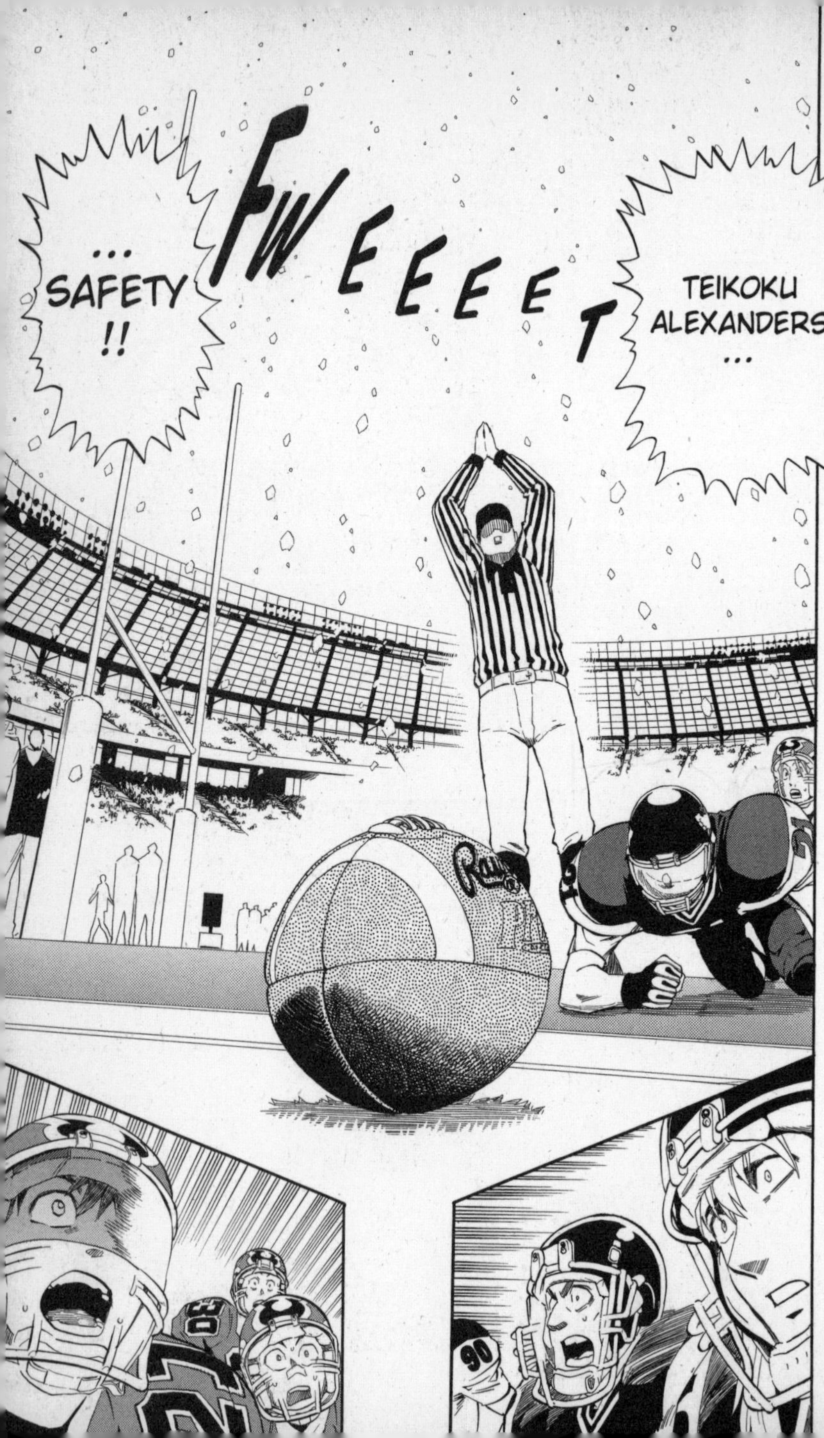
TEIKOKU ALEXANDERS ...
FWEEEET
... SAFETY !!

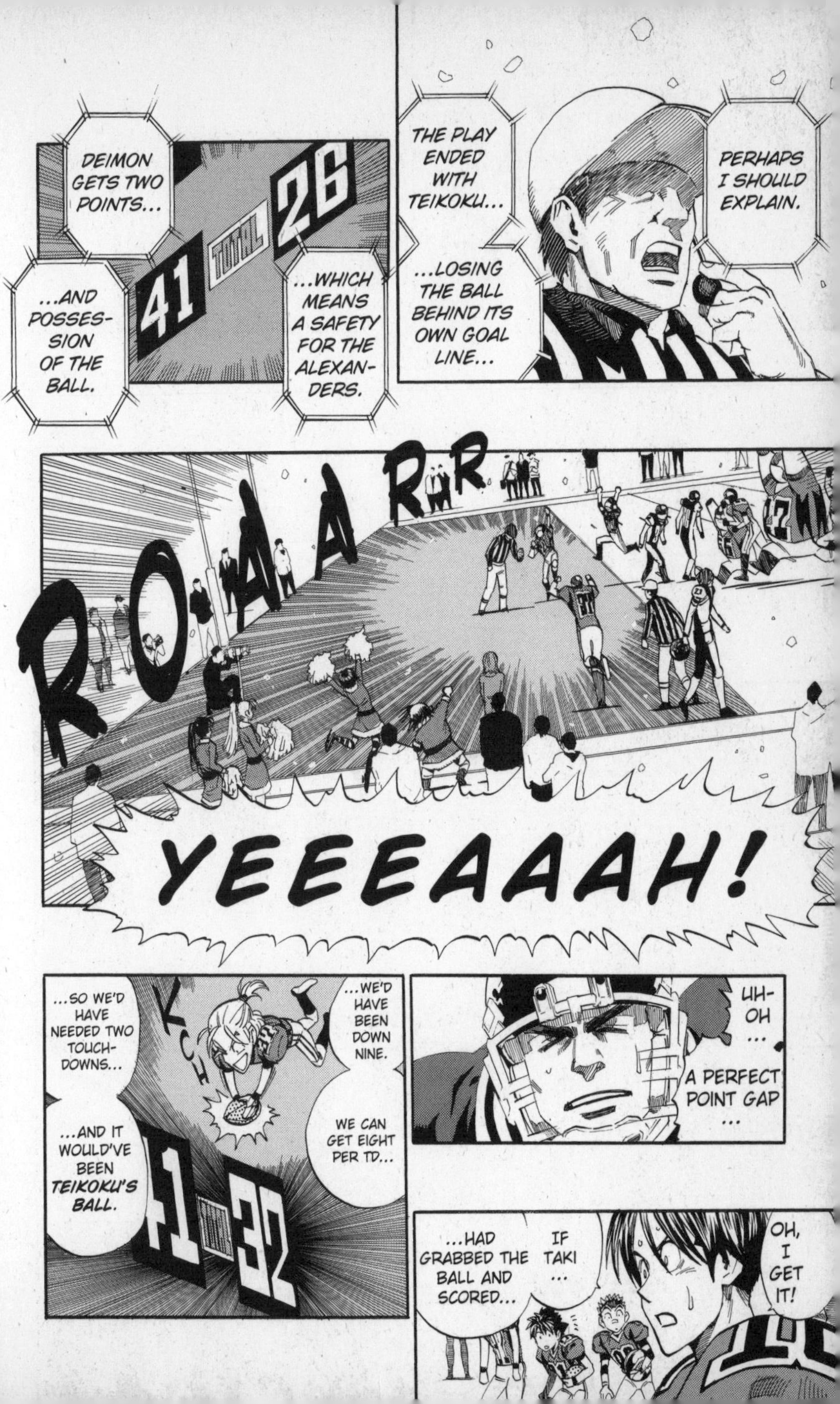
PERHAPS I SHOULD EXPLAIN.
THE PLAY ENDED WITH TEIKOKU...
...LOSING THE BALL BEHIND ITS OWN GOAL LINE...
41 TOTAL 26
...WHICH MEANS A SAFETY FOR THE ALEXANDERS.
DEIMON GETS TWO POINTS...
...AND POSSESSION OF THE BALL.
ROAARRR
YEEEAAAH!
UH-OH... A PERFECT POINT GAP...
OH, I GET IT!
IF TAKI...
...HAD GRABBED THE BALL AND SCORED...
...WE'D HAVE BEEN DOWN NINE.
...SO WE'D HAVE NEEDED TWO TOUCHDOWNS...
KCH
WE CAN GET EIGHT PER TD...
...AND IT WOULD'VE BEEN *TEIKOKU'S* BALL.

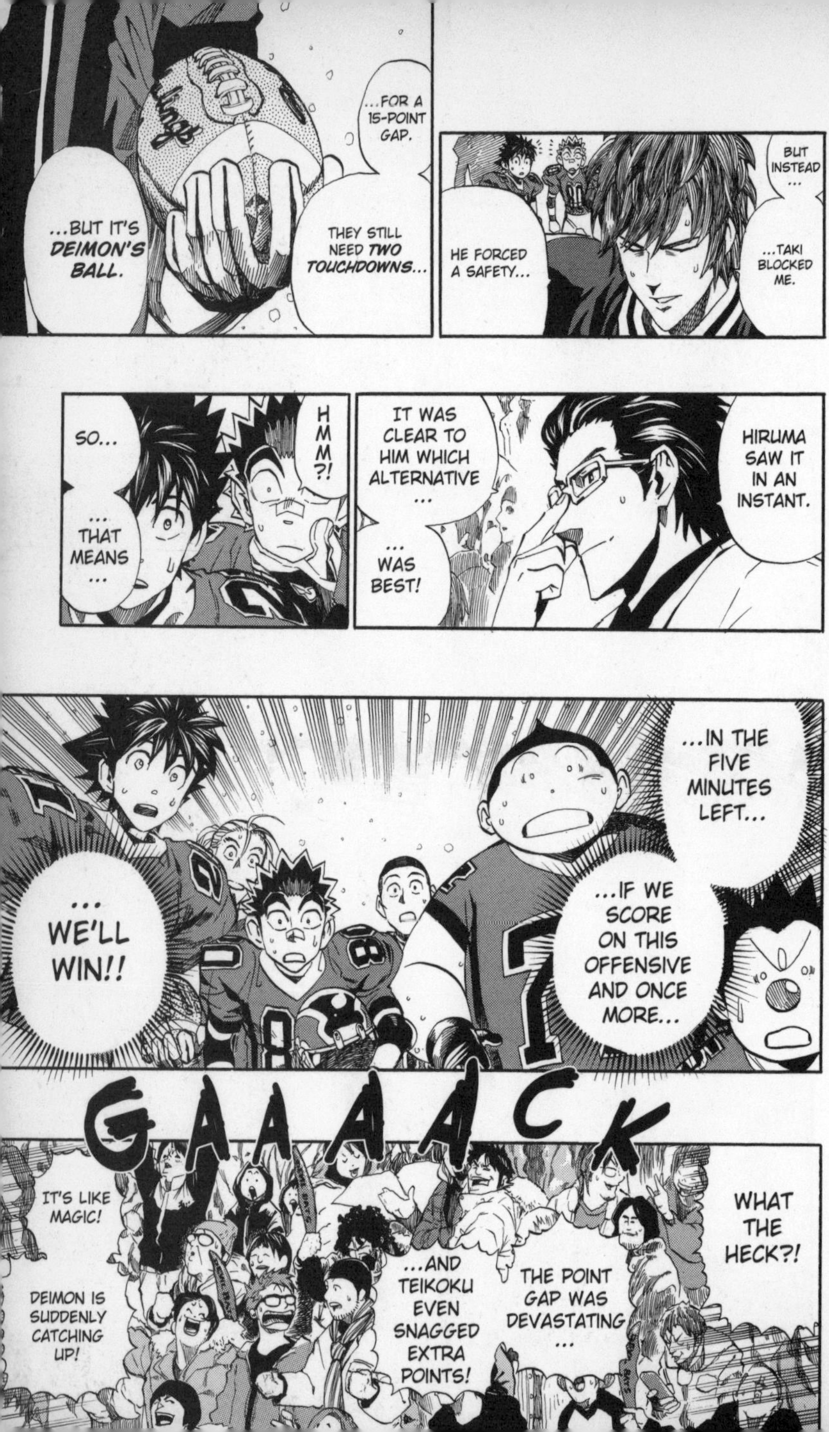
BUT INSTEAD...
...TAKI BLOCKED ME.
HE FORCED A SAFETY...
...FOR A 15-POINT GAP.
THEY STILL NEED TWO TOUCHDOWNS...
...BUT IT'S DEIMON'S BALL.
HIRUMA SAW IT IN AN INSTANT.
IT WAS CLEAR TO HIM WHICH ALTERNATIVE...
...WAS BEST!
HMM?!
SO...
...THAT MEANS...
...IN THE FIVE MINUTES LEFT...
...IF WE SCORE ON THIS OFFENSIVE AND ONCE MORE...
...WE'LL WIN!!
GAAAACK
WHAT THE HECK?!
THE POINT GAP WAS DEVASTATING...
...AND TEIKOKU EVEN SNAGGED EXTRA POINTS!
IT'S LIKE MAGIC!
DEIMON IS SUDDENLY CATCHING UP!

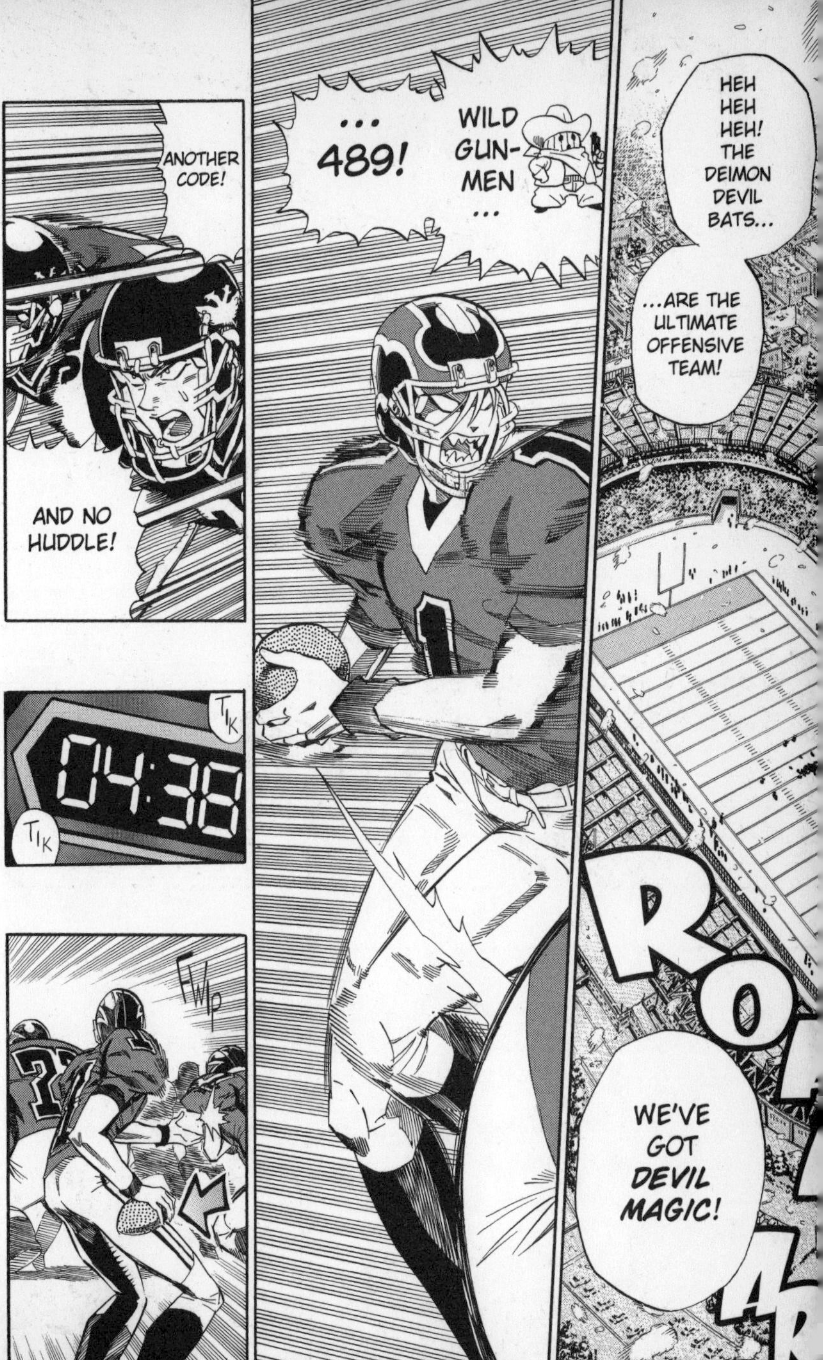
HEH HEH HEH! THE DEIMON DEVIL BATS...
...ARE THE ULTIMATE OFFENSIVE TEAM!
WE'VE GOT DEVIL MAGIC!
WILD GUN-MEN ...
... 489!
ANOTHER CODE!
AND NO HUDDLE!
TIK
04:38
TIK
FWIP

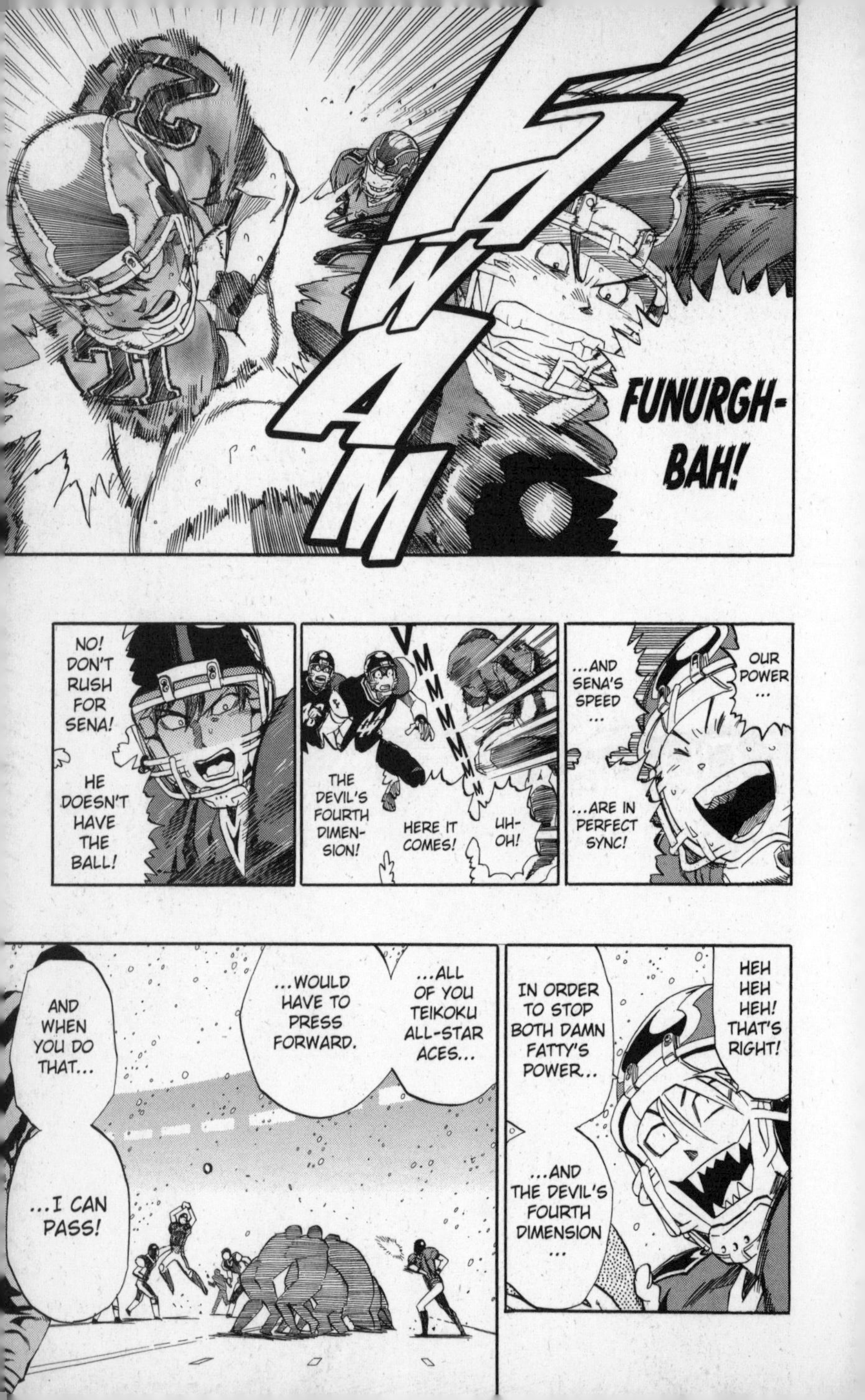
WHAM
FUNURGH-BAH!
OUR POWER...
...AND SENA'S SPEED...
...ARE IN PERFECT SYNC!
UH-OH!
VMMMMMMM
HERE IT COMES!
THE DEVIL'S FOURTH DIMENSION!
NO! DON'T RUSH FOR SENA!
HE DOESN'T HAVE THE BALL!
HEH HEH HEH! THAT'S RIGHT!
IN ORDER TO STOP BOTH DAMN FATTY'S POWER...
...AND THE DEVIL'S FOURTH DIMENSION...
...ALL OF YOU TEIKOKU ALL-STAR ACES...
...WOULD HAVE TO PRESS FORWARD.
AND WHEN YOU DO THAT...
...I CAN PASS!

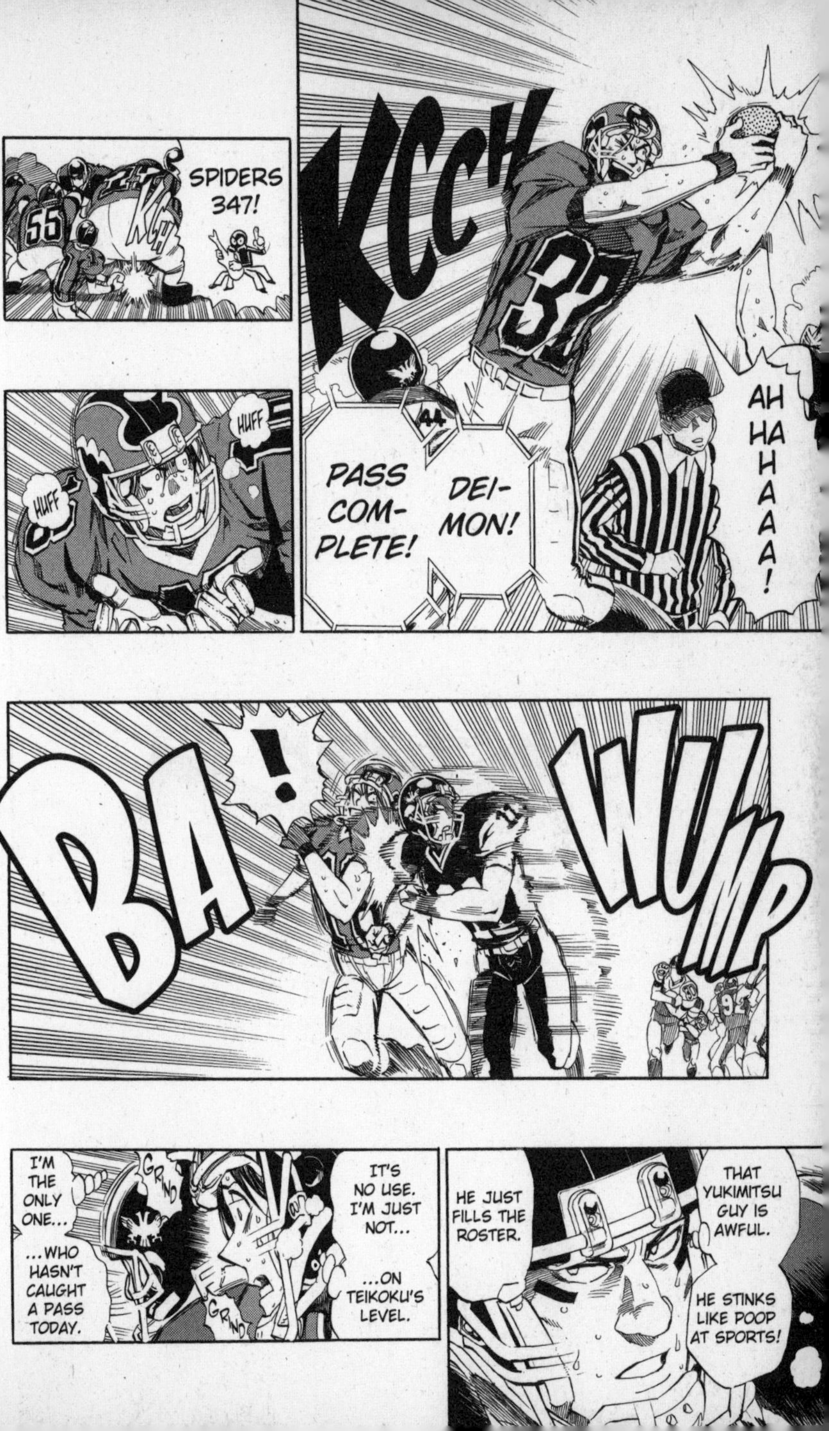
AH HA HAHAAA!
KCCH
DEI-MON!
PASS COM-PLETE!
SPIDERS 347!
KGH
HUFF
HUFF
BA!
WUMP
THAT YUKIMITSU GUY IS AWFUL.
HE JUST FILLS THE ROSTER.
HE STINKS LIKE POOP AT SPORTS!
IT'S NO USE. I'M JUST NOT...
...ON TEIKOKU'S LEVEL.
GRIND
I'M THE ONLY ONE...
...WHO HASN'T CAUGHT A PASS TODAY.
GRIND

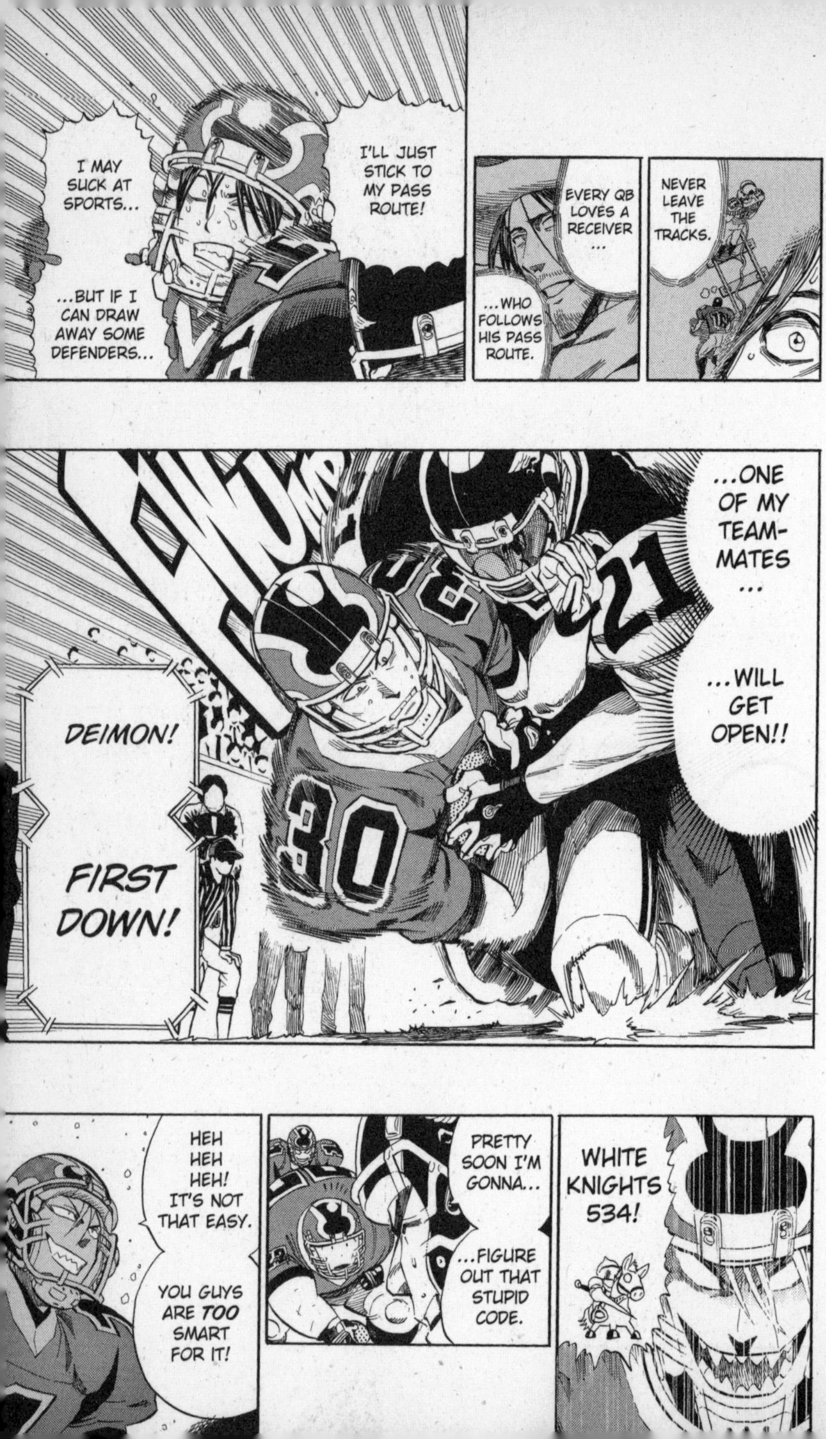
NEVER LEAVE THE TRACKS.
EVERY QB LOVES A RECEIVER...
...WHO FOLLOWS HIS PASS ROUTE.
I'LL JUST STICK TO MY PASS ROUTE!
I MAY SUCK AT SPORTS...
...BUT IF I CAN DRAW AWAY SOME DEFENDERS...
...ONE OF MY TEAM-MATES...
...WILL GET OPEN!!
DEIMON!
FIRST DOWN!
WHITE KNIGHTS 534!
PRETTY SOON I'M GONNA...
...FIGURE OUT THAT STUPID CODE.
HEH HEH HEH! IT'S NOT THAT EASY.
YOU GUYS ARE *TOO* SMART FOR IT!

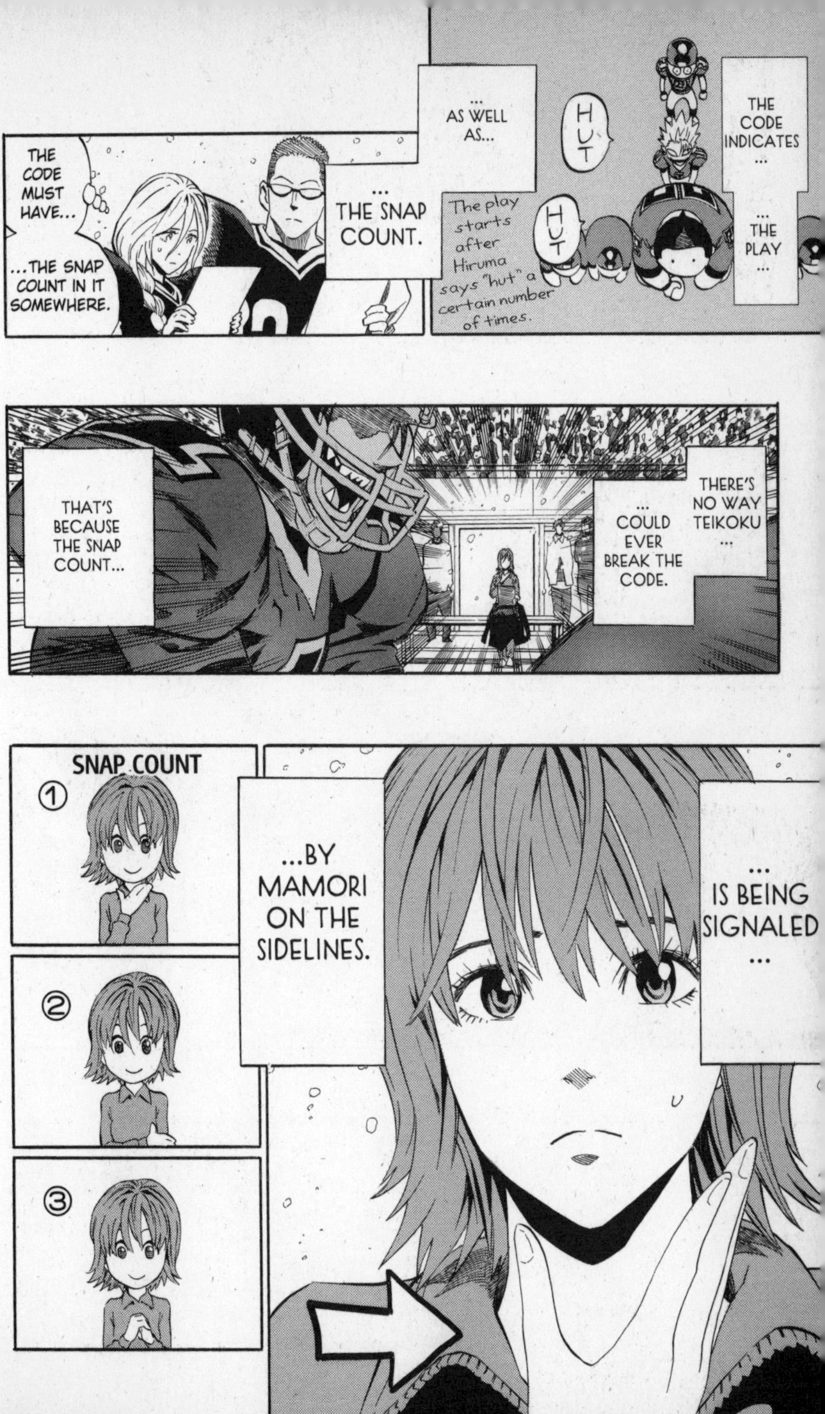
THE CODE INDICATES ... ... THE PLAY ...
HUT
HUT
... AS WELL AS...
The play starts after Hiruma says "hut" a certain number of times.
... THE SNAP COUNT.
THE CODE MUST HAVE...
...THE SNAP COUNT IN IT SOMEWHERE.
THERE'S NO WAY TEIKOKU ...
... COULD EVER BREAK THE CODE.
THAT'S BECAUSE THE SNAP COUNT...
... IS BEING SIGNALED ...
...BY MAMORI ON THE SIDELINES.
SNAP COUNT
①
②
③

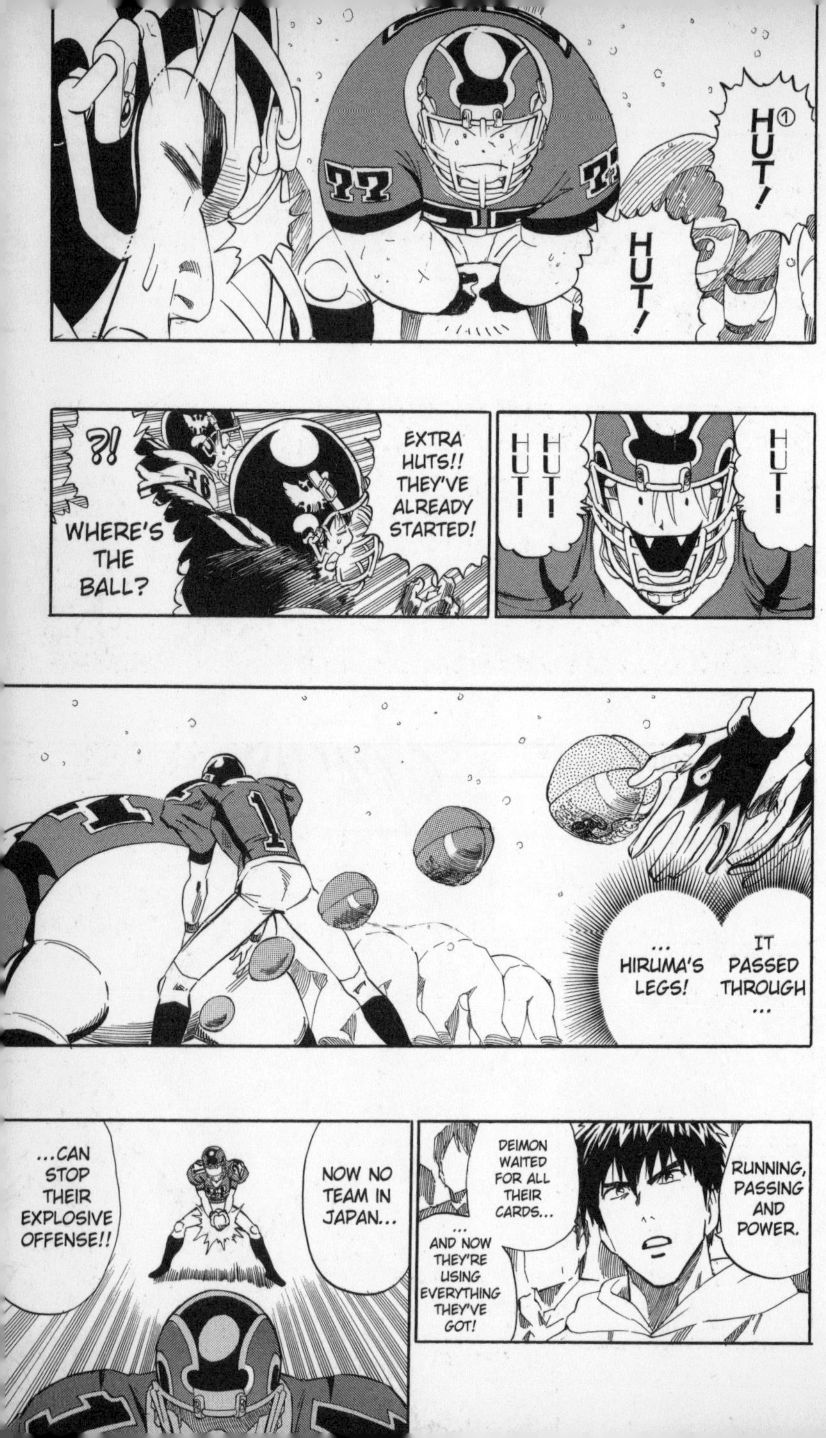
HUT! ①
HUT!
HUT!
HUT!
HUT!
EXTRA HUTS!! THEY'VE ALREADY STARTED!
?!
WHERE'S THE BALL?
IT PASSED THROUGH...
...HIRUMA'S LEGS!
RUNNING, PASSING AND POWER.
DEIMON WAITED FOR ALL THEIR CARDS...
...AND NOW THEY'RE USING EVERYTHING THEY'VE GOT!
NOW NO TEAM IN JAPAN...
...CAN STOP THEIR EXPLOSIVE OFFENSE!!

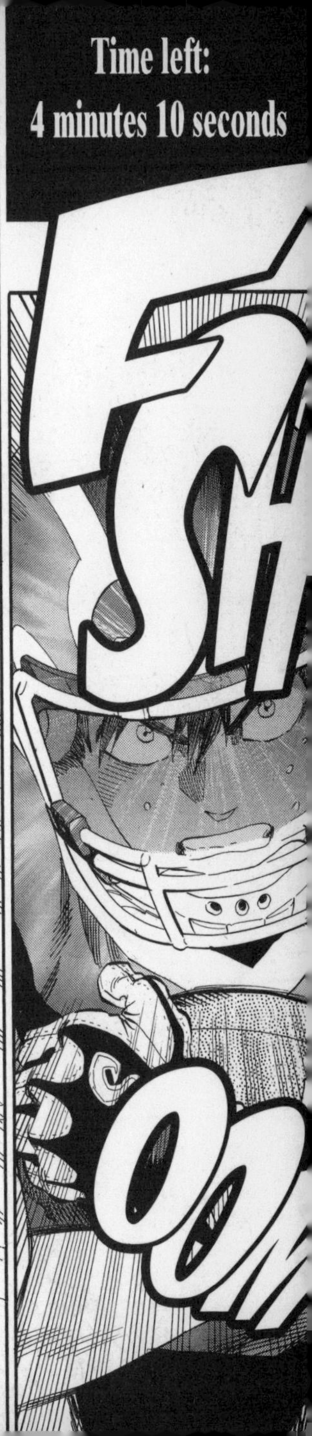
Time left:
4 minutes 10 seconds

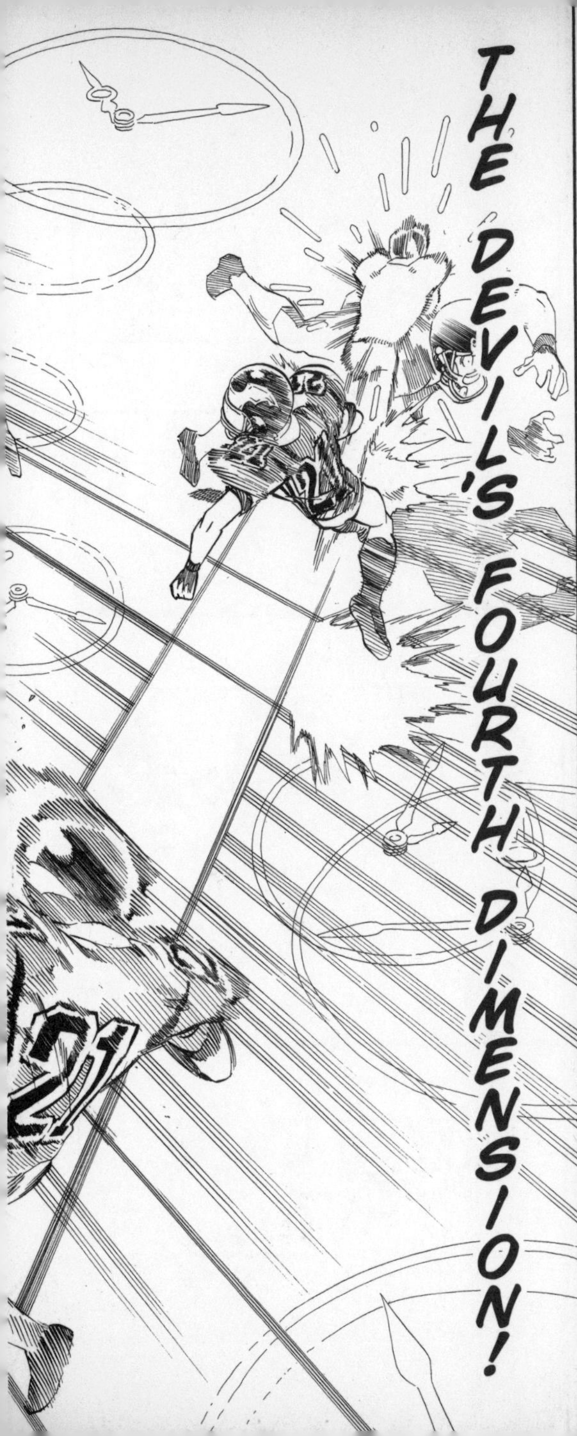
THE DEVIL'S FOURTH DIMENSION!

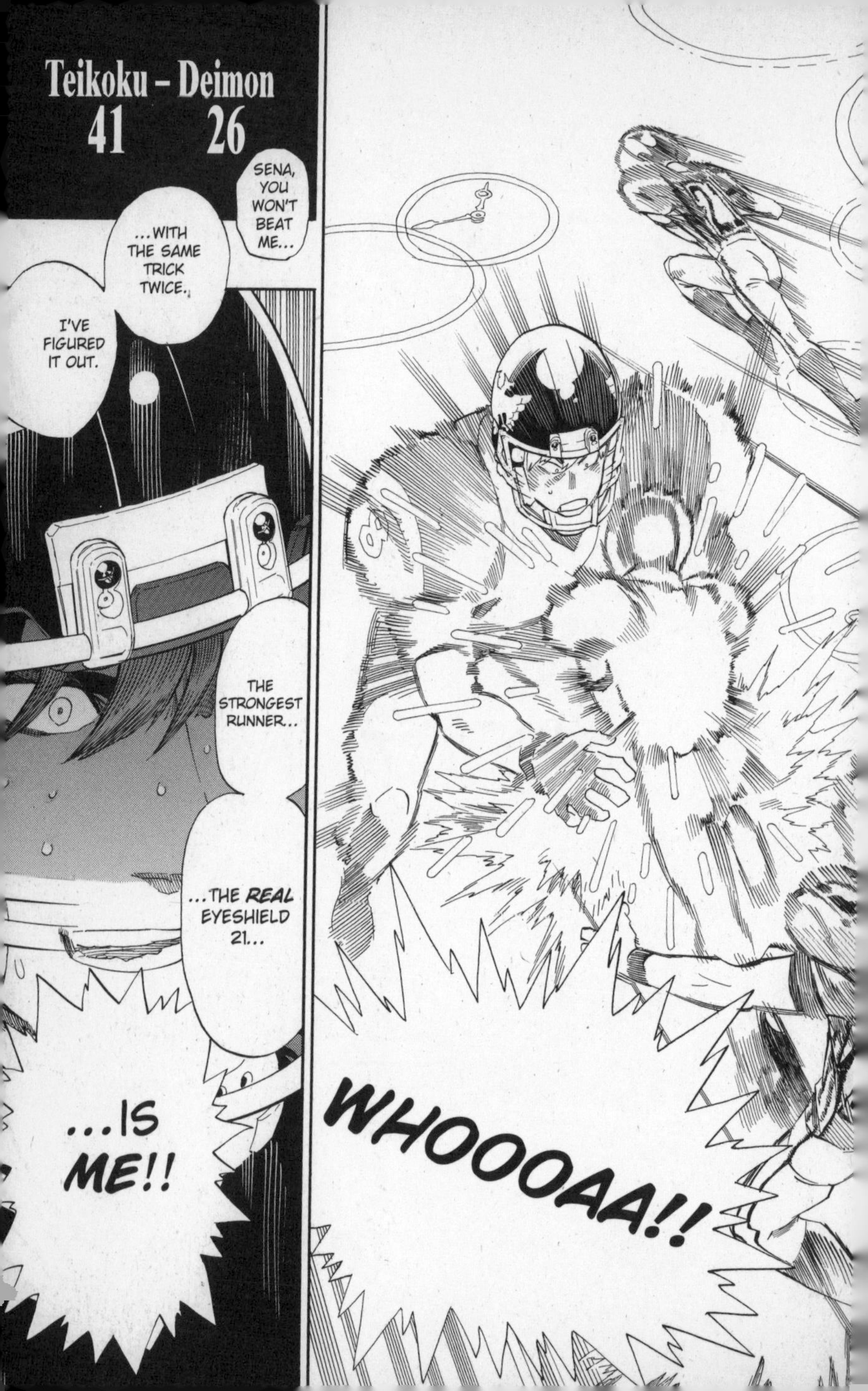
WHOOOOAA!!
Teikoku – Deimon 41 26
SENA, YOU WON'T BEAT ME...
...WITH THE SAME TRICK TWICE.
I'VE FIGURED IT OUT.
THE STRONGEST RUNNER...
...THE *REAL* EYESHIELD 21...
...IS *ME*!!

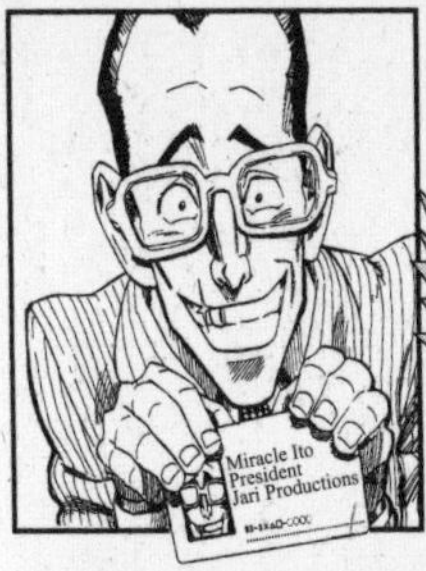
Miracle Ito
President
Jari Productions

He's still alive! Shrewd Miracle Ito's

New product!!

HIGH SCHOOL FOOTBALL STAR GOODS

Tableware for the New Football Generation!!

Seijuro Shin's "Trident Tackle"!

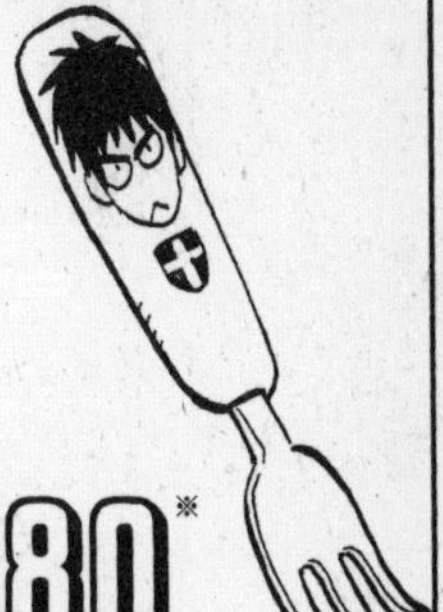

SPECIAL PRICE **¥880**※

※$9.75

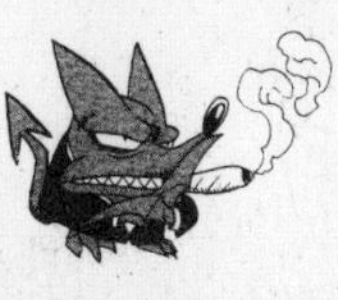

IN OTHER WORDS, A FORK.

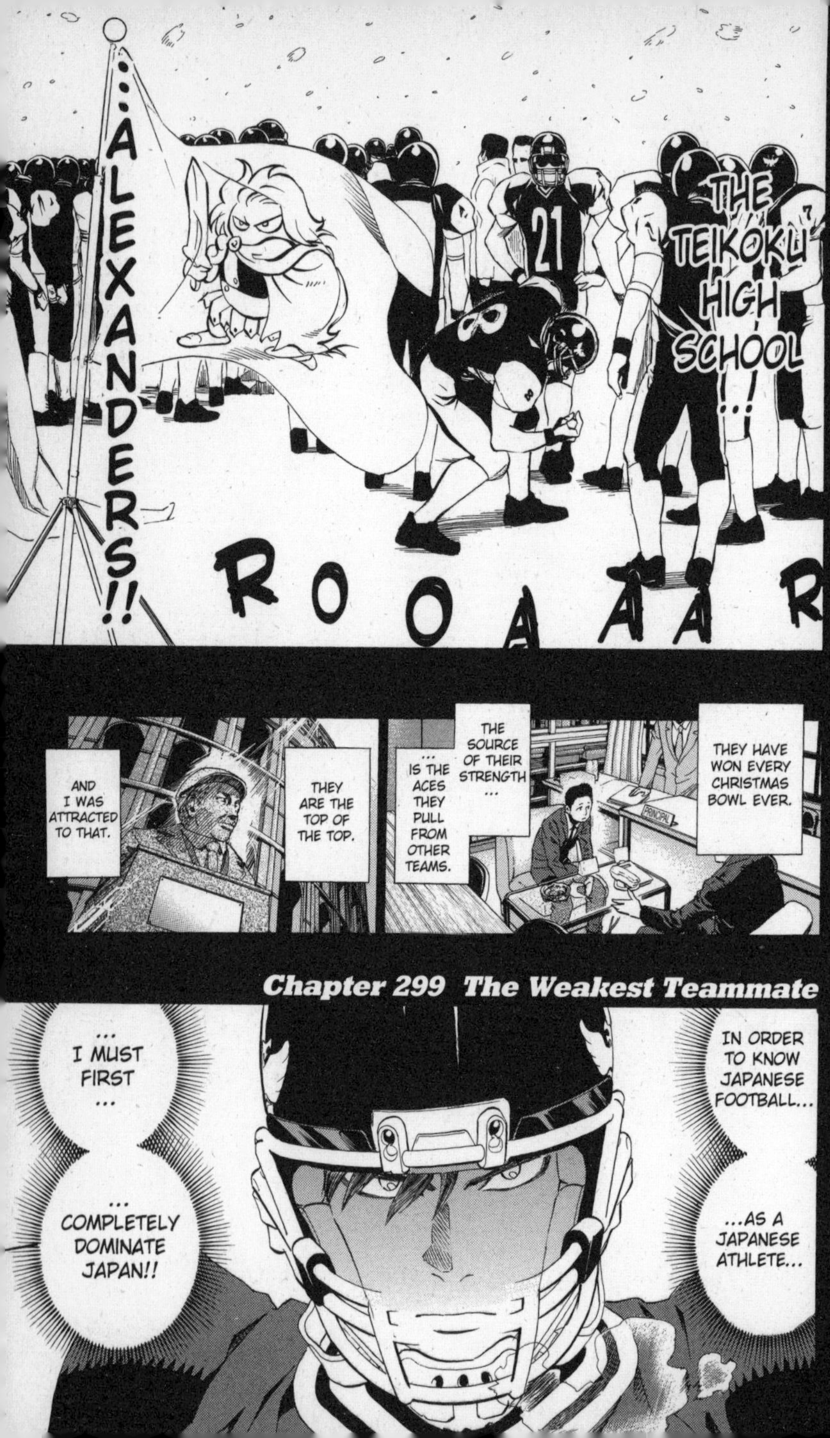
THE TEIKOKU HIGH SCHOOL ...!
...ALEXANDERS!!
ROOAAAR
THEY HAVE WON EVERY CHRISTMAS BOWL EVER.
PRINCIPAL
THE SOURCE OF THEIR STRENGTH ...
... IS THE ACES THEY PULL FROM OTHER TEAMS.
THEY ARE THE TOP OF THE TOP.
AND I WAS ATTRACTED TO THAT.
Chapter 299 The Weakest Teammate
IN ORDER TO KNOW JAPANESE FOOTBALL...
...AS A JAPANESE ATHLETE...
... I MUST FIRST ...
... COMPLETELY DOMINATE JAPAN!!

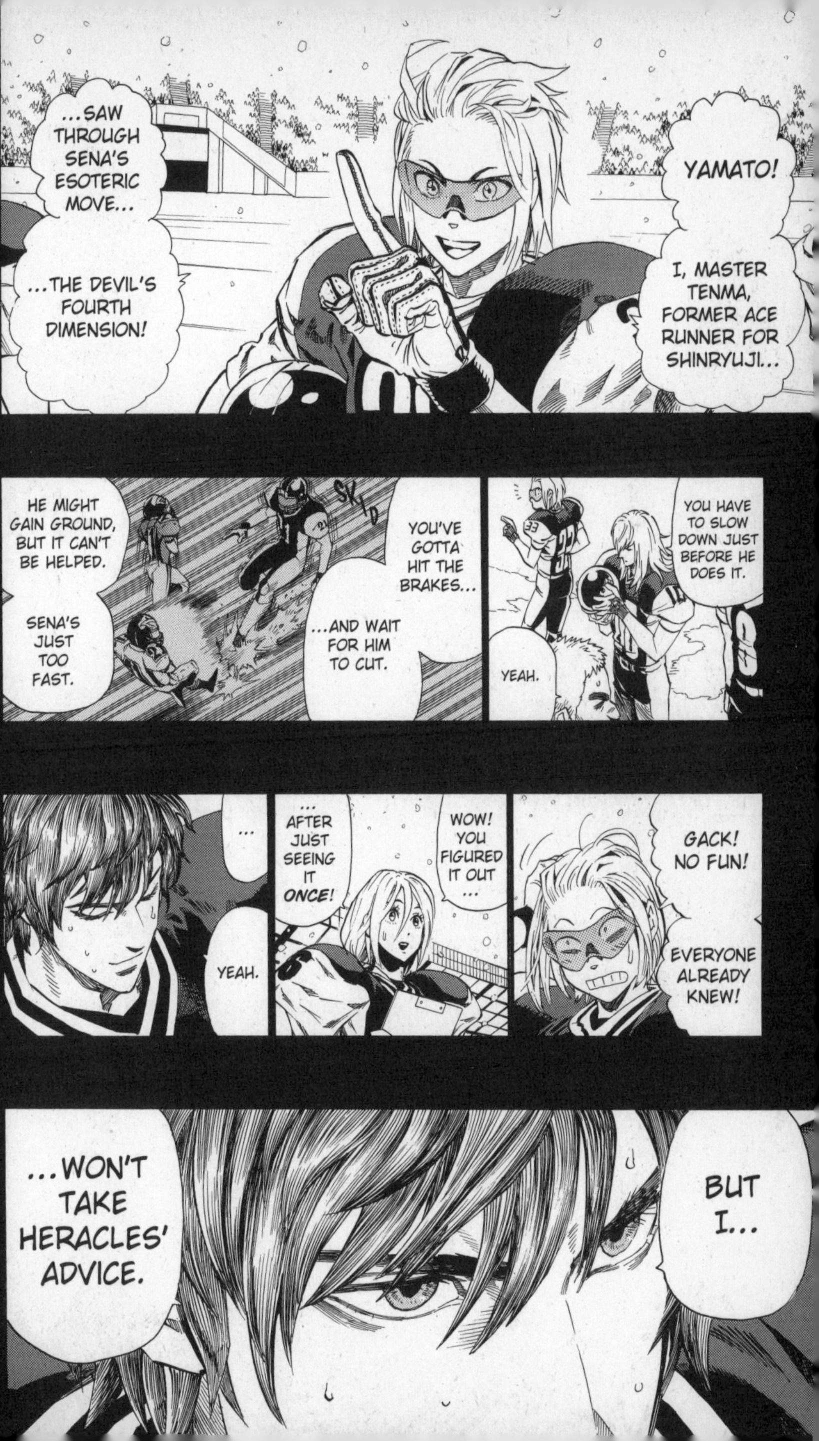
YAMATO!
I, MASTER TENMA, FORMER ACE RUNNER FOR SHINRYUJI...
...SAW THROUGH SENA'S ESOTERIC MOVE...
...THE DEVIL'S FOURTH DIMENSION!
YOU HAVE TO SLOW DOWN JUST BEFORE HE DOES IT.
YEAH.
YOU'VE GOTTA HIT THE BRAKES...
...AND WAIT FOR HIM TO CUT.
SKID
HE MIGHT GAIN GROUND, BUT IT CAN'T BE HELPED.
SENA'S JUST TOO FAST.
GACK! NO FUN!
EVERYONE ALREADY KNEW!
WOW! YOU FIGURED IT OUT...
...AFTER JUST SEEING IT *ONCE*!
...
YEAH.
BUT I...
...WON'T TAKE HERACLES' ADVICE.

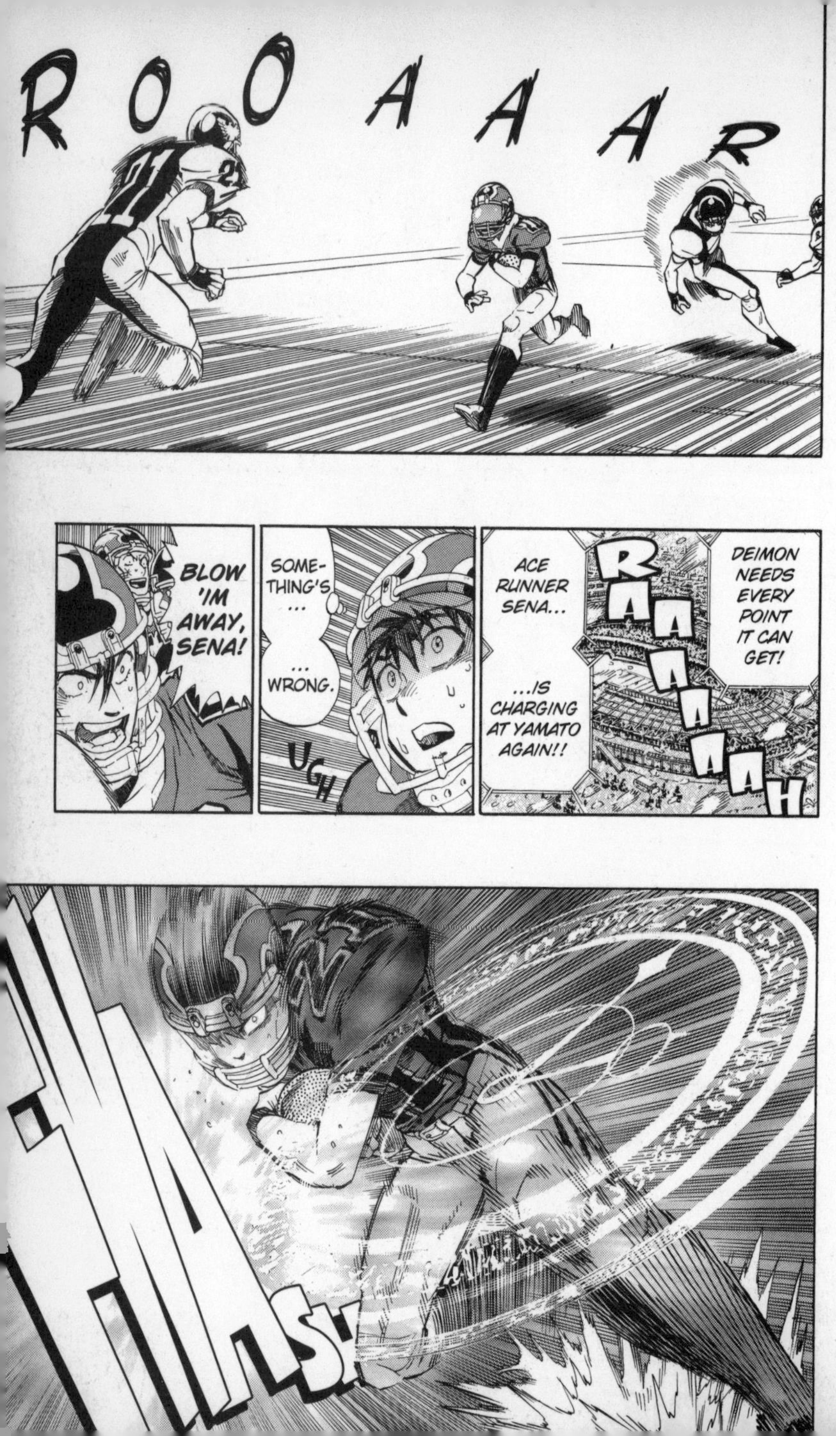
ROOAAAAR
DEIMON NEEDS EVERY POINT IT CAN GET!
RAAAAAAAH
ACE RUNNER SENA...
...IS CHARGING AT YAMATO AGAIN!!
SOME-THING'S...
...WRONG.
UGH
BLOW 'IM AWAY, SENA!

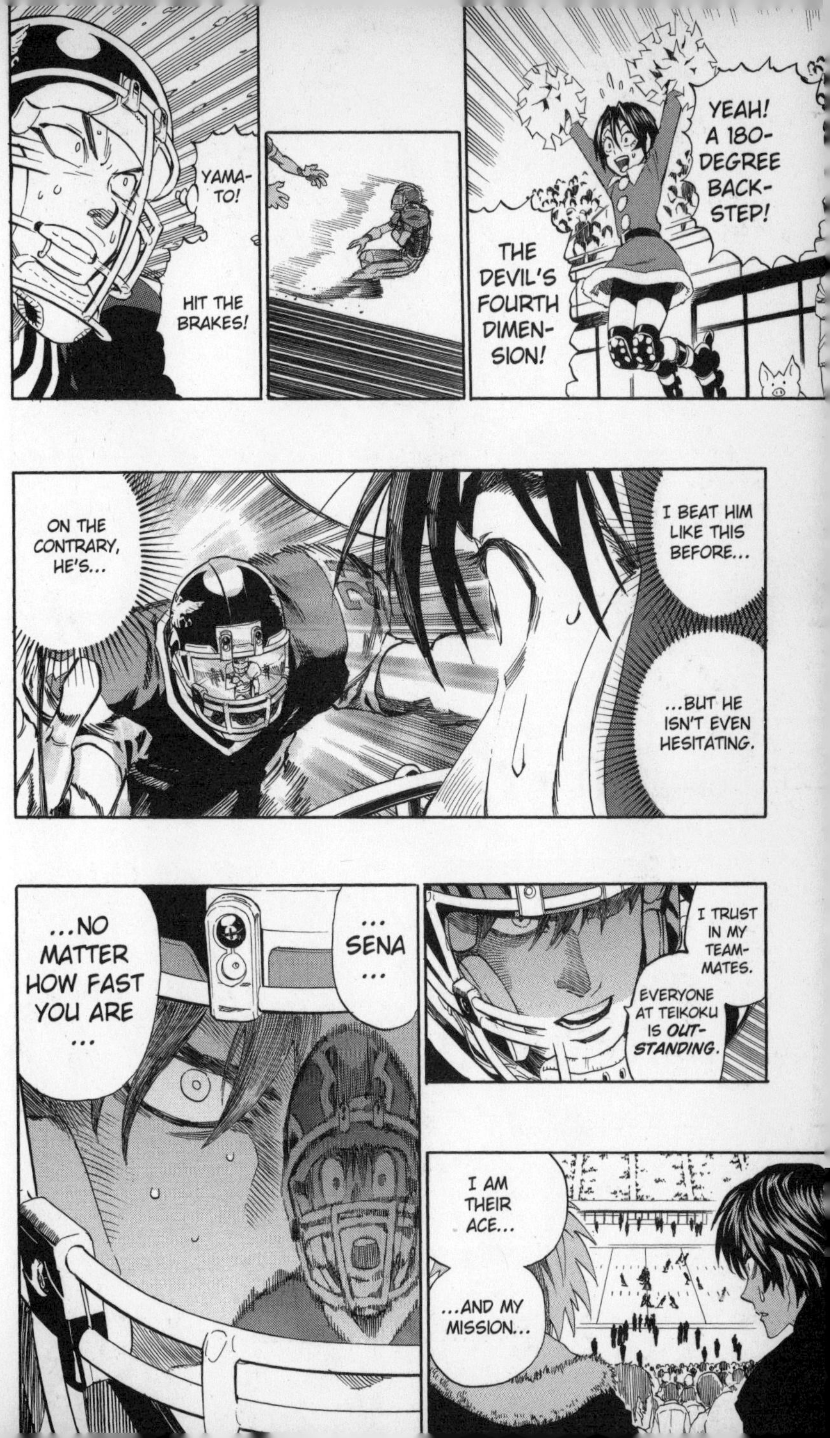
YEAH! A 180-DEGREE BACK-STEP!
THE DEVIL'S FOURTH DIMEN-SION!
YAMA-TO!
HIT THE BRAKES!
I BEAT HIM LIKE THIS BEFORE...
...BUT HE ISN'T EVEN HESITATING.
ON THE CONTRARY, HE'S...
I TRUST IN MY TEAM-MATES.
EVERYONE AT TEIKOKU IS *OUT-STANDING*.
I AM THEIR ACE...
...AND MY MISSION...
...SENA...
...NO MATTER HOW FAST YOU ARE...

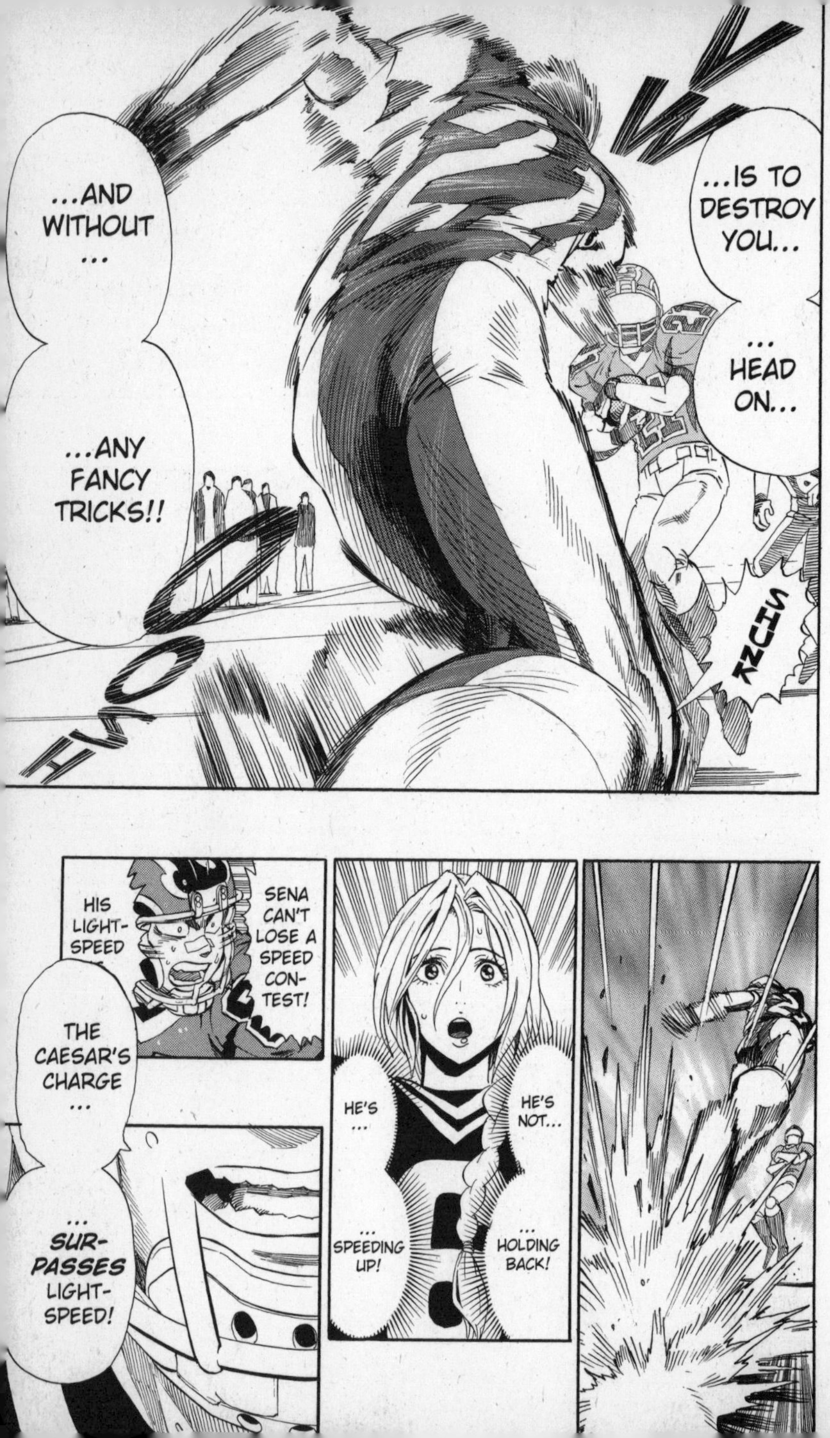
...IS TO DESTROY YOU...
... HEAD ON...
...AND WITHOUT ...
...ANY FANCY TRICKS!!
SHUNK
HE'S NOT...
... HOLDING BACK!
HE'S ...
... SPEEDING UP!
SENA CAN'T LOSE A SPEED CON-TEST!
HIS LIGHT-SPEED
THE CAESAR'S CHARGE ...
... SUR-PASSES LIGHT-SPEED!

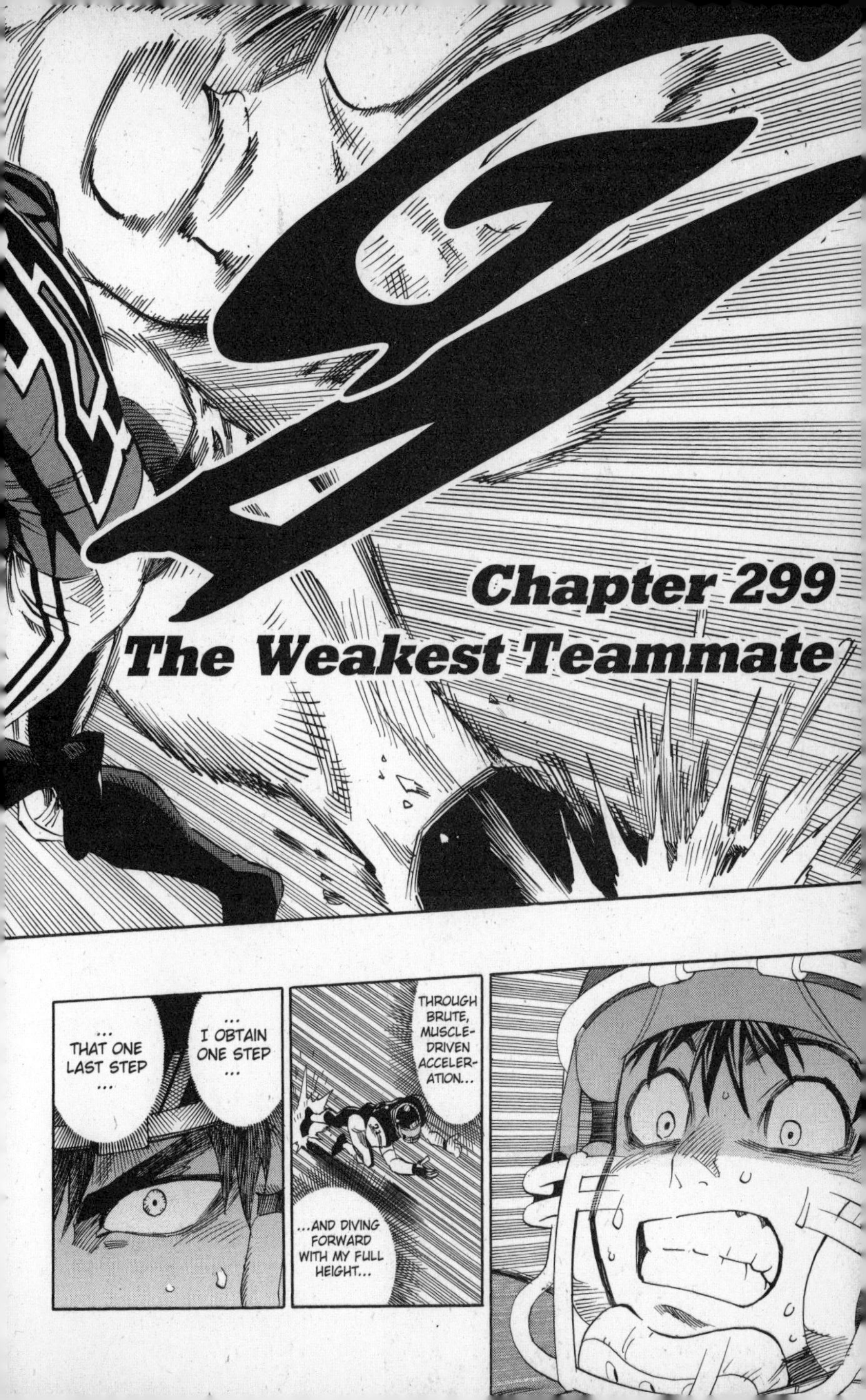
Chapter 299
The Weakest Teammate
THROUGH BRUTE, MUSCLE-DRIVEN ACCELERATION...
...AND DIVING FORWARD WITH MY FULL HEIGHT...
... I OBTAIN ONE STEP ...
... THAT ONE LAST STEP ...

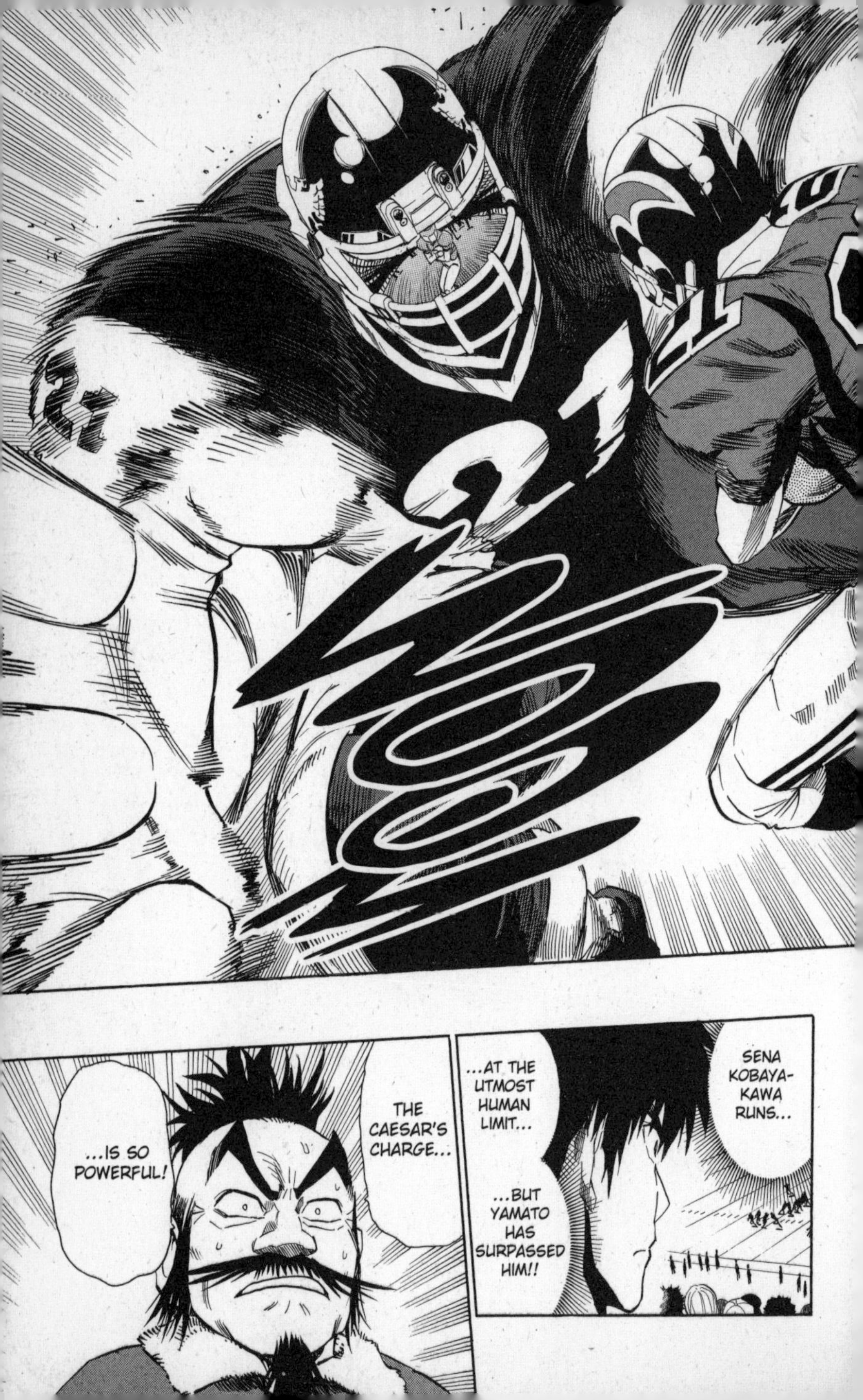
SENA KOBAYA-KAWA RUNS...
...AT THE UTMOST HUMAN LIMIT...
...BUT YAMATO HAS SURPASSED HIM!!
THE CAESAR'S CHARGE...
...IS SO POWERFUL!

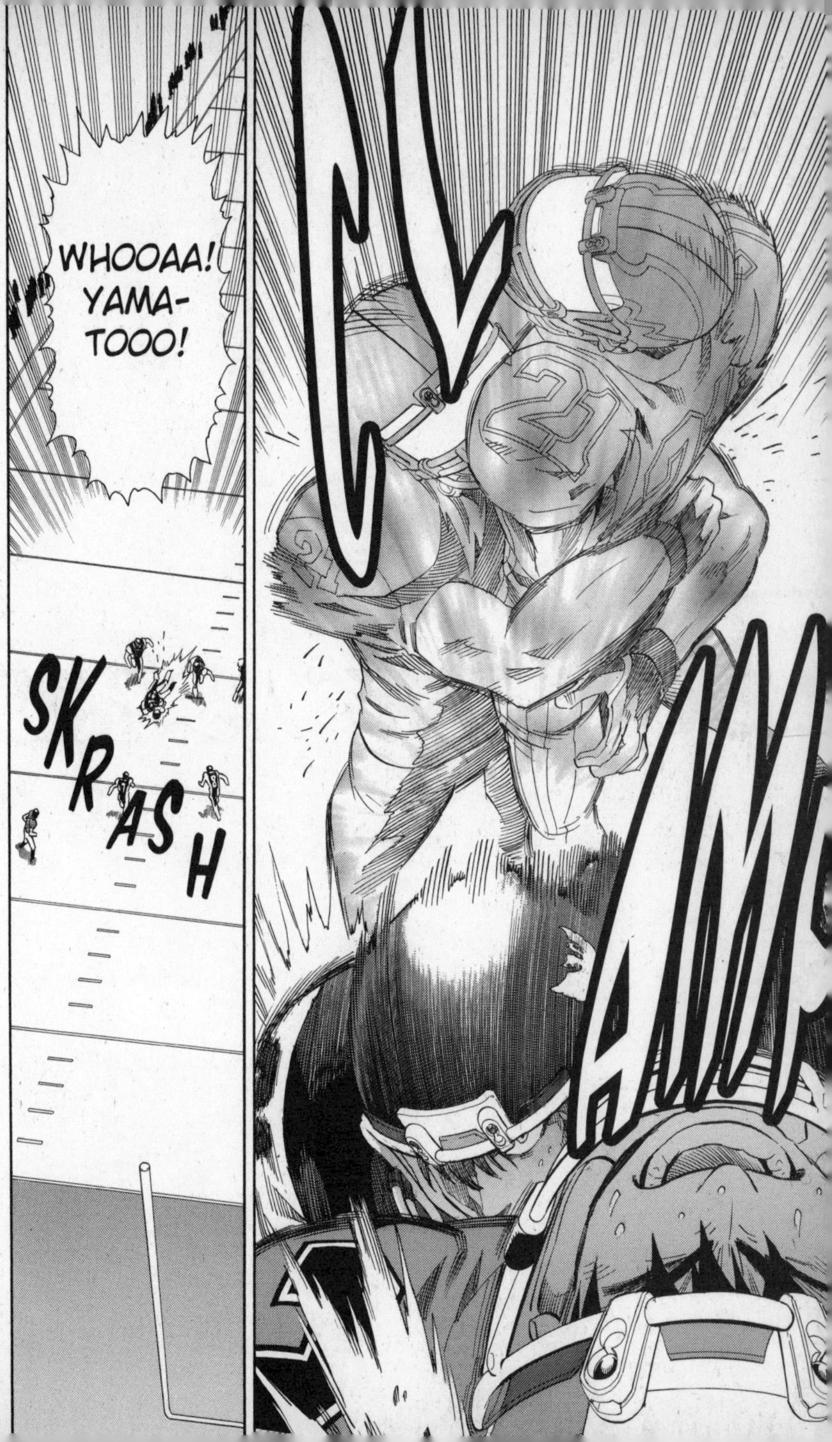
WHOOAA! YAMA-TOOO!
SKRASH

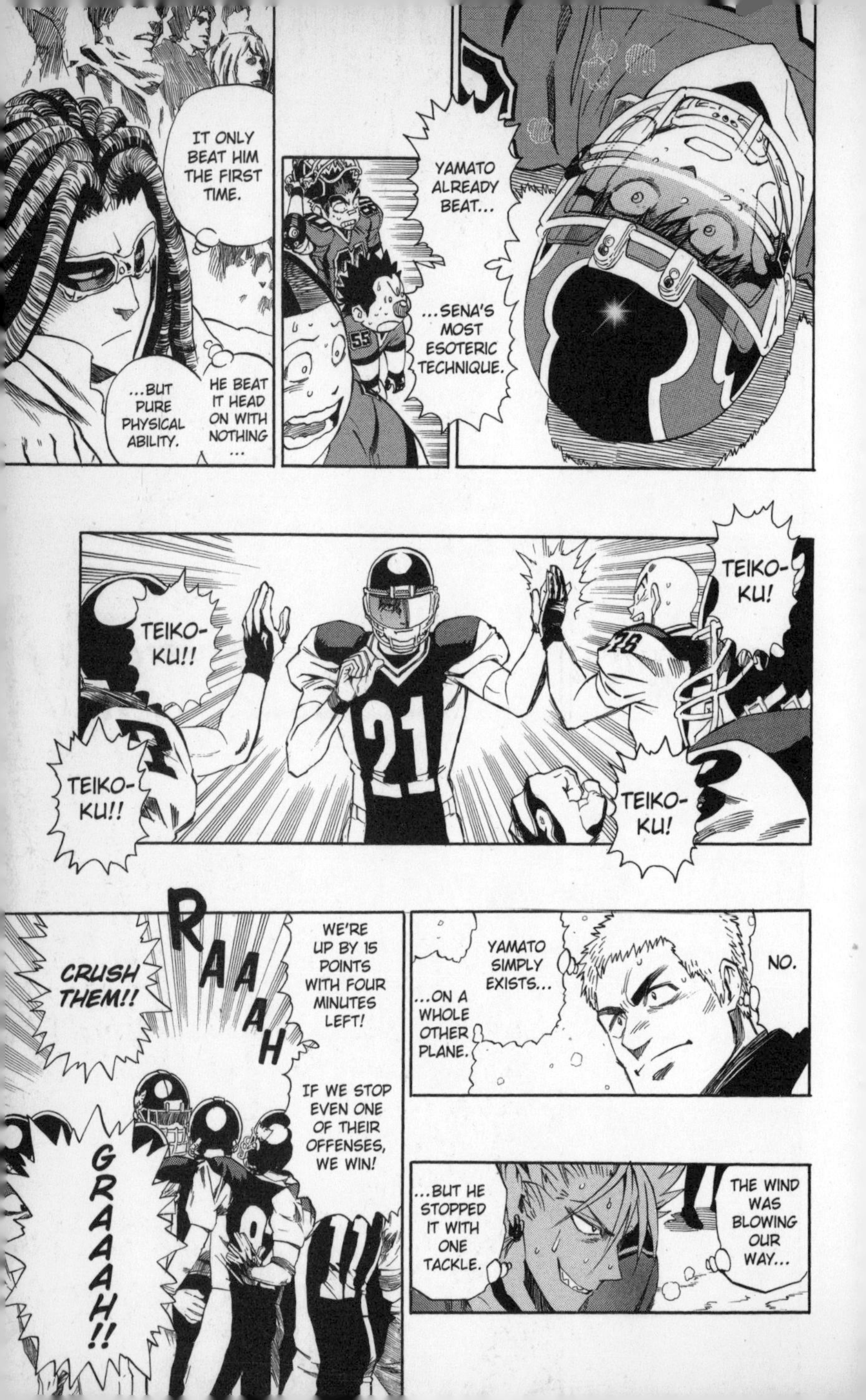

YAMATO ALREADY BEAT...
...SENA'S MOST ESOTERIC TECHNIQUE.
IT ONLY BEAT HIM THE FIRST TIME.
HE BEAT IT HEAD ON WITH NOTHING...
...BUT PURE PHYSICAL ABILITY.
TEIKO-KU!
TEIKO-KU!
TEIKO-KU!!
TEIKO-KU!!
NO.
YAMATO SIMPLY EXISTS...
...ON A WHOLE OTHER PLANE.
THE WIND WAS BLOWING OUR WAY...
...BUT HE STOPPED IT WITH ONE TACKLE.
WE'RE UP BY 15 POINTS WITH FOUR MINUTES LEFT!
IF WE STOP EVEN ONE OF THEIR OFFENSES, WE WIN!
RAAAH
CRUSH THEM!!
GRAAAAH!!

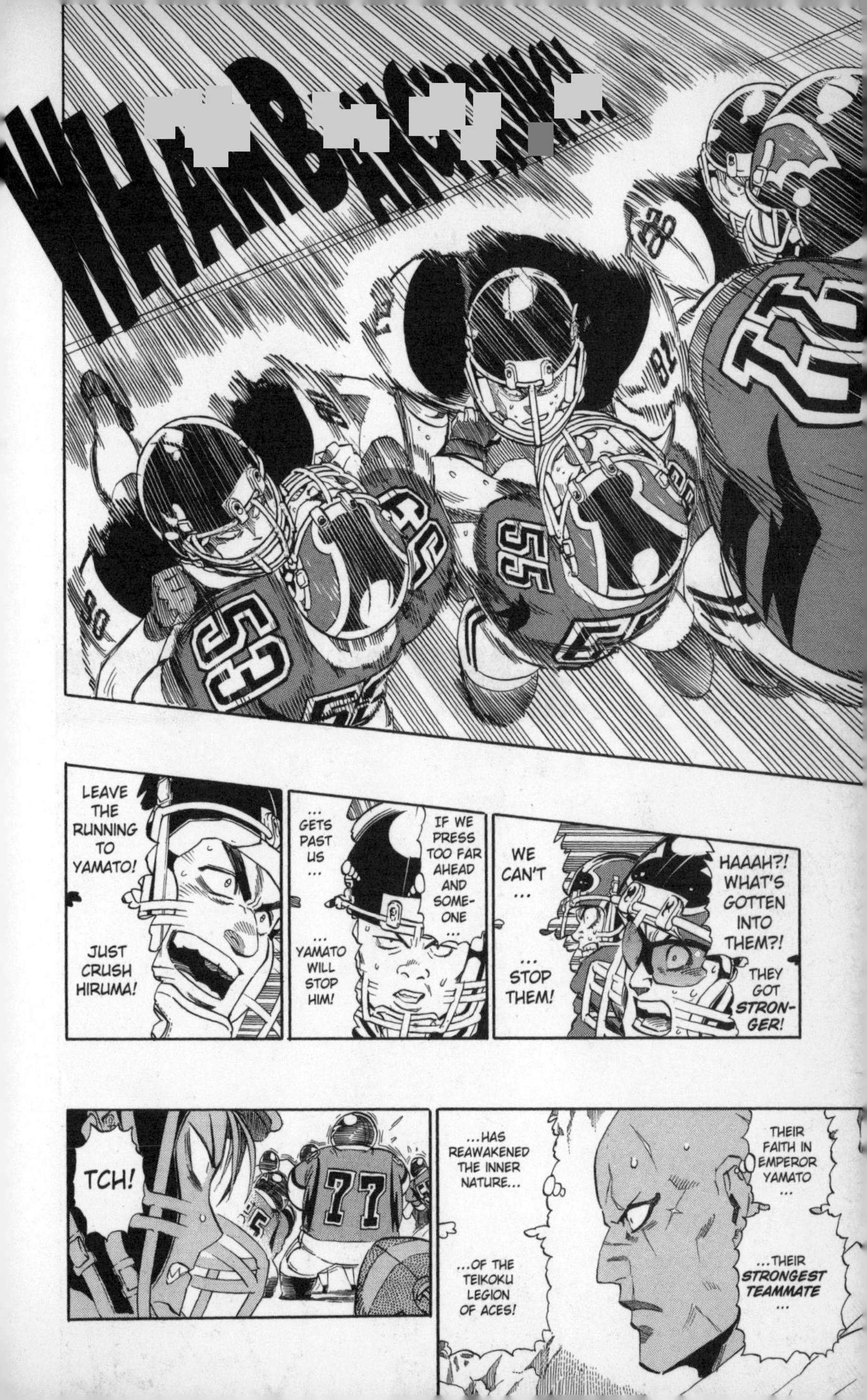
HAAAH?! WHAT'S GOTTEN INTO THEM?!
THEY GOT STRONGER!
WE CAN'T ...
... STOP THEM!
IF WE PRESS TOO FAR AHEAD AND SOMEONE ...
... GETS PAST US ...
... YAMATO WILL STOP HIM!
LEAVE THE RUNNING TO YAMATO!
JUST CRUSH HIRUMA!
THEIR FAITH IN EMPEROR YAMATO ...
...THEIR STRONGEST TEAMMATE ...
...HAS REAWAKENED THE INNER NATURE...
...OF THE TEIKOKU LEGION OF ACES!
TCH!

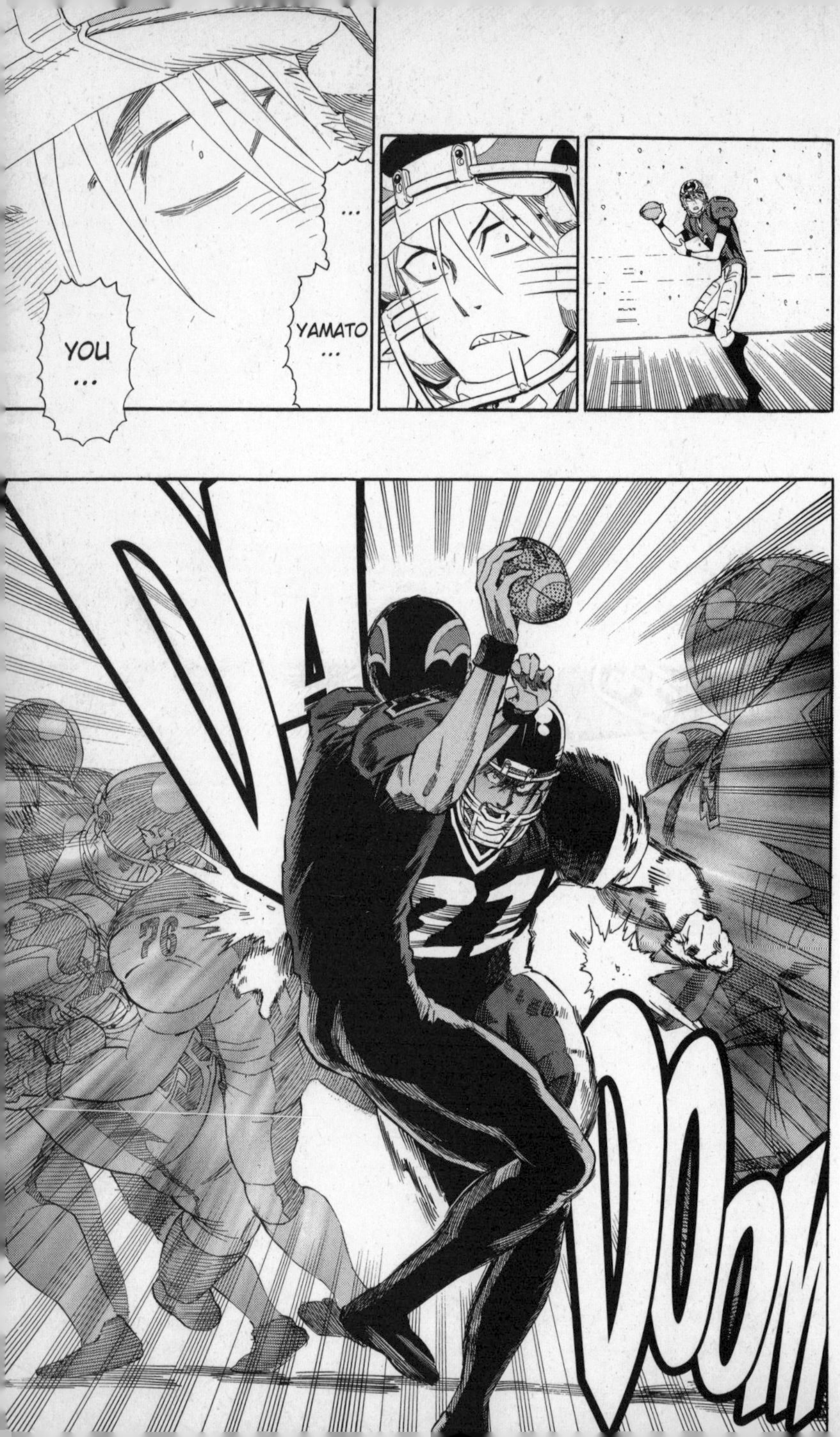
...
YAMATO ...
YOU ...
DOOM

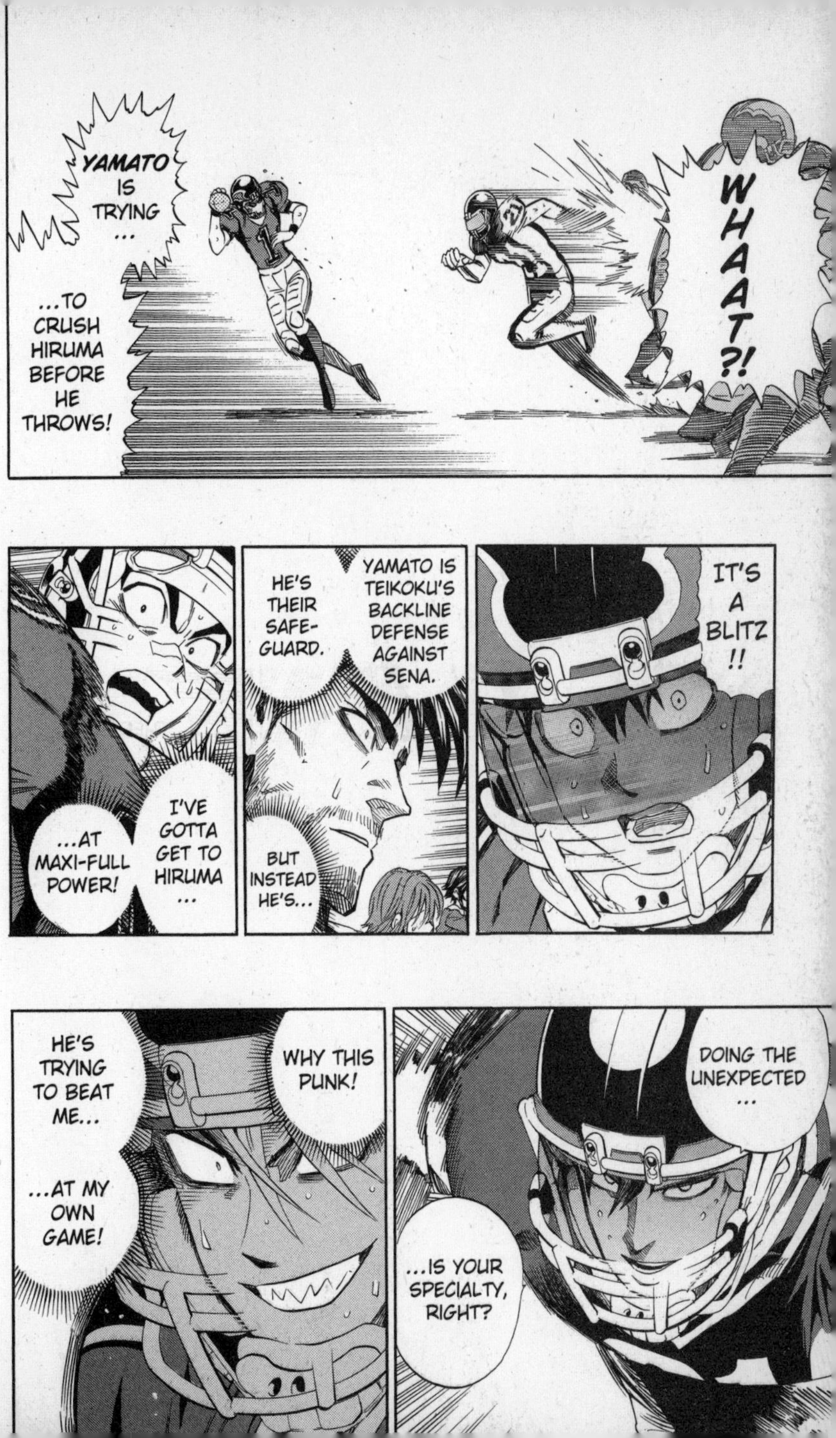
WHAAT?!
YAMATO IS TRYING...
...TO CRUSH HIRUMA BEFORE HE THROWS!
IT'S A BLITZ!!
YAMATO IS TEIKOKU'S BACKLINE DEFENSE AGAINST SENA.
HE'S THEIR SAFE-GUARD.
BUT INSTEAD HE'S...
I'VE GOTTA GET TO HIRUMA...
...AT MAXI-FULL POWER!
DOING THE UNEXPECTED...
...IS YOUR SPECIALTY, RIGHT?
WHY THIS PUNK!
HE'S TRYING TO BEAT ME...
...AT MY OWN GAME!

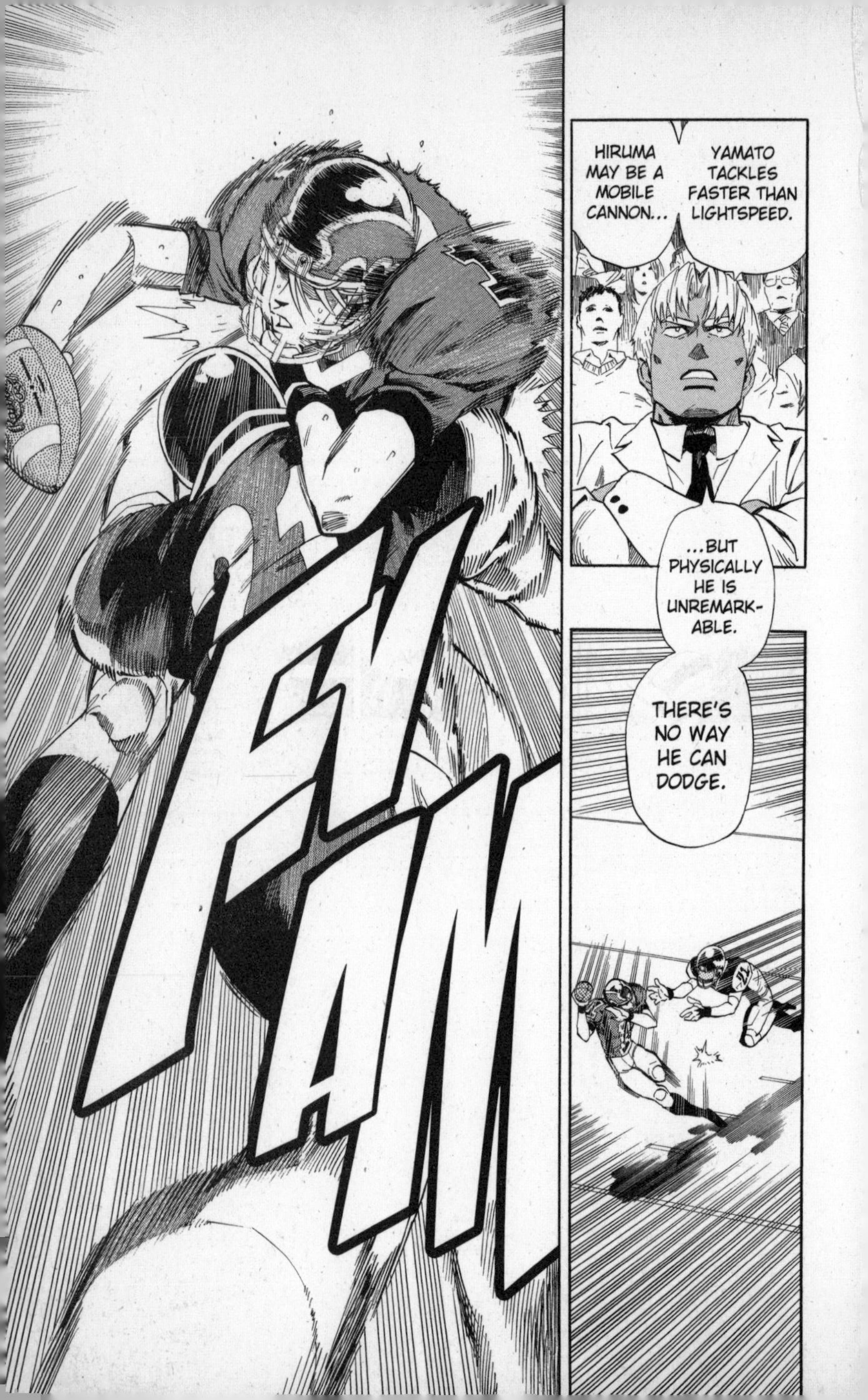
YAMATO TACKLES FASTER THAN LIGHTSPEED.
HIRUMA MAY BE A MOBILE CANNON...
...BUT PHYSICALLY HE IS UNREMARK-ABLE.
THERE'S NO WAY HE CAN DODGE.

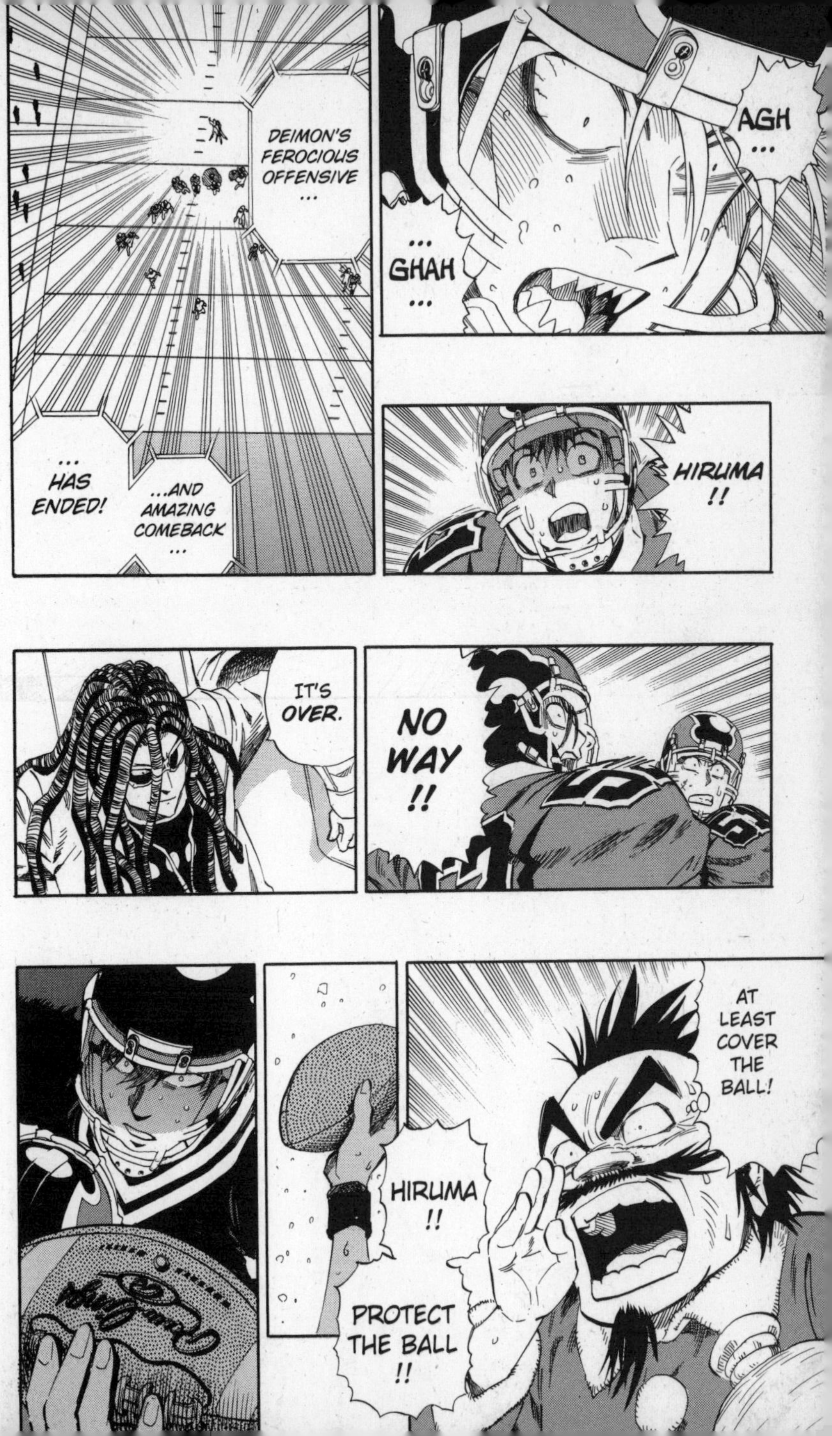
AGH ...
... GHAH ...
HIRUMA !!
DEIMON'S FEROCIOUS OFFENSIVE ...
...AND AMAZING COMEBACK ...
... HAS ENDED!
NO WAY !!
IT'S OVER.
AT LEAST COVER THE BALL!
HIRUMA !!
PROTECT THE BALL !!

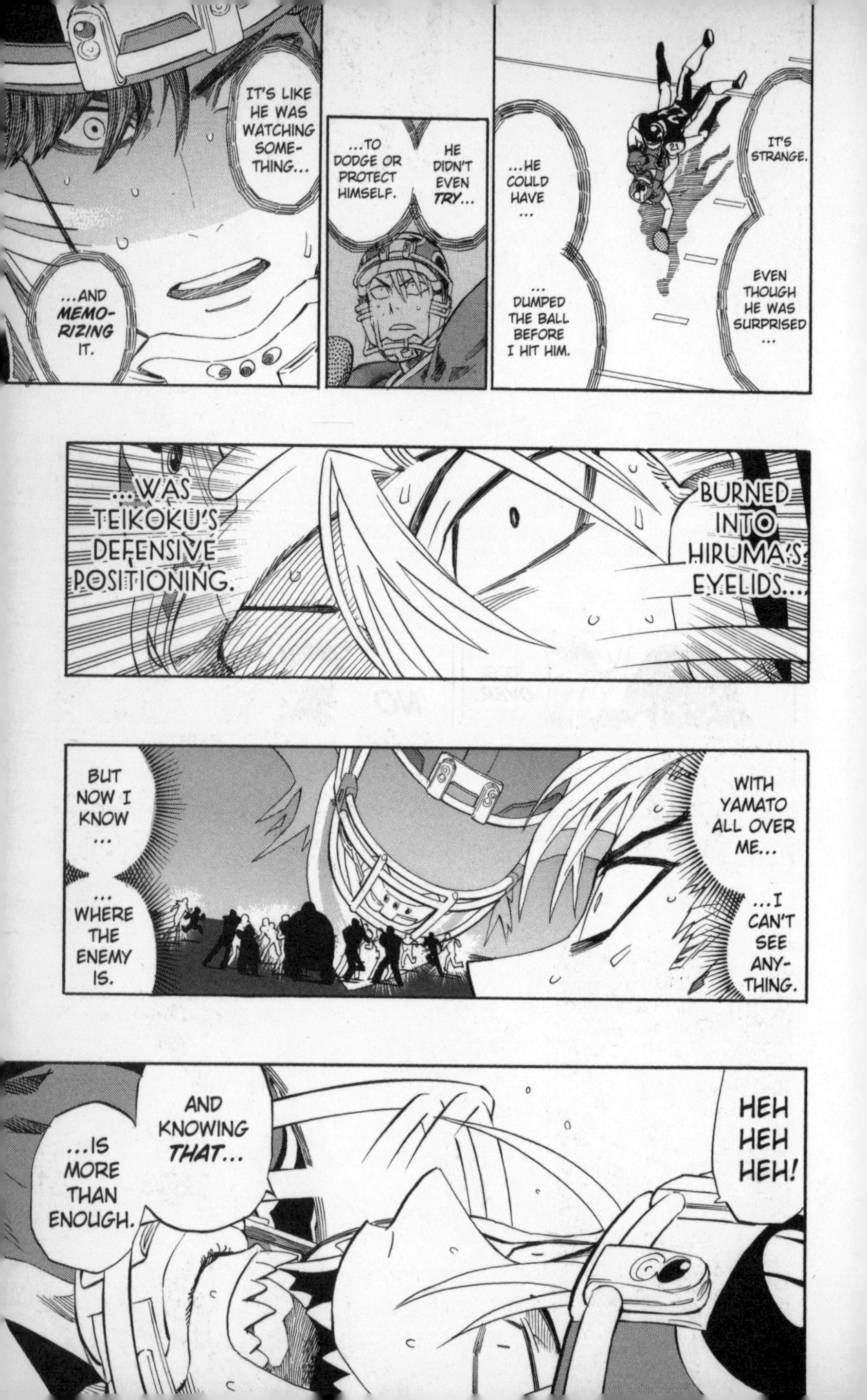
IT'S STRANGE.
EVEN THOUGH HE WAS SURPRISED...
...HE COULD HAVE...
...DUMPED THE BALL BEFORE I HIT HIM.
HE DIDN'T EVEN *TRY*...
...TO DODGE OR PROTECT HIMSELF.
IT'S LIKE HE WAS WATCHING SOME-THING...
...AND *MEMORIZING* IT.
BURNED INTO HIRUMA'S EYELIDS...
...WAS TEIKOKU'S DEFENSIVE POSITIONING.
WITH YAMATO ALL OVER ME...
...I CAN'T SEE ANYTHING.
BUT NOW I KNOW...
...WHERE THE ENEMY IS.
HEH HEH HEH!
AND KNOWING *THAT*...
...IS MORE THAN ENOUGH.

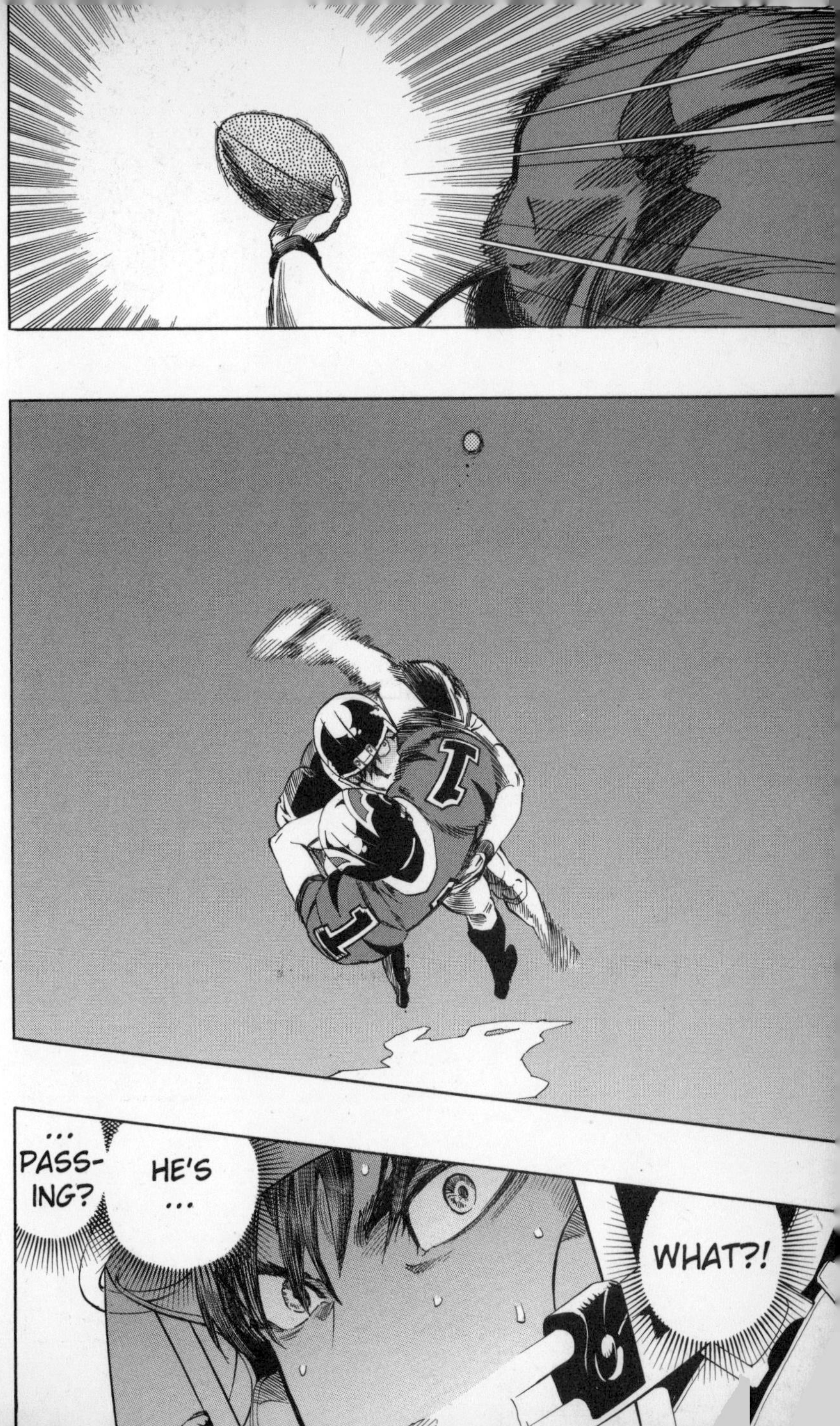
WHAT?!
HE'S ...
... PASSING?

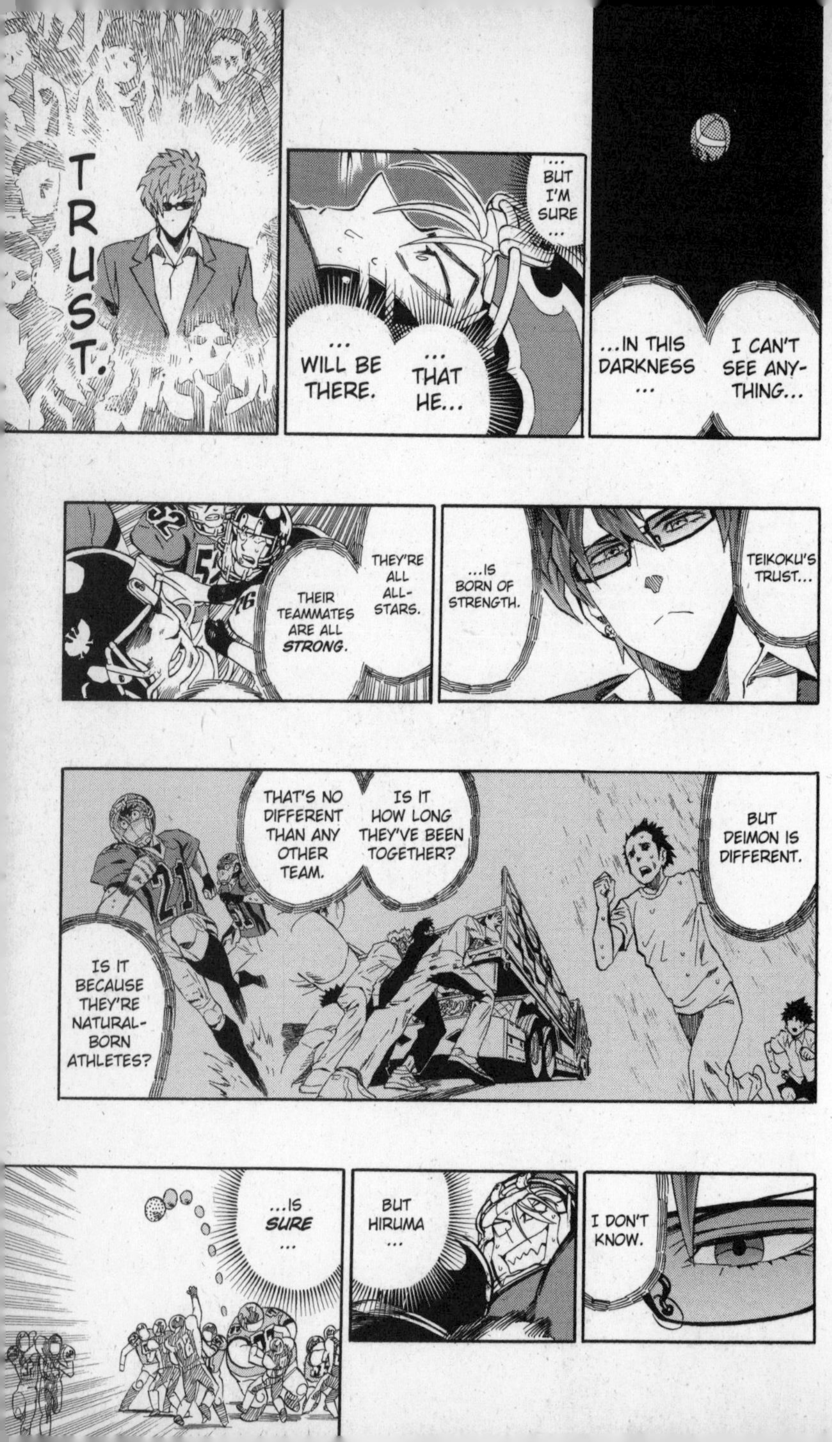
I CAN'T SEE ANYTHING...
...IN THIS DARKNESS...
...BUT I'M SURE...
...THAT HE...
...WILL BE THERE.
TRUST.
TEIKOKU'S TRUST...
...IS BORN OF STRENGTH.
THEY'RE ALL ALL-STARS.
THEIR TEAMMATES ARE ALL STRONG.
BUT DEIMON IS DIFFERENT.
IS IT HOW LONG THEY'VE BEEN TOGETHER?
THAT'S NO DIFFERENT THAN ANY OTHER TEAM.
IS IT BECAUSE THEY'RE NATURAL-BORN ATHLETES?
I DON'T KNOW.
BUT HIRUMA...
...IS SURE...

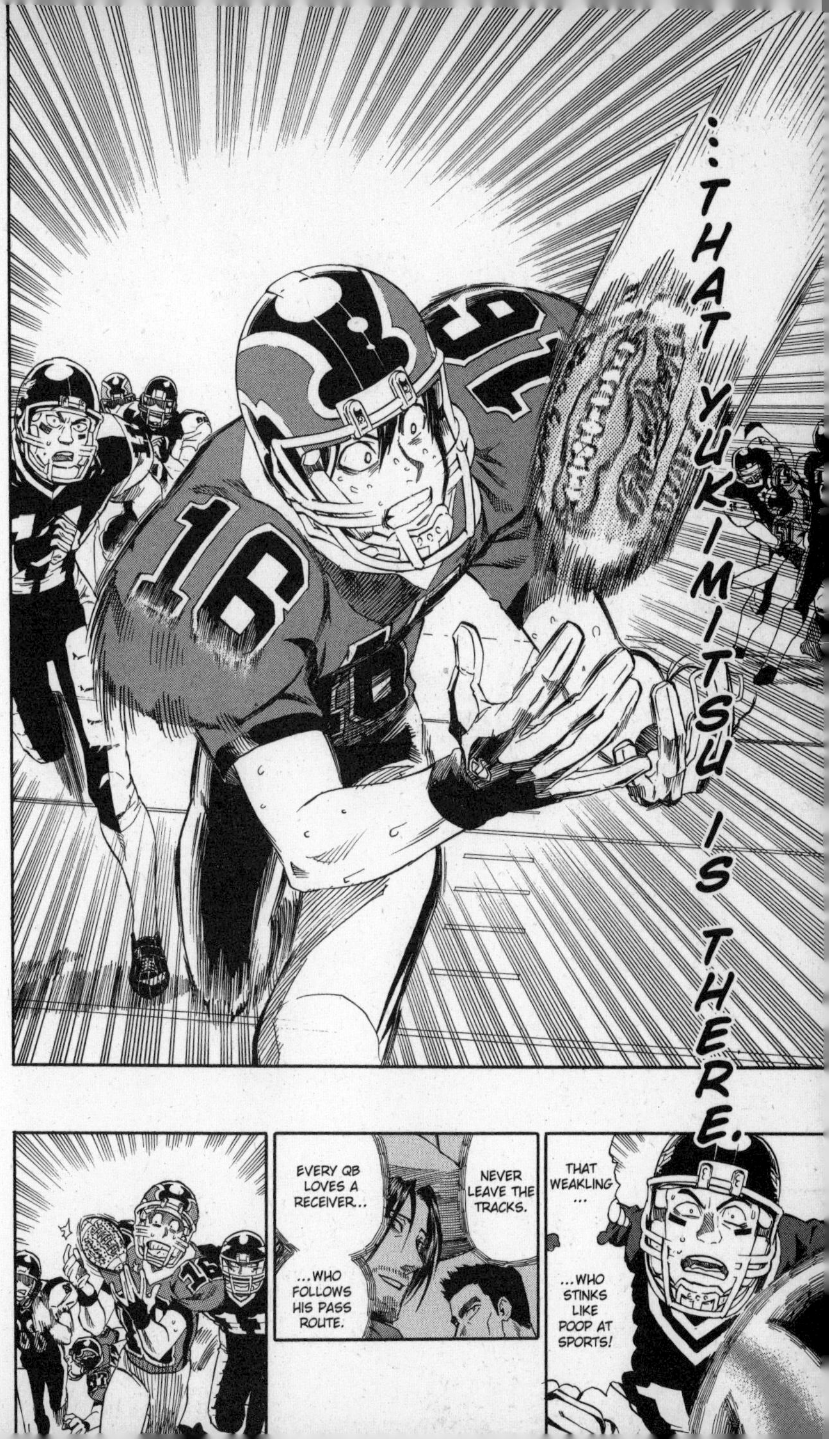
...THAT YUKIMITSU IS THERE.
THAT WEAKLING ...
...WHO STINKS LIKE POOP AT SPORTS!
EVERY QB LOVES A RECEIVER...
...WHO FOLLOWS HIS PASS ROUTE.
NEVER LEAVE THE TRACKS.

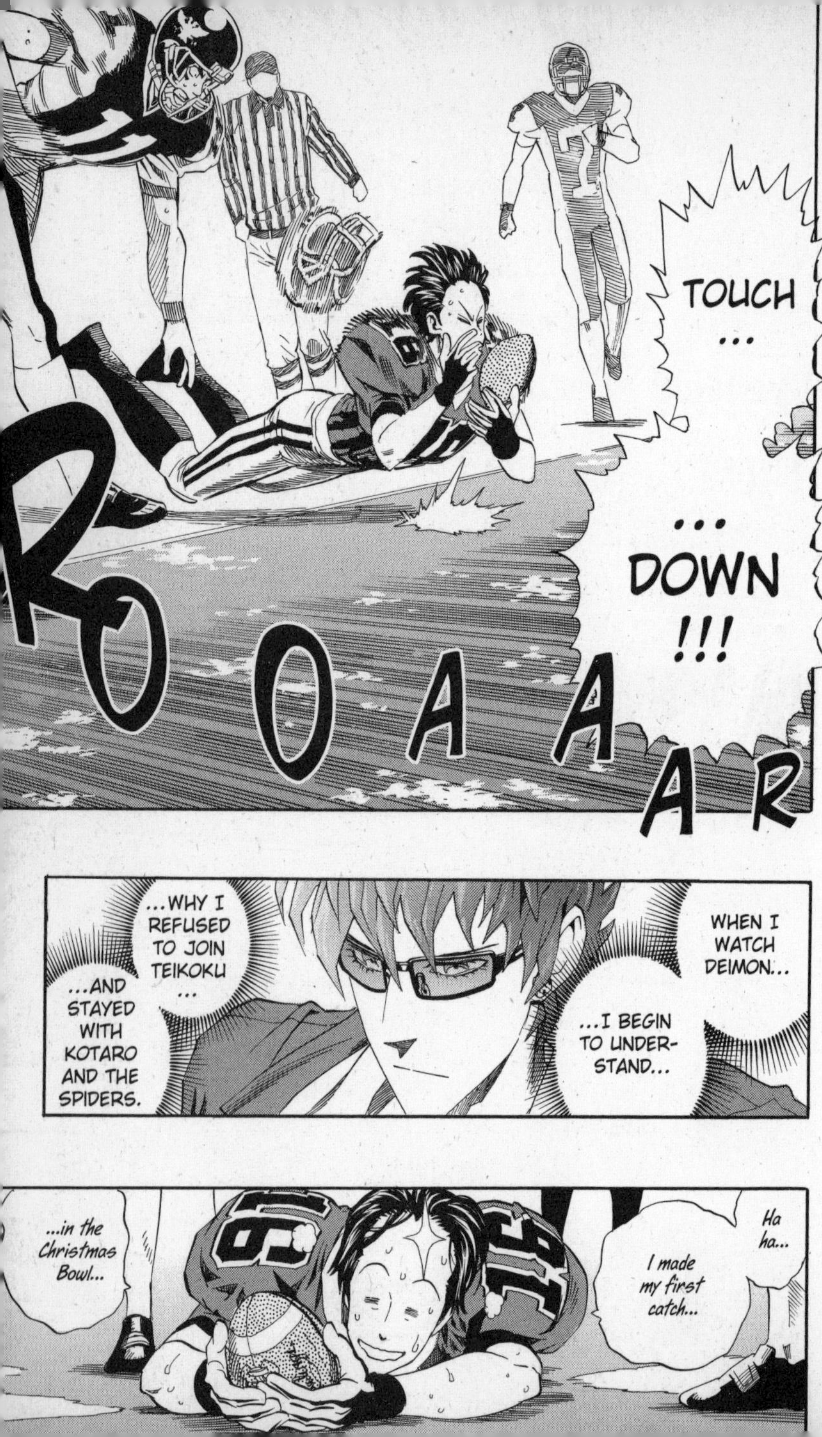
TOUCH...
...DOWN!!!
ROOOAAAAR
WHEN I WATCH DEIMON...
...I BEGIN TO UNDER-STAND...
...WHY I REFUSED TO JOIN TEIKOKU...
...AND STAYED WITH KOTARO AND THE SPIDERS.
Ha ha...
I made my first catch...
...in the Christmas Bowl...

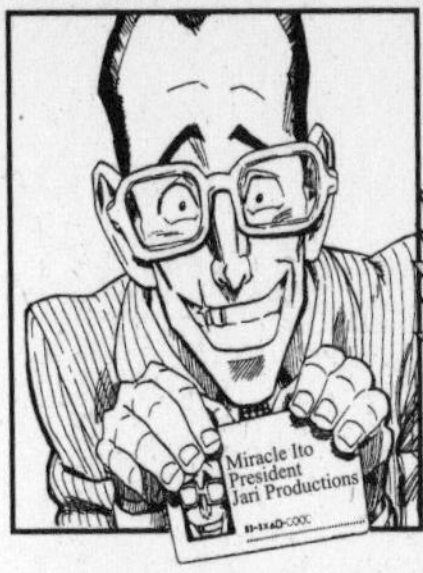
Miracle Ito
President
Jari Productions

He's still alive! Shrewd Miracle Ito's

New product !!

HIGH SCHOOL FOOTBALL STAR GOODS

Eyeshield 21 Model

Ultra Lightspeed Rotating Fan

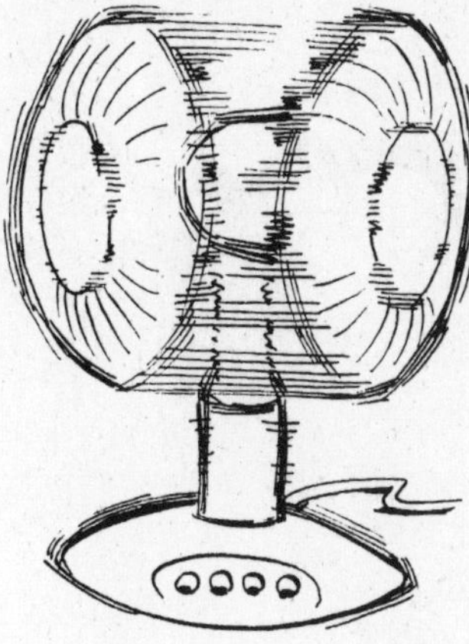

When someone to the right is cool, someone on the left is hot…

When someone on the left is cool, someone on the right is hot…

Say good-bye to this dilemma!

Just like with the Devil Bat Ghost, the fan's rotating head **looks like it has split in two**. It rotates faster than the blade spins! No more fighting for a spot in front of the fan!

※It's incredibly, incredibly dangerous, so don't put your hand anywhere near it.

SPECIAL PRICE **¥6,980**※

※$77.40

Chapter 300
Teikoku's Triumphal Parade

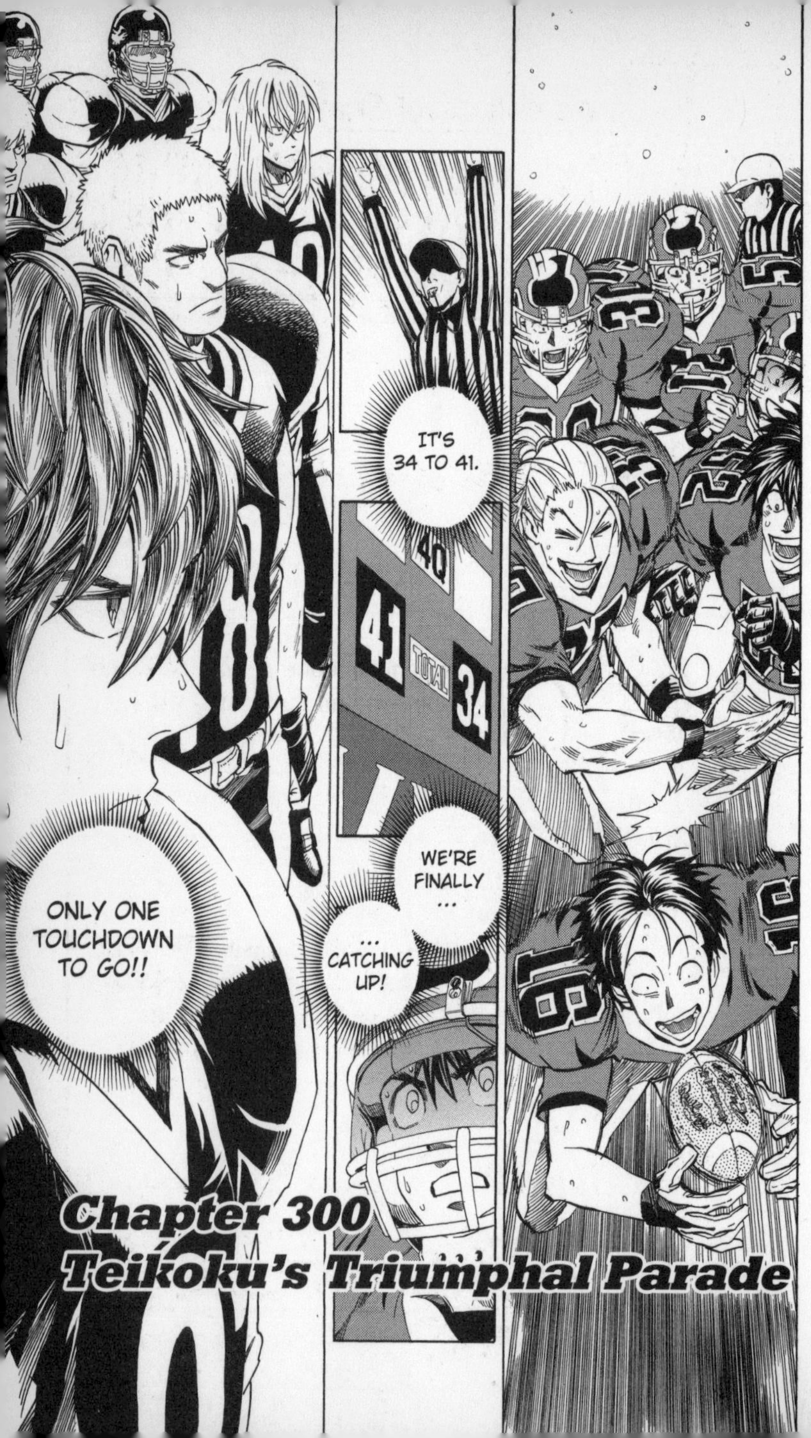
IT'S 34 TO 41.
4Q
41
TOTAL
34
WE'RE FINALLY ...
... CATCHING UP!
ONLY ONE TOUCHDOWN TO GO!!

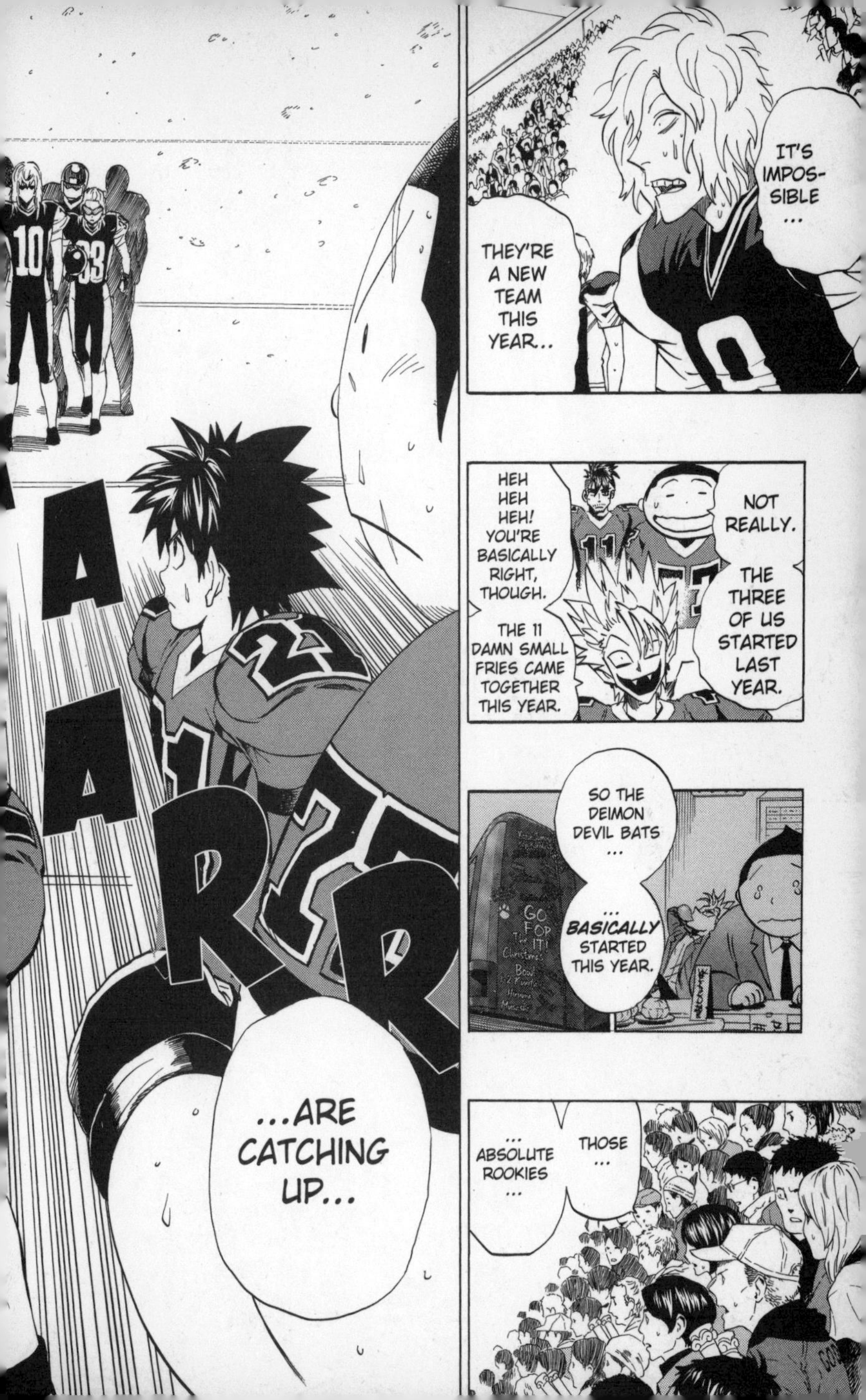
IT'S IMPOSSIBLE...
THEY'RE A NEW TEAM THIS YEAR...
NOT REALLY.
THE THREE OF US STARTED LAST YEAR.
HEH HEH HEH! YOU'RE BASICALLY RIGHT, THOUGH.
THE 11 DAMN SMALL FRIES CAME TOGETHER THIS YEAR.
SO THE DEIMON DEVIL BATS...
...BASICALLY STARTED THIS YEAR.
THOSE...
...ABSOLUTE ROOKIES...
...ARE CATCHING UP...

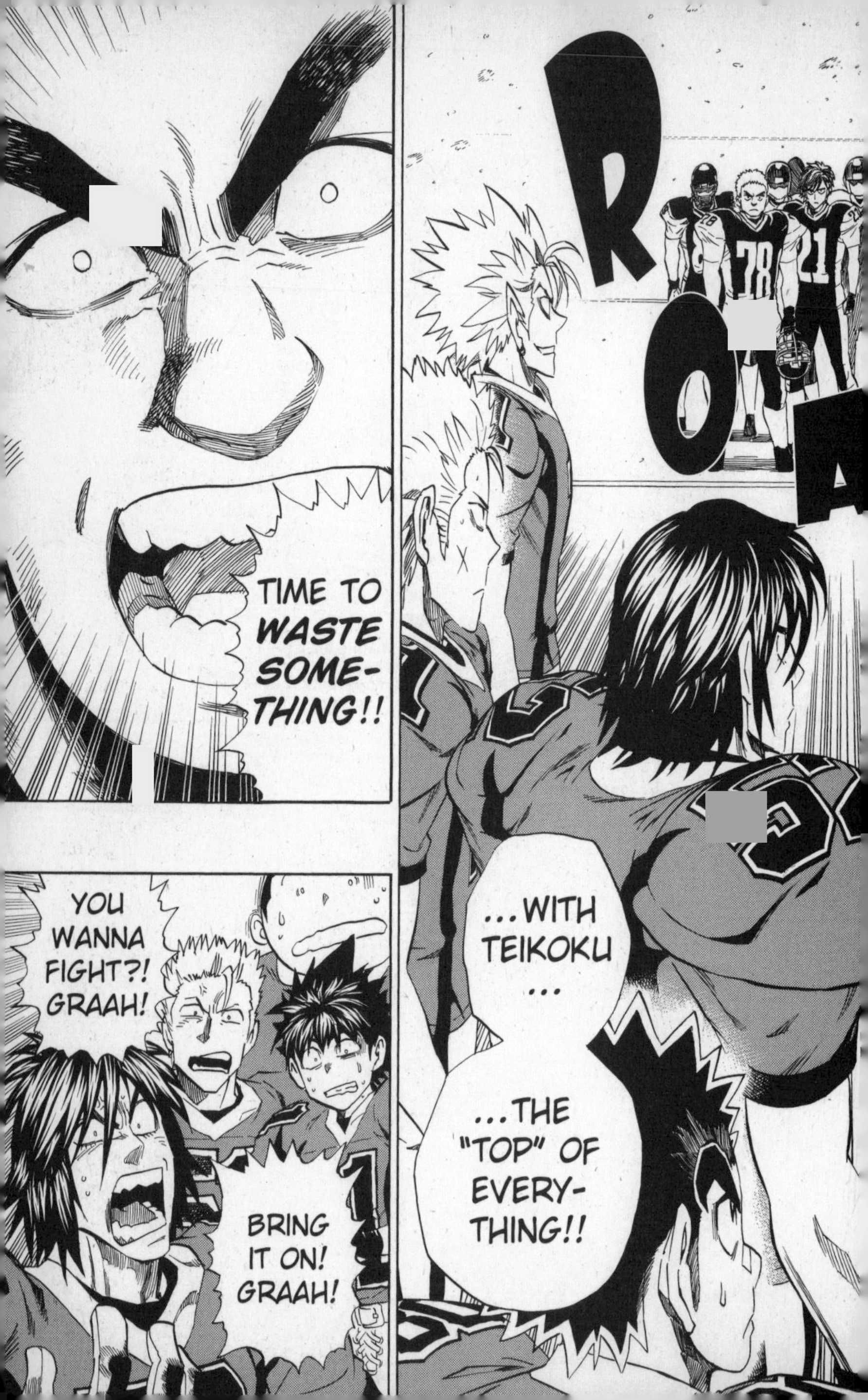
ROA
...WITH TEIKOKU...
...THE "TOP" OF EVERYTHING!!
TIME TO WASTE SOMETHING!!
YOU WANNA FIGHT?! GRAAH!
BRING IT ON! GRAAH!

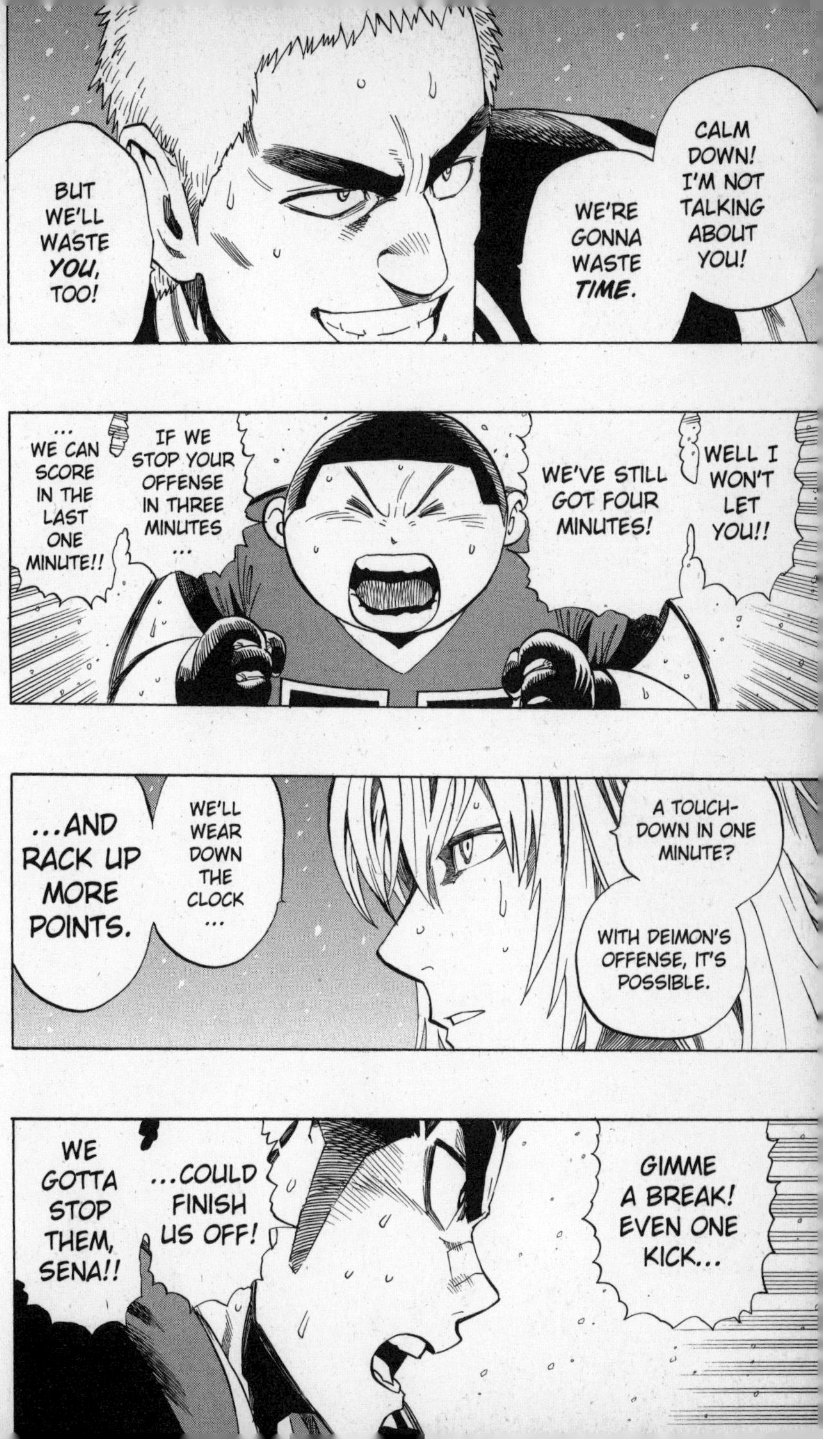
CALM DOWN! I'M NOT TALKING ABOUT YOU!
WE'RE GONNA WASTE *TIME*.
BUT WE'LL WASTE *YOU*, TOO!
WELL I WON'T LET YOU!!
WE'VE STILL GOT FOUR MINUTES!
IF WE STOP YOUR OFFENSE IN THREE MINUTES...
...WE CAN SCORE IN THE LAST ONE MINUTE!!
A TOUCH-DOWN IN ONE MINUTE?
WITH DEIMON'S OFFENSE, IT'S POSSIBLE.
WE'LL WEAR DOWN THE CLOCK...
...AND RACK UP MORE POINTS.
GIMME A BREAK! EVEN ONE KICK...
...COULD FINISH US OFF!
WE GOTTA STOP THEM, SENA!!

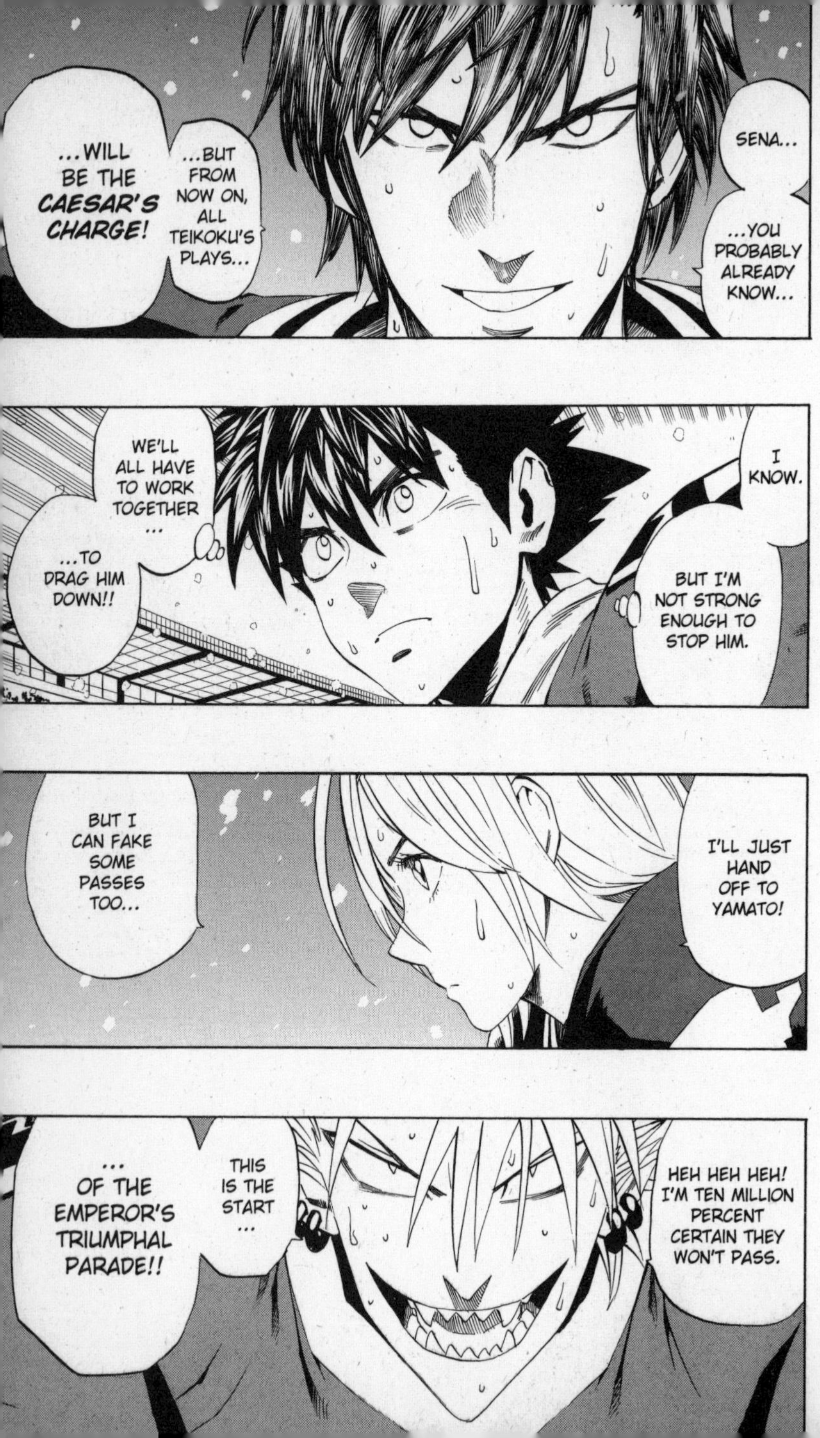
SENA...
...YOU PROBABLY ALREADY KNOW...
...BUT FROM NOW ON, ALL TEIKOKU'S PLAYS...
...WILL BE THE *CAESAR'S CHARGE*!
I KNOW.
BUT I'M NOT STRONG ENOUGH TO STOP HIM.
WE'LL ALL HAVE TO WORK TOGETHER...
...TO DRAG HIM DOWN!!
I'LL JUST HAND OFF TO YAMATO!
BUT I CAN FAKE SOME PASSES TOO...
HEH HEH HEH! I'M TEN MILLION PERCENT CERTAIN THEY WON'T PASS.
THIS IS THE START...
...OF THE EMPEROR'S TRIUMPHAL PARADE!!

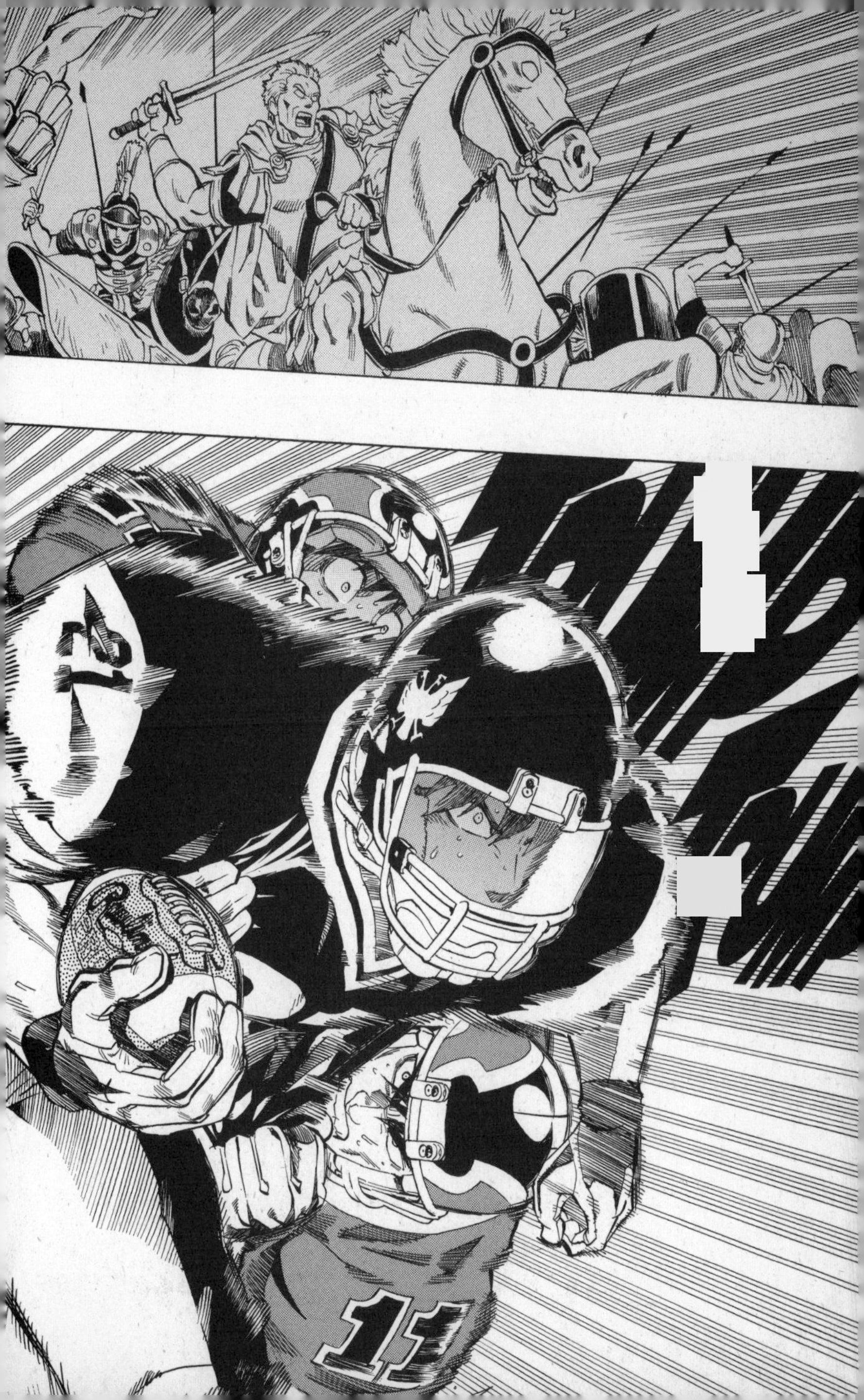

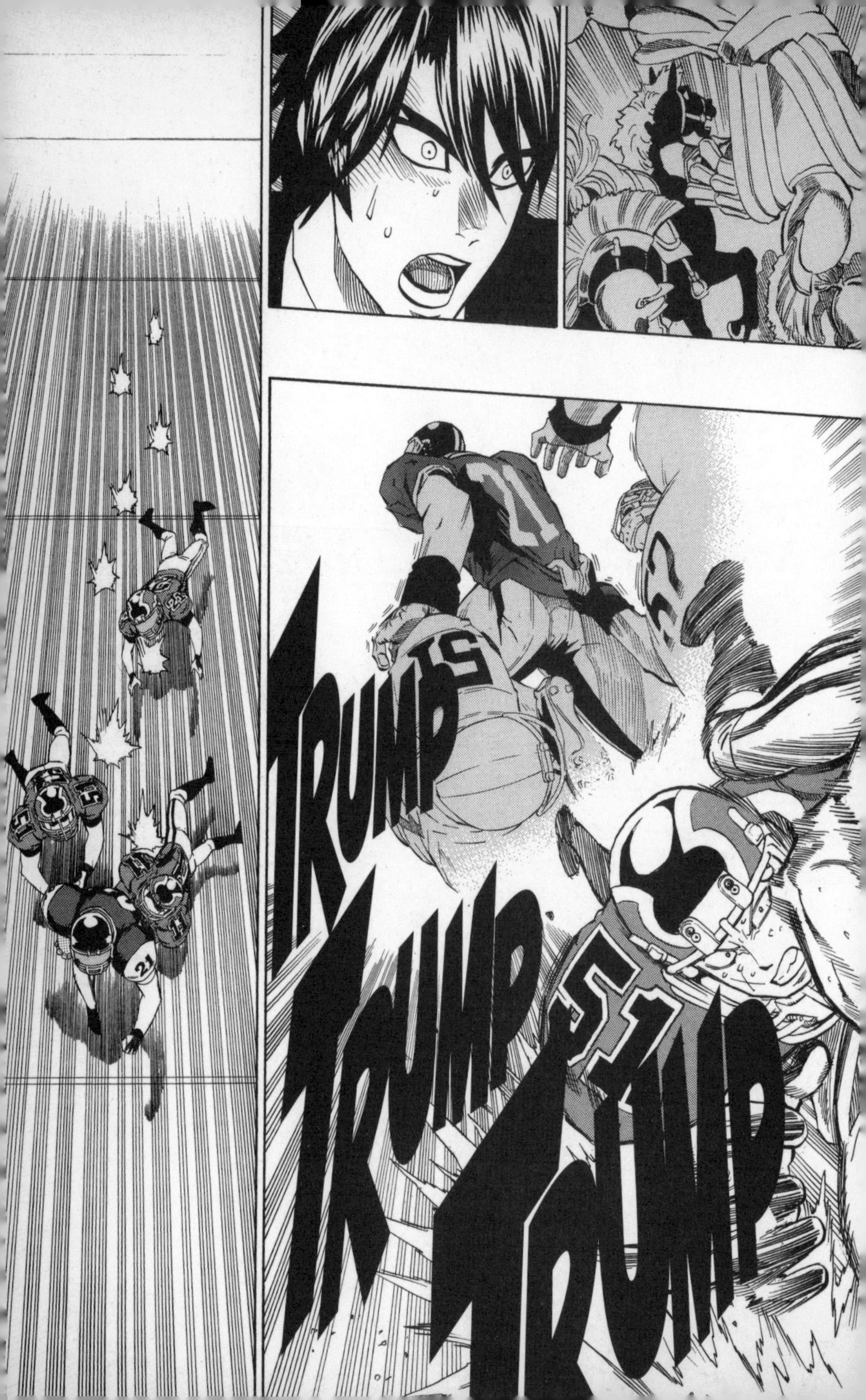
TRUMP
TRUMP
TRUMP

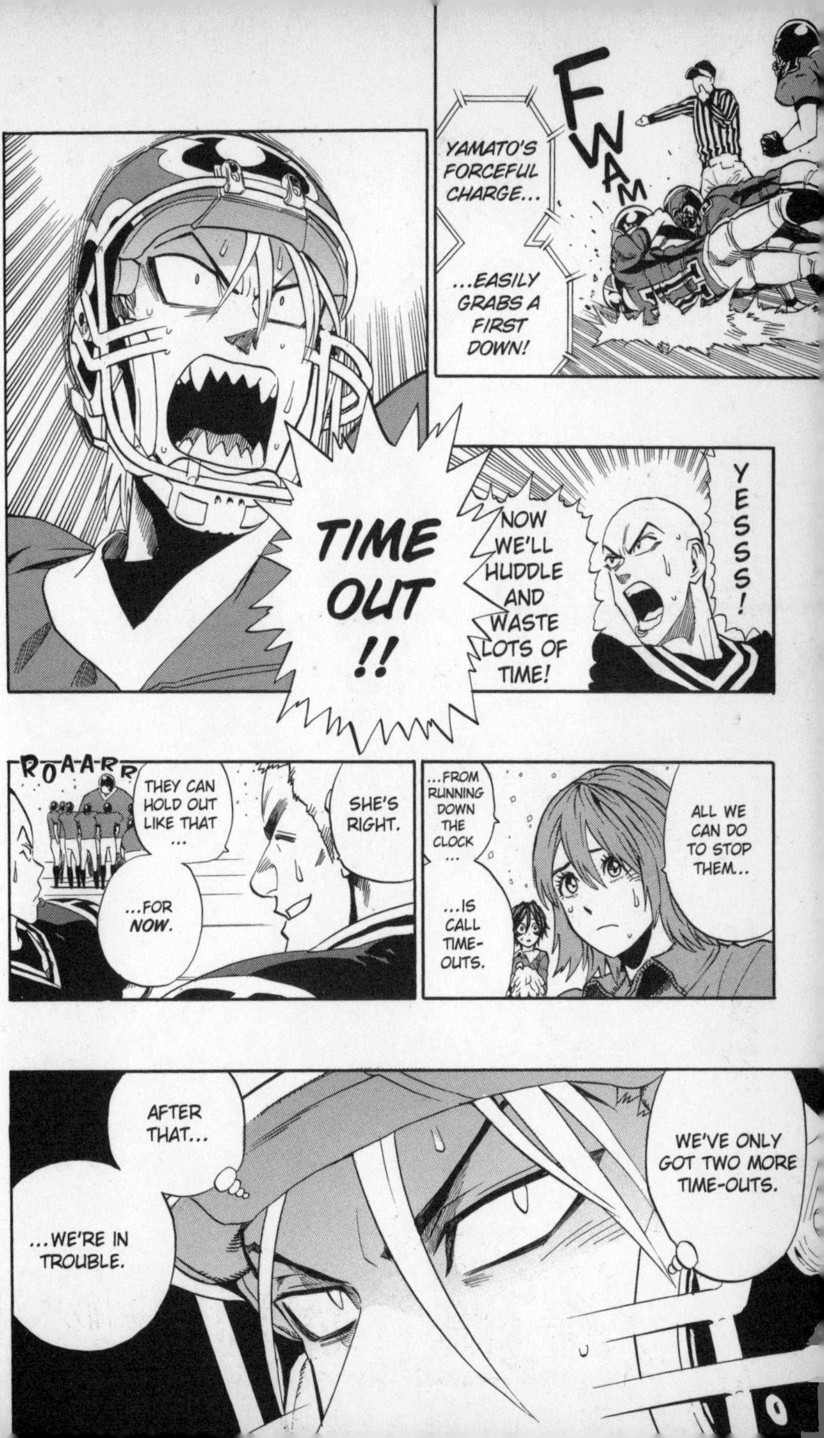
FWAM
YAMATO'S FORCEFUL CHARGE...
...EASILY GRABS A FIRST DOWN!
YESSS!
NOW WE'LL HUDDLE AND WASTE LOTS OF TIME!
TIME OUT!!
ALL WE CAN DO TO STOP THEM...
...FROM RUNNING DOWN THE CLOCK...
...IS CALL TIME-OUTS.
SHE'S RIGHT.
THEY CAN HOLD OUT LIKE THAT...
...FOR *NOW.*
ROAARR
WE'VE ONLY GOT TWO MORE TIME-OUTS.
AFTER THAT...
...WE'RE IN TROUBLE.

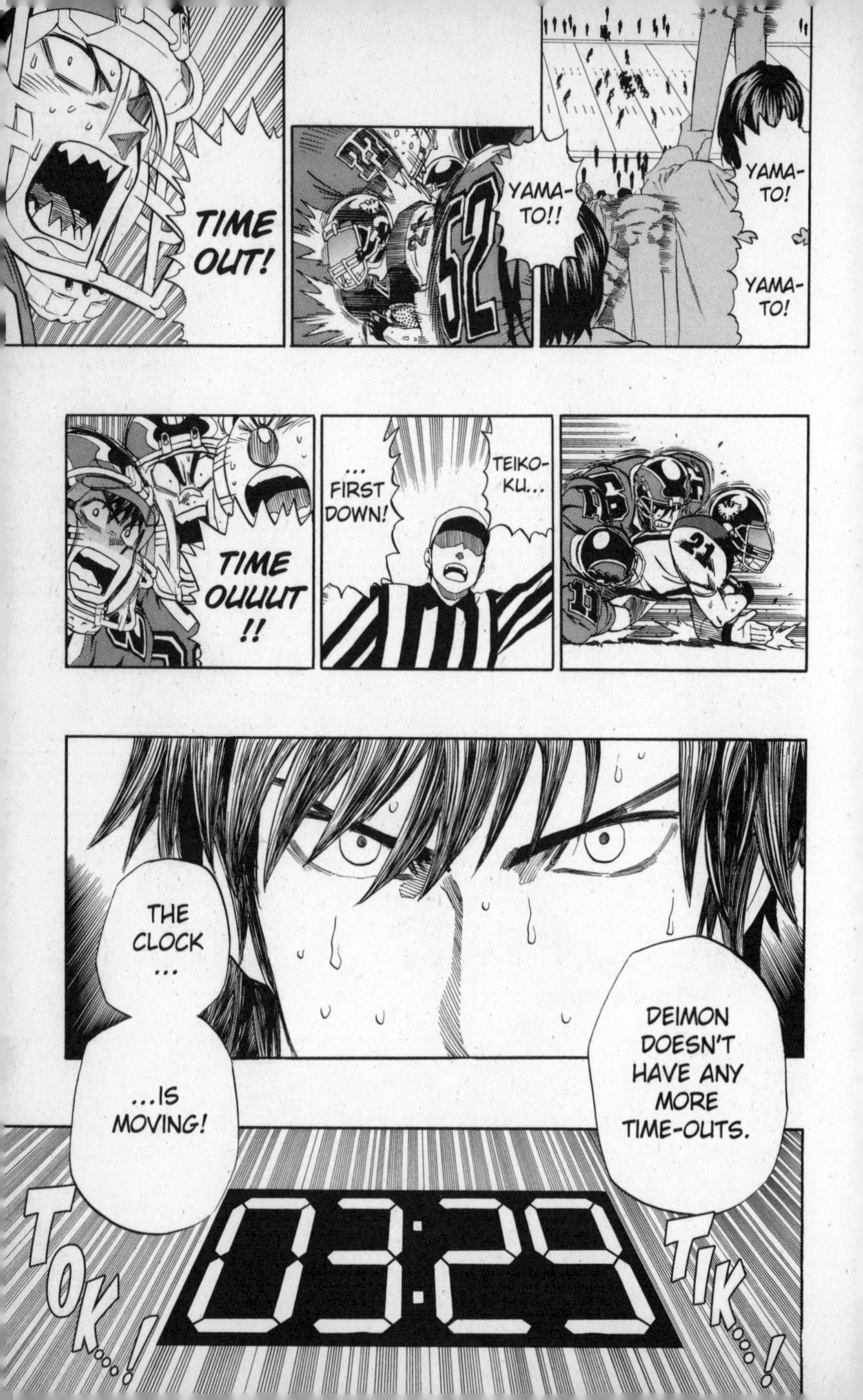
YAMA-TO!
YAMA-TO!
YAMA-TO!!
TIME OUT!
TEIKO-KU...
...FIRST DOWN!
TIME OUUUT!!
DEIMON DOESN'T HAVE ANY MORE TIME-OUTS.
THE CLOCK...
...IS MOVING!
03:25
TIK...!
TOK...!

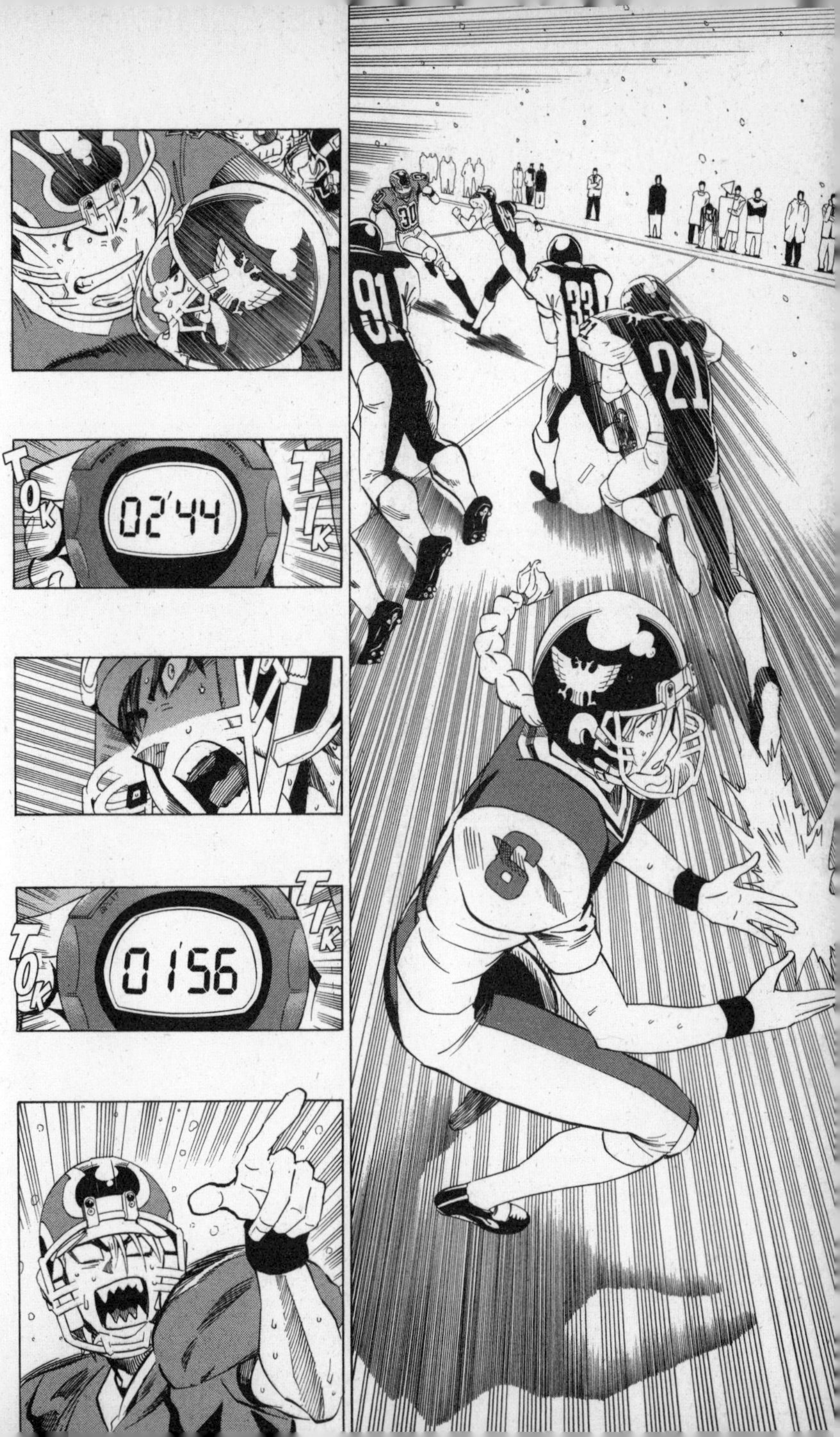

TIK
02'44
TOK
TIK
01'56
TOK

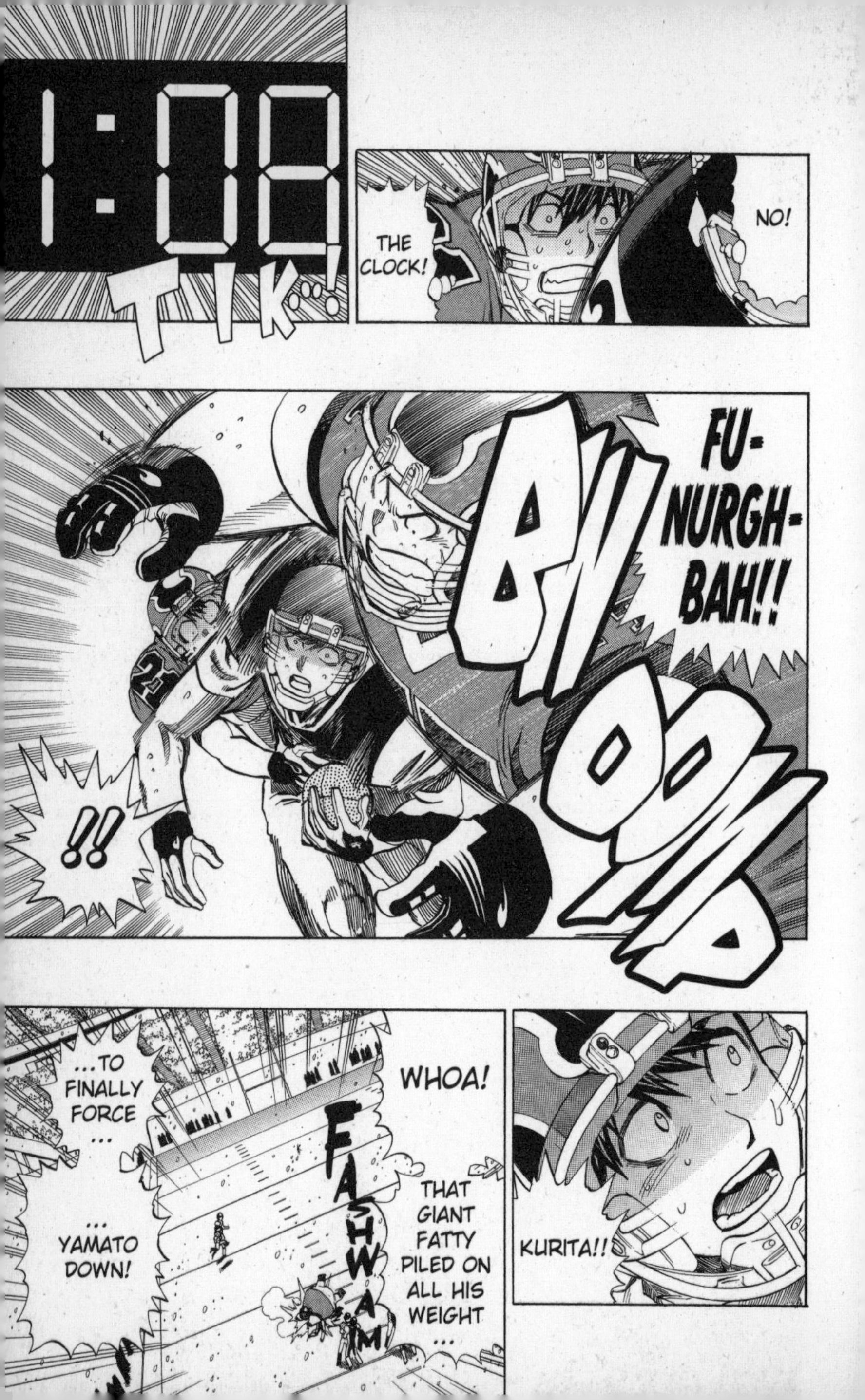
NO!
THE CLOCK!
TIK..!
FU-NURGH-BAH!!
!!
KURITA!!
WHOA!
THAT GIANT FATTY PILED ON ALL HIS WEIGHT ...
...TO FINALLY FORCE ...
... YAMATO DOWN!
FASHWAM

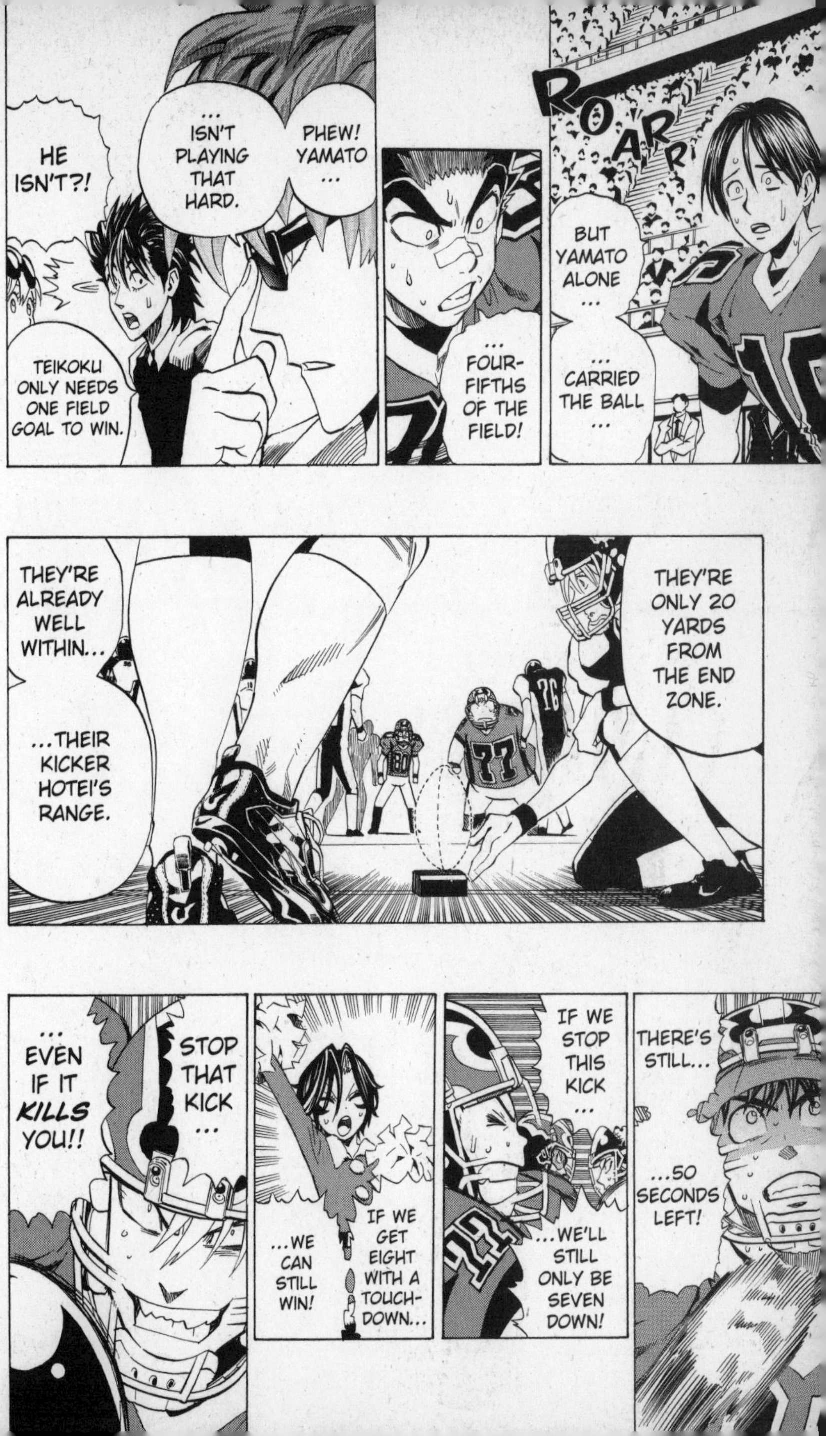
ROARR
BUT YAMATO ALONE ...
... CARRIED THE BALL ...
... FOUR-FIFTHS OF THE FIELD!
PHEW! YAMATO ...
... ISN'T PLAYING THAT HARD.
HE ISN'T?!
TEIKOKU ONLY NEEDS ONE FIELD GOAL TO WIN.
THEY'RE ONLY 20 YARDS FROM THE END ZONE.
THEY'RE ALREADY WELL WITHIN...
...THEIR KICKER HOTEI'S RANGE.
THERE'S STILL...
...50 SECONDS LEFT!
IF WE STOP THIS KICK ...
...WE'LL STILL ONLY BE SEVEN DOWN!
IF WE GET EIGHT WITH A TOUCHDOWN...
...WE CAN STILL WIN!
STOP THAT KICK ...
... EVEN IF IT ***KILLS*** YOU!!

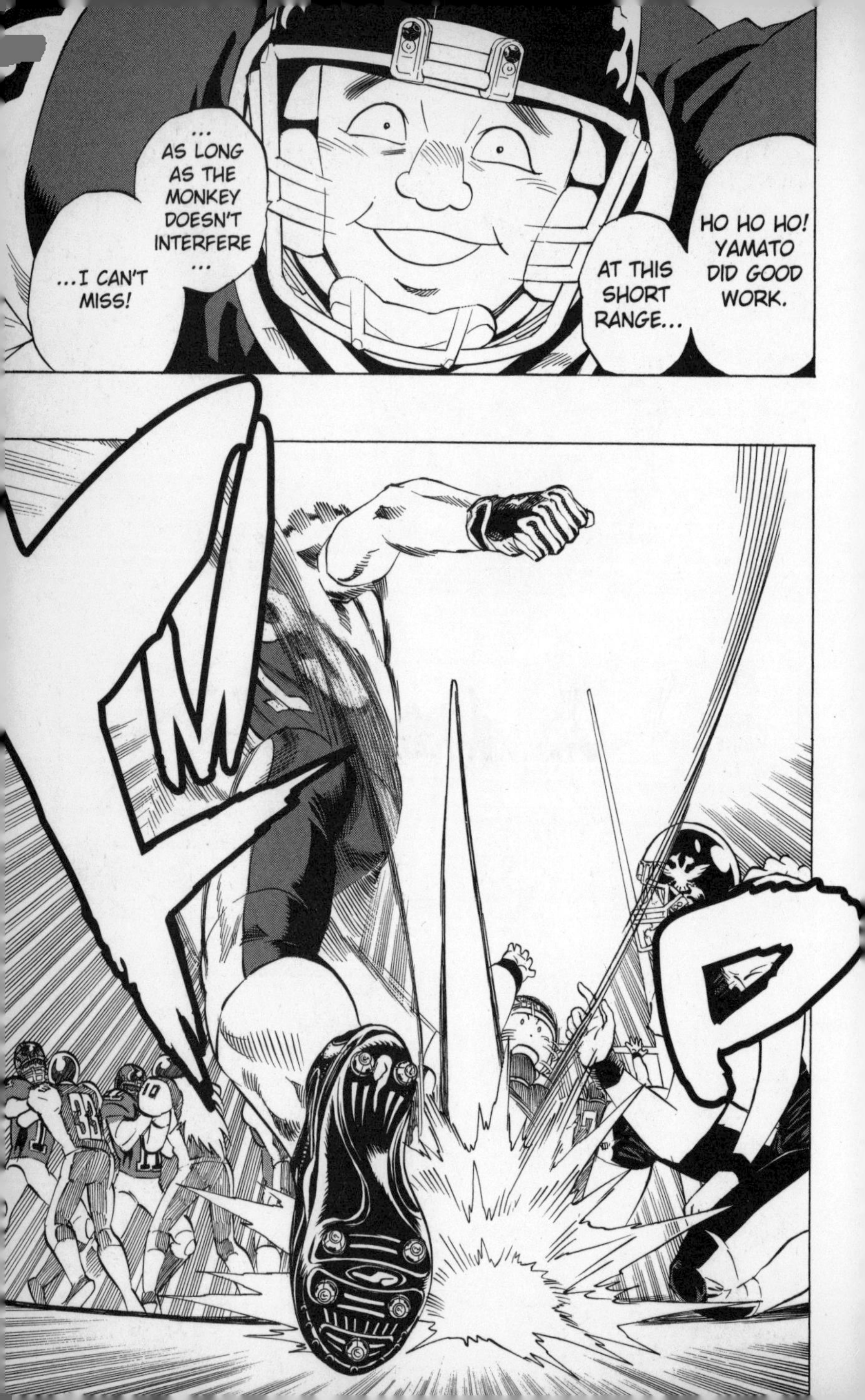
HO HO HO! YAMATO DID GOOD WORK.
AT THIS SHORT RANGE...
... AS LONG AS THE MONKEY DOESN'T INTERFERE ...
...I CAN'T MISS!

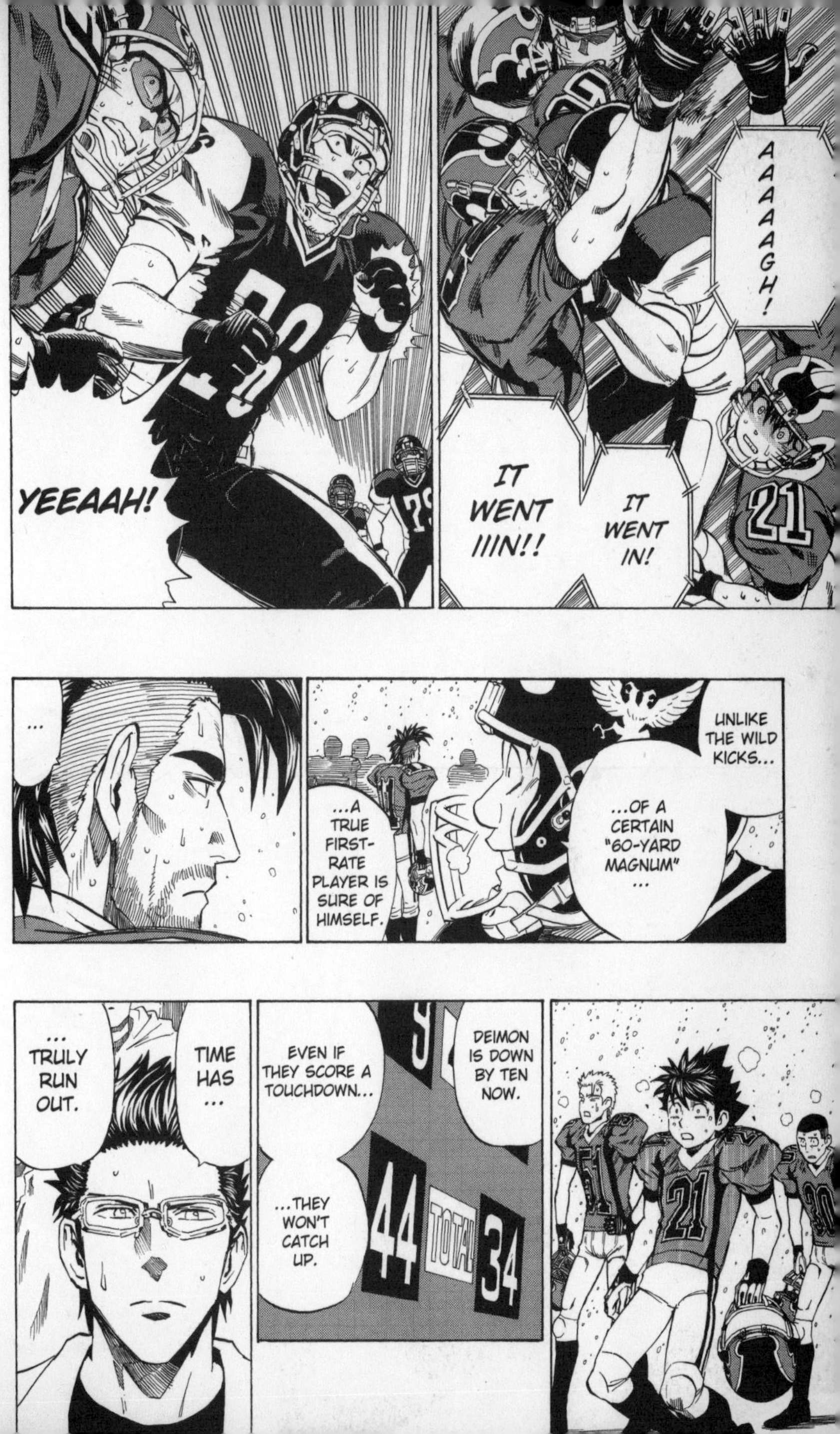
AAAAAAGH!
IT WENT IN!
IT WENT IIIN!!
YEEAAH!
UNLIKE THE WILD KICKS...
...OF A CERTAIN "60-YARD MAGNUM"...
...A TRUE FIRST-RATE PLAYER IS SURE OF HIMSELF.
...
DEIMON IS DOWN BY TEN NOW.
EVEN IF THEY SCORE A TOUCHDOWN...
...THEY WON'T CATCH UP.
44
TOTAL
34
TIME HAS...
...TRULY RUN OUT.

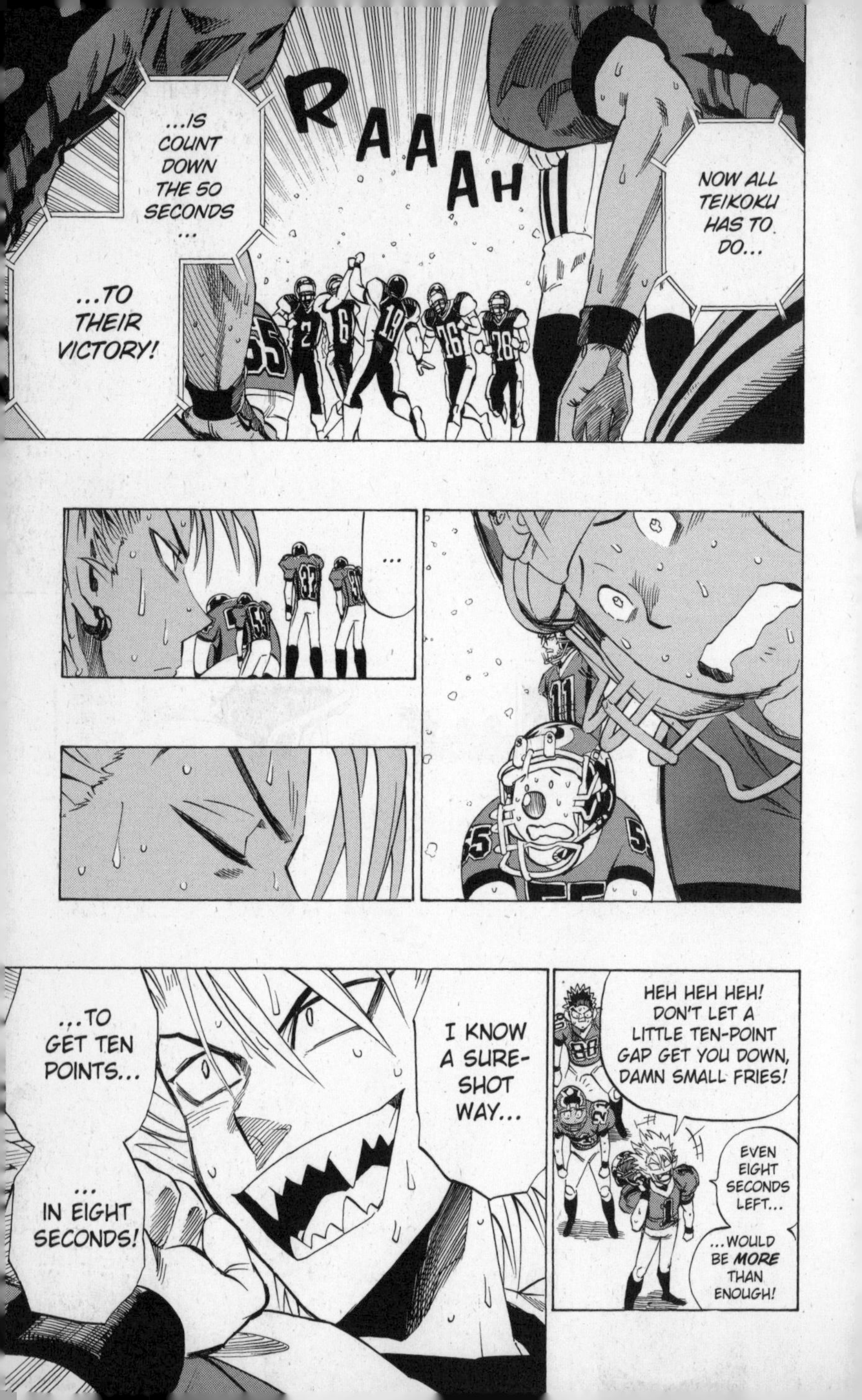
NOW ALL TEIKOKU HAS TO DO...
RAAAAH
...IS COUNT DOWN THE 50 SECONDS ...
...TO THEIR VICTORY!
...
HEH HEH HEH! DON'T LET A LITTLE TEN-POINT GAP GET YOU DOWN, DAMN SMALL FRIES!
EVEN EIGHT SECONDS LEFT...
...WOULD BE MORE THAN ENOUGH!
I KNOW A SURE-SHOT WAY...
...TO GET TEN POINTS...
... IN EIGHT SECONDS!

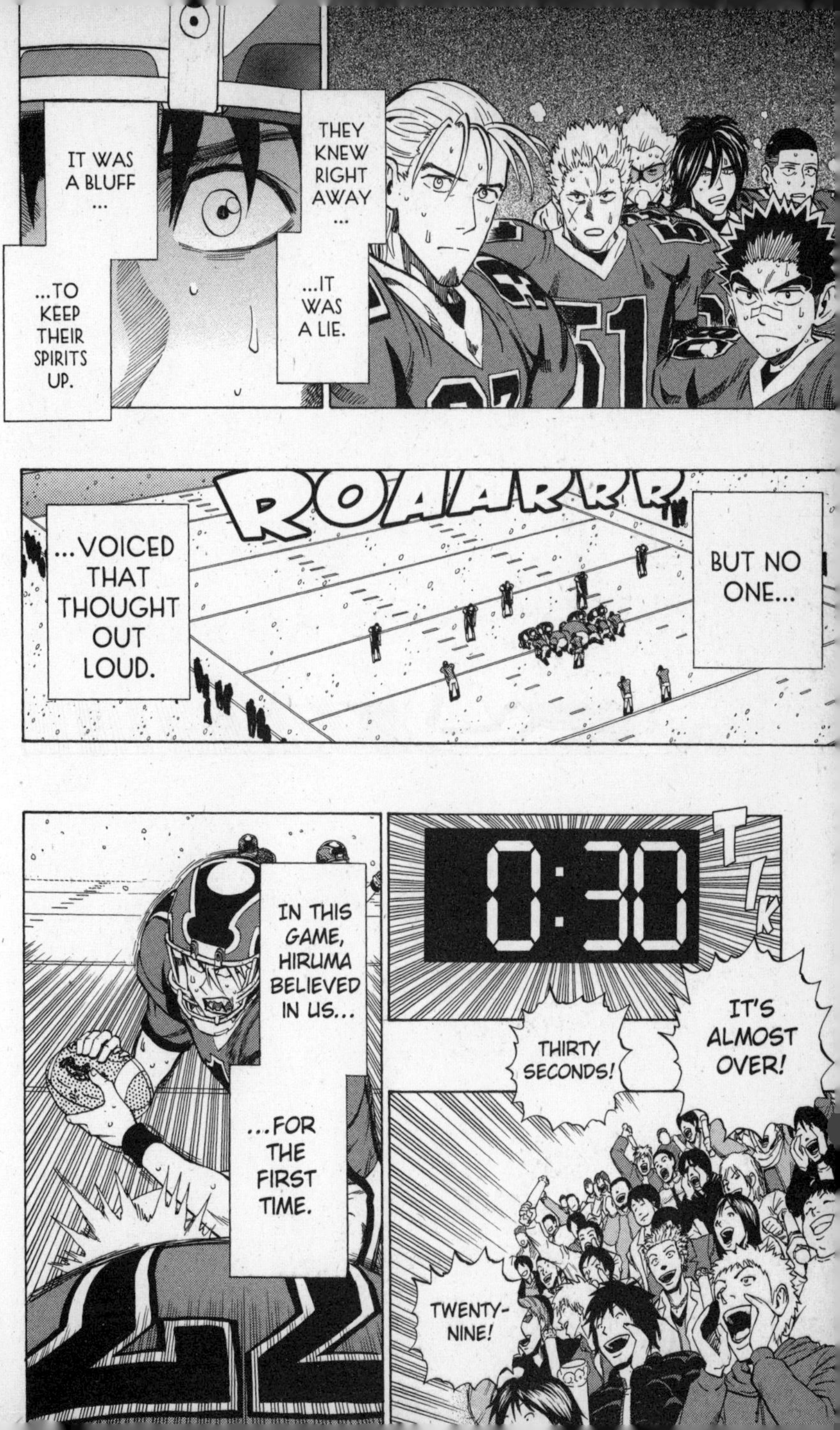
THEY KNEW RIGHT AWAY ...
...IT WAS A LIE.
IT WAS A BLUFF ...
...TO KEEP THEIR SPIRITS UP.
ROAARRR
BUT NO ONE...
...VOICED THAT THOUGHT OUT LOUD.
0:30
TIK
IT'S ALMOST OVER!
THIRTY SECONDS!
TWENTY-NINE!
IN THIS GAME, HIRUMA BELIEVED IN US...
...FOR THE FIRST TIME.

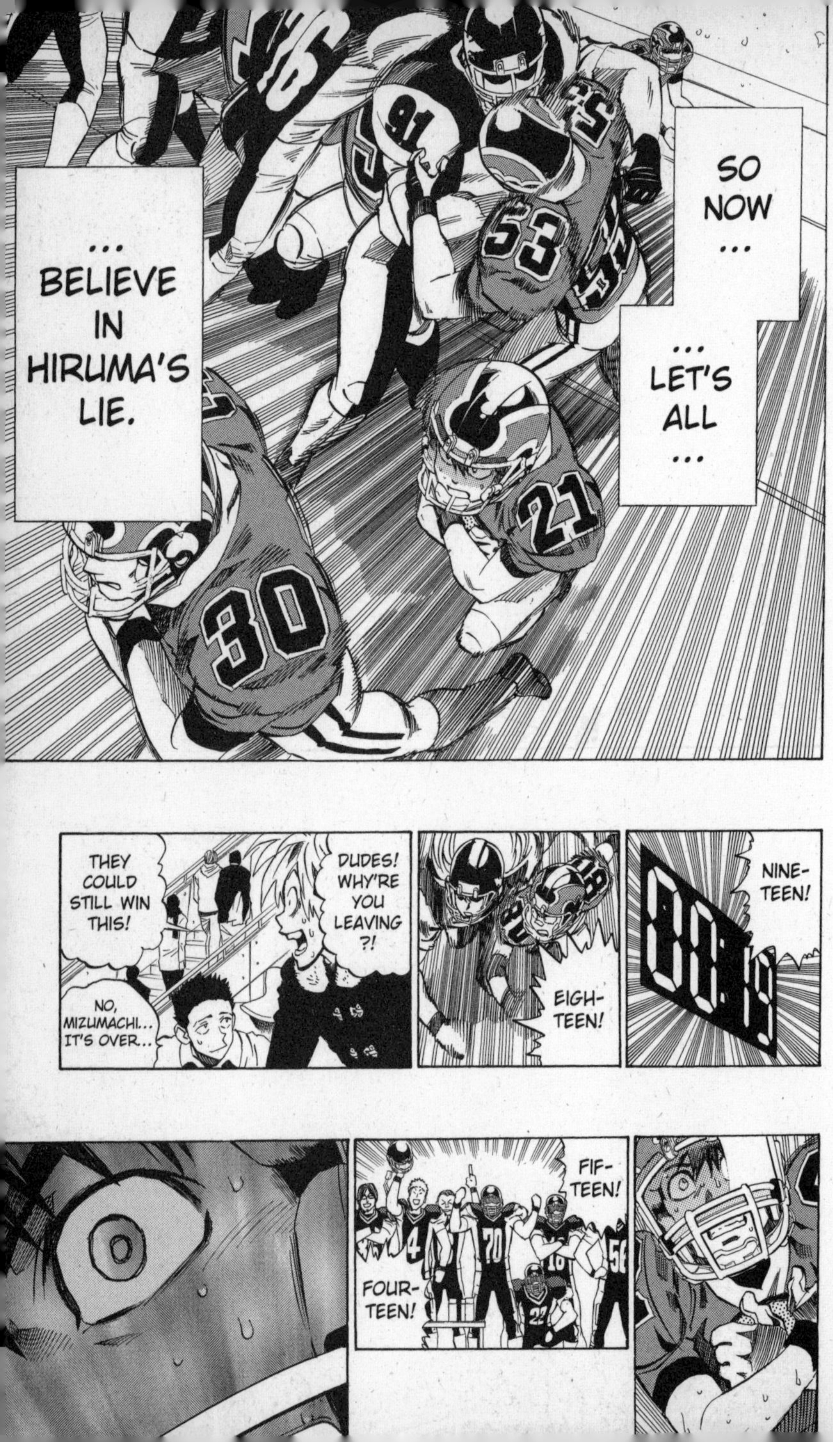
SO NOW ...
... LET'S ALL ...
... BELIEVE IN HIRUMA'S LIE.
NINE-TEEN!
EIGH-TEEN!
DUDES! WHY'RE YOU LEAVING ?!
THEY COULD STILL WIN THIS!
NO, MIZUMACHI... IT'S OVER...
FIF-TEEN!
FOUR-TEEN!

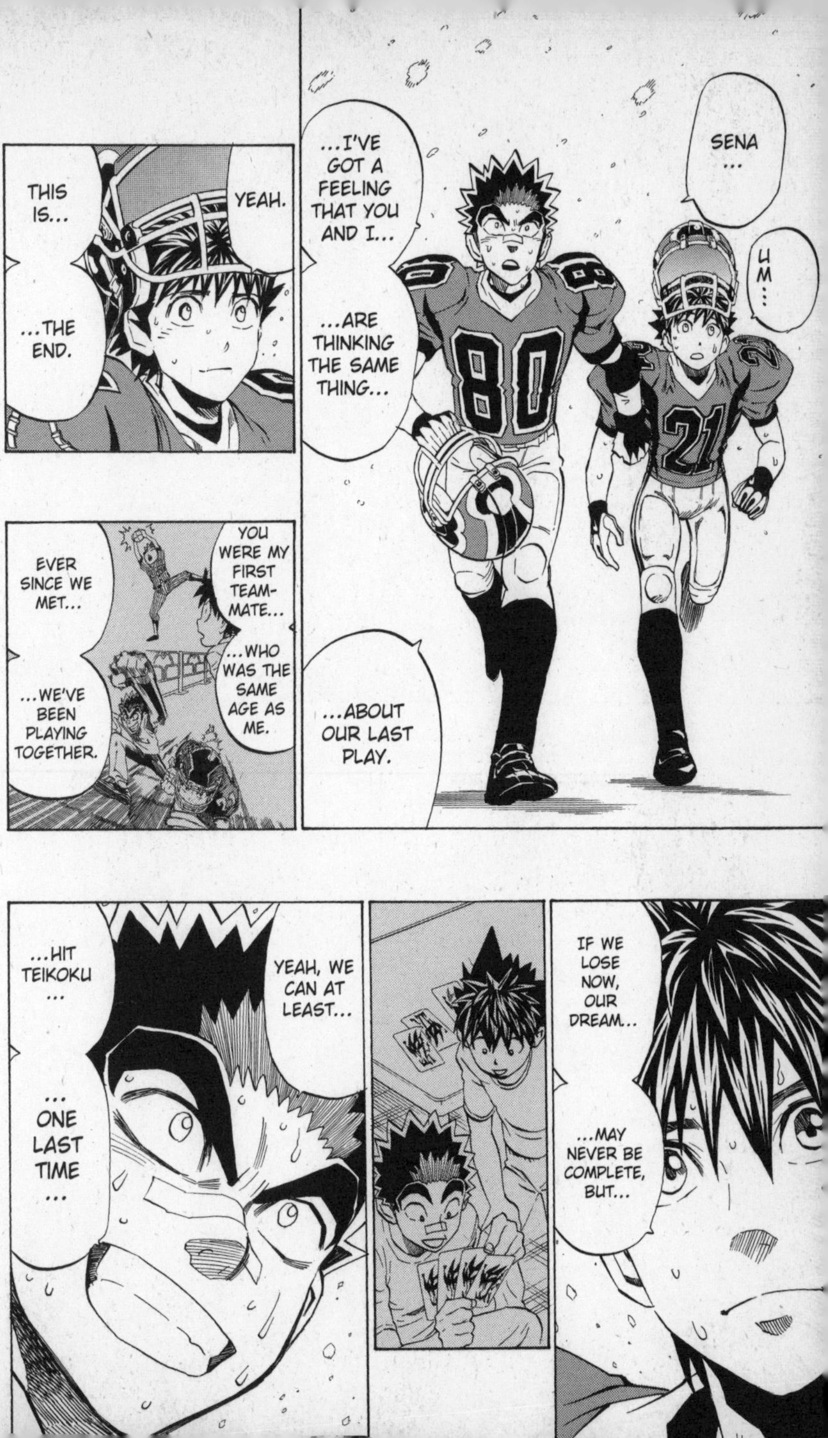
SENA ...
UM...
...I'VE GOT A FEELING THAT YOU AND I...
...ARE THINKING THE SAME THING...
...ABOUT OUR LAST PLAY.
YEAH.
THIS IS...
...THE END.
YOU WERE MY FIRST TEAM-MATE...
...WHO WAS THE SAME AGE AS ME.
EVER SINCE WE MET...
...WE'VE BEEN PLAYING TOGETHER.
IF WE LOSE NOW, OUR DREAM...
...MAY NEVER BE COMPLETE, BUT...
YEAH, WE CAN AT LEAST...
...HIT TEIKOKU ...
... ONE LAST TIME ...

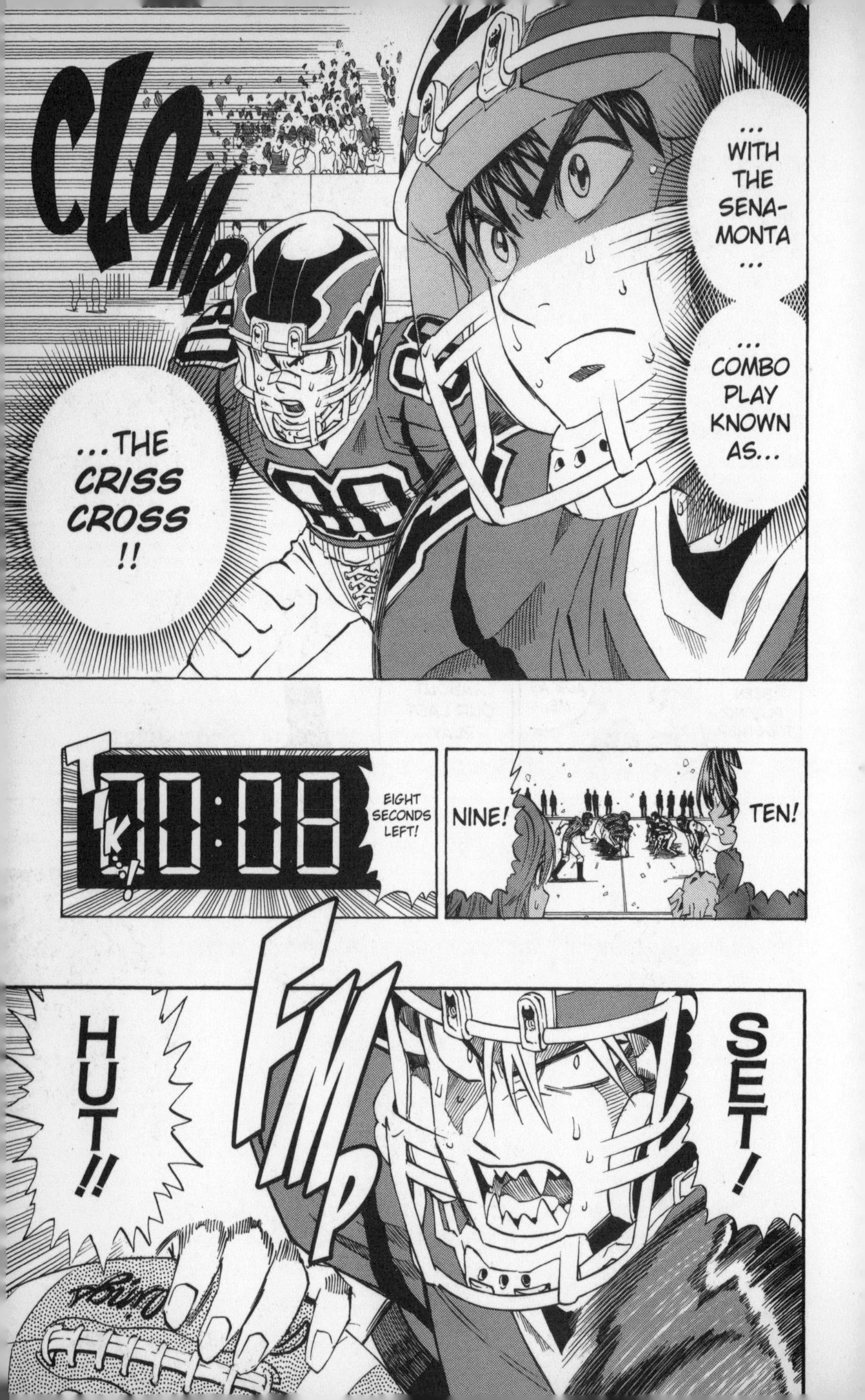
...WITH THE SENA-MONTA...
...COMBO PLAY KNOWN AS...
CLOMP
...THE CRISS CROSS!!
TEN!
NINE!
EIGHT SECONDS LEFT!
00:08
TIK..!
SET!
FMP
HUT!!

Devil Bat 021

Investigation File #144

Reveal Teikoku High School's entrance exam!

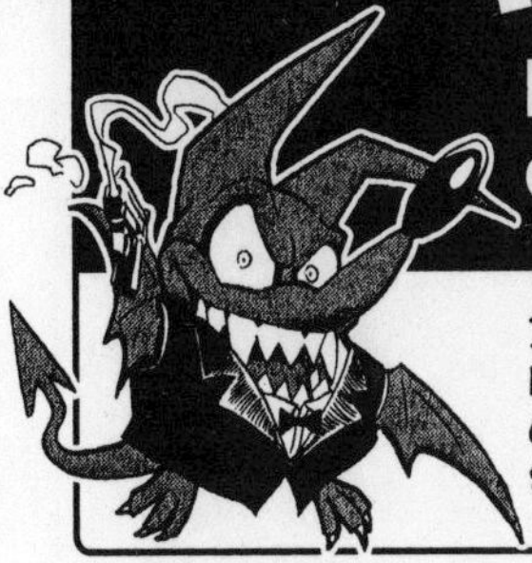

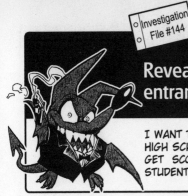

I WANT TO GO TO TEIKOKU HIGH SCHOOL. FOOTBALL ACES GET SCOUTED, BUT HOW DO STUDENTS NORMALLY ENROLL?

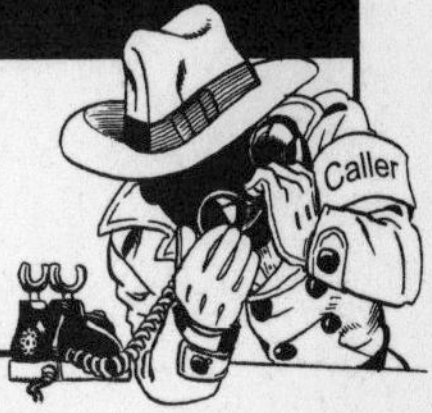
Caller

Caller name: T.M. in Toyama Prefecture

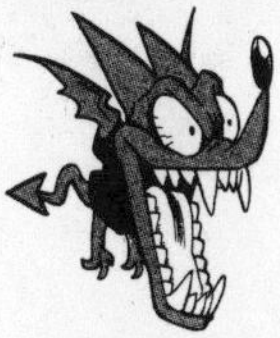

THERE IS A NORMAL ENTRANCE EXAM... BUT FOR SOME REASON FOOTBALL QUESTIONS ARE MIXED IN!

Q: Which of the following is not a violation of football rules? Answer with the number.

(1) Confusing your opponent by drawing a football on your uniform

(2) Deliberately tripping an opponent carrying the ball

(3) Linking arms with your teammates and running at your opponent

(4) A team's coach smoking on the sidelines

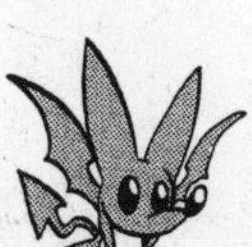

THAT'S PRETTY HARD... THE ANSWER IS BELOW! IF YOU GET THE RIGHT ANSWER, MAYBE YOU CAN BECOME A STUDENT AT TEIKOKU HIGH SCHOOL!!

A: (2) Just about anything is allowed against an opposing runner.

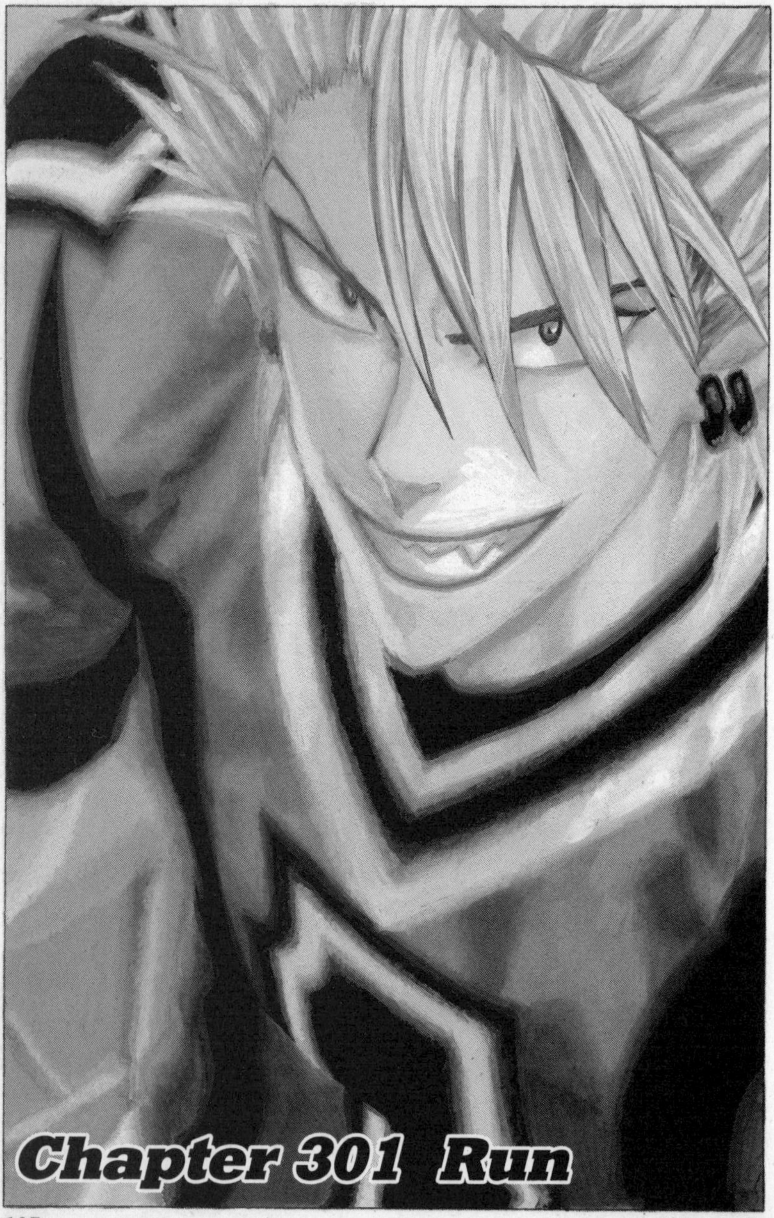
Chapter 301 Run

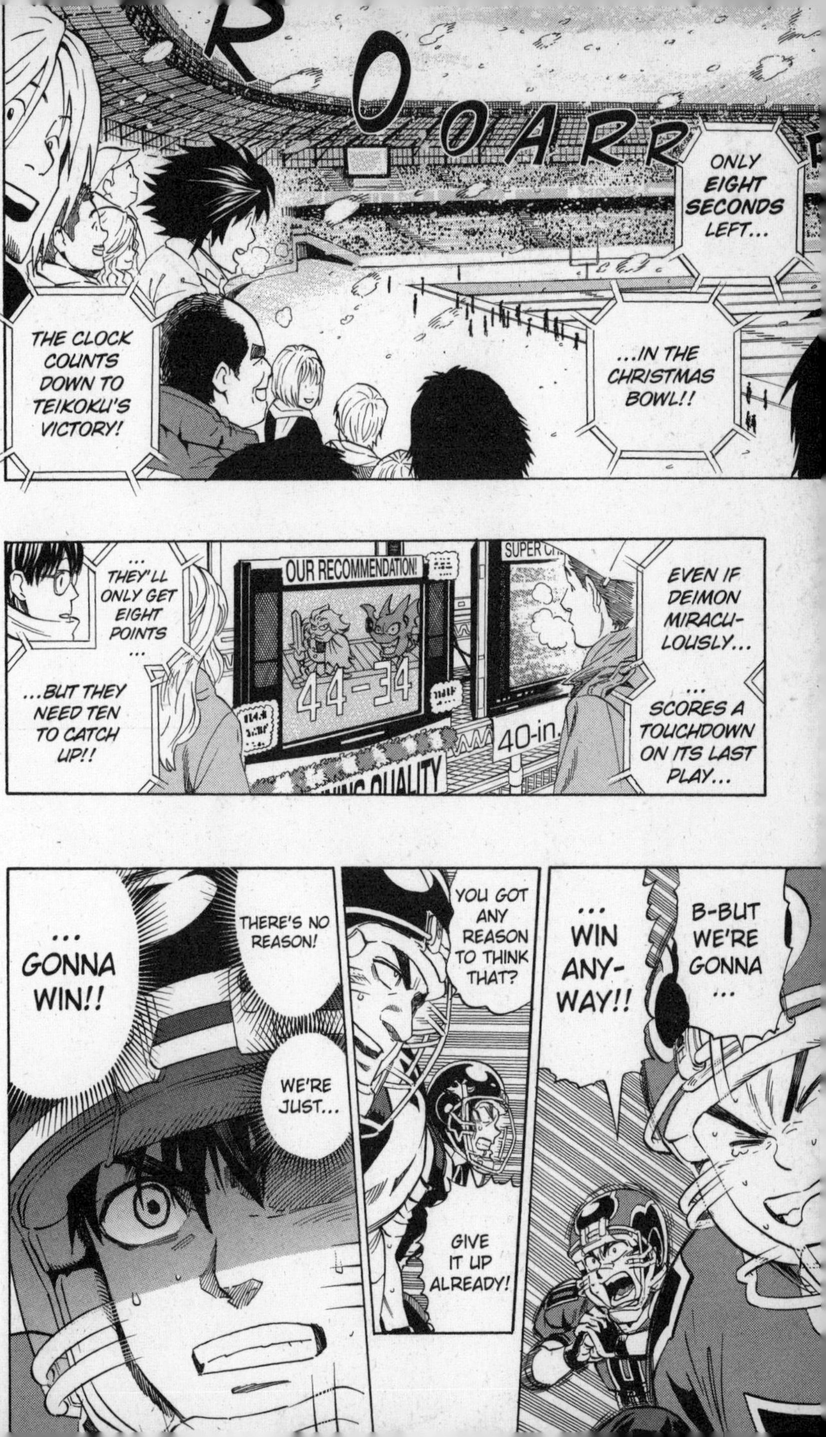
ROOOARR
ONLY EIGHT SECONDS LEFT...
...IN THE CHRISTMAS BOWL!!
THE CLOCK COUNTS DOWN TO TEIKOKU'S VICTORY!
EVEN IF DEIMON MIRACULOUSLY...
...SCORES A TOUCHDOWN ON ITS LAST PLAY...
OUR RECOMMENDATION!
44-34
40-in.
...THEY'LL ONLY GET EIGHT POINTS...
...BUT THEY NEED TEN TO CATCH UP!!
B-BUT WE'RE GONNA...
...WIN ANYWAY!!
YOU GOT ANY REASON TO THINK THAT?
GIVE IT UP ALREADY!
THERE'S NO REASON!
WE'RE JUST...
...GONNA WIN!!

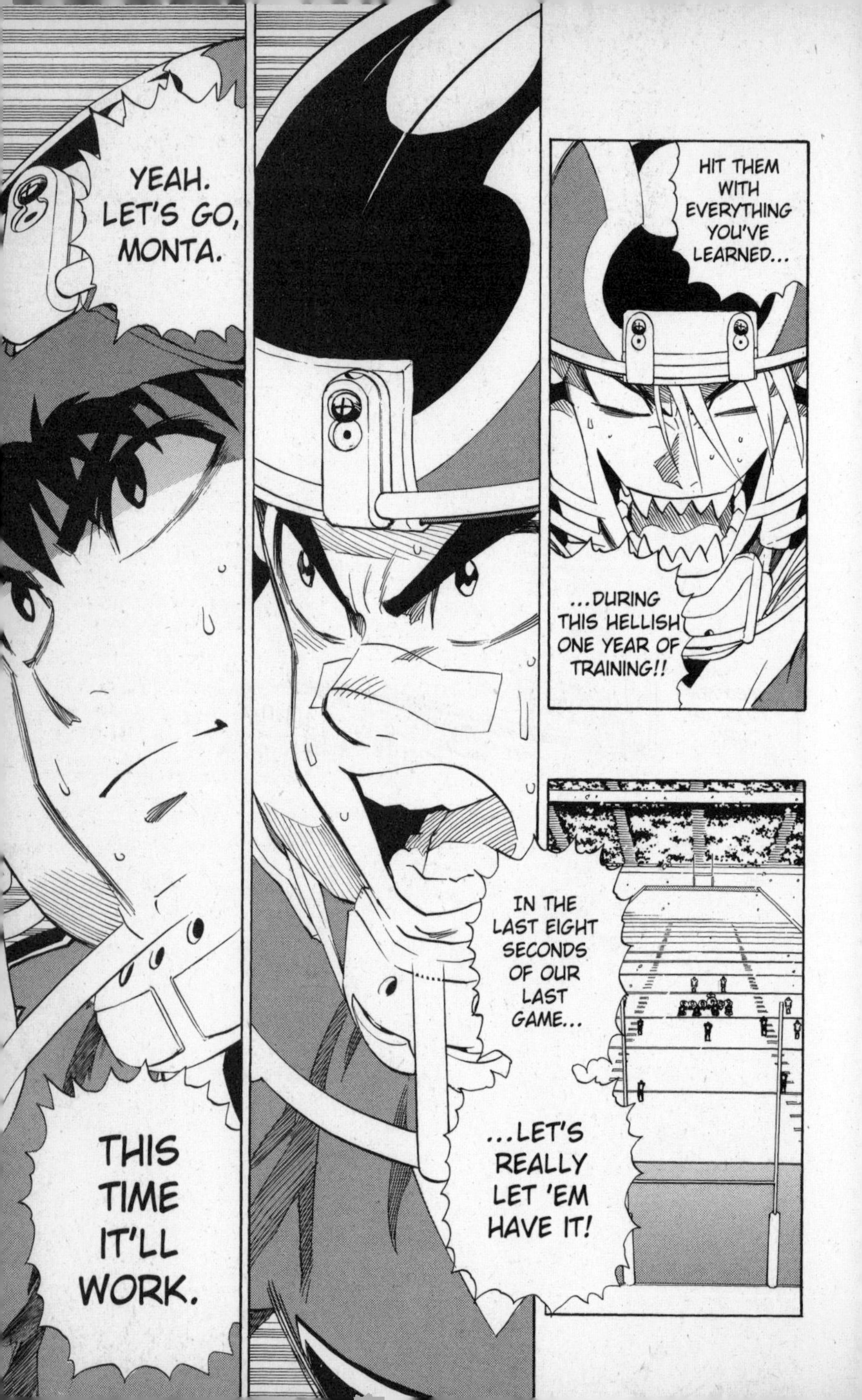
HIT THEM WITH EVERYTHING YOU'VE LEARNED...
...DURING THIS HELLISH ONE YEAR OF TRAINING!!
IN THE LAST EIGHT SECONDS OF OUR LAST GAME...
...LET'S REALLY LET 'EM HAVE IT!
YEAH. LET'S GO, MONTA.
THIS TIME IT'LL WORK.

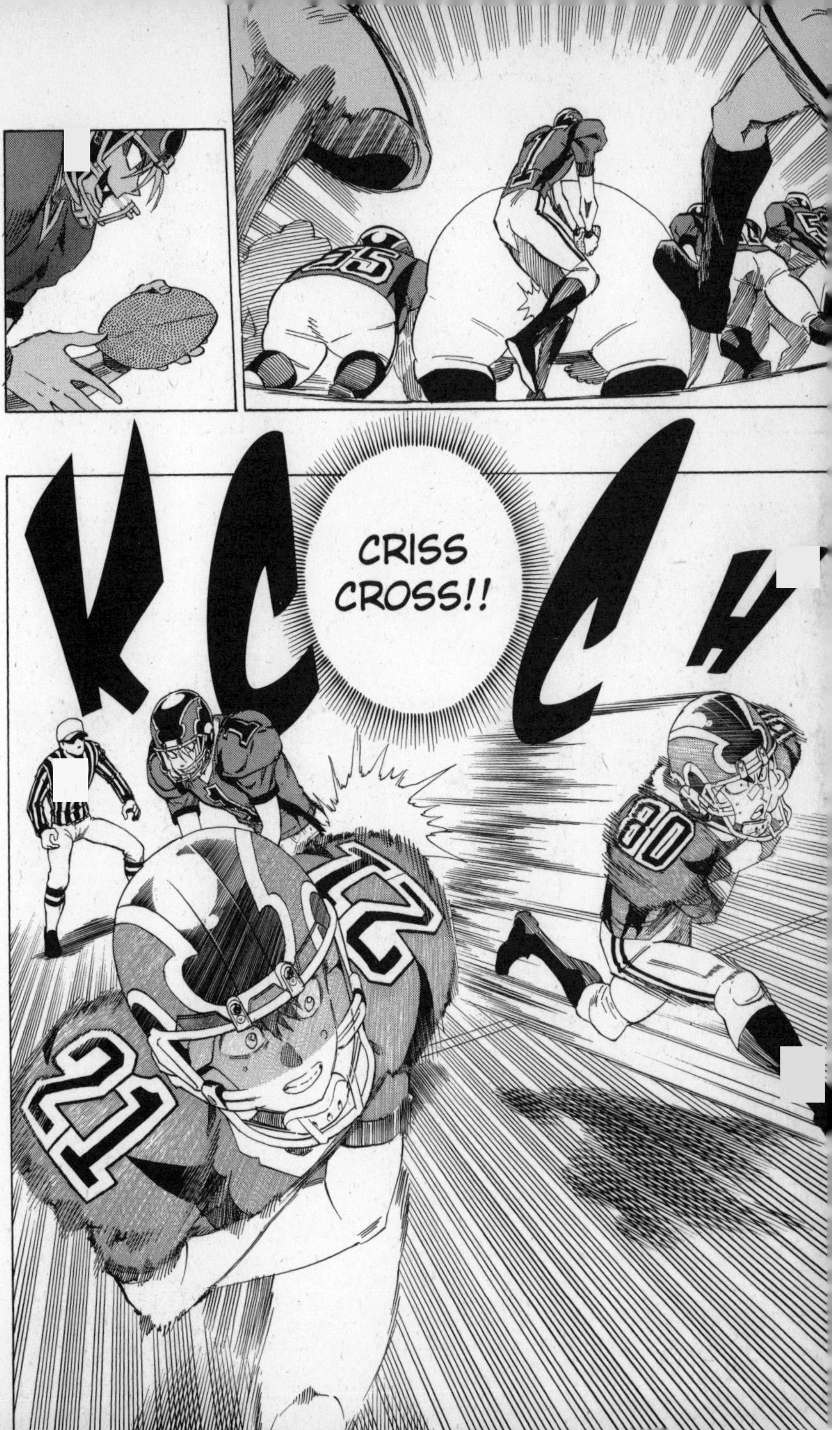
CRISS CROSS!!
KCCH

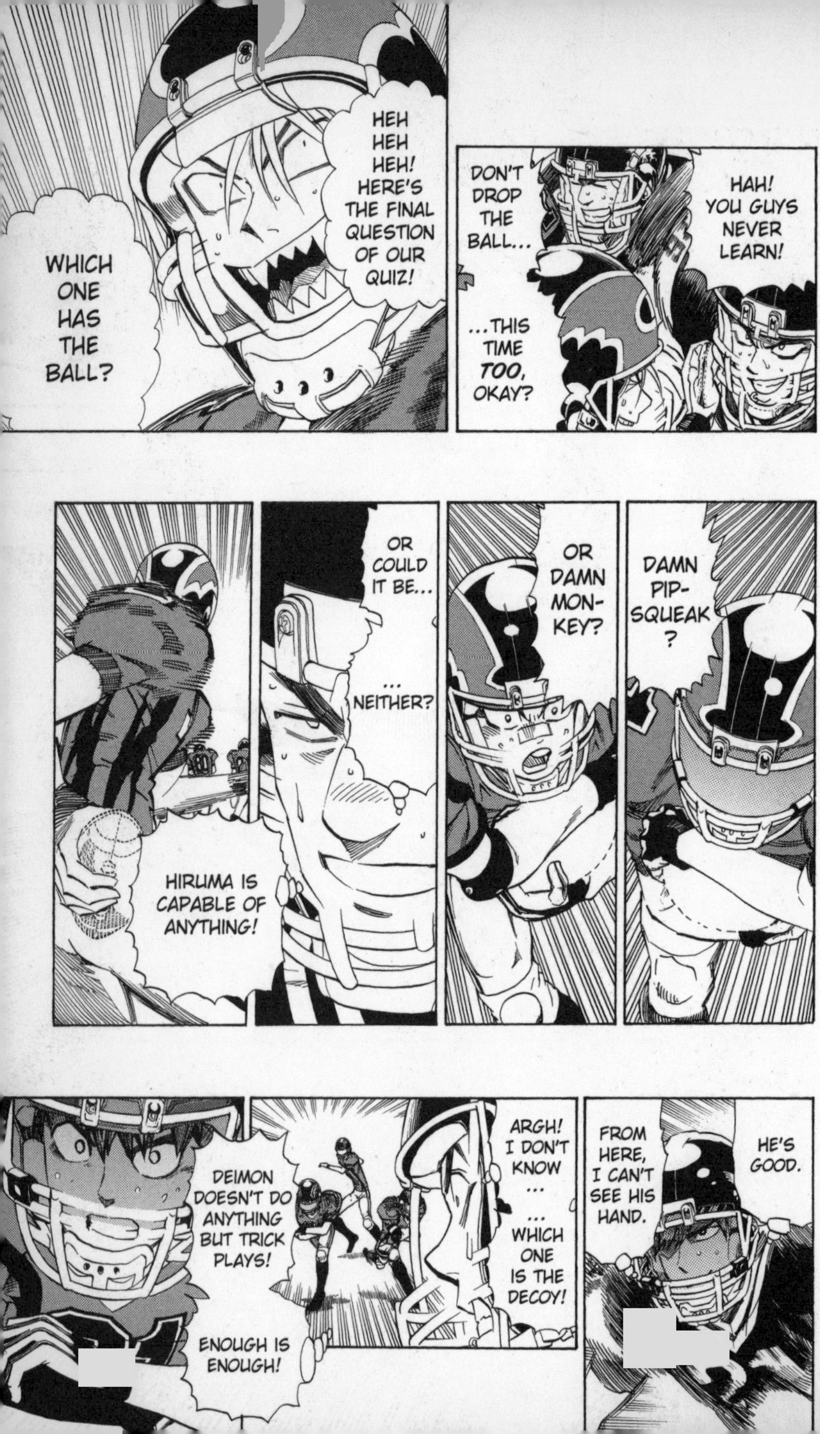
HAH! YOU GUYS NEVER LEARN!
DON'T DROP THE BALL...
...THIS TIME *TOO*, OKAY?
HEH HEH HEH! HERE'S THE FINAL QUESTION OF OUR QUIZ!
WHICH ONE HAS THE BALL?
DAMN PIP-SQUEAK?
OR DAMN MON-KEY?
OR COULD IT BE...
...NEITHER?
HIRUMA IS CAPABLE OF ANYTHING!
HE'S GOOD.
FROM HERE, I CAN'T SEE HIS HAND.
ARGH! I DON'T KNOW...
...WHICH ONE IS THE DECOY!
DEIMON DOESN'T DO ANYTHING BUT TRICK PLAYS!
ENOUGH IS ENOUGH!

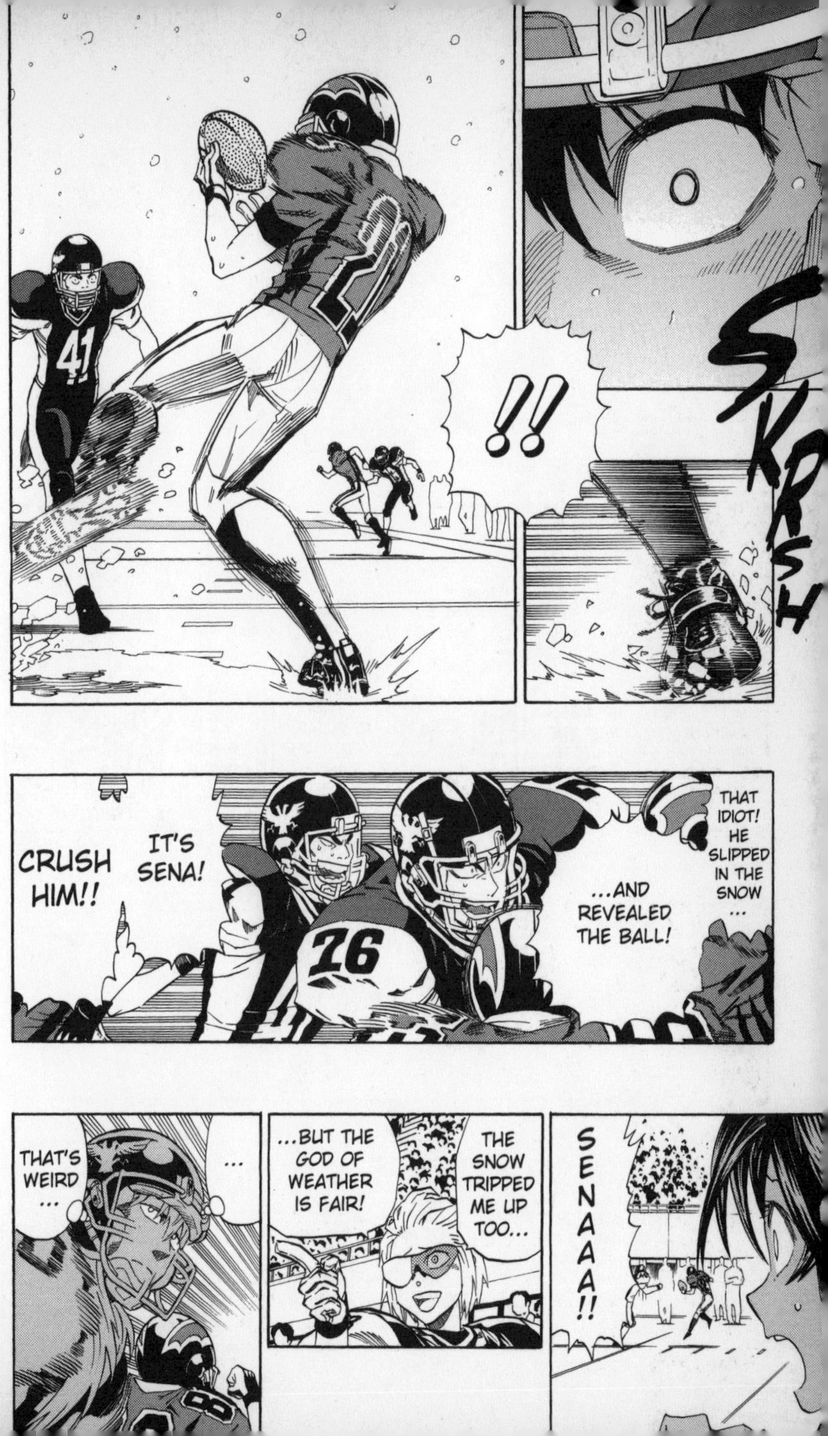
SKRSH
!!
THAT IDIOT! HE SLIPPED IN THE SNOW...
...AND REVEALED THE BALL!
IT'S SENA!
CRUSH HIM!!
SENAAAA!!
THE SNOW TRIPPED ME UP TOO...
...BUT THE GOD OF WEATHER IS FAIR!
...
THAT'S WEIRD...

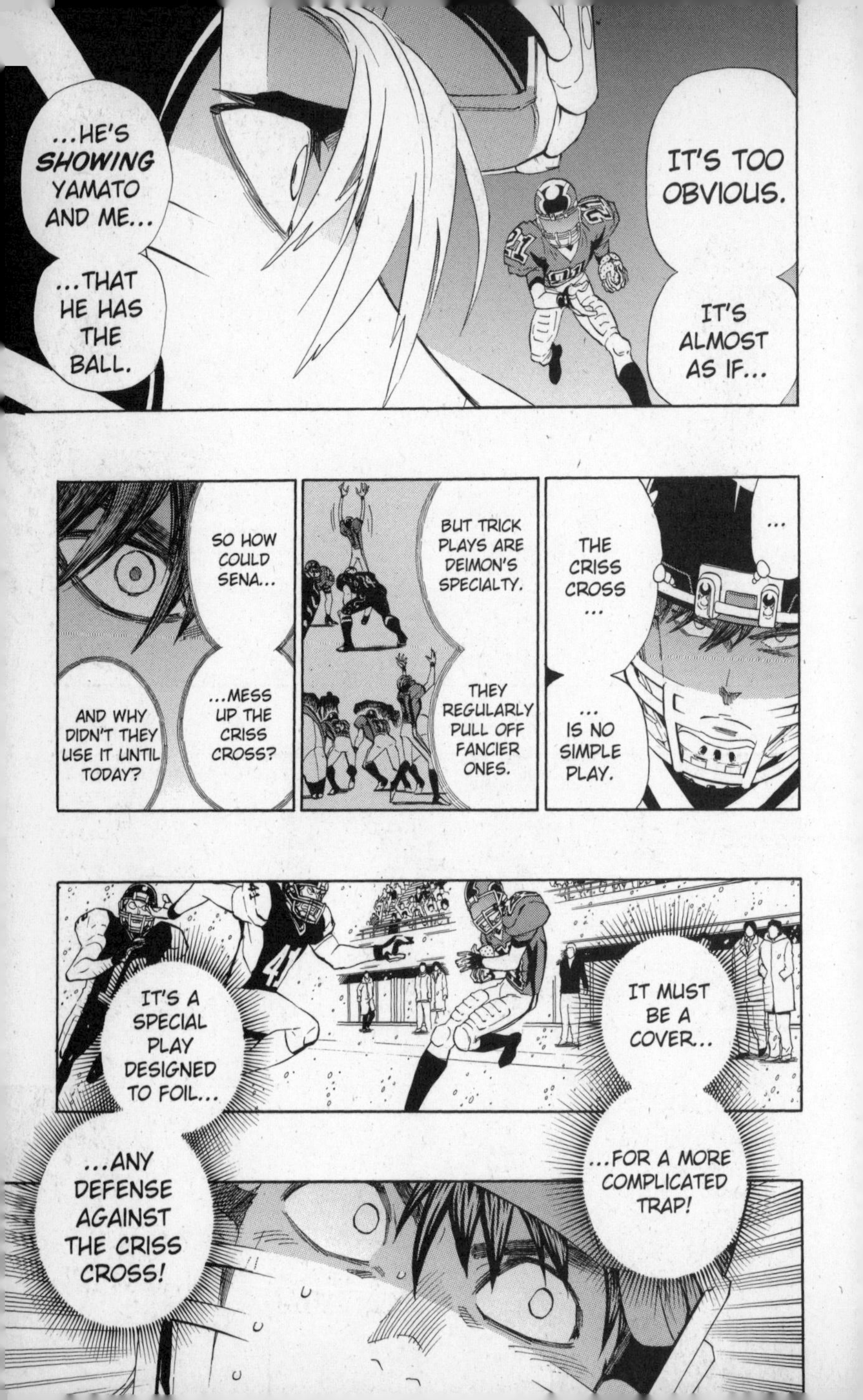
IT'S TOO OBVIOUS.
IT'S ALMOST AS IF...
...HE'S *SHOWING* YAMATO AND ME...
...THAT HE HAS THE BALL.
...
THE CRISS CROSS ...
... IS NO SIMPLE PLAY.
BUT TRICK PLAYS ARE DEIMON'S SPECIALTY.
THEY REGULARLY PULL OFF FANCIER ONES.
SO HOW COULD SENA...
...MESS UP THE CRISS CROSS?
AND WHY DIDN'T THEY USE IT UNTIL TODAY?
IT MUST BE A COVER...
...FOR A MORE COMPLICATED TRAP!
IT'S A SPECIAL PLAY DESIGNED TO FOIL...
...ANY DEFENSE AGAINST THE CRISS CROSS!

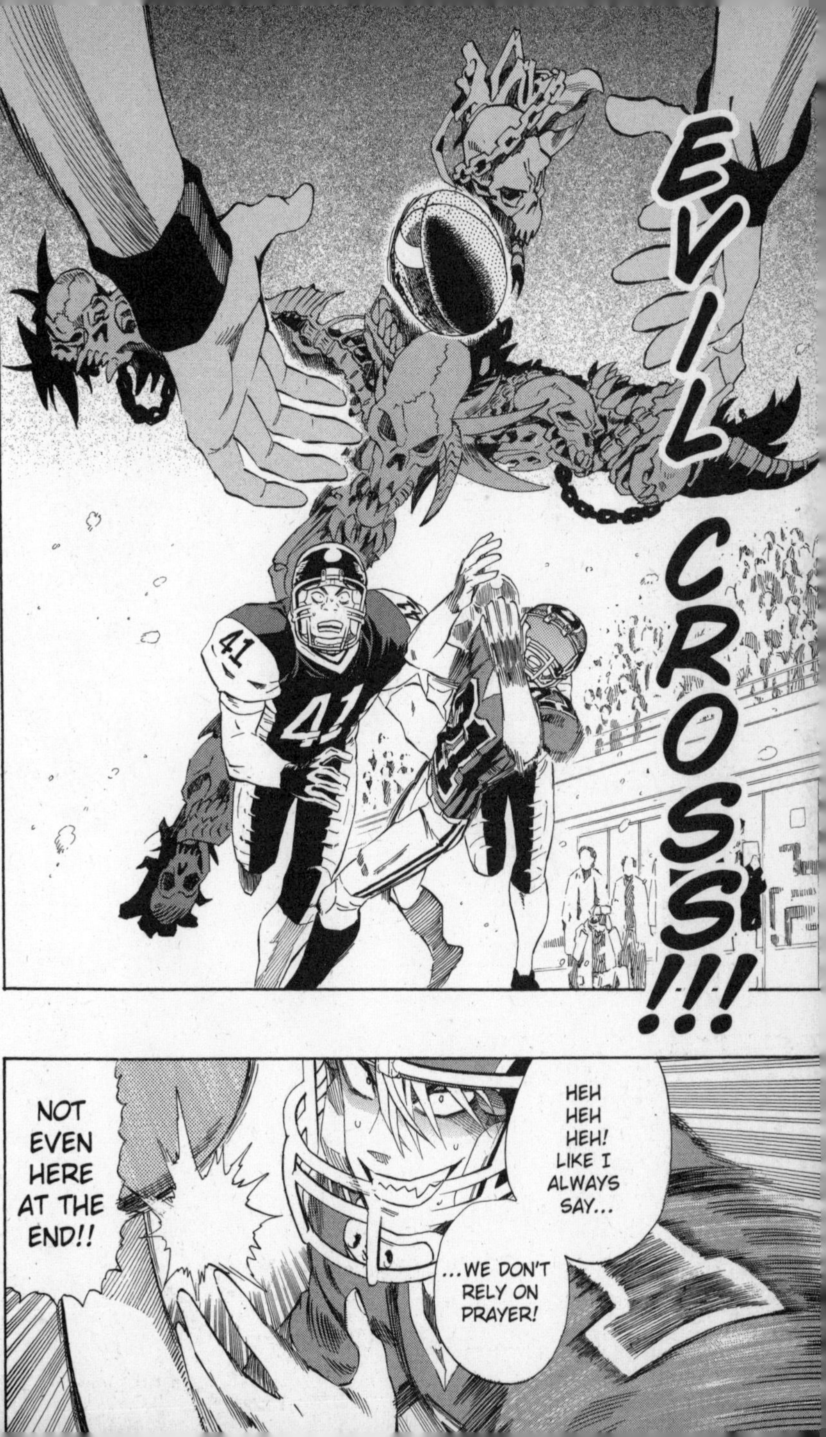
EVIL CROSS!!!
HEH HEH HEH! LIKE I ALWAYS SAY...
...WE DON'T RELY ON PRAYER!
NOT EVEN HERE AT THE END!!

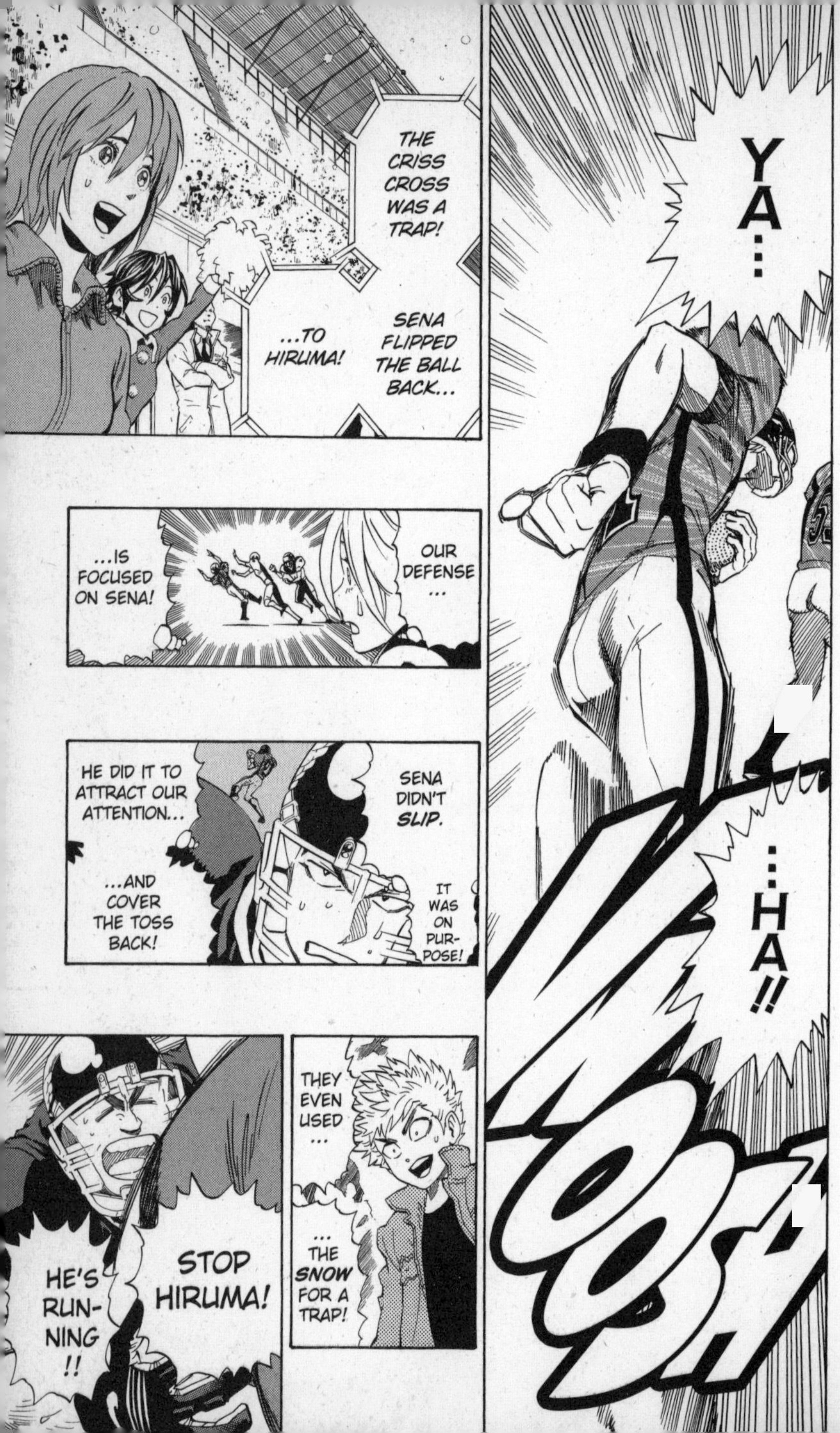
YA...
...HA!!
THE CRISS CROSS WAS A TRAP!
SENA FLIPPED THE BALL BACK...
...TO HIRUMA!
OUR DEFENSE...
...IS FOCUSED ON SENA!
SENA DIDN'T *SLIP*.
IT WAS ON PURPOSE!
HE DID IT TO ATTRACT OUR ATTENTION...
...AND COVER THE TOSS BACK!
THEY EVEN USED...
...THE *SNOW* FOR A TRAP!
STOP HIRUMA!
HE'S RUNNING!!

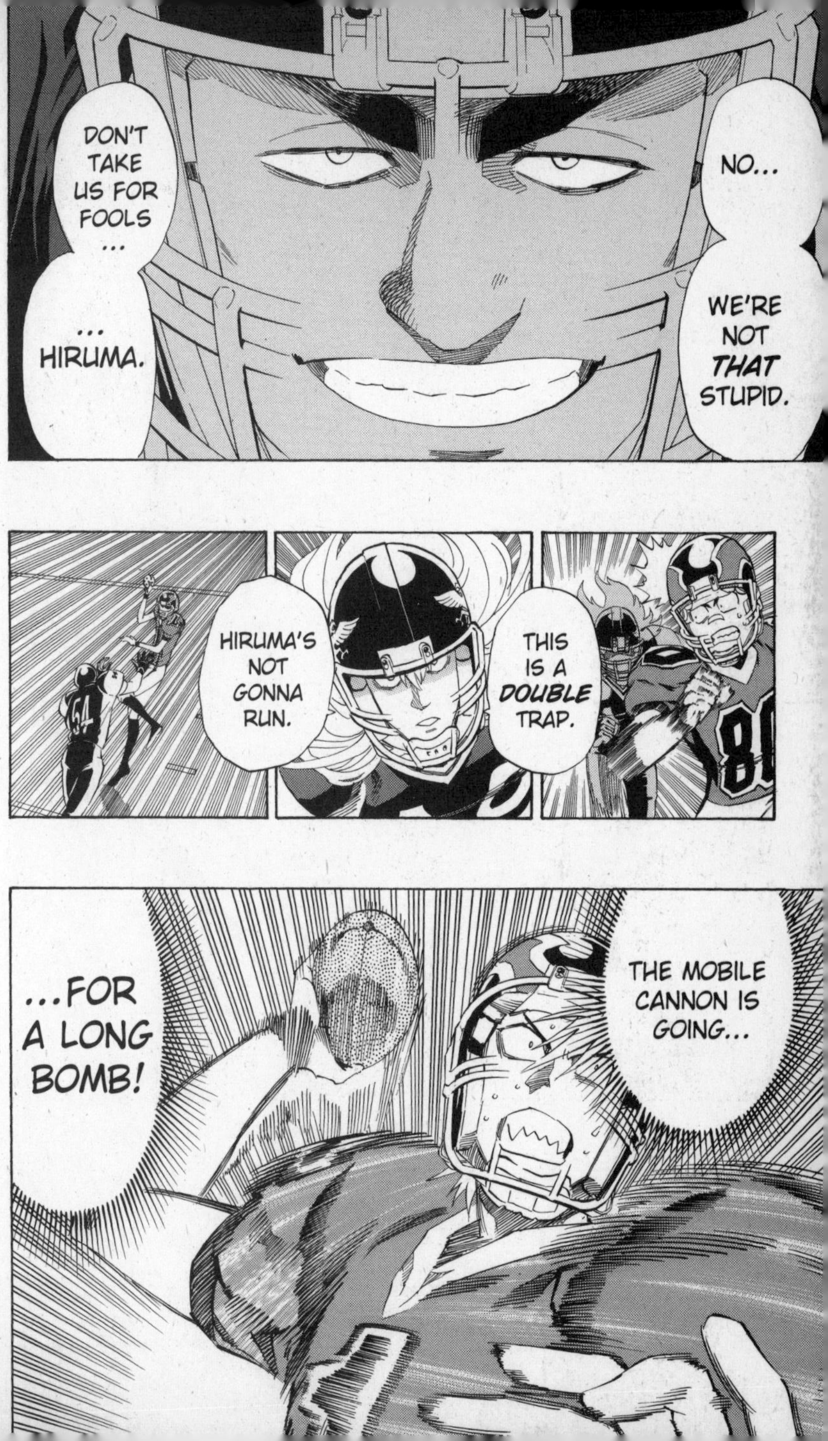
NO...
WE'RE NOT *THAT* STUPID.
DON'T TAKE US FOR FOOLS...
...HIRUMA.
THIS IS A *DOUBLE* TRAP.
HIRUMA'S NOT GONNA RUN.
THE MOBILE CANNON IS GOING...
...FOR A LONG BOMB!

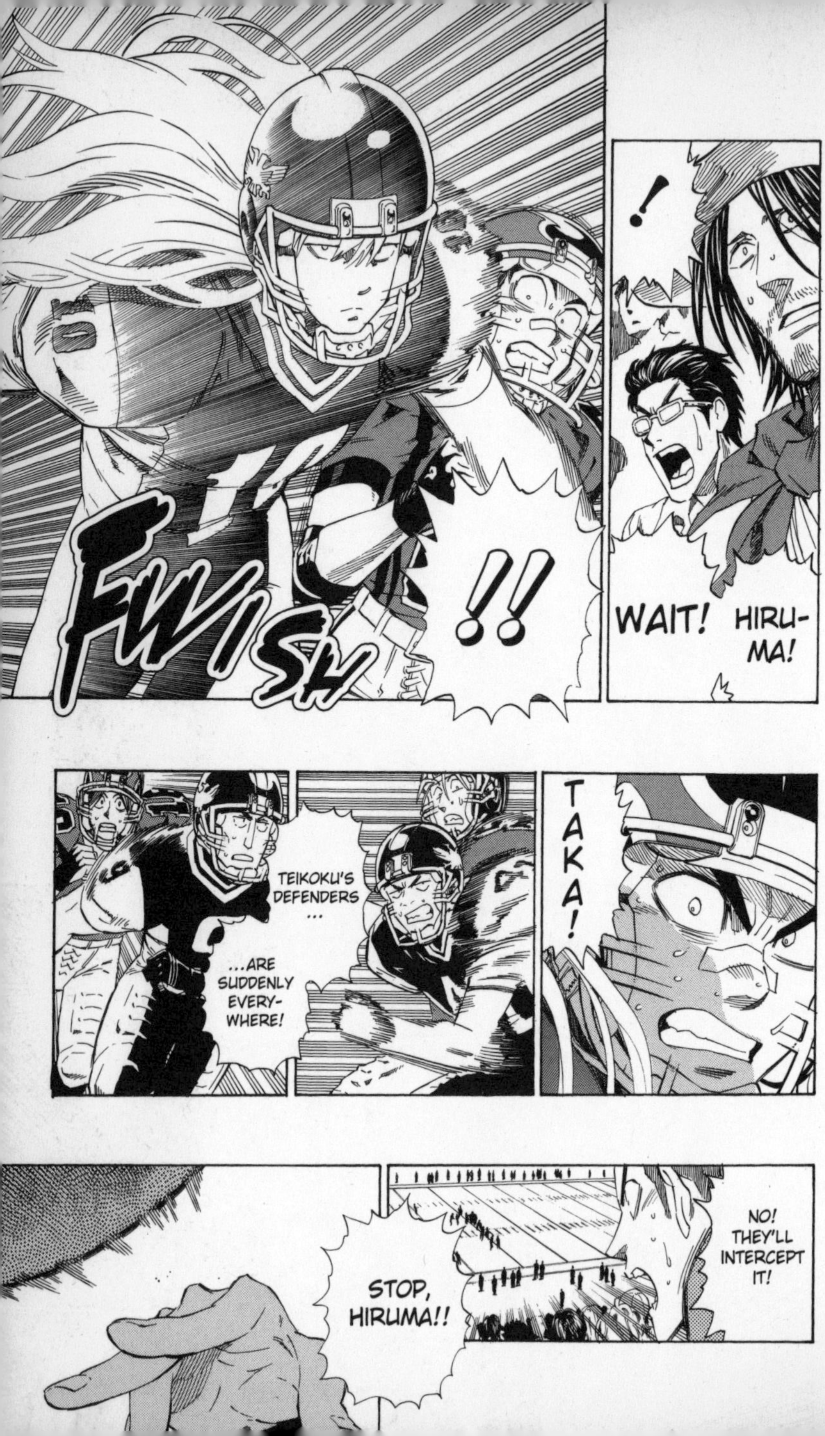
!
HIRU-MA!
WAIT!
!!
FWISH
TAKA!
TEIKOKU'S DEFENDERS ...
...ARE SUDDENLY EVERY-WHERE!
NO! THEY'LL INTERCEPT IT!
STOP, HIRUMA!!

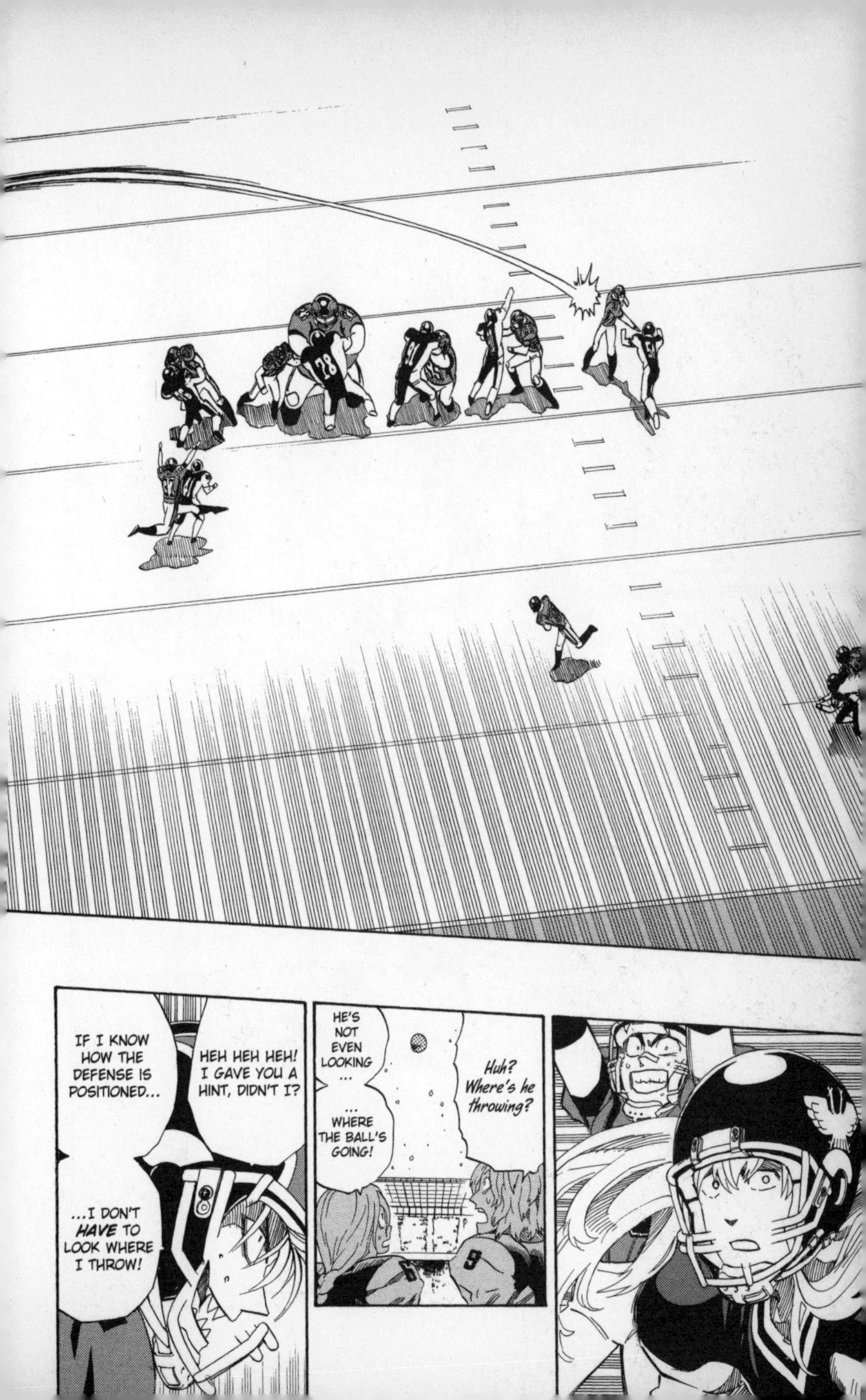

Huh? Where's he throwing?
HE'S NOT EVEN LOOKING...
...WHERE THE BALL'S GOING!
HEH HEH HEH! I GAVE YOU A HINT, DIDN'T I?
IF I KNOW HOW THE DEFENSE IS POSITIONED...
...I DON'T *HAVE* TO LOOK WHERE I THROW!

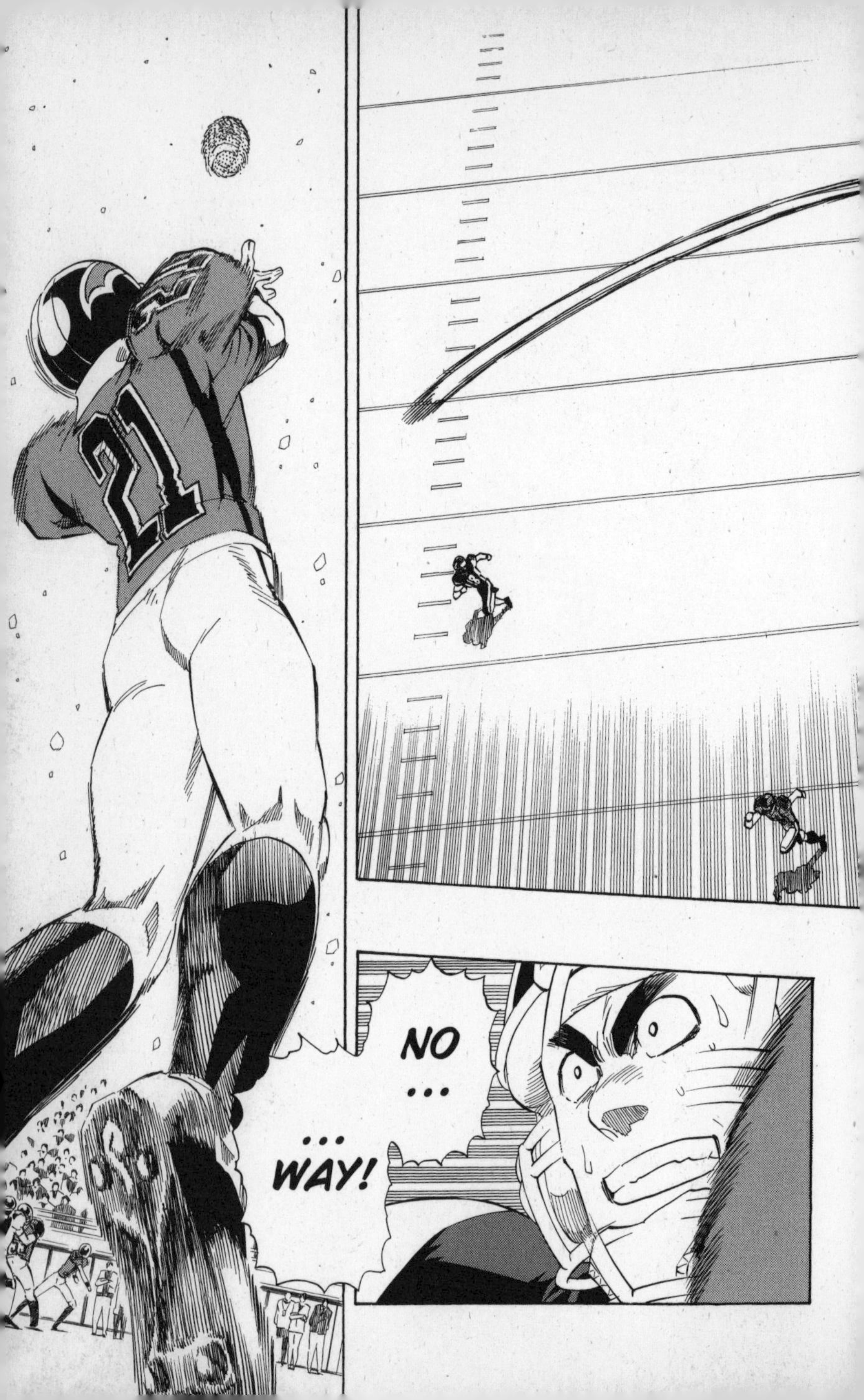
NO ...
... WAY!

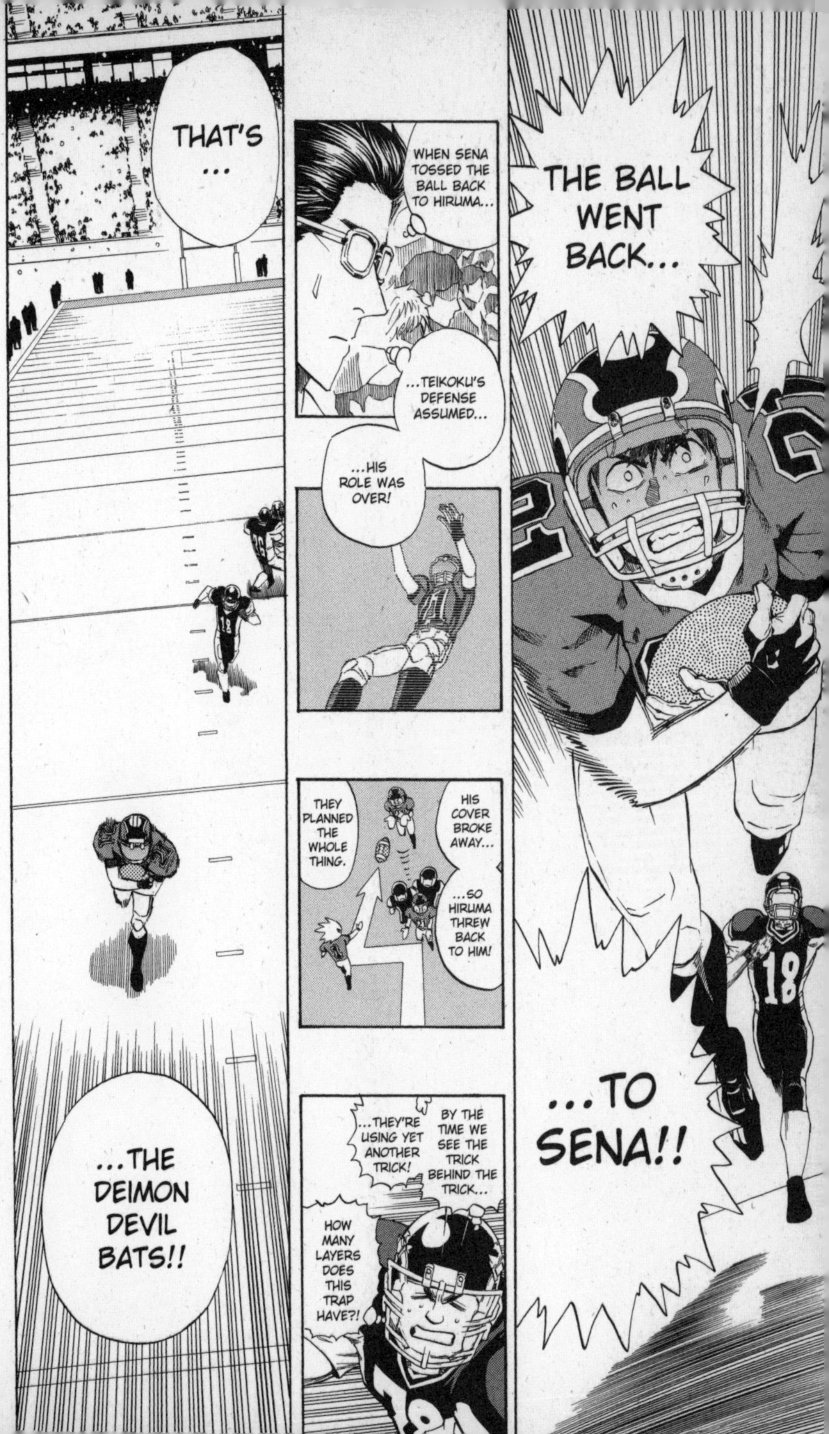
THE BALL WENT BACK...
...TO SENA!!
WHEN SENA TOSSED THE BALL BACK TO HIRUMA...
...TEIKOKU'S DEFENSE ASSUMED...
...HIS ROLE WAS OVER!
HIS COVER BROKE AWAY...
...SO HIRUMA THREW BACK TO HIM!
THEY PLANNED THE WHOLE THING.
BY THE TIME WE SEE THE TRICK BEHIND THE TRICK...
...THEY'RE USING YET ANOTHER TRICK!
HOW MANY LAYERS DOES THIS TRAP HAVE?!
THAT'S ...
...THE DEIMON DEVIL BATS!!

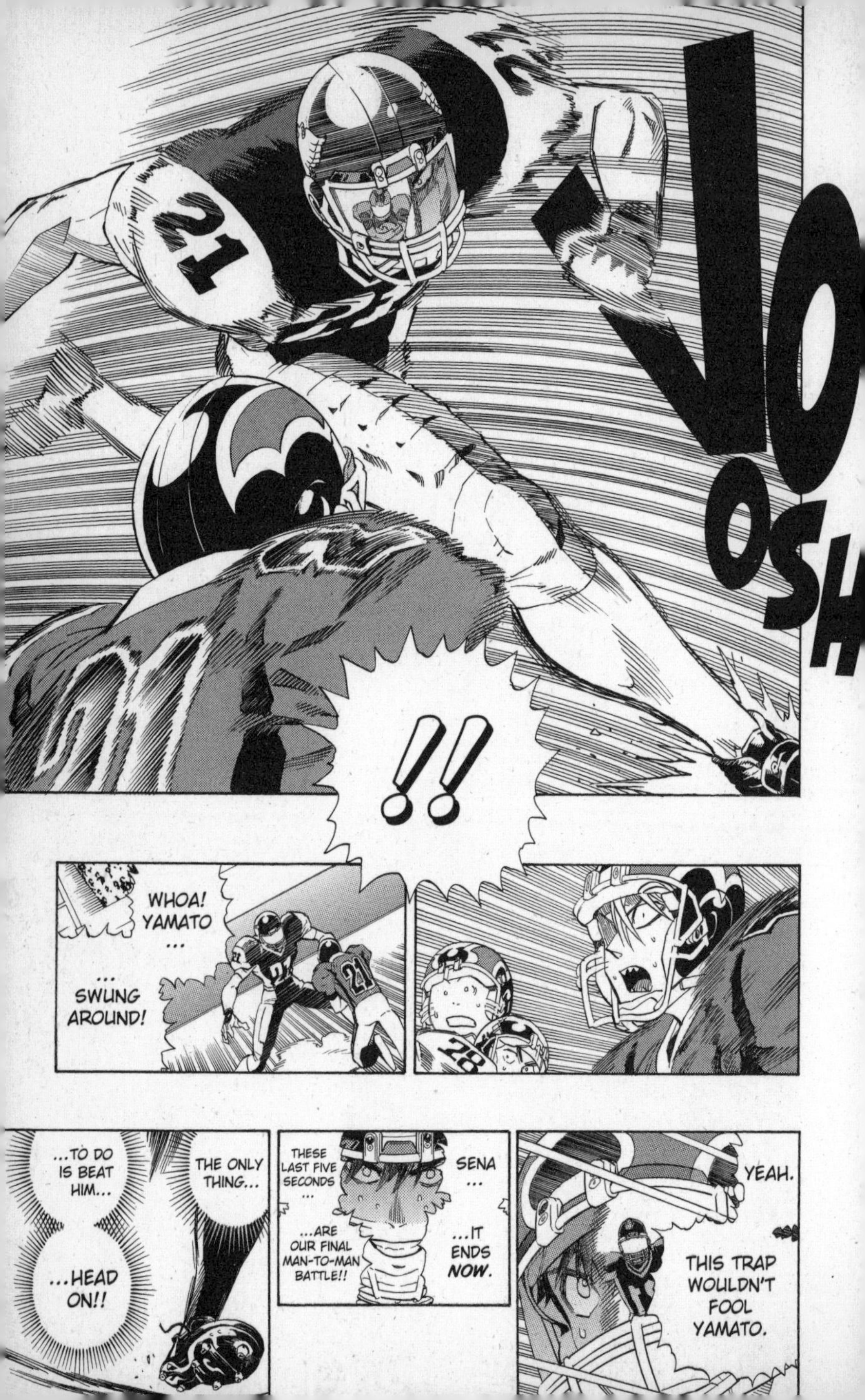
VOOSH
!!
WHOA! YAMATO ...
... SWUNG AROUND!
YEAH.
THIS TRAP WOULDN'T FOOL YAMATO.
SENA ...
... IT ENDS NOW.
THESE LAST FIVE SECONDS ...
...ARE OUR FINAL MAN-TO-MAN BATTLE!!
THE ONLY THING...
...TO DO IS BEAT HIM...
...HEAD ON!!

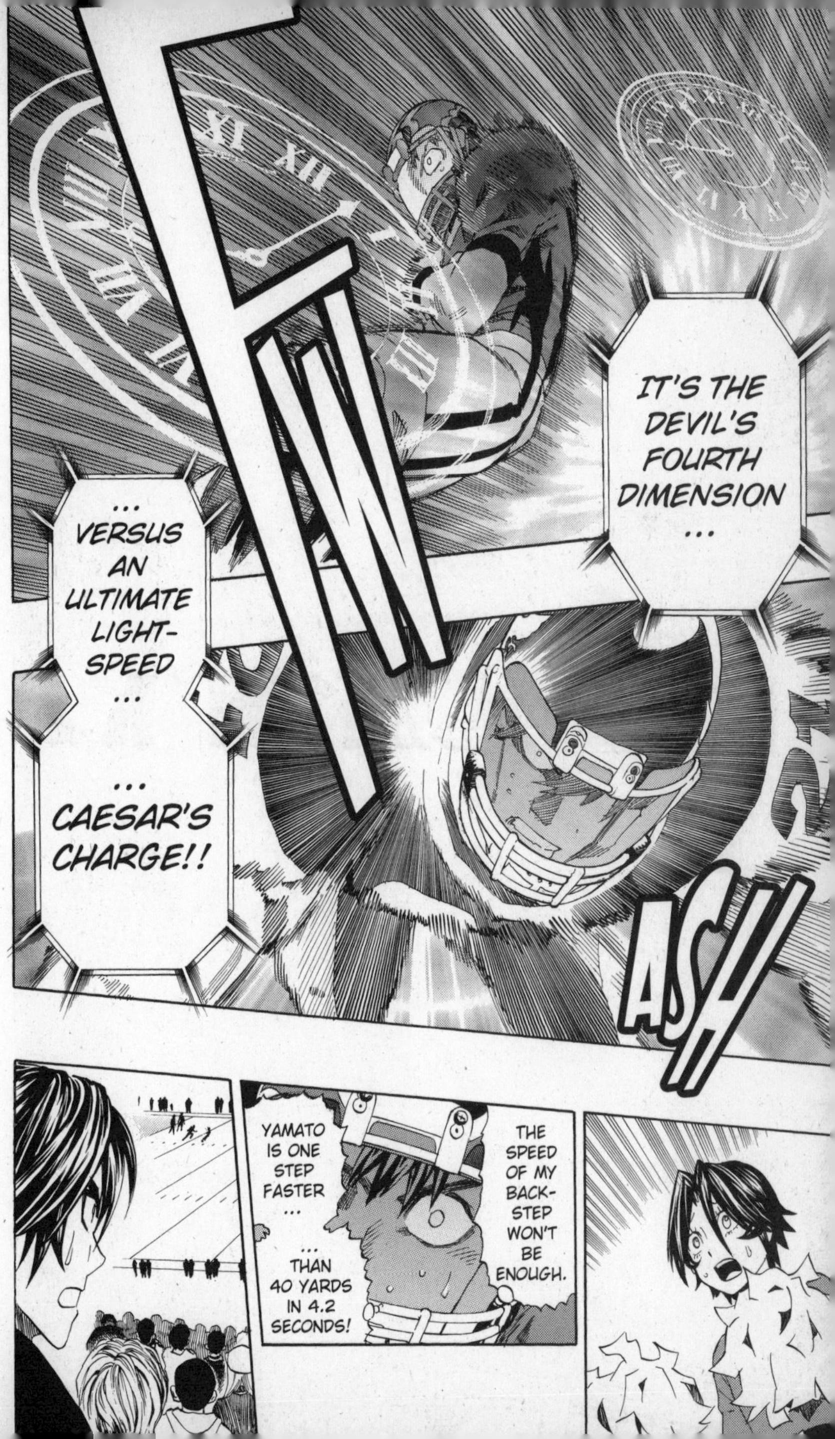
IT'S THE DEVIL'S FOURTH DIMENSION ...
... VERSUS AN ULTIMATE LIGHT-SPEED ...
... CAESAR'S CHARGE!!
ASH
THE SPEED OF MY BACK-STEP WON'T BE ENOUGH.
YAMATO IS ONE STEP FASTER ...
... THAN 40 YARDS IN 4.2 SECONDS!

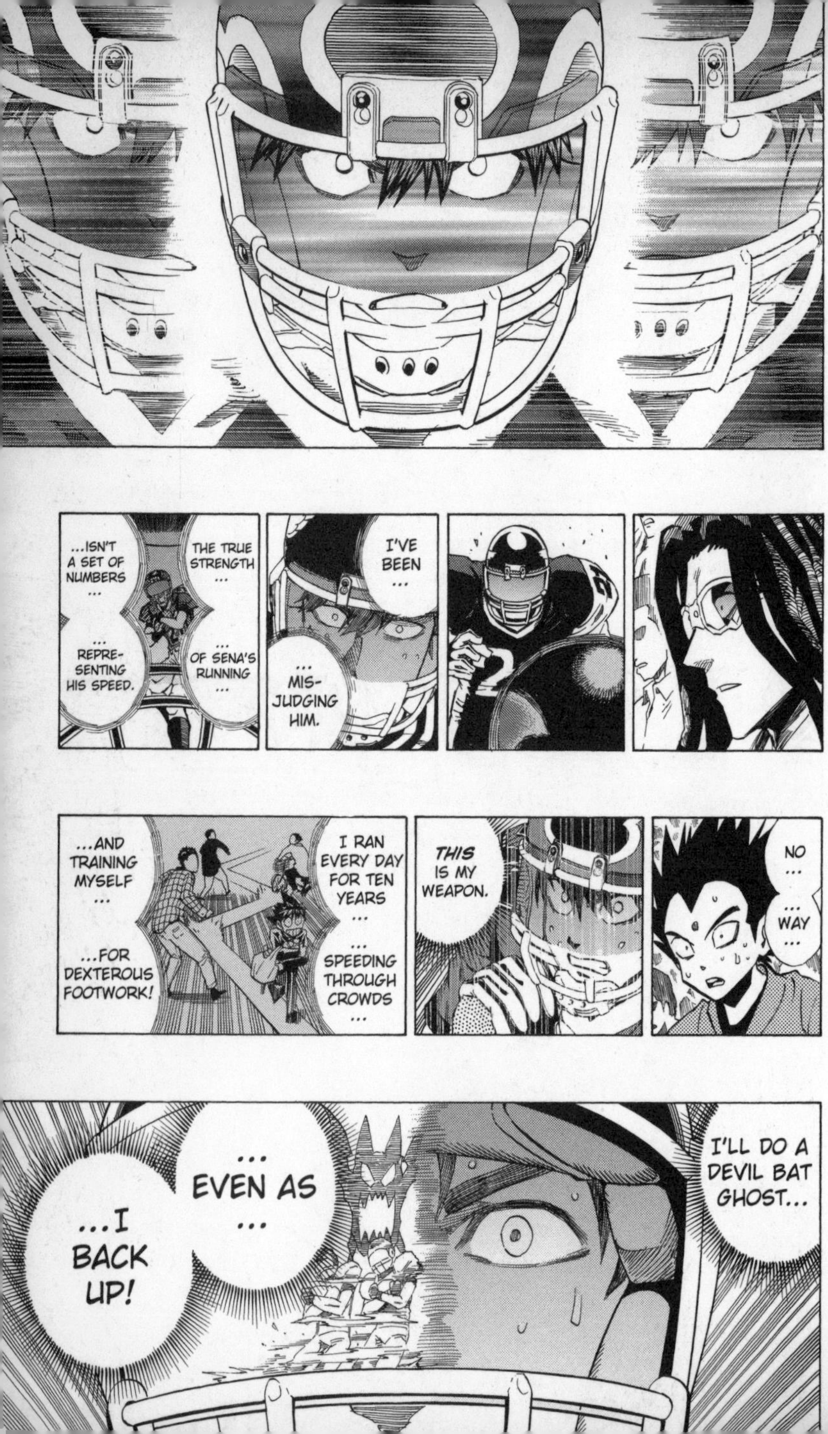
I'VE BEEN ...
... MIS-JUDGING HIM.
THE TRUE STRENGTH ...
... OF SENA'S RUNNING ...
...ISN'T A SET OF NUMBERS ...
... REPRE-SENTING HIS SPEED.
NO ...
... WAY ...
THIS IS MY WEAPON.
I RAN EVERY DAY FOR TEN YEARS ...
... SPEEDING THROUGH CROWDS ...
...AND TRAINING MYSELF ...
...FOR DEXTEROUS FOOTWORK!
I'LL DO A DEVIL BAT GHOST...
... EVEN AS ...
...I BACK UP!

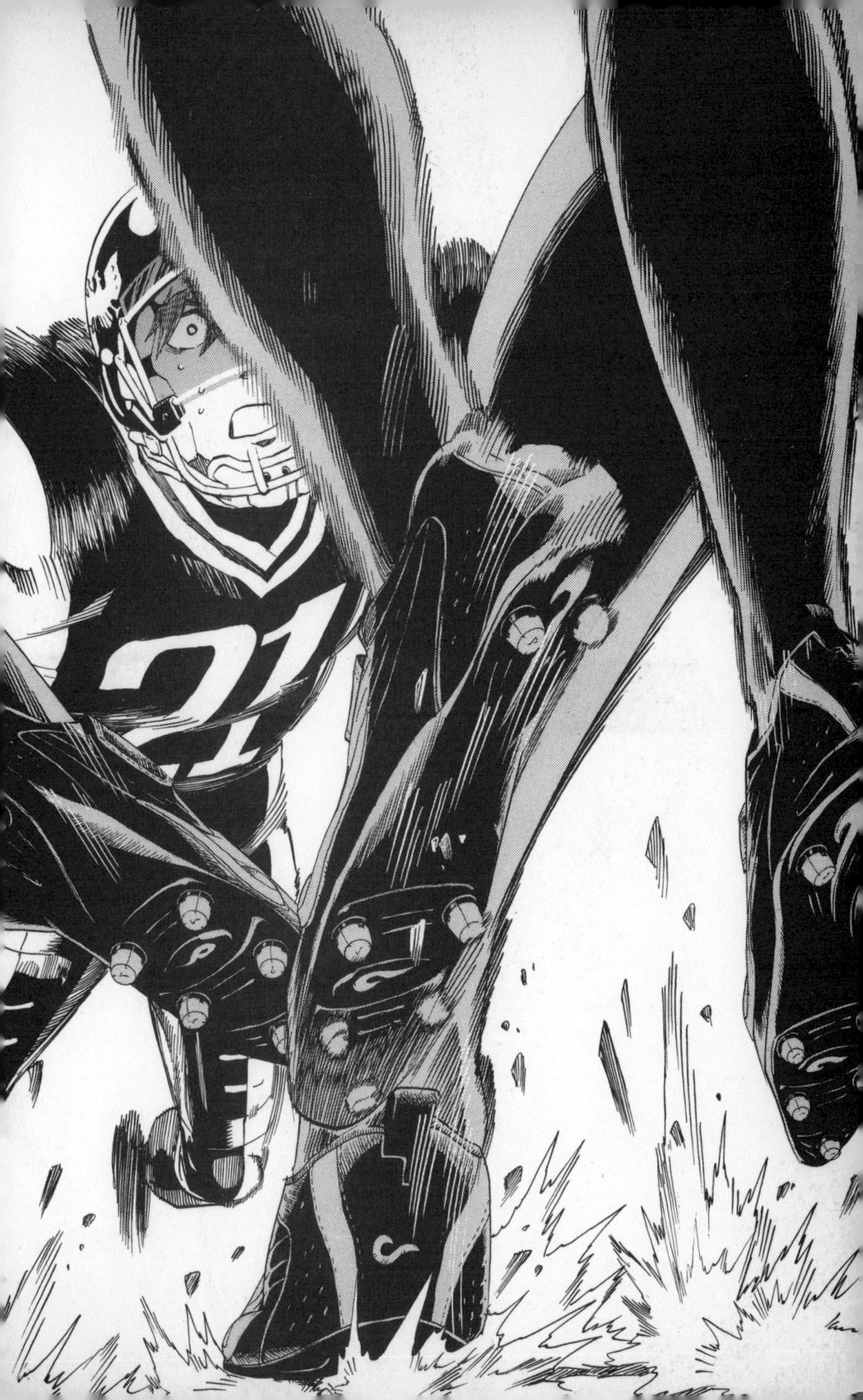

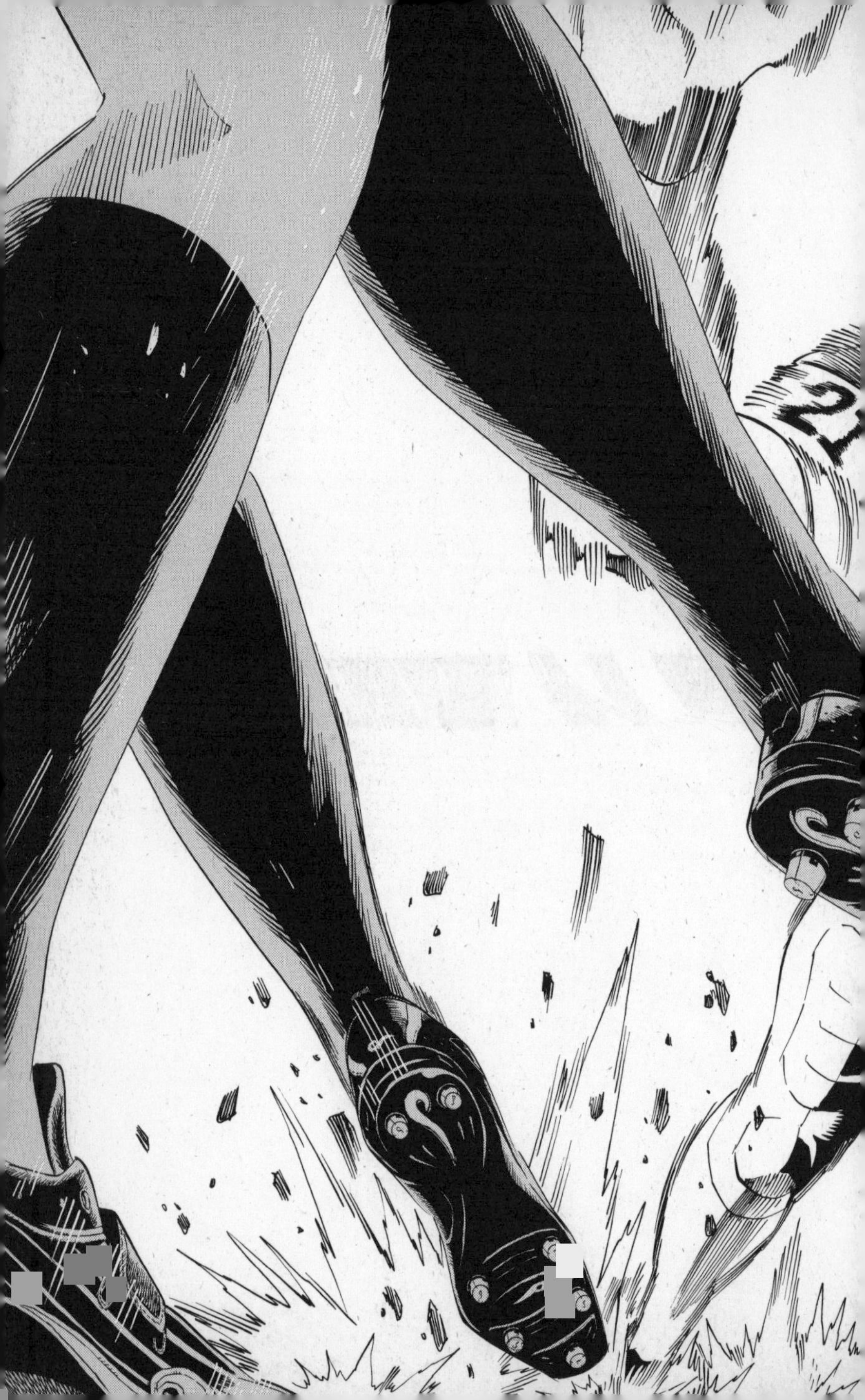

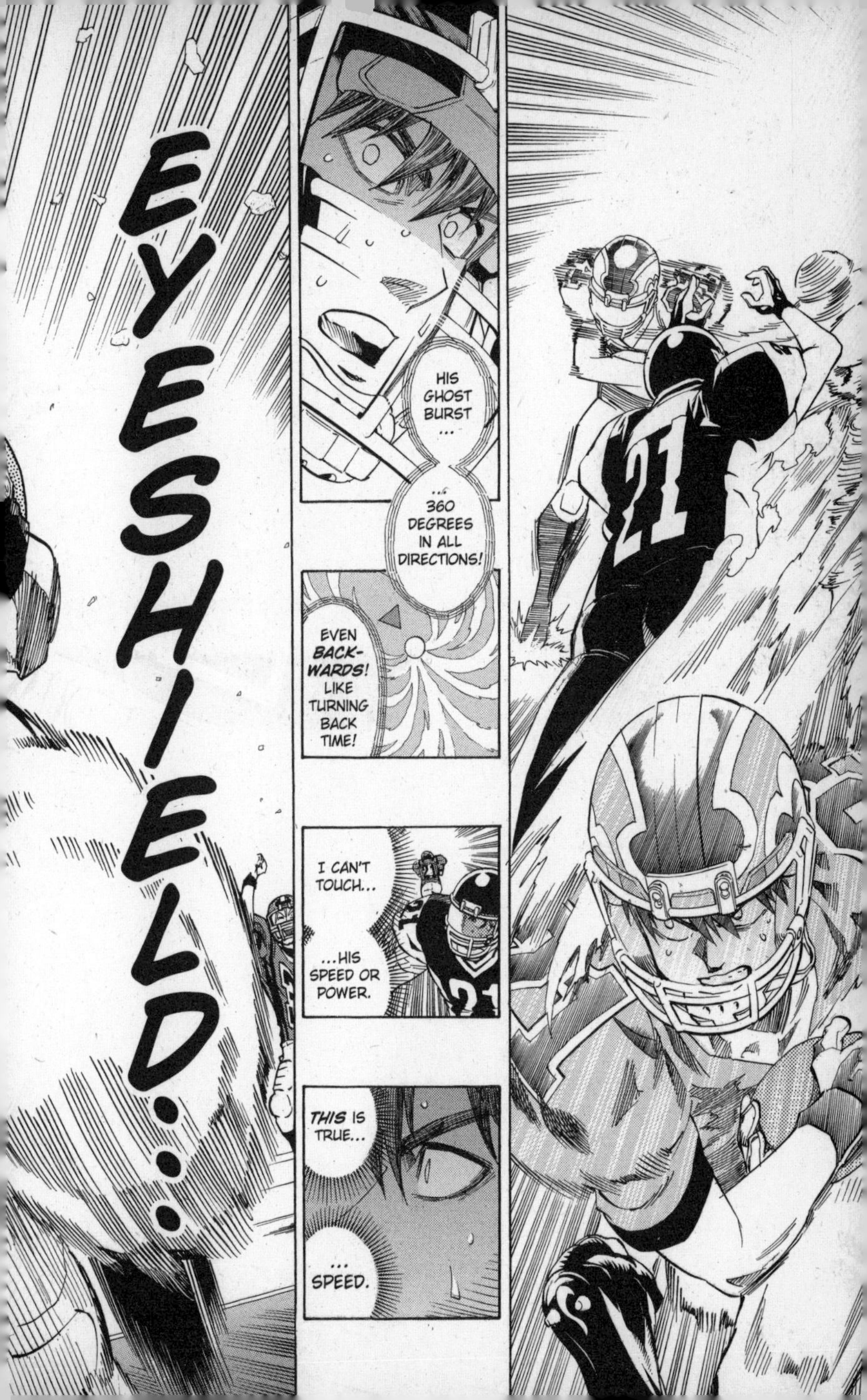

HIS GHOST BURST...
...360 DEGREES IN ALL DIRECTIONS!
EVEN *BACKWARDS!* LIKE TURNING BACK TIME!
I CAN'T TOUCH...
...HIS SPEED OR POWER.
THIS is TRUE...
...SPEED.
EYESHIELD...

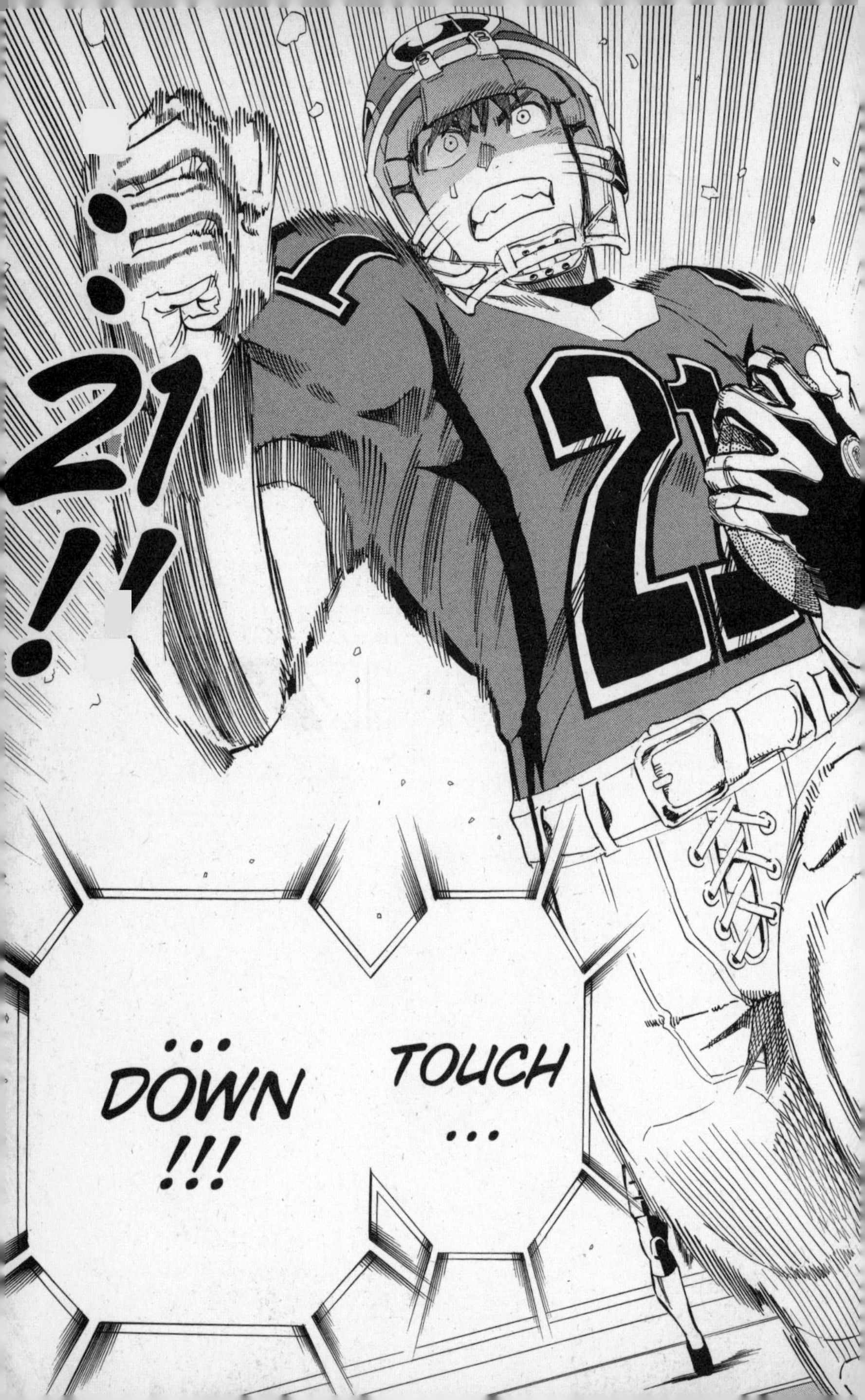
Z!!
TOUCH ...
... DOWN !!!

Devil Bat 021

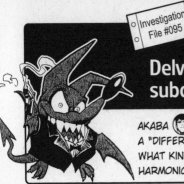

Investigation File #095

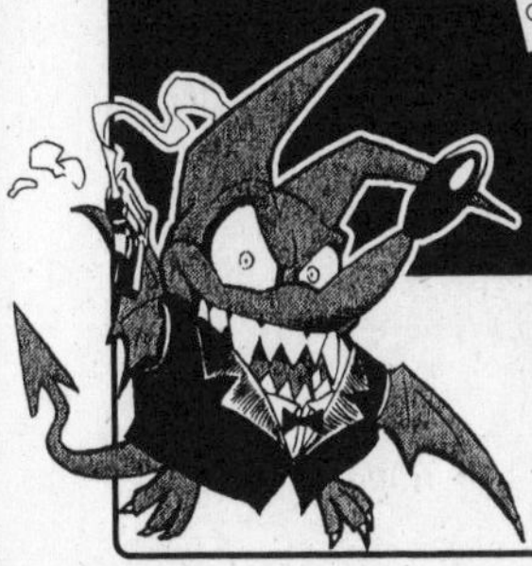

Delve into Akaba's subconscious mind!!

AKABA ALWAYS TALKS ABOUT A "DIFFERENCE IN HARMONICS." WHAT KIND OF PEOPLE DO HIS HARMONICS MATCH WITH?

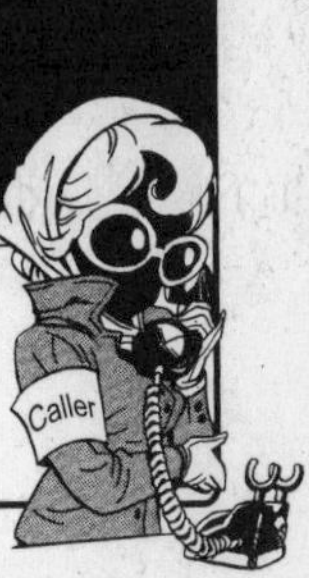
Caller

Caller name: M.M. in Iwate Prefecture

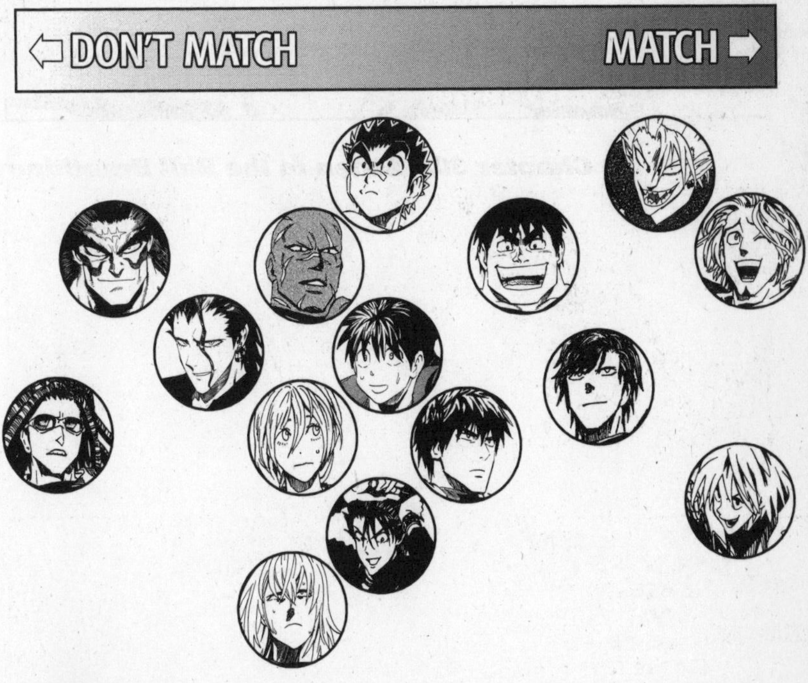
DON'T MATCH
MATCH

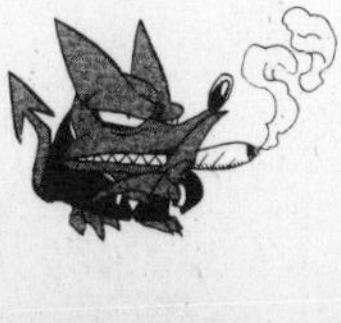

AT A ROUGH GLANCE, IT LOOKS LIKE HE MATCHES WELL WITH ***ENERGETIC WEIRDOS***.

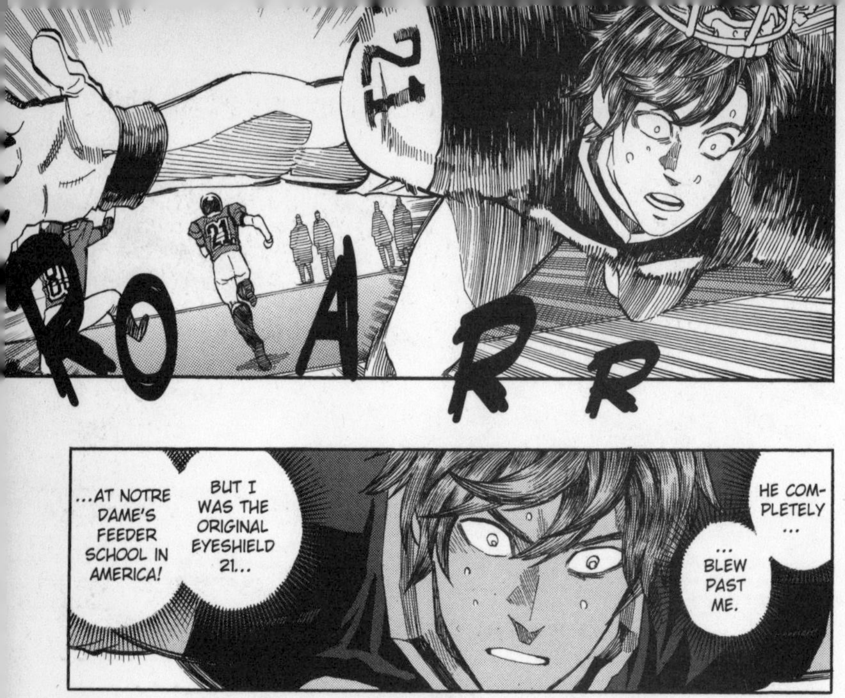
ROARR
HE COMPLETELY...
...BLEW PAST ME.
BUT I WAS THE ORIGINAL EYESHIELD 21...
...AT NOTRE DAME'S FEEDER SCHOOL IN AMERICA!

Chapter 302 Listen to the Ball Breathing

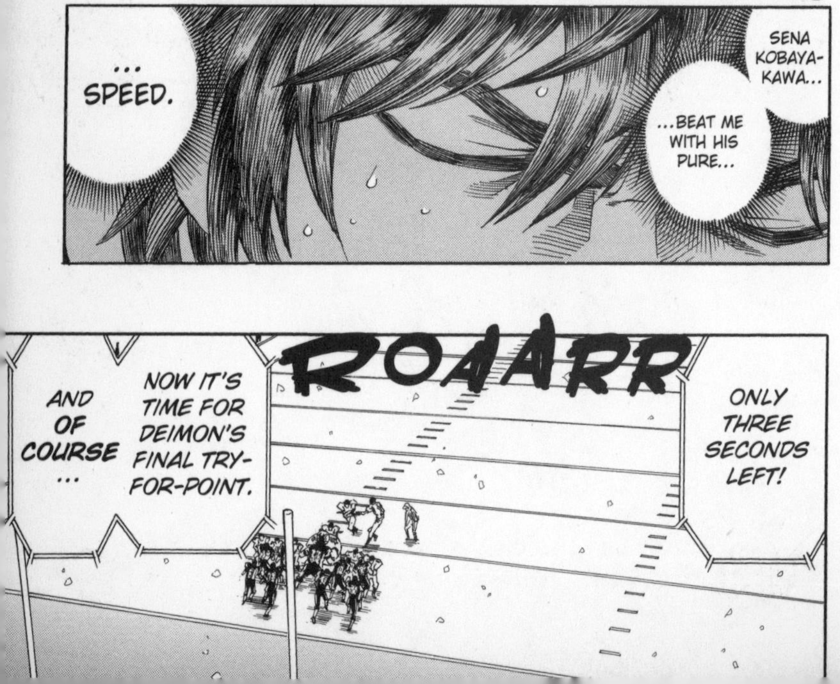
SENA KOBAYAKAWA...
...BEAT ME WITH HIS PURE...
...SPEED.
ROAARR
ONLY THREE SECONDS LEFT!
NOW IT'S TIME FOR DEIMON'S FINAL TRY-FOR-POINT.
AND OF COURSE...

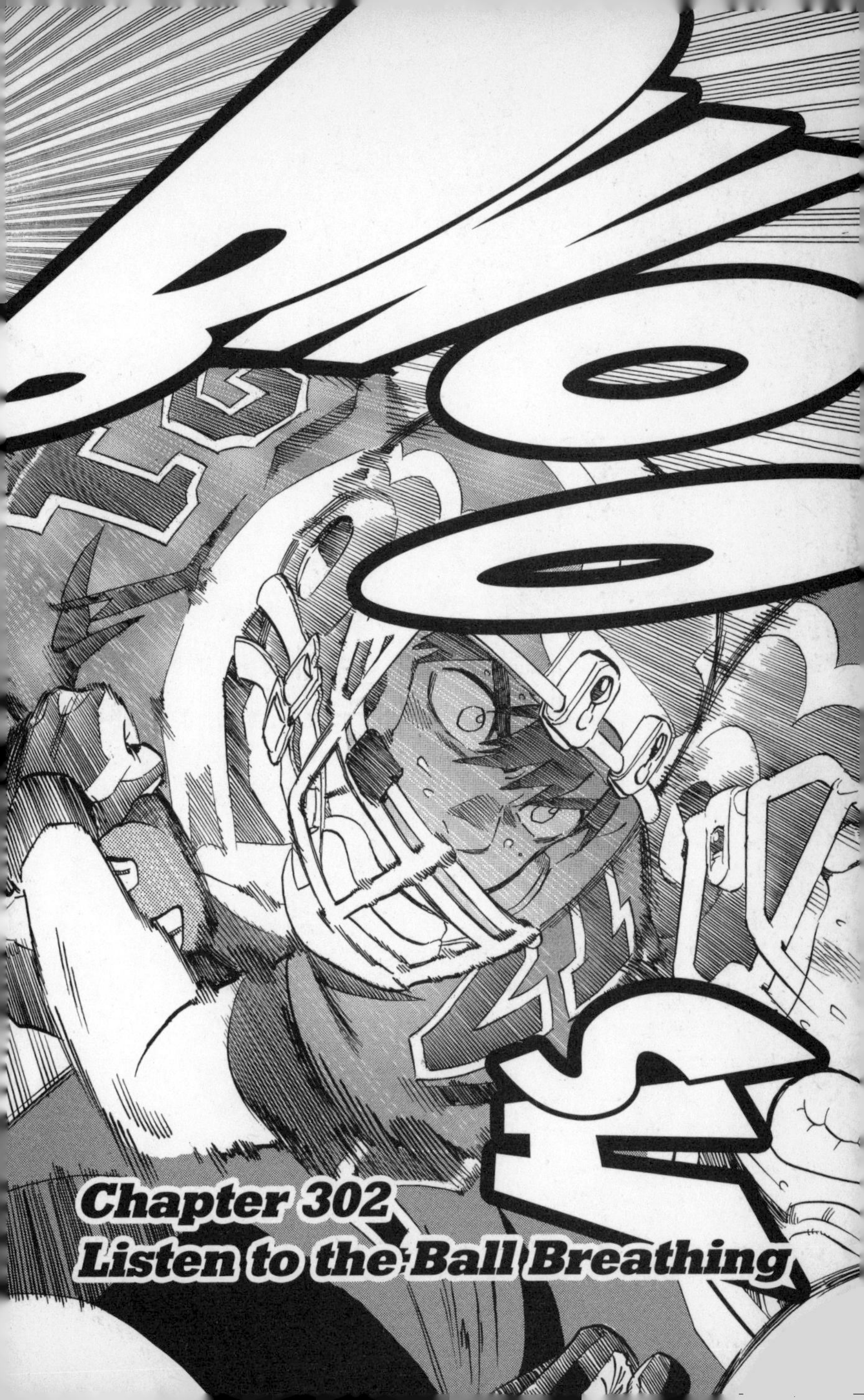

Chapter 302
Listen to the Ball Breathing

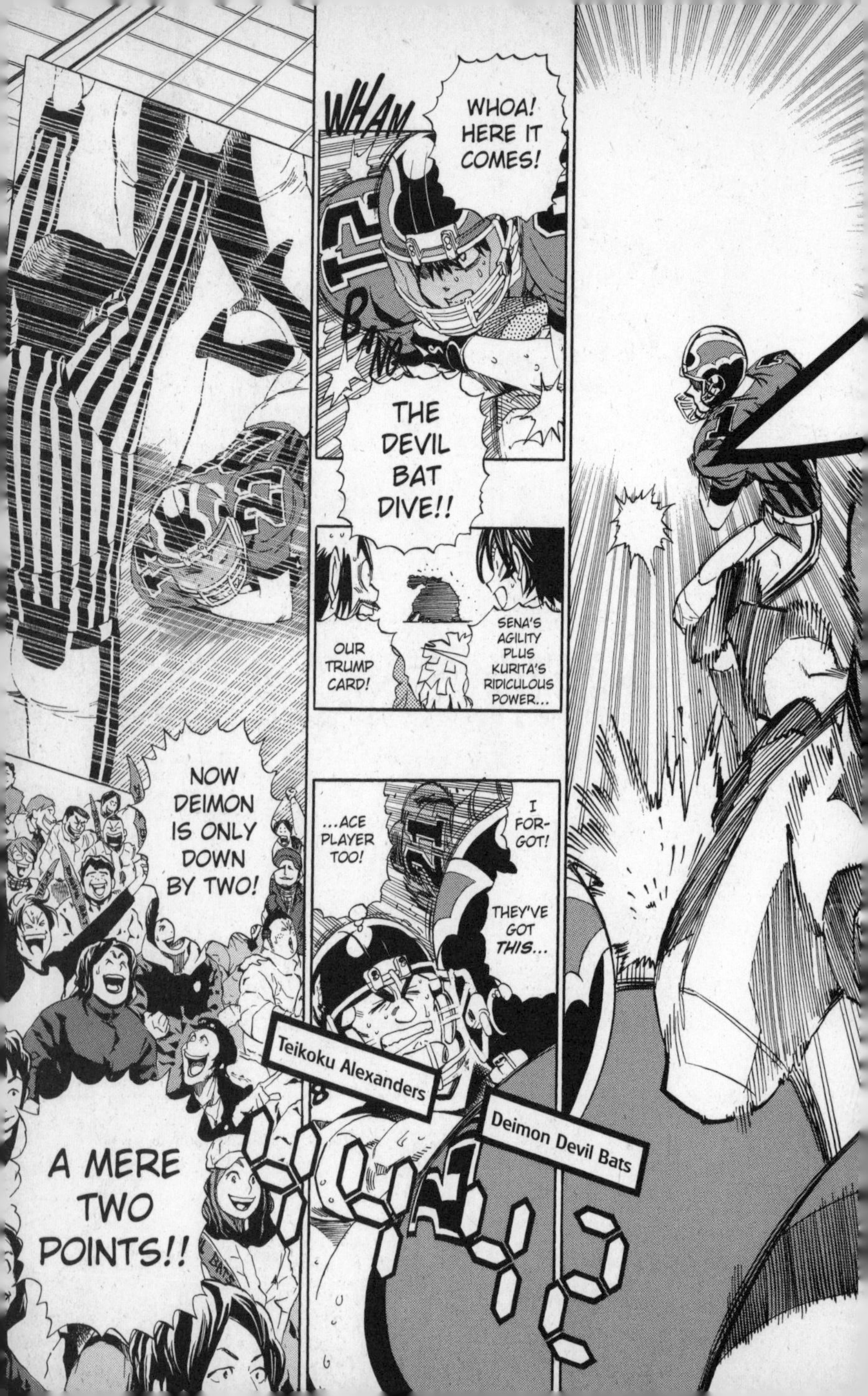
WHAM
WHOA! HERE IT COMES!
BANG
THE DEVIL BAT DIVE!!
SENA'S AGILITY PLUS KURITA'S RIDICULOUS POWER...
OUR TRUMP CARD!
I FOR-GOT!
THEY'VE GOT *THIS*...
...ACE PLAYER TOO!
Teikoku Alexanders
Deimon Devil Bats
NOW DEIMON IS ONLY DOWN BY TWO!
A MERE TWO POINTS!!

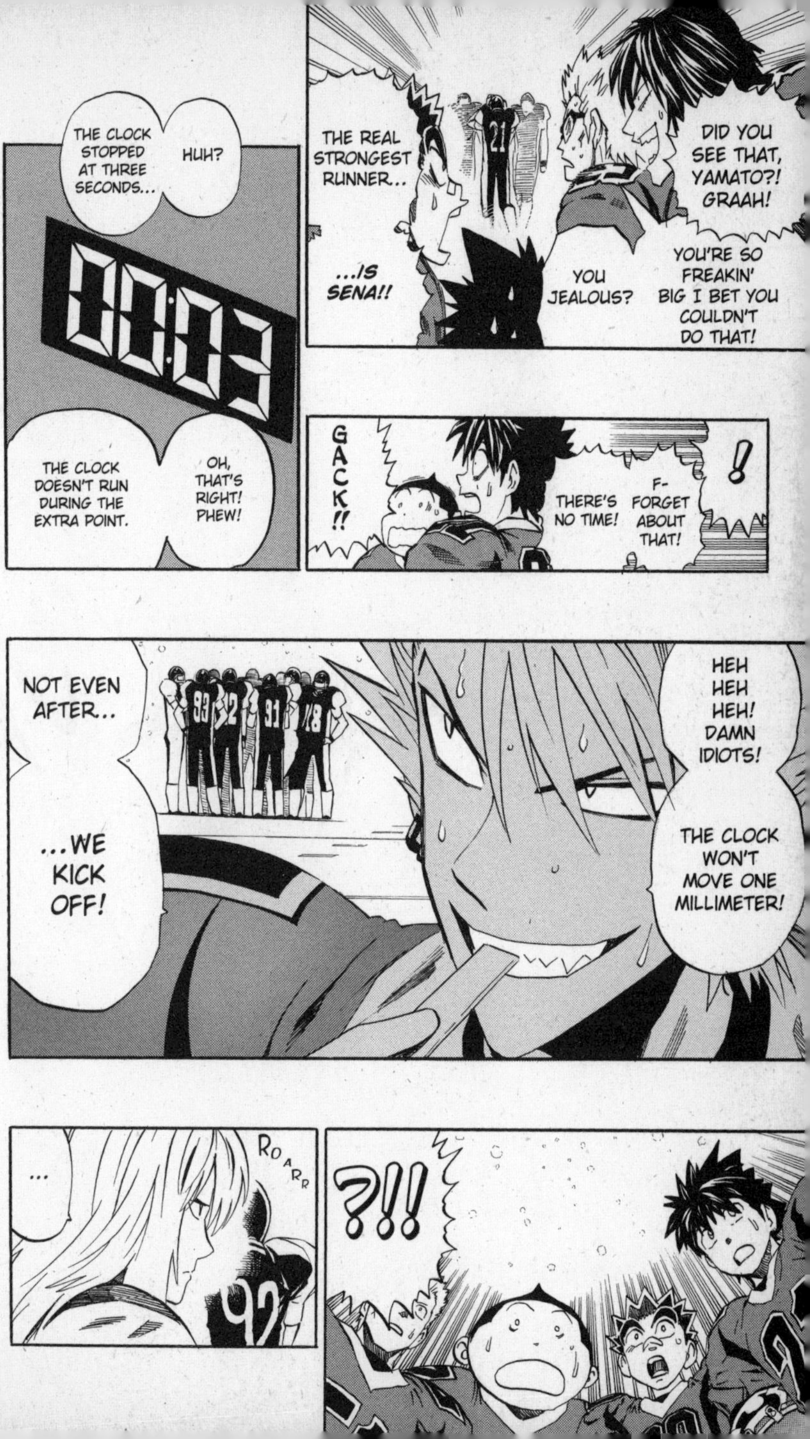
DID YOU SEE THAT, YAMATO?! GRAAH!
YOU'RE SO FREAKIN' BIG I BET YOU COULDN'T DO THAT!
YOU JEALOUS?
THE REAL STRONGEST RUNNER...
...IS SENA!!
!
F- FORGET ABOUT THAT!
THERE'S NO TIME!
GACK!!
HUH?
THE CLOCK STOPPED AT THREE SECONDS...
OH, THAT'S RIGHT! PHEW!
THE CLOCK DOESN'T RUN DURING THE EXTRA POINT.
HEH HEH HEH! DAMN IDIOTS!
THE CLOCK WON'T MOVE ONE MILLIMETER!
NOT EVEN AFTER...
...WE KICK OFF!
?!!
ROARR
...

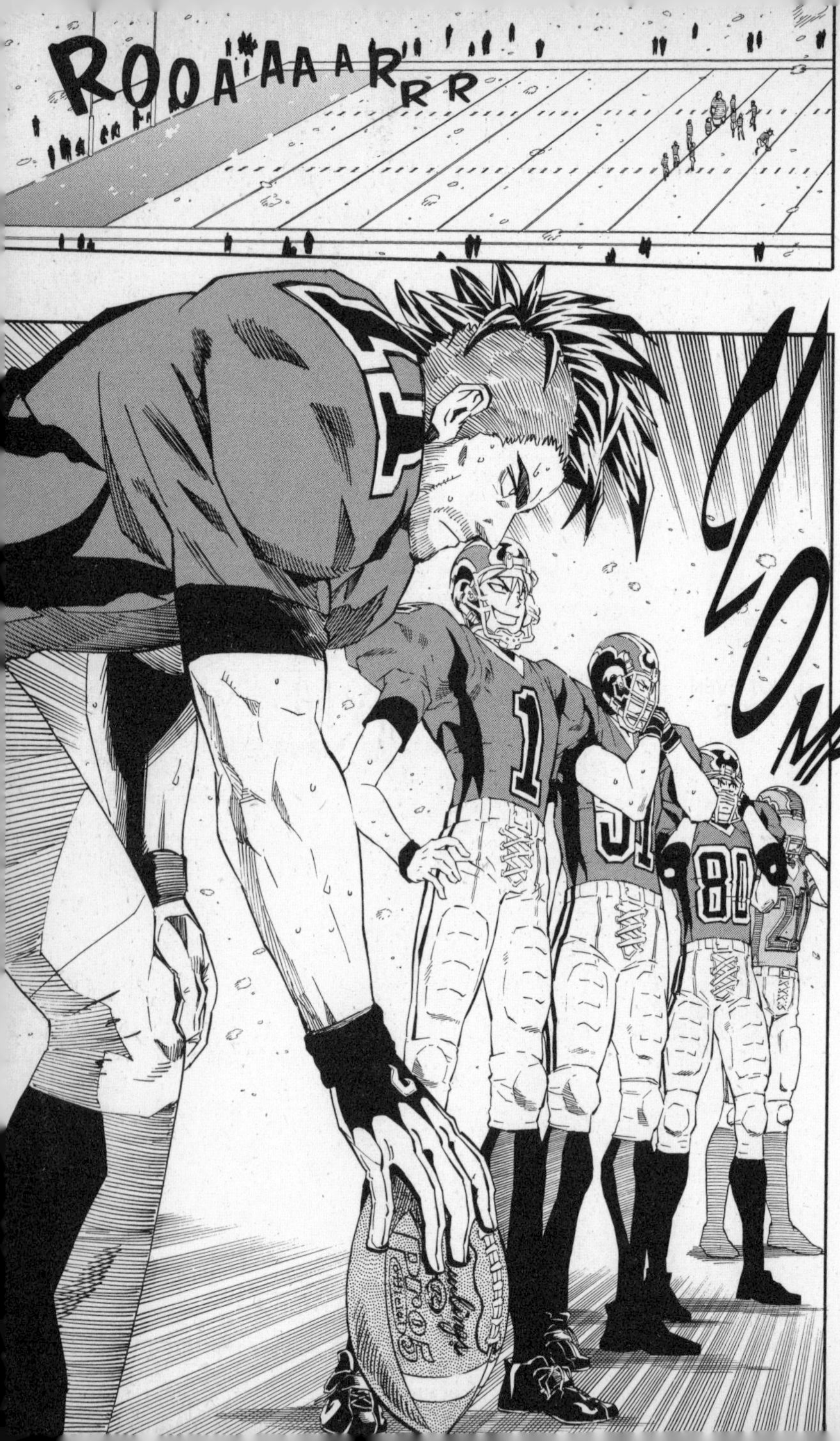
ROOAAAARRR

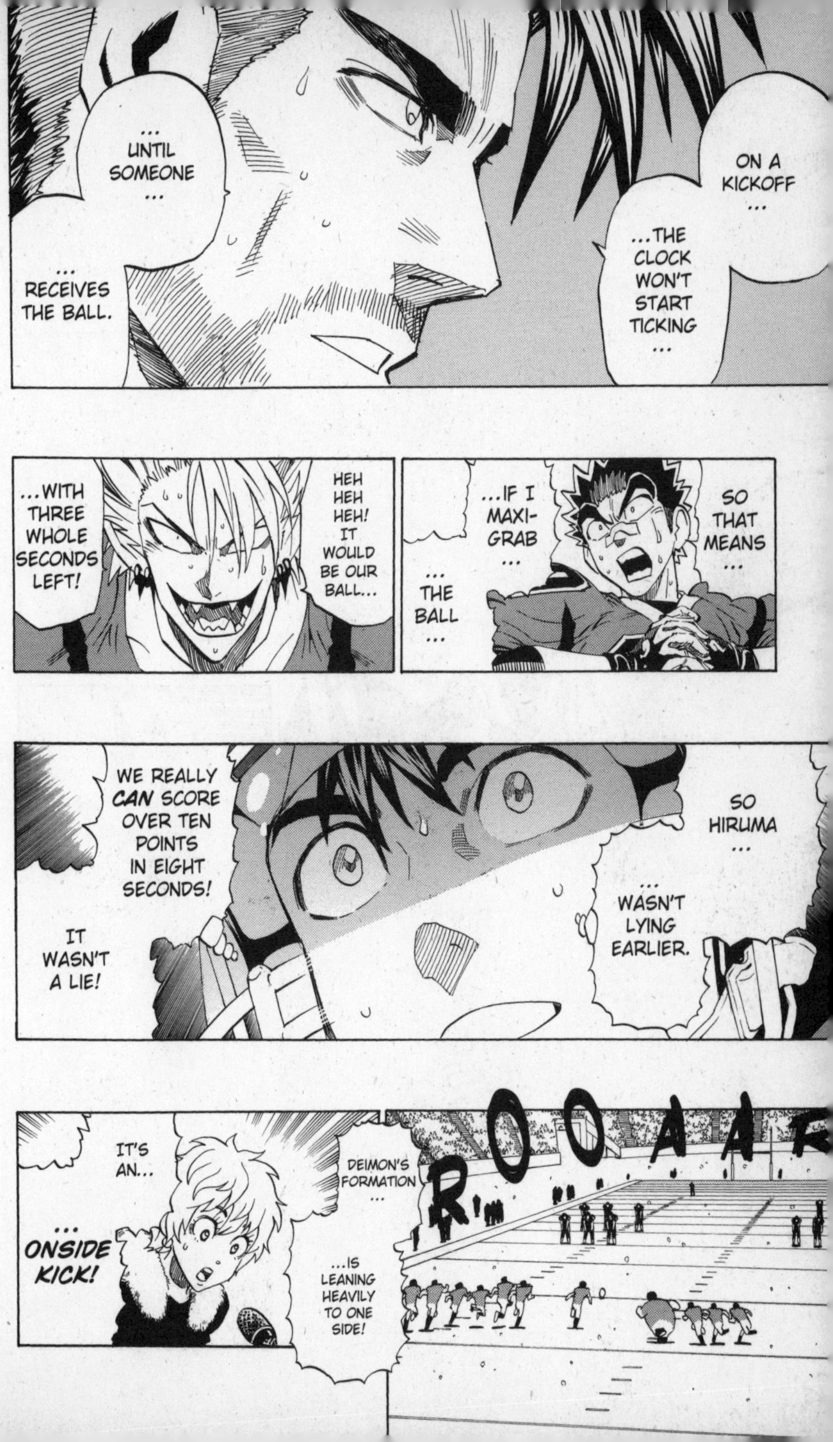
ON A KICKOFF...
...THE CLOCK WON'T START TICKING...
...UNTIL SOMEONE...
...RECEIVES THE BALL.
SO THAT MEANS...
...IF I MAXI-GRAB...
...THE BALL...
HEH HEH HEH! IT WOULD BE OUR BALL...
...WITH THREE WHOLE SECONDS LEFT!
SO HIRUMA...
...WASN'T LYING EARLIER.
WE REALLY CAN SCORE OVER TEN POINTS IN EIGHT SECONDS!
IT WASN'T A LIE!
ROOAAR
DEIMON'S FORMATION...
...IS LEANING HEAVILY TO ONE SIDE!
IT'S AN...
...ONSIDE KICK!

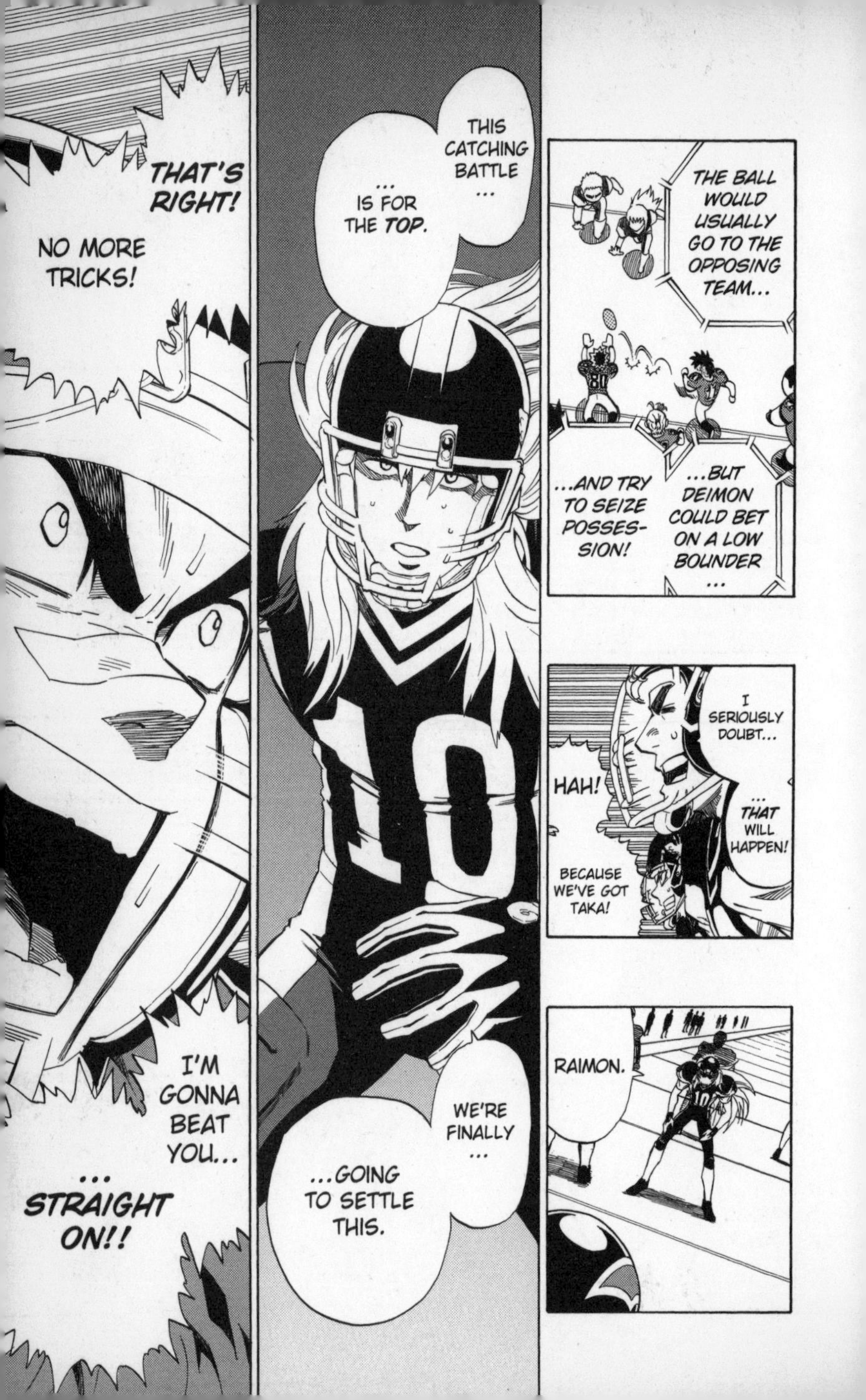
THE BALL WOULD USUALLY GO TO THE OPPOSING TEAM...
...BUT DEIMON COULD BET ON A LOW BOUNDER...
...AND TRY TO SEIZE POSSESSION!
I SERIOUSLY DOUBT...
...THAT WILL HAPPEN!
HAH!
BECAUSE WE'VE GOT TAKA!
RAIMON.
THIS CATCHING BATTLE...
...IS FOR THE TOP.
WE'RE FINALLY...
...GOING TO SETTLE THIS.
THAT'S RIGHT!
NO MORE TRICKS!
I'M GONNA BEAT YOU...
...STRAIGHT ON!!

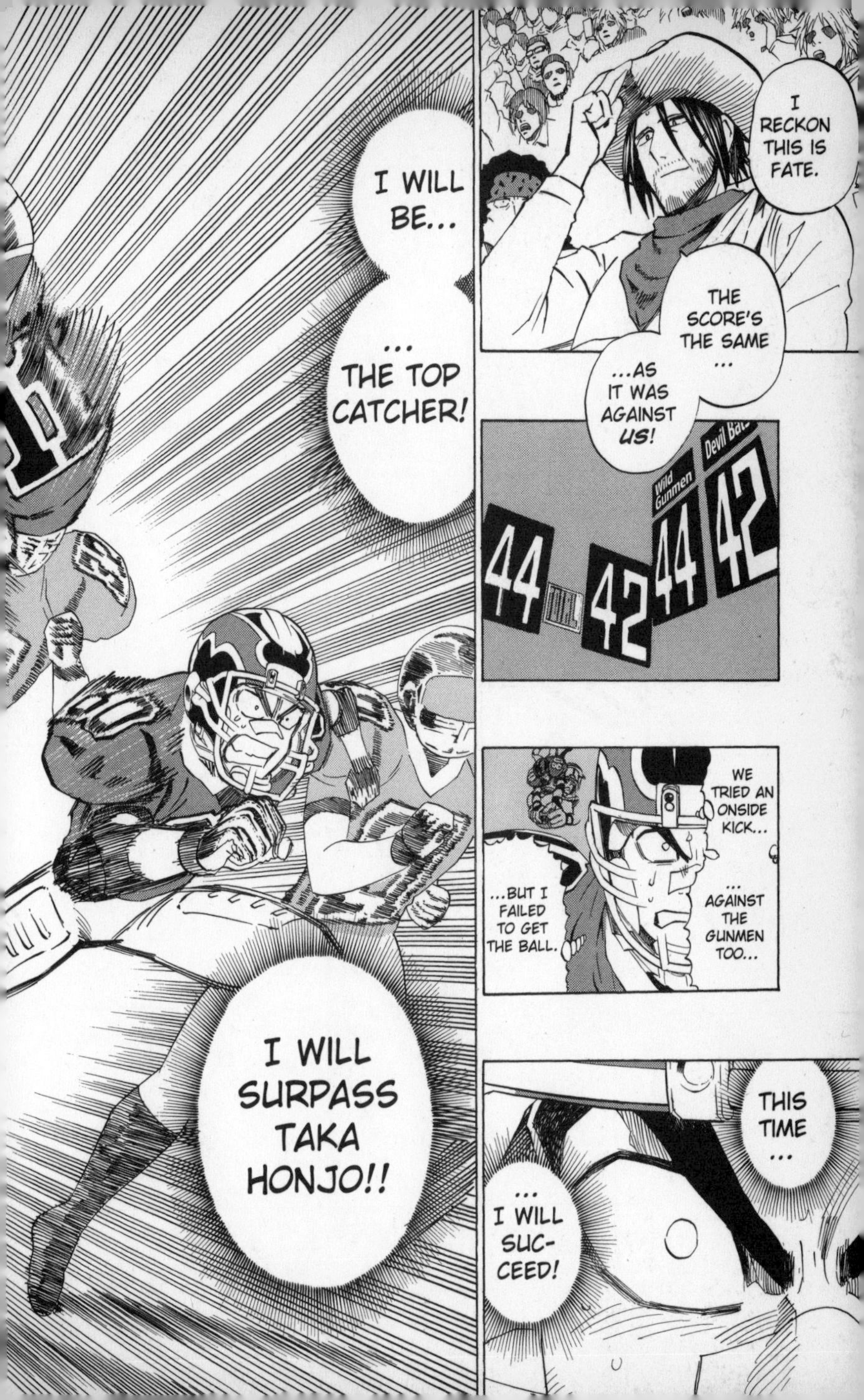
I RECKON THIS IS FATE.
THE SCORE'S THE SAME...
...AS IT WAS AGAINST US!
Wild Gunmen
44
42
44
42
WE TRIED AN ONSIDE KICK...
...AGAINST THE GUNMEN TOO...
...BUT I FAILED TO GET THE BALL.
THIS TIME...
...I WILL SUC-CEED!
I WILL BE...
...THE TOP CATCHER!
I WILL SURPASS TAKA HONJO!!

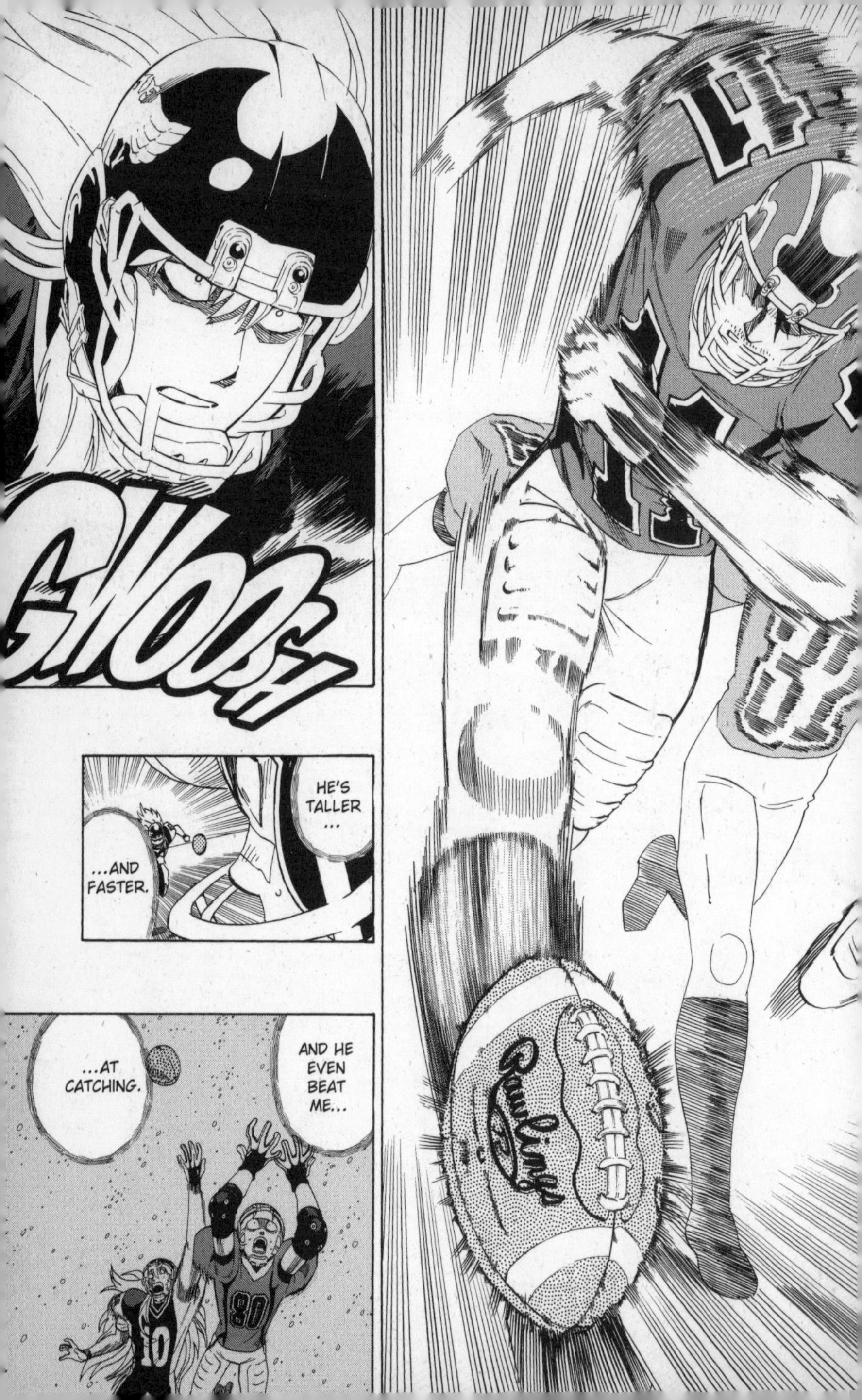
HE'S TALLER ...
...AND FASTER.
AND HE EVEN BEAT ME...
...AT CATCHING.

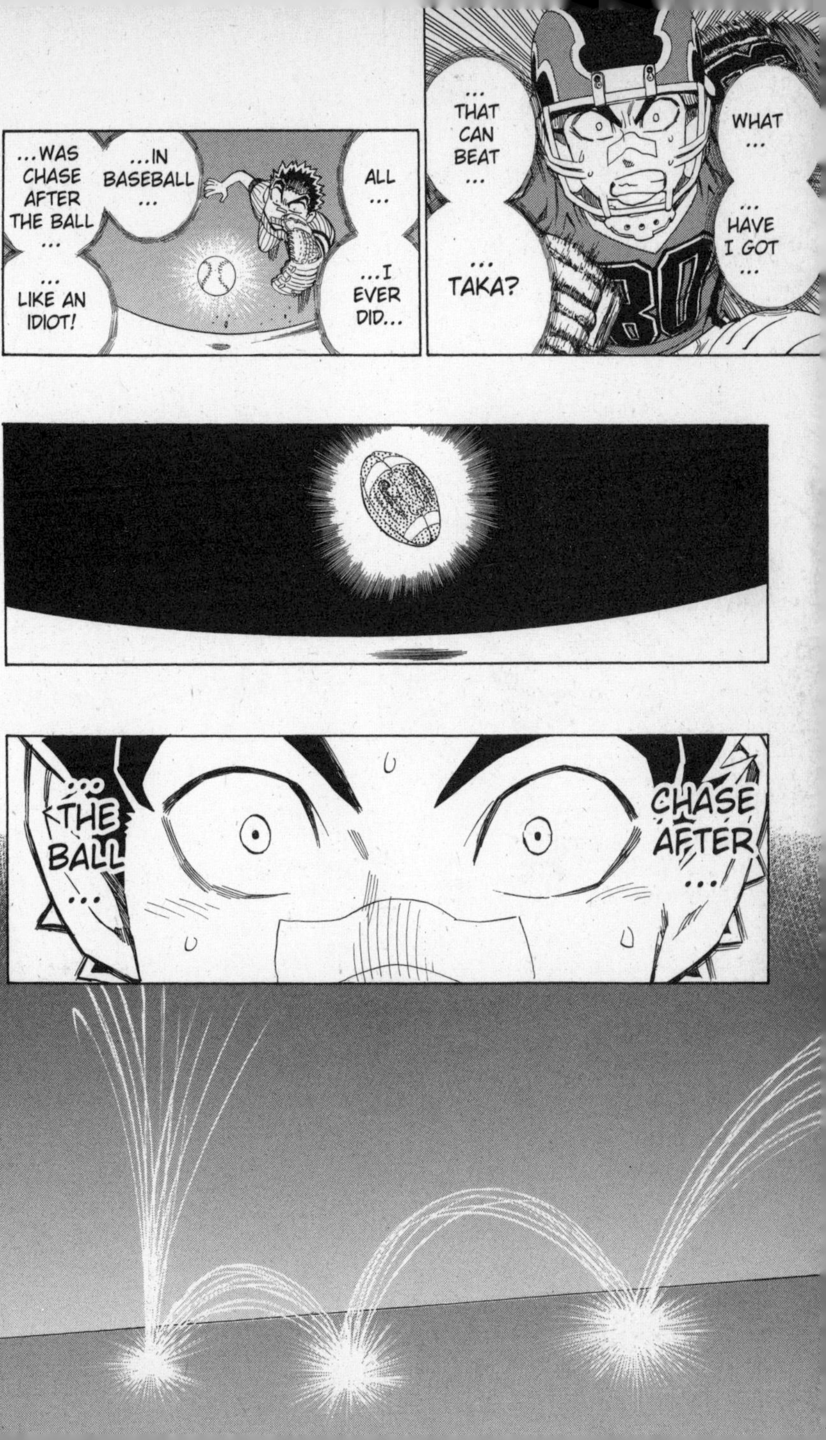
WHAT...
...HAVE I GOT...
...THAT CAN BEAT...
...TAKA?
ALL...
...I EVER DID...
...IN BASEBALL...
...WAS CHASE AFTER THE BALL...
...LIKE AN IDIOT!
CHASE AFTER...
...THE BALL...

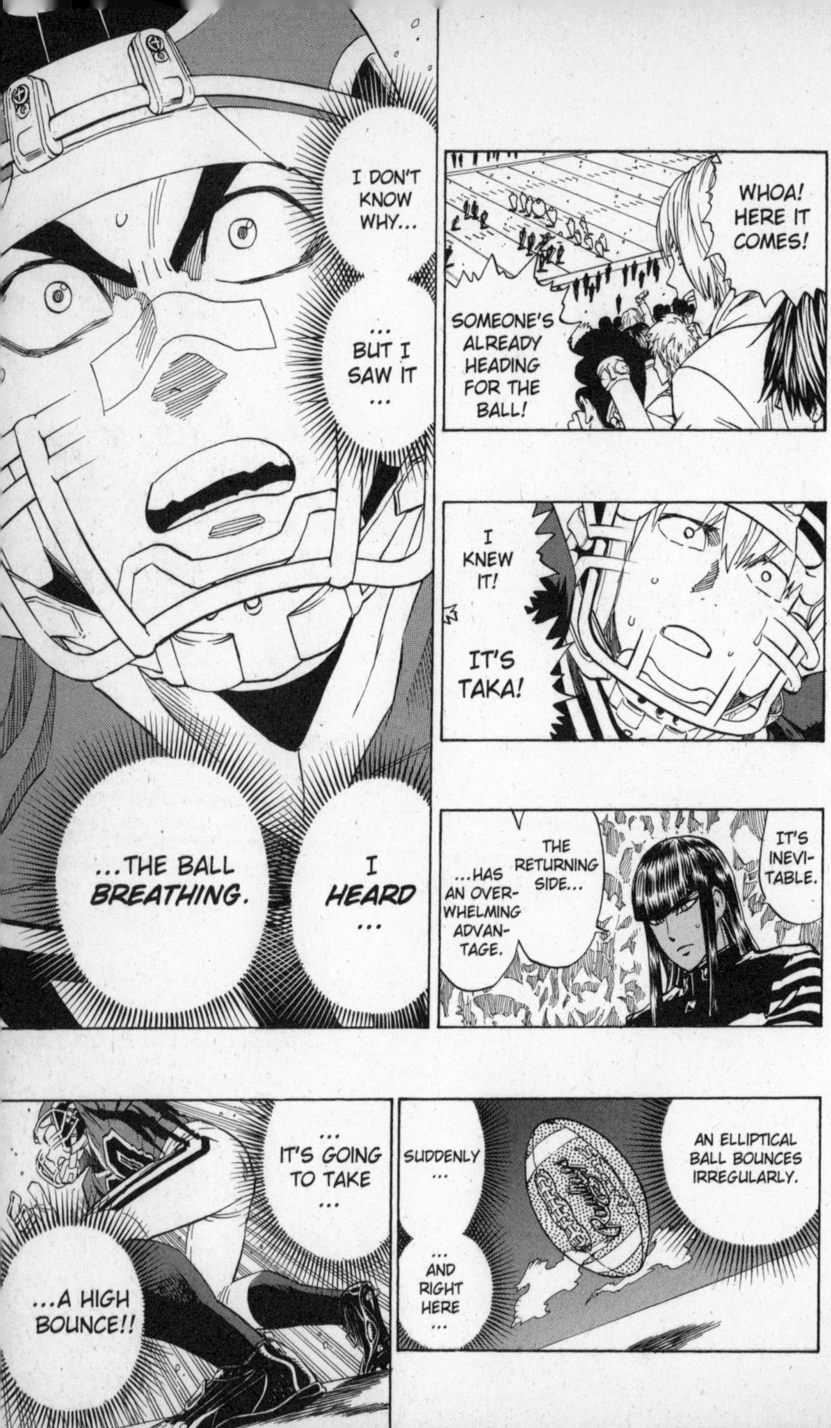
WHOA! HERE IT COMES!
SOMEONE'S ALREADY HEADING FOR THE BALL!
I KNEW IT!
IT'S TAKA!
IT'S INEVITABLE.
THE RETURNING SIDE...
...HAS AN OVERWHELMING ADVANTAGE.
I DON'T KNOW WHY...
...BUT I SAW IT...
I HEARD...
...THE BALL BREATHING.
AN ELLIPTICAL BALL BOUNCES IRREGULARLY.
SUDDENLY...
...AND RIGHT HERE...
...IT'S GOING TO TAKE...
...A HIGH BOUNCE!!

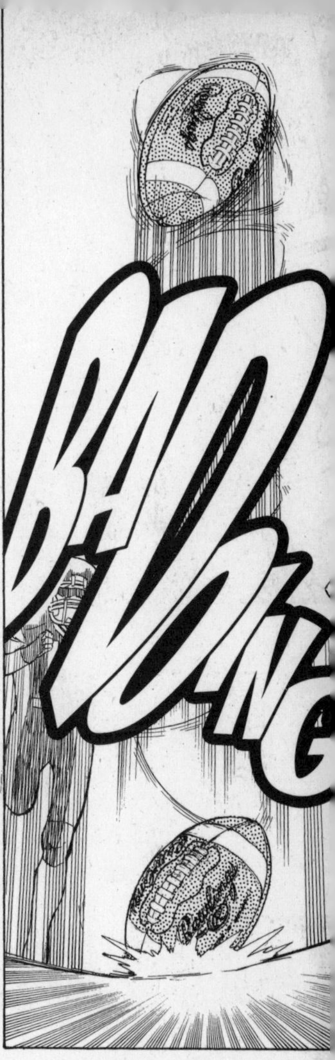
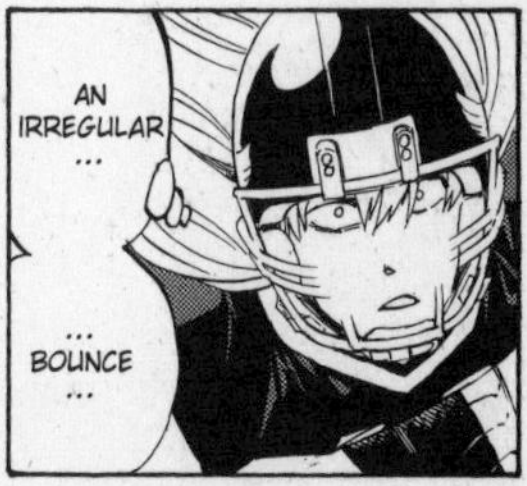
AN IRREGULAR ...
... BOUNCE ...
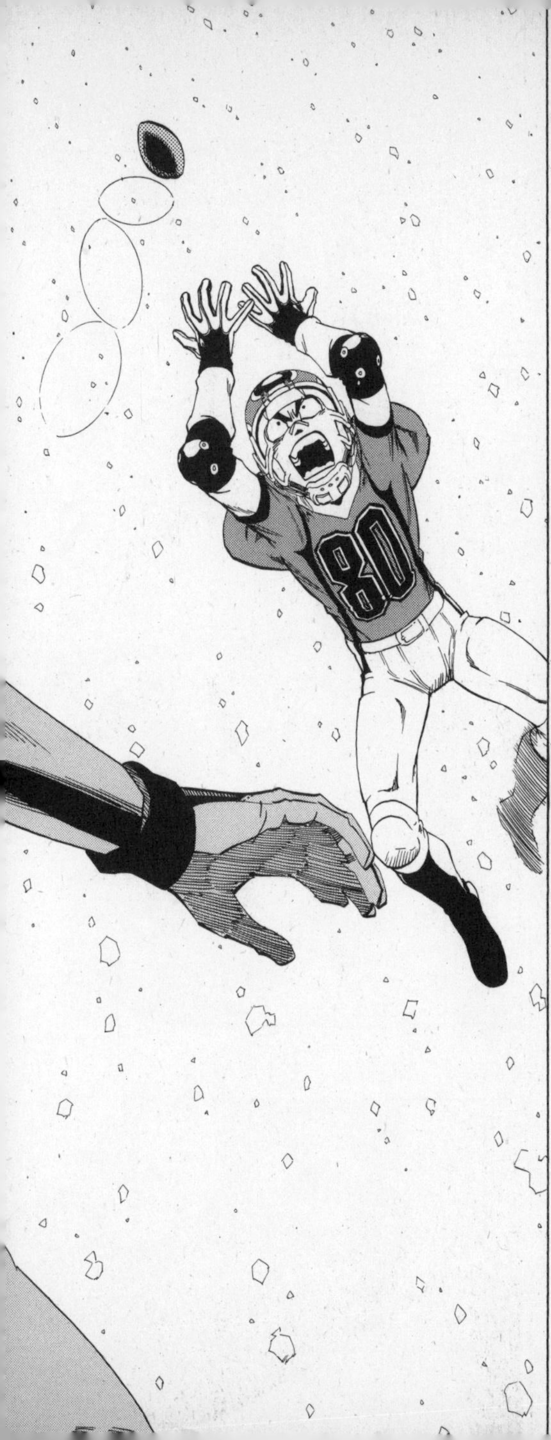

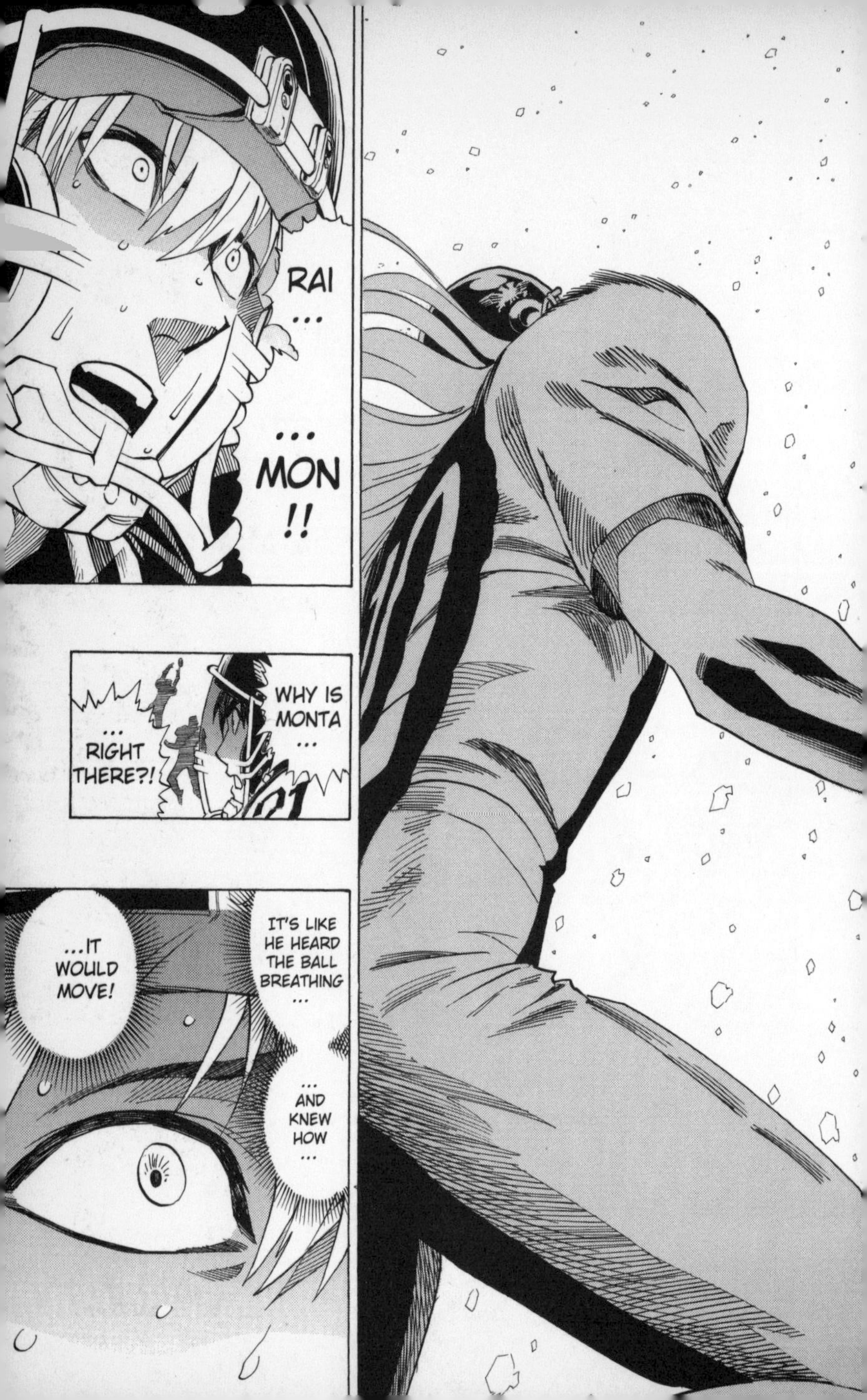
RAI ...
... MON !!
WHY IS MONTA ...
... RIGHT THERE?!
IT'S LIKE HE HEARD THE BALL BREATHING ...
... AND KNEW HOW ...
...IT WOULD MOVE!

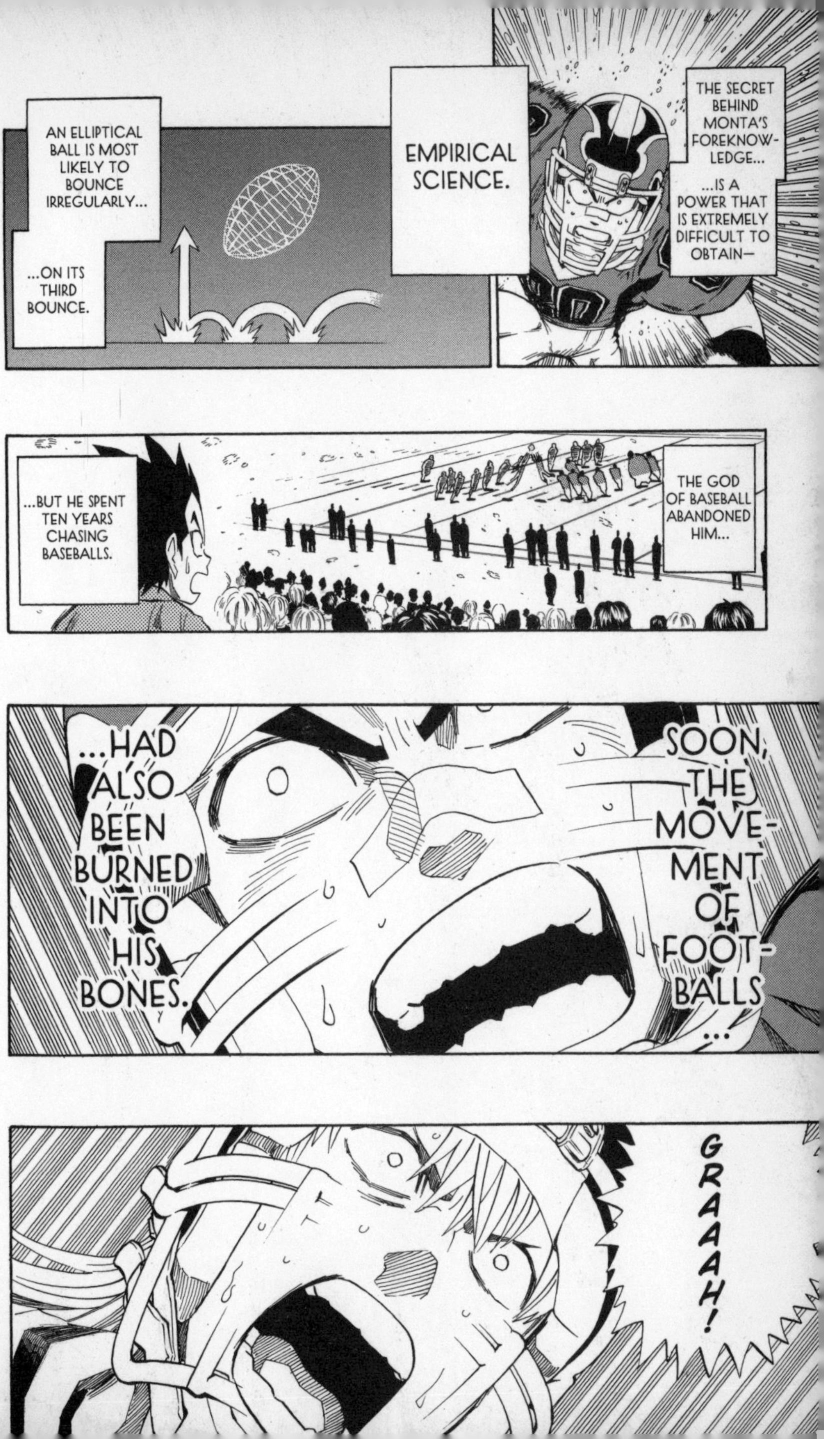
THE SECRET BEHIND MONTA'S FOREKNOW-LEDGE...
...IS A POWER THAT IS EXTREMELY DIFFICULT TO OBTAIN—
EMPIRICAL SCIENCE.
AN ELLIPTICAL BALL IS MOST LIKELY TO BOUNCE IRREGULARLY...
...ON ITS THIRD BOUNCE.
THE GOD OF BASEBALL ABANDONED HIM...
...BUT HE SPENT TEN YEARS CHASING BASEBALLS.
SOON, THE MOVE-MENT OF FOOT-BALLS...
...HAD ALSO BEEN BURNED INTO HIS BONES.
GRAAAH!

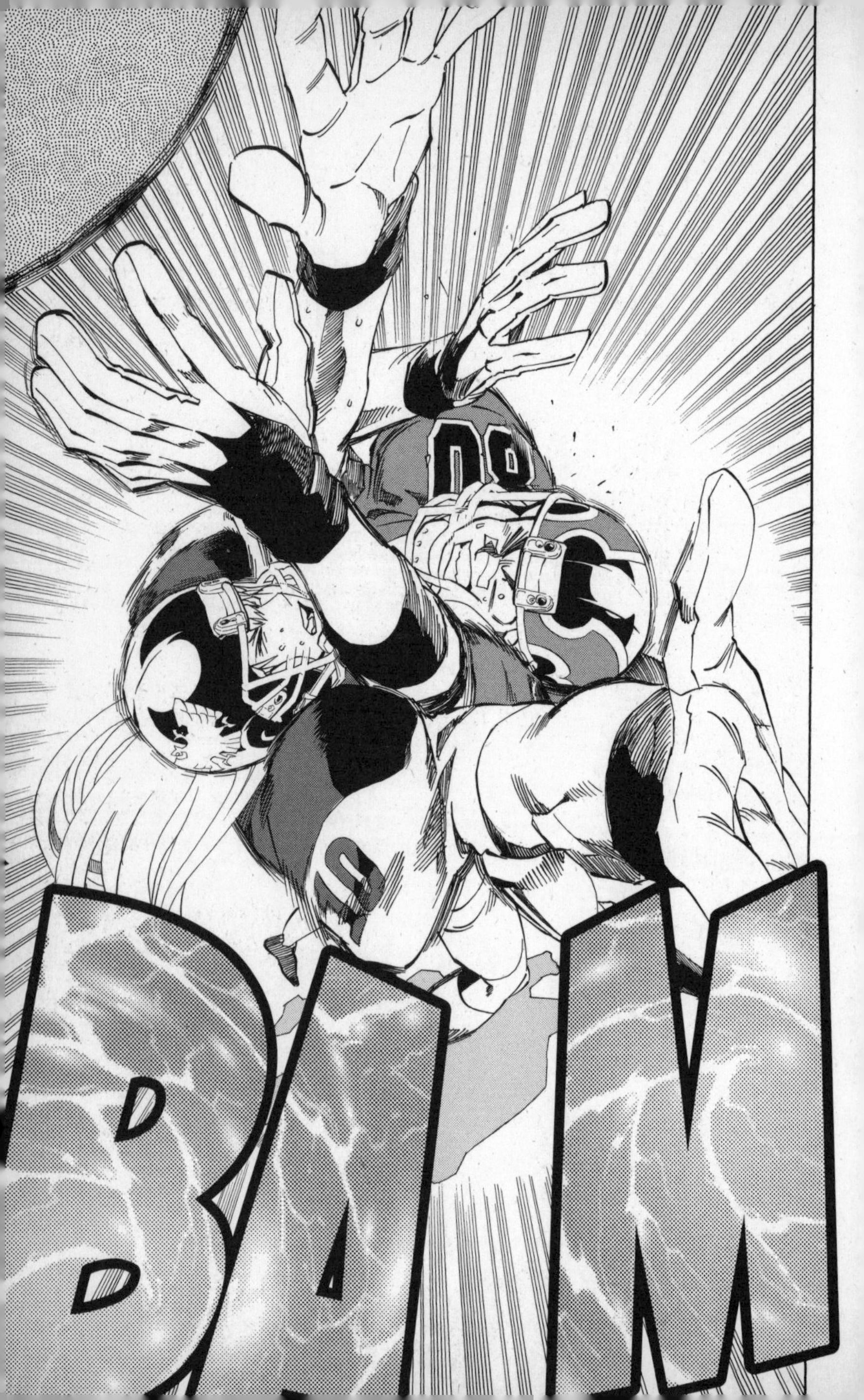

BAM

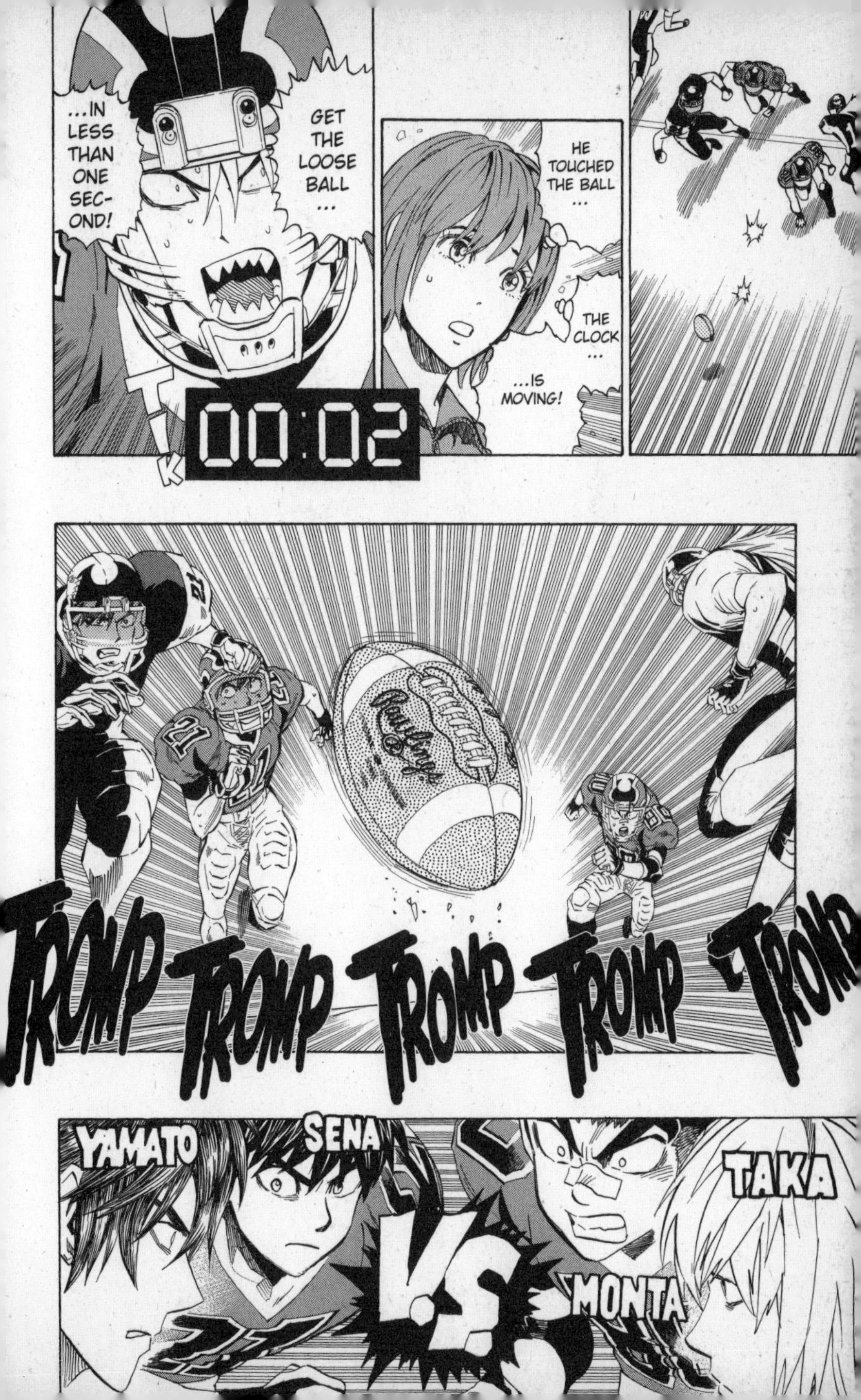
HE TOUCHED THE BALL...
THE CLOCK...
...IS MOVING!
GET THE LOOSE BALL...
...IN LESS THAN ONE SEC-OND!
00:02
TROMP TROMP TROMP TROMP TROMP
TAKA
MONTA
VS
SENA
YAMATO

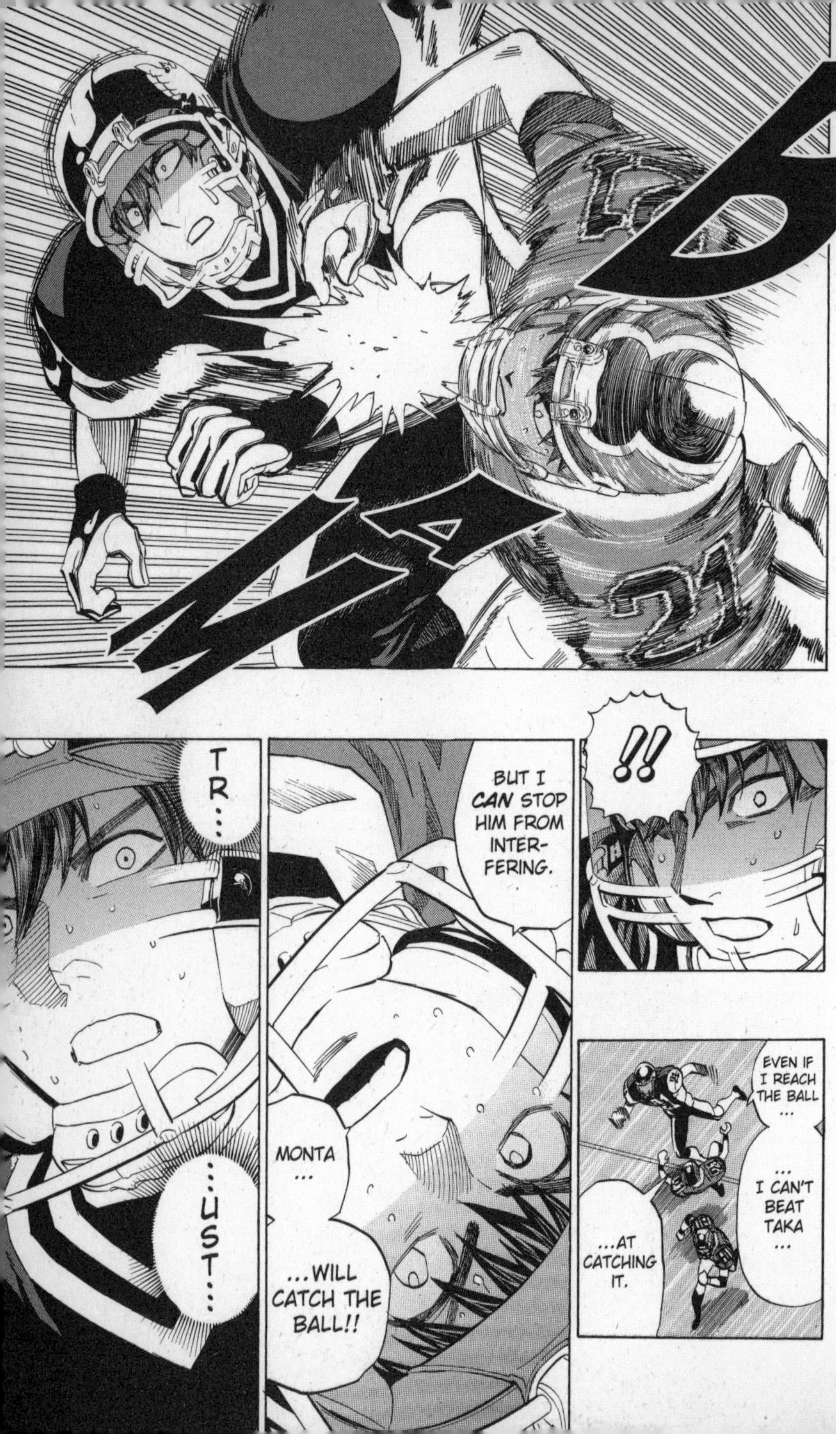
BAM
!!
EVEN IF I REACH THE BALL...
...I CAN'T BEAT TAKA...
...AT CATCHING IT.
BUT I CAN STOP HIM FROM INTER-FERING.
MONTA...
...WILL CATCH THE BALL!!
TR...
...UST...

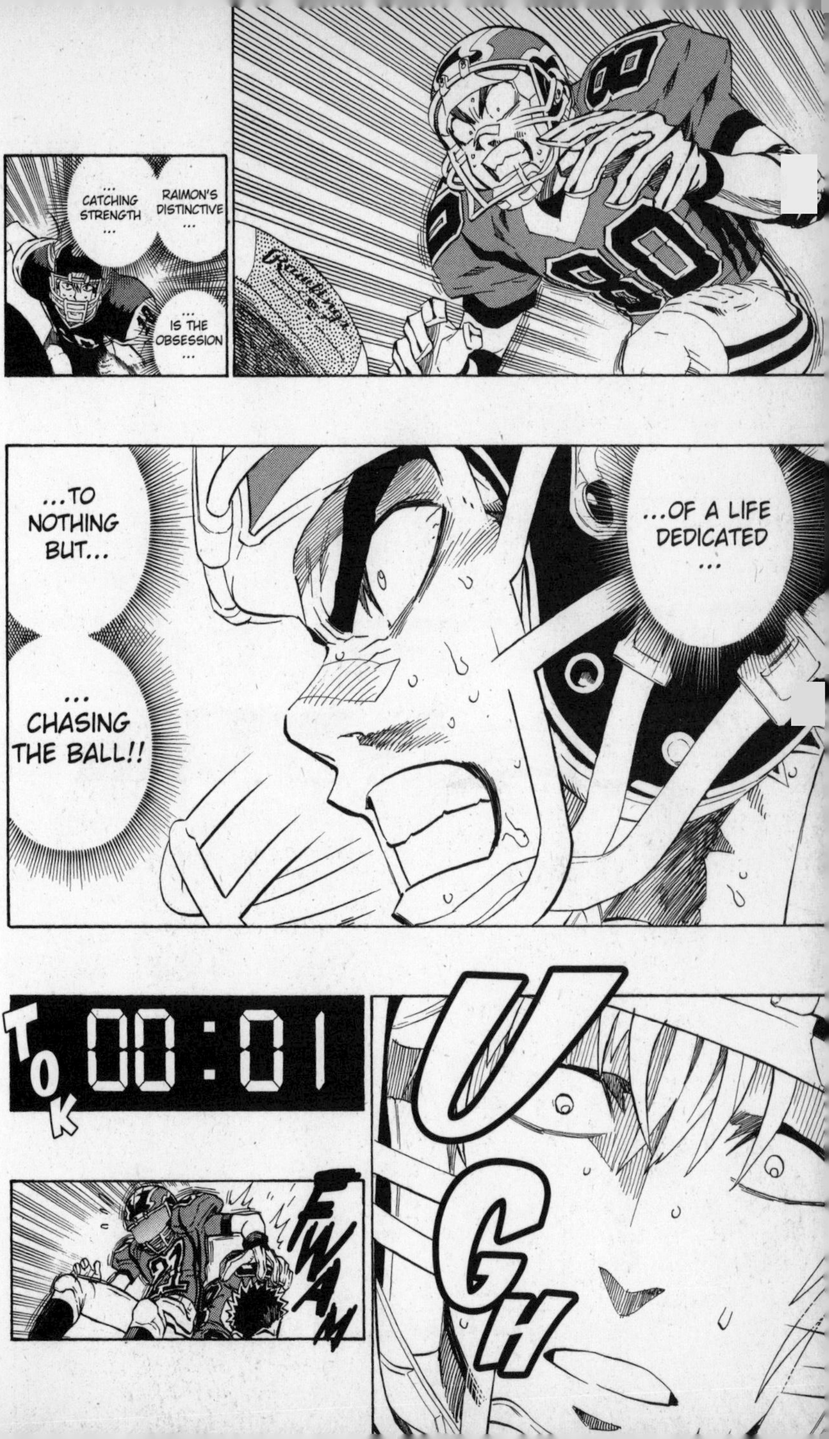
... RAIMON'S DISTINCTIVE ...
... CATCHING STRENGTH ...
... IS THE OBSESSION ...
...OF A LIFE DEDICATED ...
...TO NOTHING BUT...
... CHASING THE BALL!!
UGH
TOK
00:01
FWAM

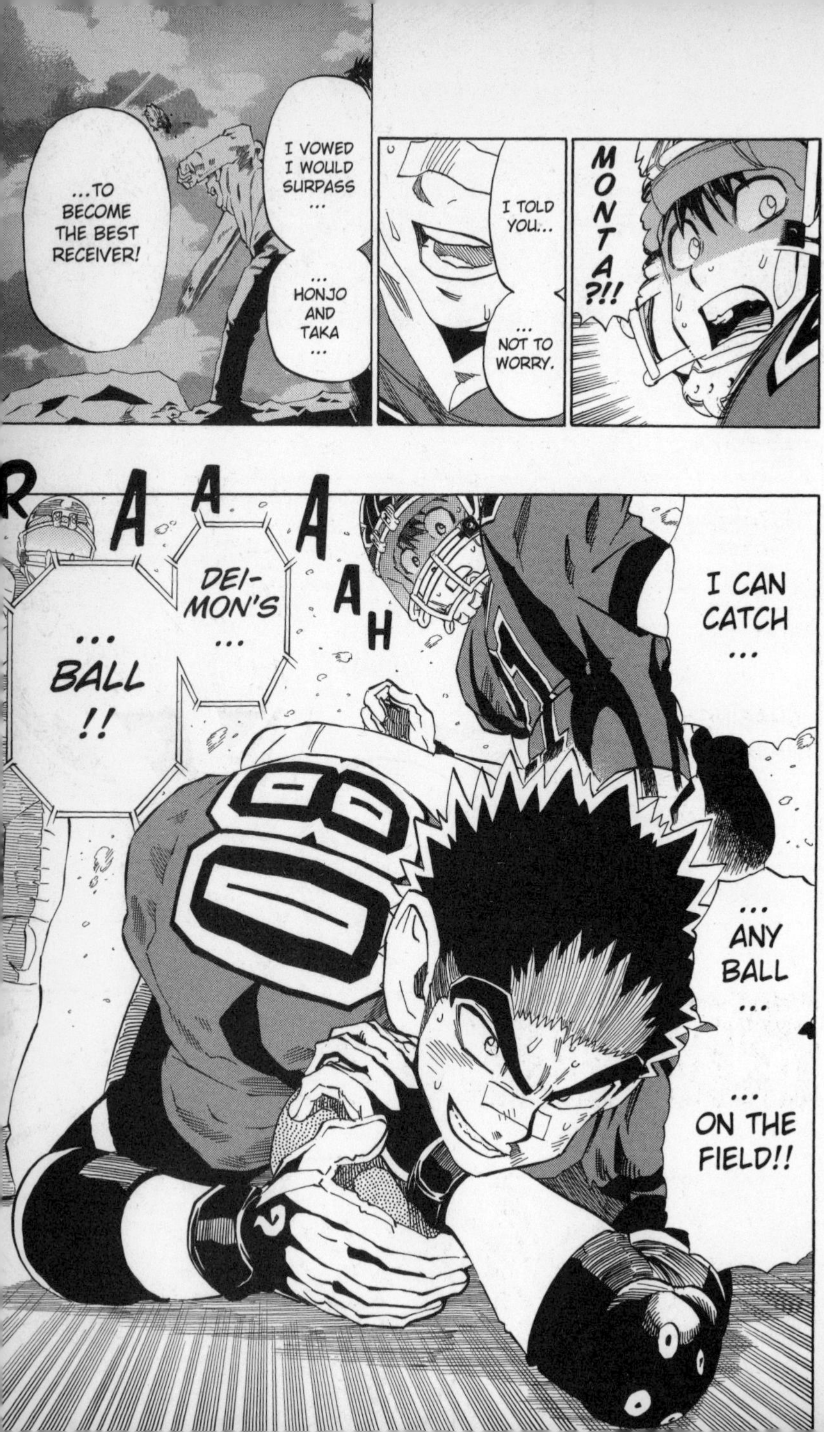
MONTA?!!
I TOLD YOU...
...NOT TO WORRY.
I VOWED I WOULD SURPASS...
...HONJO AND TAKA...
...TO BECOME THE BEST RECEIVER!
I CAN CATCH...
...ANY BALL...
...ON THE FIELD!!
RAAAAAH
DEI-MON'S...
...BALL!!

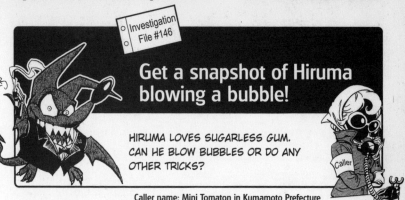

Investigation File #146

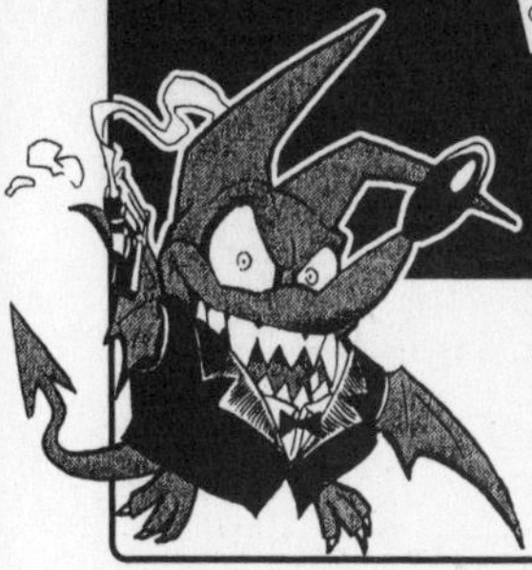

Get a snapshot of Hiruma blowing a bubble!

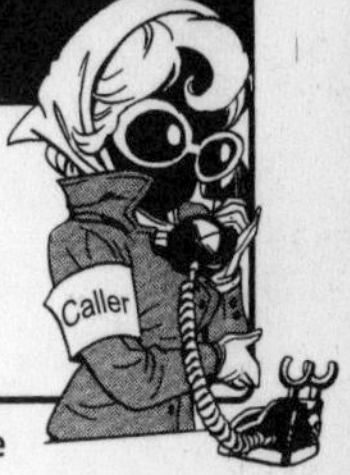
Caller

HIRUMA LOVES SUGARLESS GUM. CAN HE BLOW BUBBLES OR DO ANY OTHER TRICKS?

Caller name: Mini Tomaton in Kumamoto Prefecture

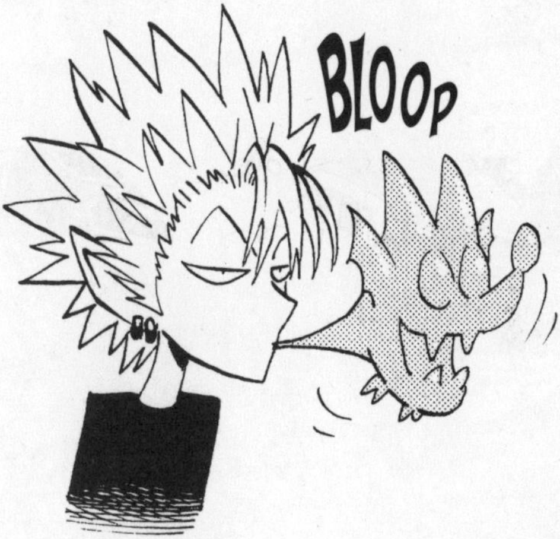
BLOOP

HOW DOES HE *DO* THAT?!!

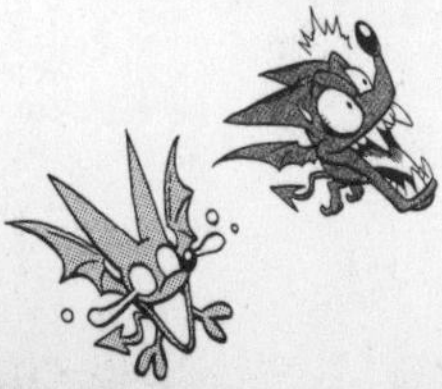

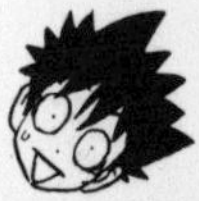

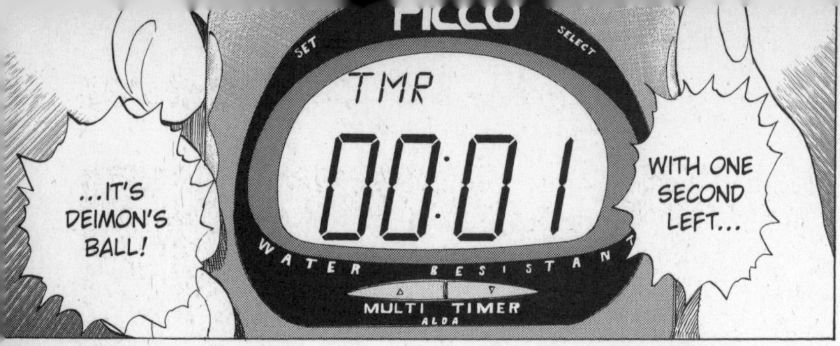
WITH ONE SECOND LEFT...
SET
SELECT
TMR
00:01
WATER RESISTANT
MULTI TIMER
ALDA
...IT'S DEIMON'S BALL!

Chapter 303 The Last of the Deimon Devil Bats

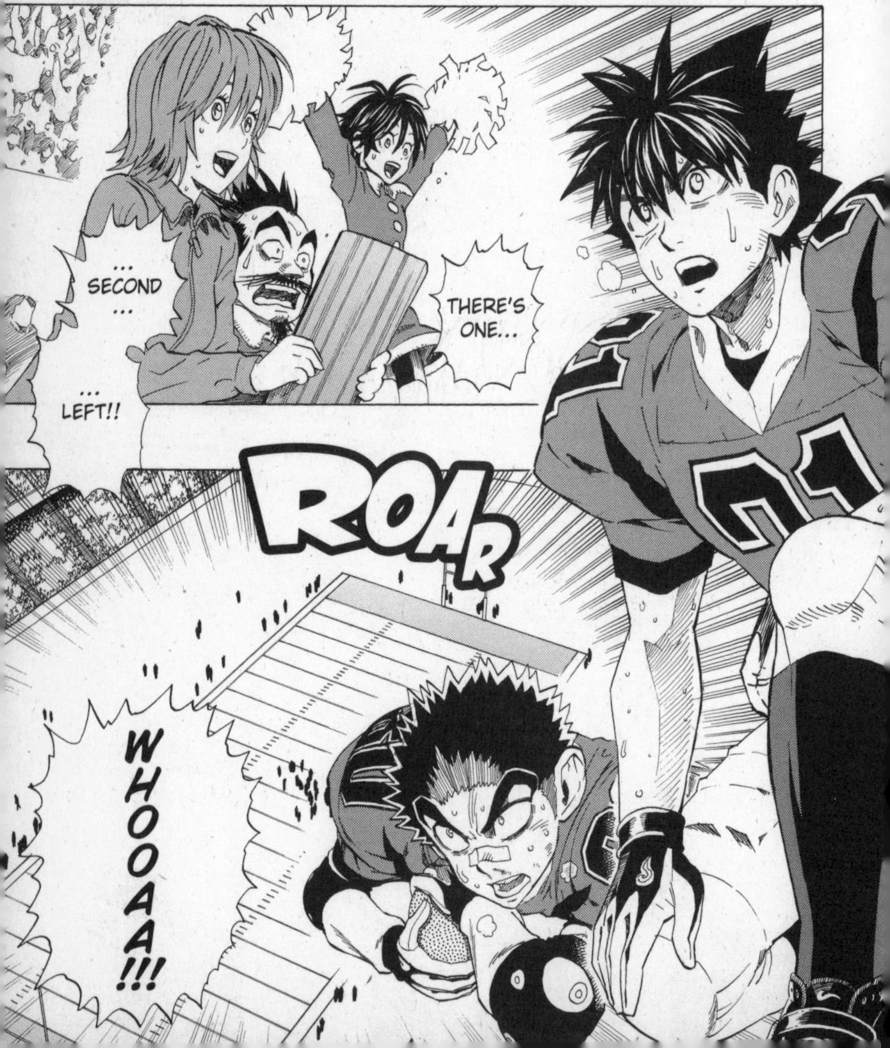
THERE'S ONE...
... SECOND ...
... LEFT!!
ROAR
WHOOAAA!!!

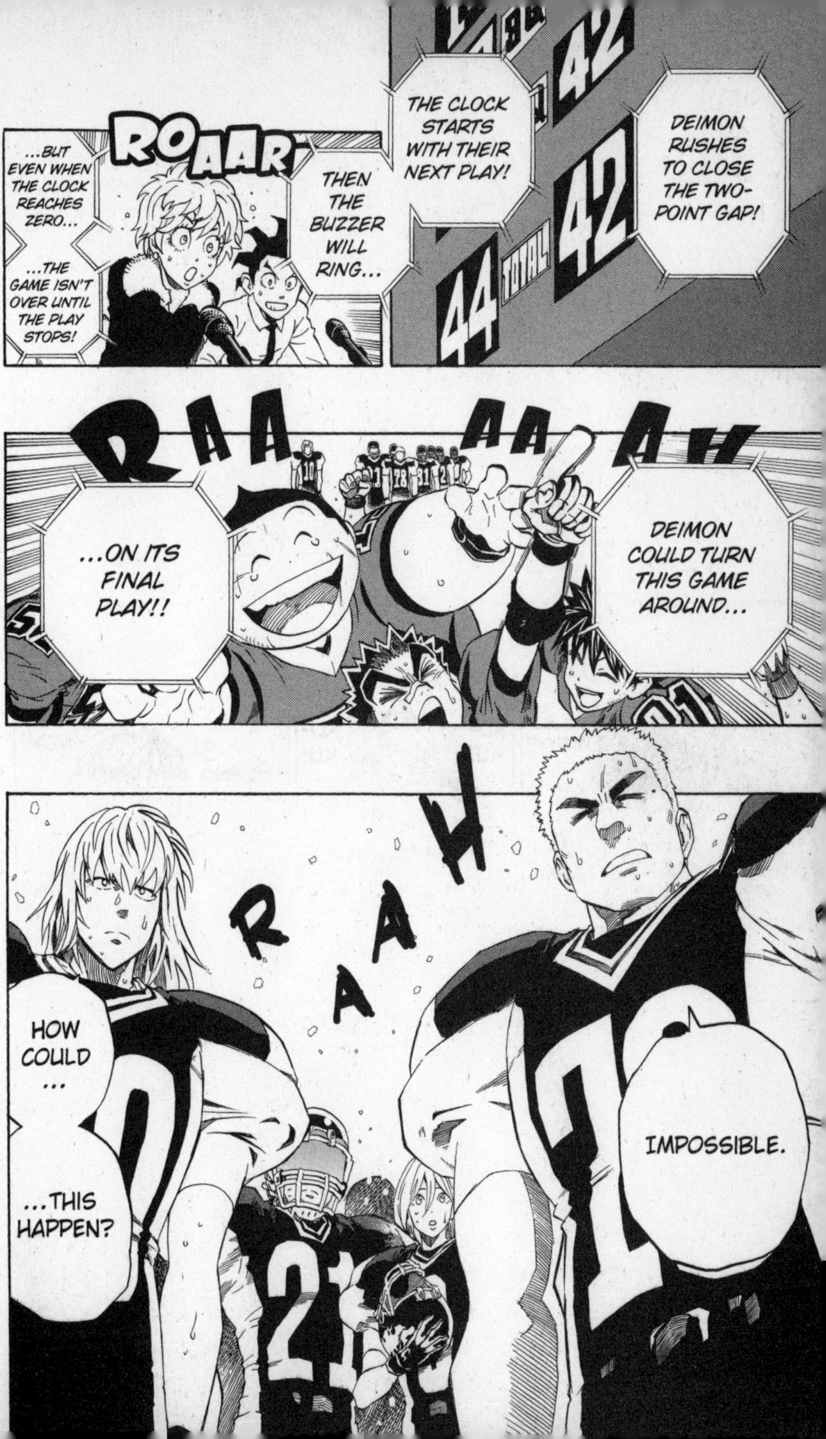
44
TOTAL
42
DEIMON RUSHES TO CLOSE THE TWO-POINT GAP!
THE CLOCK STARTS WITH THEIR NEXT PLAY!
THEN THE BUZZER WILL RING...
ROAAAR
...BUT EVEN WHEN THE CLOCK REACHES ZERO...
...THE GAME ISN'T OVER UNTIL THE PLAY STOPS!
RAAAAAAAH
DEIMON COULD TURN THIS GAME AROUND...
...ON ITS FINAL PLAY!!
RAAAH
IMPOSSIBLE.
HOW COULD...
...THIS HAPPEN?

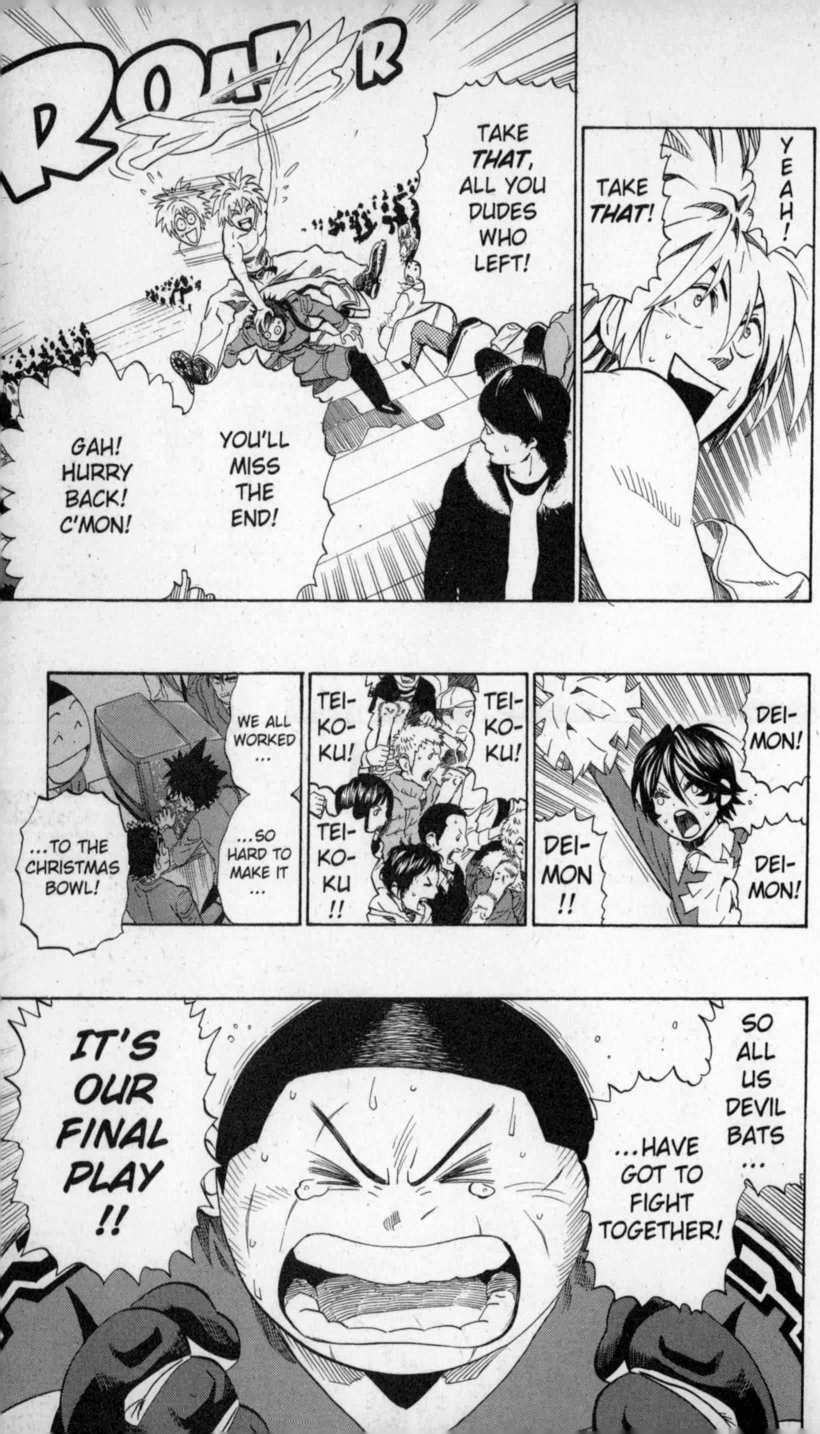
YEAH!
TAKE THAT!
ROAR
TAKE THAT, ALL YOU DUDES WHO LEFT!
YOU'LL MISS THE END!
GAH! HURRY BACK! C'MON!
DEI-MON!
DEI-MON!
DEI-MON!!
TEI-KO-KU!
TEI-KO-KU!
TEI-KO-KU!!
WE ALL WORKED...
...SO HARD TO MAKE IT...
...TO THE CHRISTMAS BOWL!
SO ALL US DEVIL BATS...
...HAVE GOT TO FIGHT TOGETHER!
IT'S OUR FINAL PLAY!!

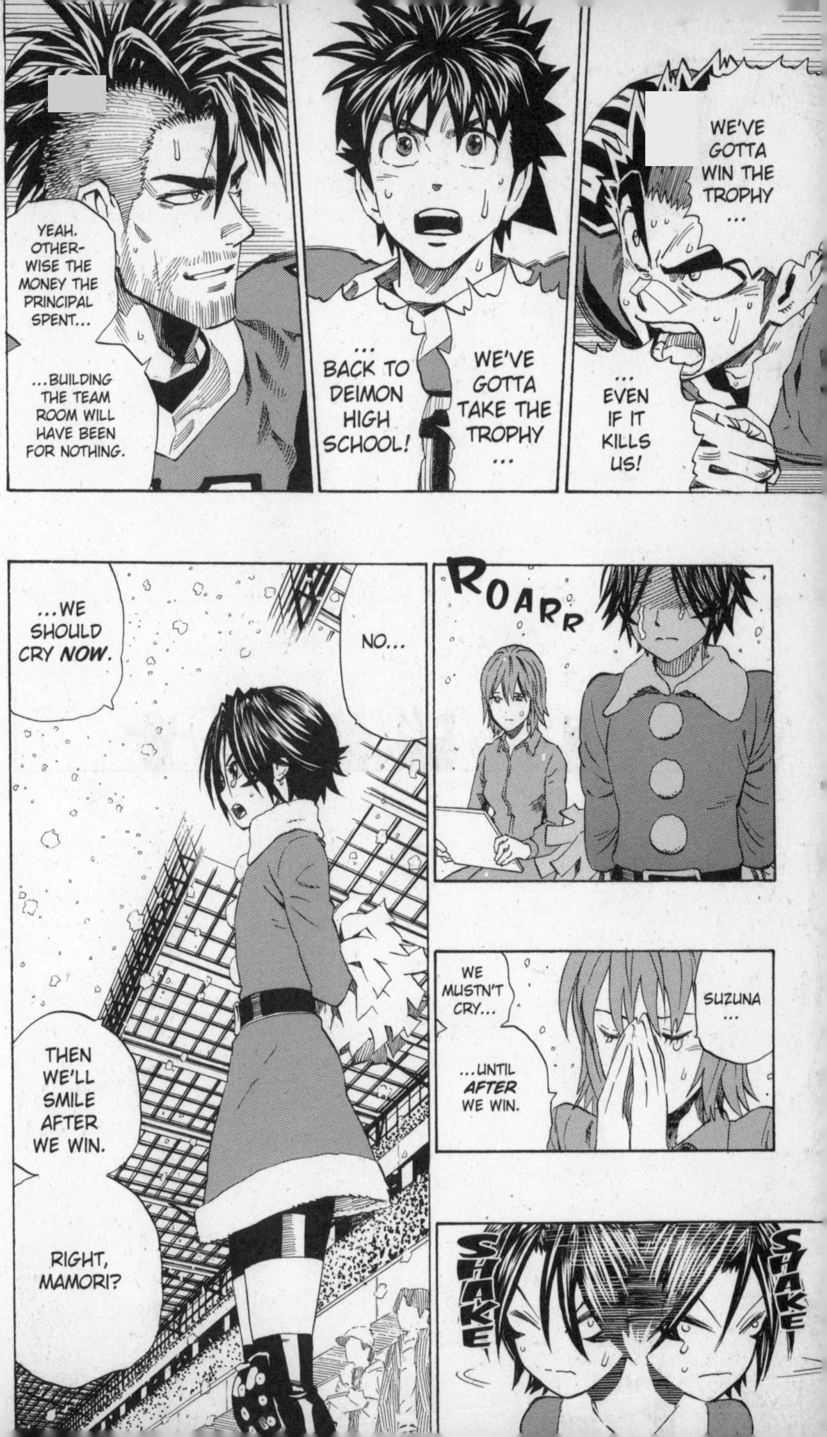
WE'VE GOTTA WIN THE TROPHY ...
... EVEN IF IT KILLS US!
WE'VE GOTTA TAKE THE TROPHY ...
... BACK TO DEIMON HIGH SCHOOL!
YEAH. OTHER-WISE THE MONEY THE PRINCIPAL SPENT...
...BUILDING THE TEAM ROOM WILL HAVE BEEN FOR NOTHING.
ROARR
SUZUNA ...
WE MUSTN'T CRY...
...UNTIL AFTER WE WIN.
SHAKE
SHAKE
NO...
...WE SHOULD CRY NOW.
THEN WE'LL SMILE AFTER WE WIN.
RIGHT, MAMORI?

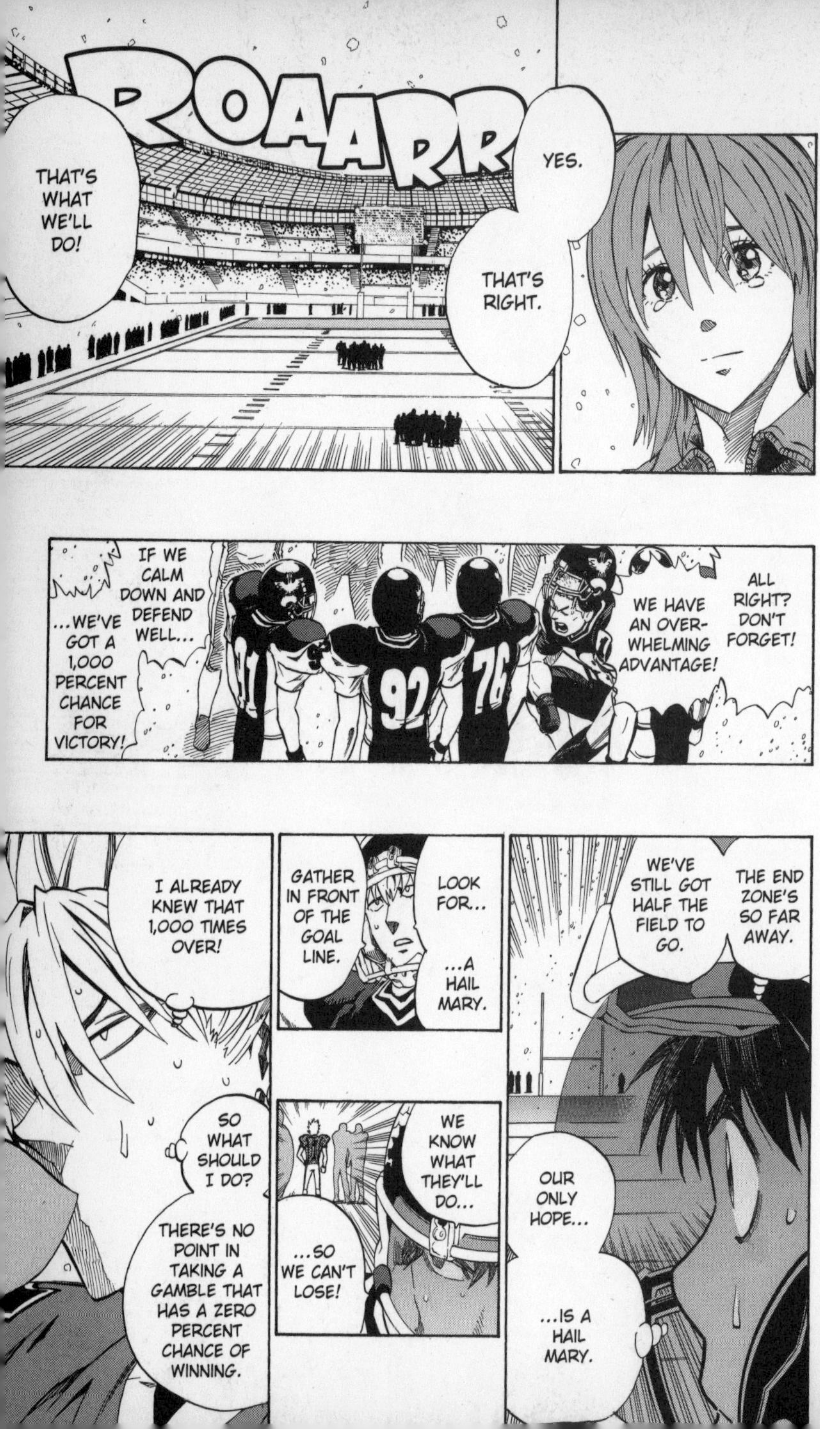
YES.
THAT'S RIGHT.
ROAARR
THAT'S WHAT WE'LL DO!
ALL RIGHT? DON'T FORGET!
WE HAVE AN OVER-WHELMING ADVANTAGE!
IF WE CALM DOWN AND DEFEND WELL...
...WE'VE GOT A 1,000 PERCENT CHANCE FOR VICTORY!
THE END ZONE'S SO FAR AWAY.
WE'VE STILL GOT HALF THE FIELD TO GO.
OUR ONLY HOPE...
...IS A HAIL MARY.
LOOK FOR...
...A HAIL MARY.
GATHER IN FRONT OF THE GOAL LINE.
WE KNOW WHAT THEY'LL DO...
...SO WE CAN'T LOSE!
I ALREADY KNEW THAT 1,000 TIMES OVER!
SO WHAT SHOULD I DO?
THERE'S NO POINT IN TAKING A GAMBLE THAT HAS A ZERO PERCENT CHANCE OF WINNING.

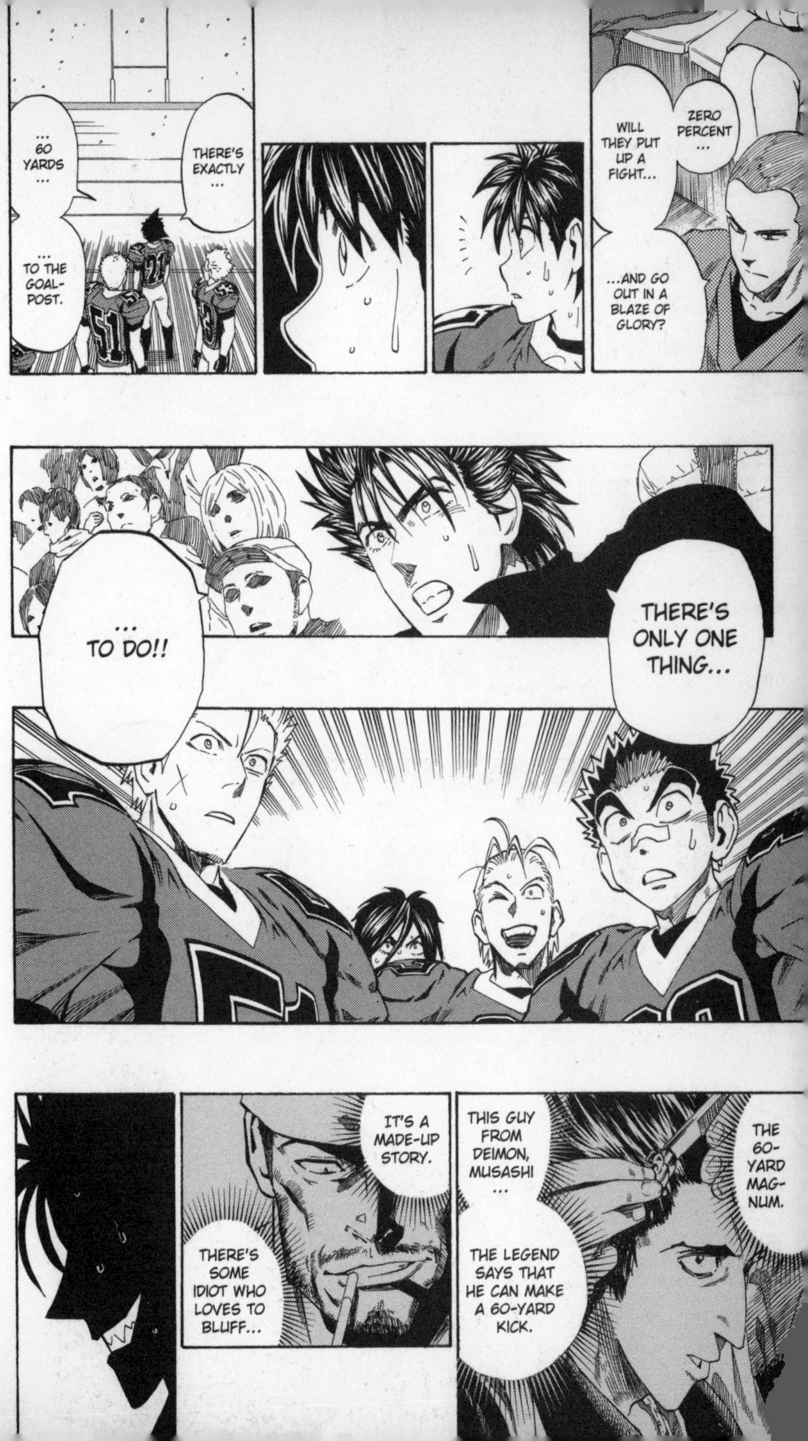

ZERO PERCENT...
WILL THEY PUT UP A FIGHT...
...AND GO OUT IN A BLAZE OF GLORY?
THERE'S EXACTLY...
...60 YARDS...
...TO THE GOAL-POST.
THERE'S ONLY ONE THING...
...TO DO!!
THE 60-YARD MAGNUM.
THIS GUY FROM DEIMON, MUSASHI...
THE LEGEND SAYS THAT HE CAN MAKE A 60-YARD KICK.
IT'S A MADE-UP STORY.
THERE'S SOME IDIOT WHO LOVES TO BLUFF...

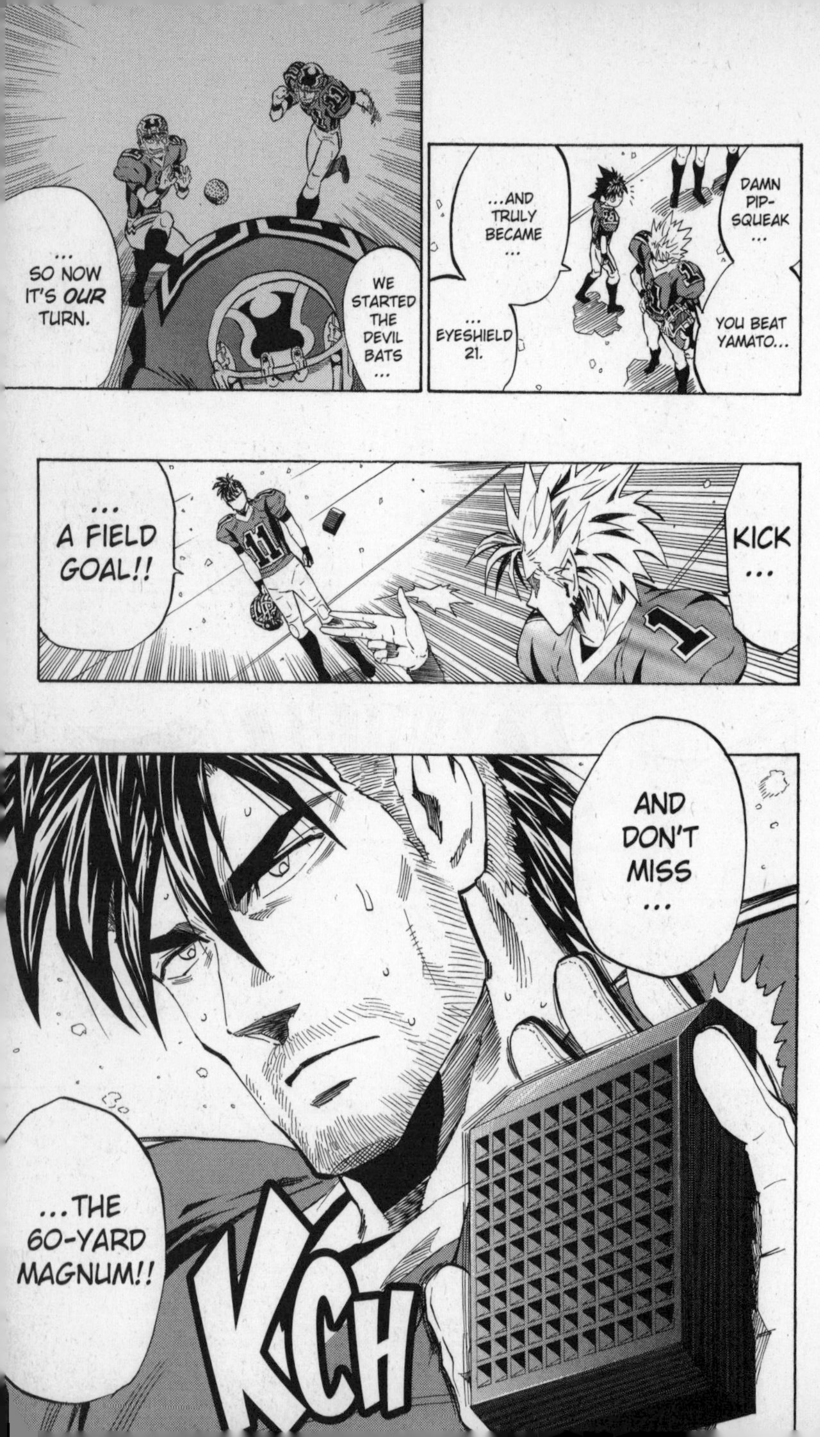
DAMN PIP-SQUEAK...
YOU BEAT YAMATO...
...AND TRULY BECAME...
...EYESHIELD 21.
WE STARTED THE DEVIL BATS...
...SO NOW IT'S *OUR* TURN.
KICK...
...A FIELD GOAL!!
AND DON'T MISS...
...THE 60-YARD MAGNUM!!
KCH

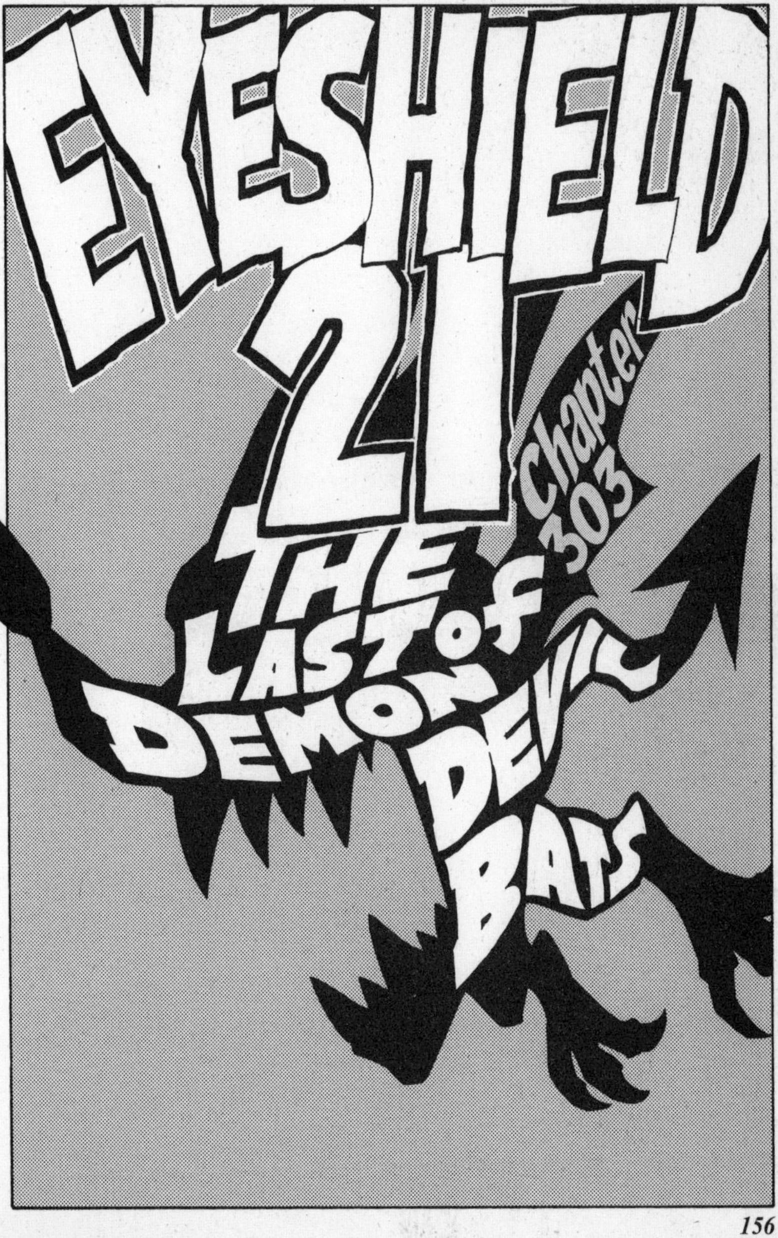
EYESHIELD 21
Chapter 303
THE LAST OF DEMON DEVIL BATS

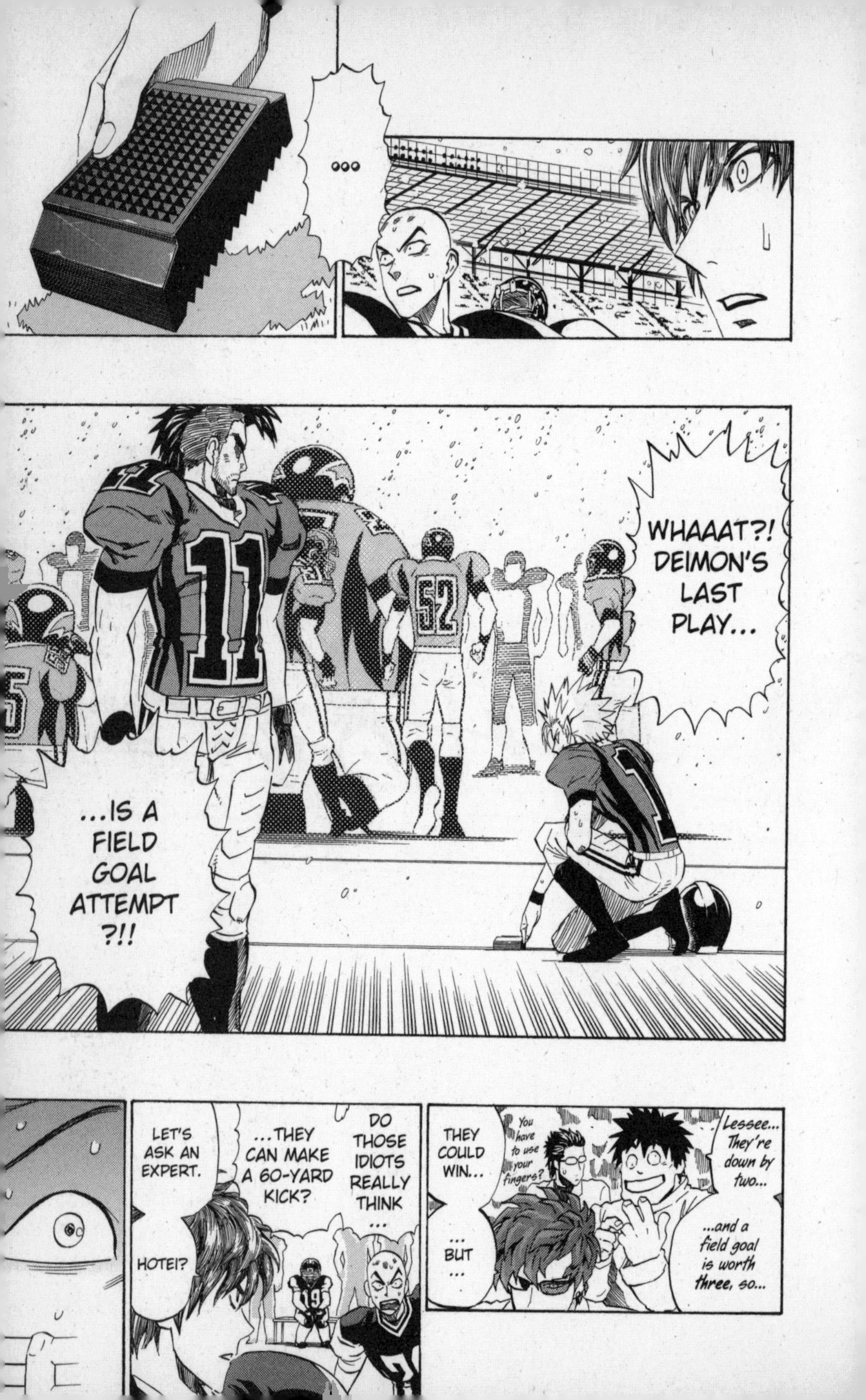
...
WHAAAT?! DEIMON'S LAST PLAY...
...IS A FIELD GOAL ATTEMPT ?!!
Lessee... They're down by two...
You have to use your fingers?
...and a field goal is worth three, so...
THEY COULD WIN...
... BUT ...
DO THOSE IDIOTS REALLY THINK ...
...THEY CAN MAKE A 60-YARD KICK?
LET'S ASK AN EXPERT.
HOTEI?

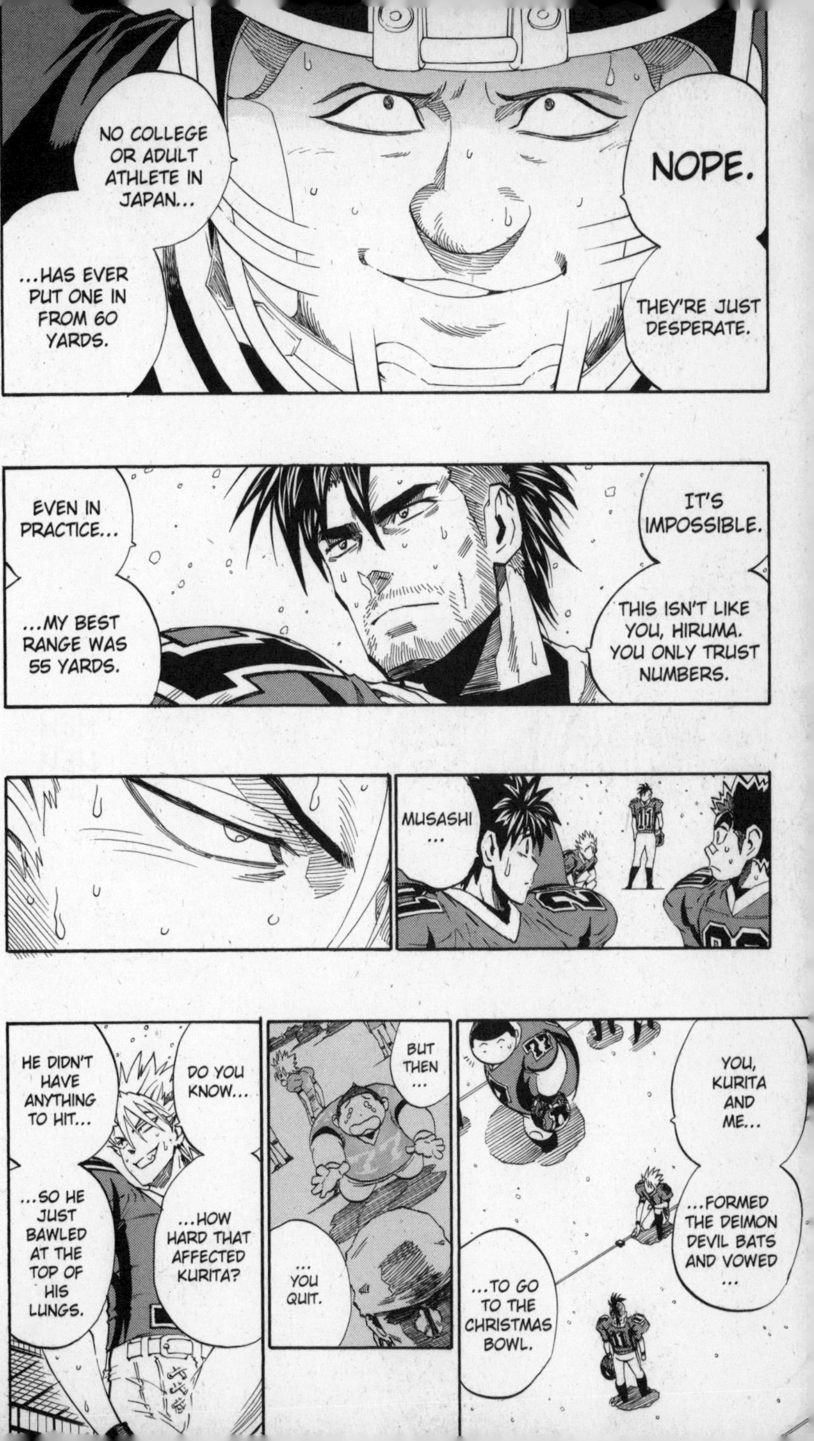
NOPE.
THEY'RE JUST DESPERATE.
NO COLLEGE OR ADULT ATHLETE IN JAPAN...
...HAS EVER PUT ONE IN FROM 60 YARDS.
IT'S IMPOSSIBLE.
THIS ISN'T LIKE YOU, HIRUMA. YOU ONLY TRUST NUMBERS.
EVEN IN PRACTICE...
...MY BEST RANGE WAS 55 YARDS.
MUSASHI ...
YOU, KURITA AND ME...
...FORMED THE DEIMON DEVIL BATS AND VOWED ...
...TO GO TO THE CHRISTMAS BOWL.
BUT THEN ...
... YOU QUIT.
DO YOU KNOW...
...HOW HARD THAT AFFECTED KURITA?
HE DIDN'T HAVE ANYTHING TO HIT...
...SO HE JUST BAWLED AT THE TOP OF HIS LUNGS.

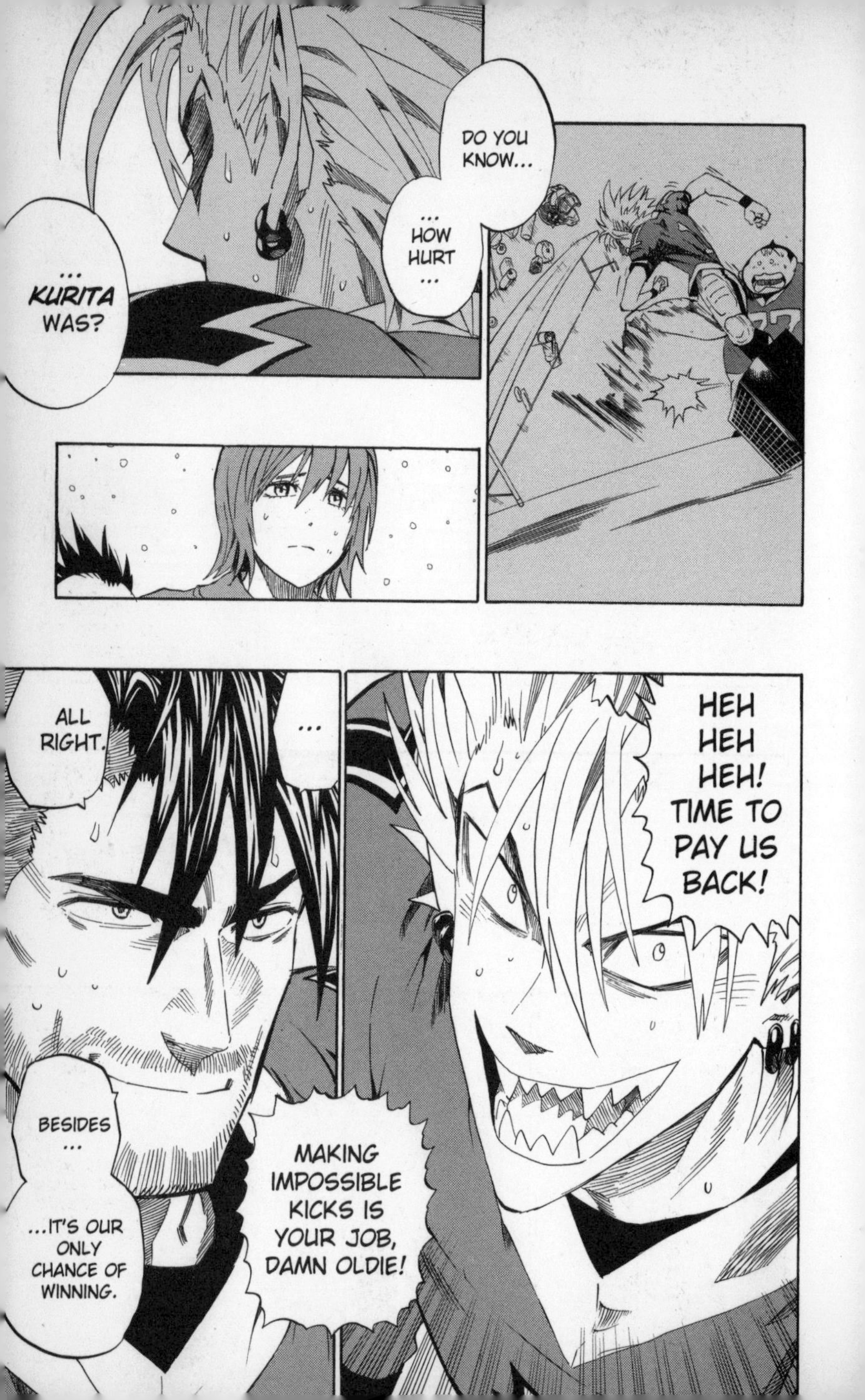
DO YOU KNOW...
...HOW HURT...
...KURITA WAS?
HEH HEH HEH! TIME TO PAY US BACK!
MAKING IMPOSSIBLE KICKS IS YOUR JOB, DAMN OLDIE!
...
ALL RIGHT.
BESIDES...
...IT'S OUR ONLY CHANCE OF WINNING.

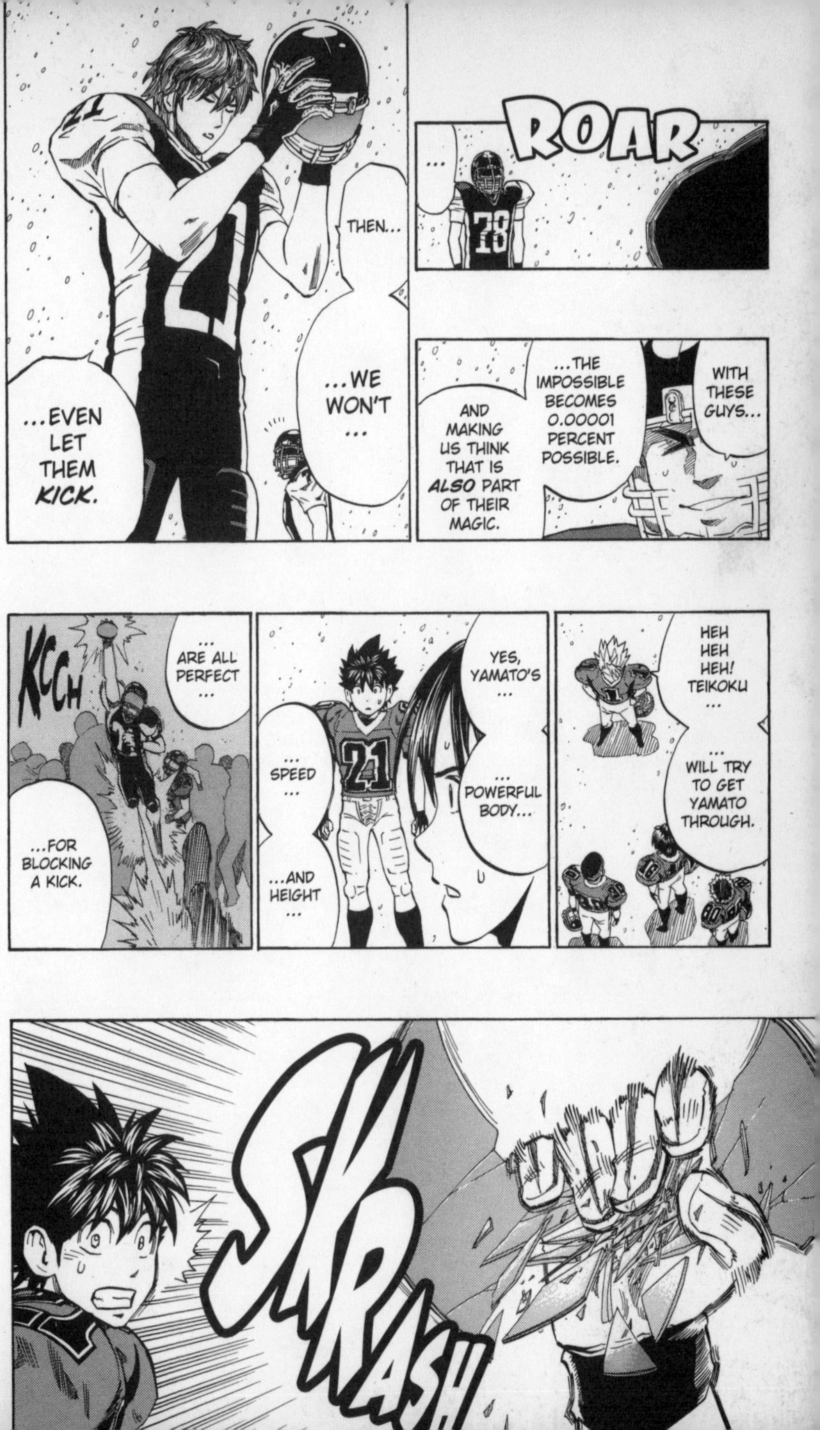
ROAR
...
WITH THESE GUYS...
...THE IMPOSSIBLE BECOMES 0.00001 PERCENT POSSIBLE.
AND MAKING US THINK THAT IS *ALSO* PART OF THEIR MAGIC.
THEN...
...WE WON'T ...
...EVEN LET THEM *KICK*.
HEH HEH HEH! TEIKOKU ...
... WILL TRY TO GET YAMATO THROUGH.
YES, YAMATO'S ...
... POWERFUL BODY...
... SPEED ...
...AND HEIGHT ...
KCCH
... ARE ALL PERFECT ...
...FOR BLOCKING A KICK.
SKRASH

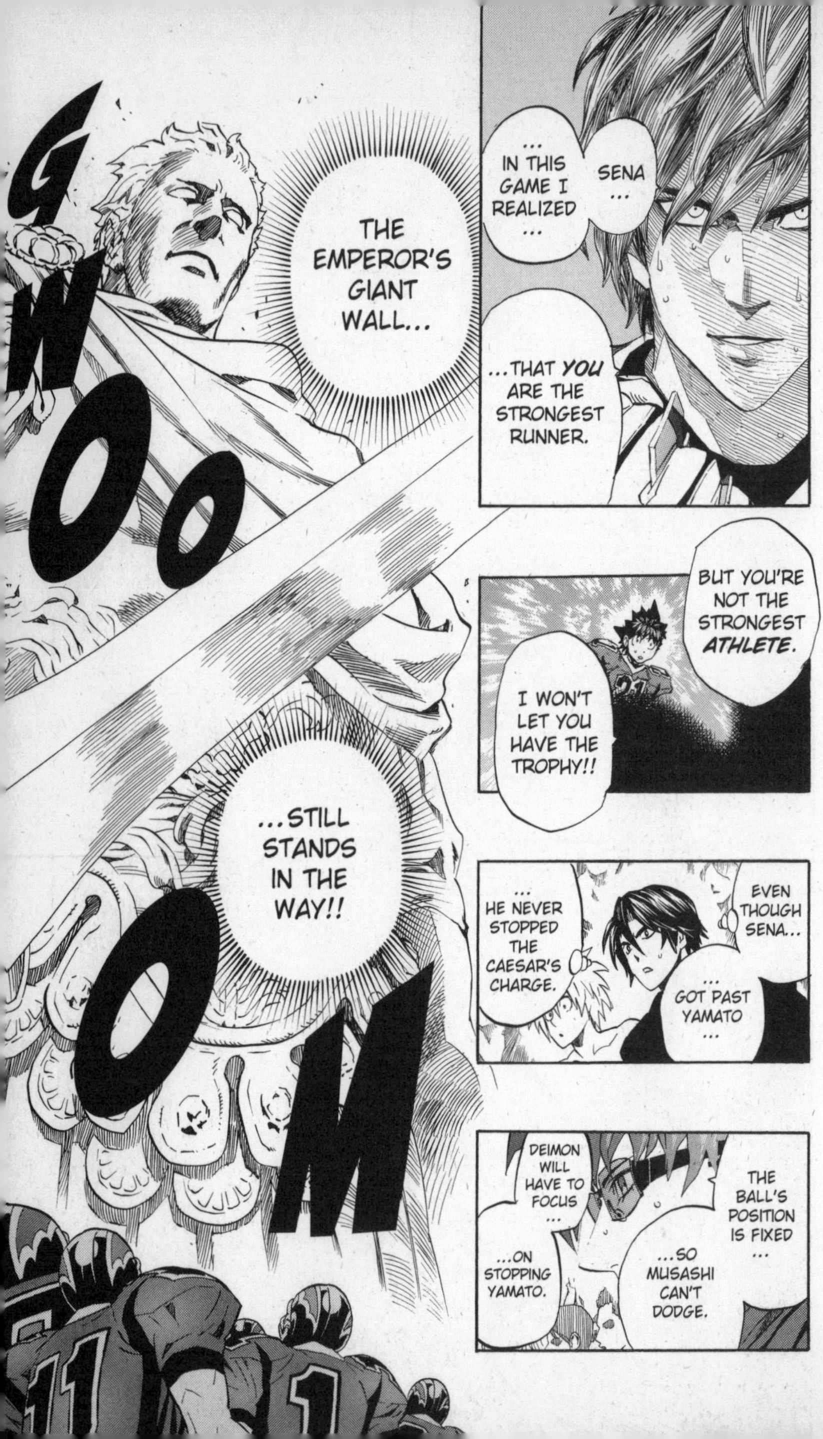
SENA ...
... IN THIS GAME I REALIZED ...
...THAT YOU ARE THE STRONGEST RUNNER.
BUT YOU'RE NOT THE STRONGEST ATHLETE.
I WON'T LET YOU HAVE THE TROPHY!!
EVEN THOUGH SENA...
... GOT PAST YAMATO ...
... HE NEVER STOPPED THE CAESAR'S CHARGE.
THE BALL'S POSITION IS FIXED ...
...SO MUSASHI CAN'T DODGE.
DEIMON WILL HAVE TO FOCUS ...
...ON STOPPING YAMATO.
THE EMPEROR'S GIANT WALL...
...STILL STANDS IN THE WAY!!
GWOOOOM

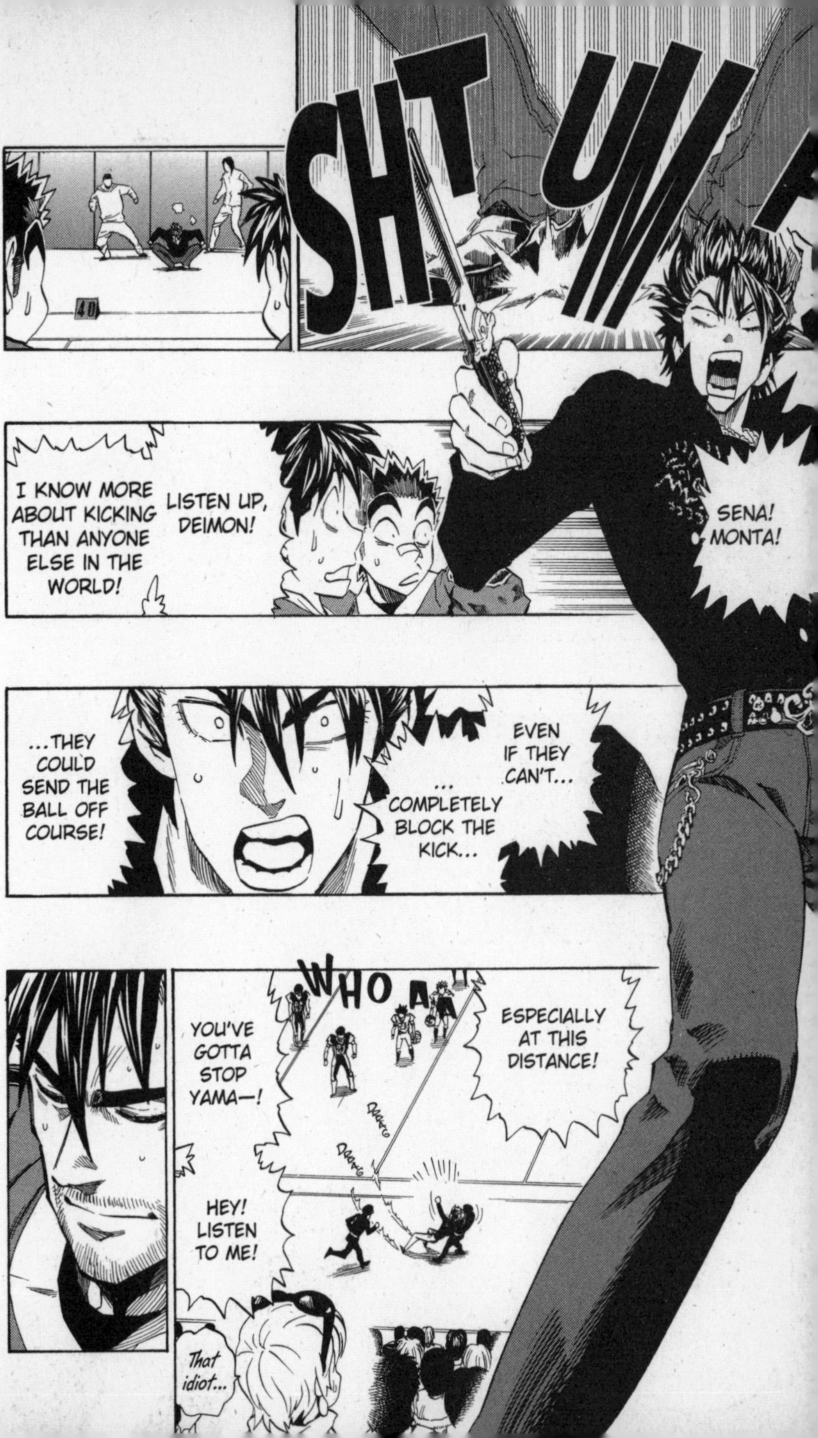
SHTUWM
SENA! MONTA!
LISTEN UP, DEIMON!
I KNOW MORE ABOUT KICKING THAN ANYONE ELSE IN THE WORLD!
EVEN IF THEY CAN'T...
...COMPLETELY BLOCK THE KICK...
...THEY COULD SEND THE BALL OFF COURSE!
WHOA
ESPECIALLY AT THIS DISTANCE!
YOU'VE GOTTA STOP YAMA—!
HEY! LISTEN TO ME!
That idiot...

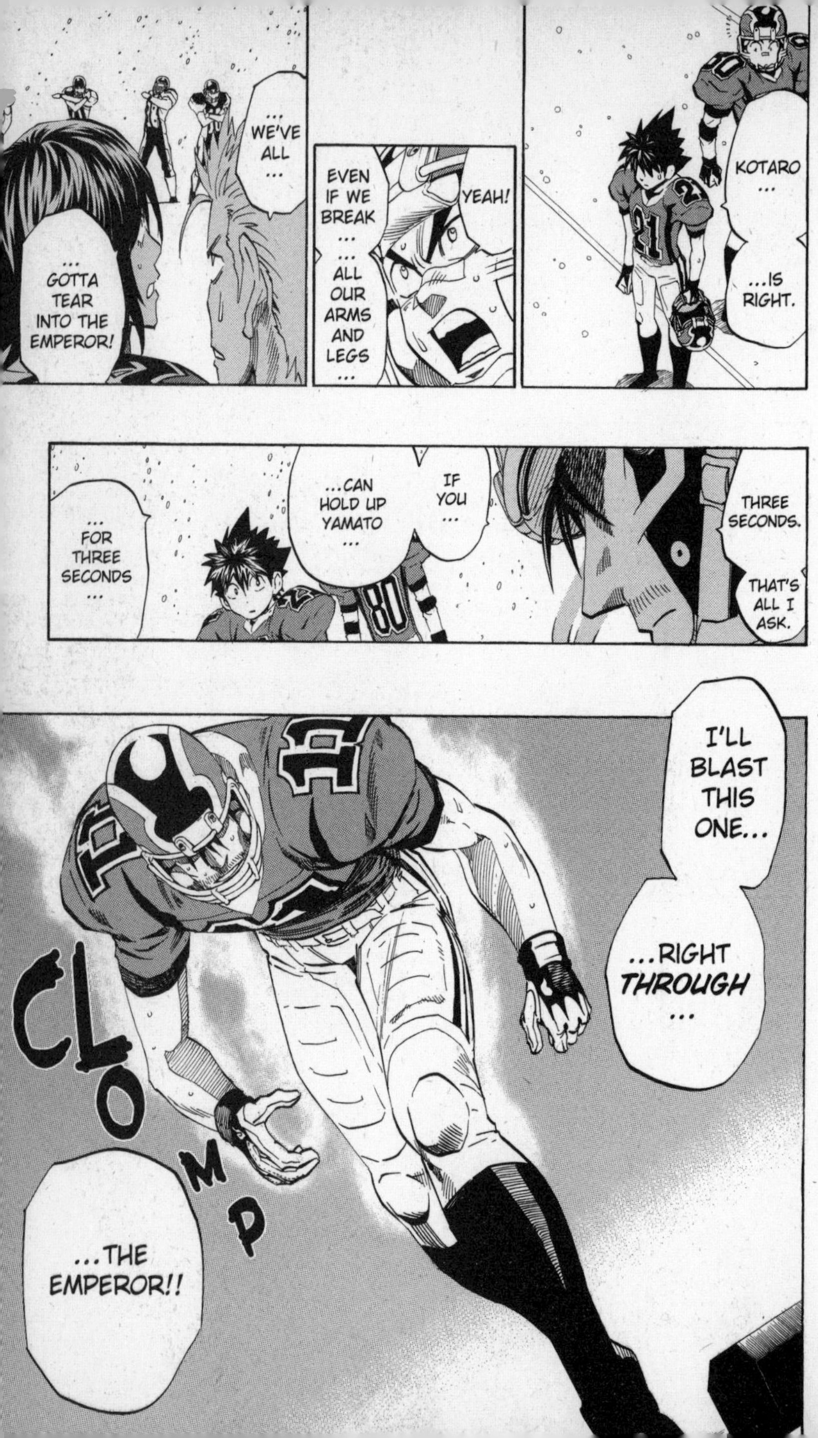
KOTARO ...
...IS RIGHT.
YEAH!
EVEN IF WE BREAK ... ... ALL OUR ARMS AND LEGS ...
... WE'VE ALL ...
... GOTTA TEAR INTO THE EMPEROR!
THREE SECONDS.
THAT'S ALL I ASK.
IF YOU ...
...CAN HOLD UP YAMATO ...
... FOR THREE SECONDS ...
I'LL BLAST THIS ONE...
...RIGHT THROUGH ...
CLOMP
...THE EMPEROR!!

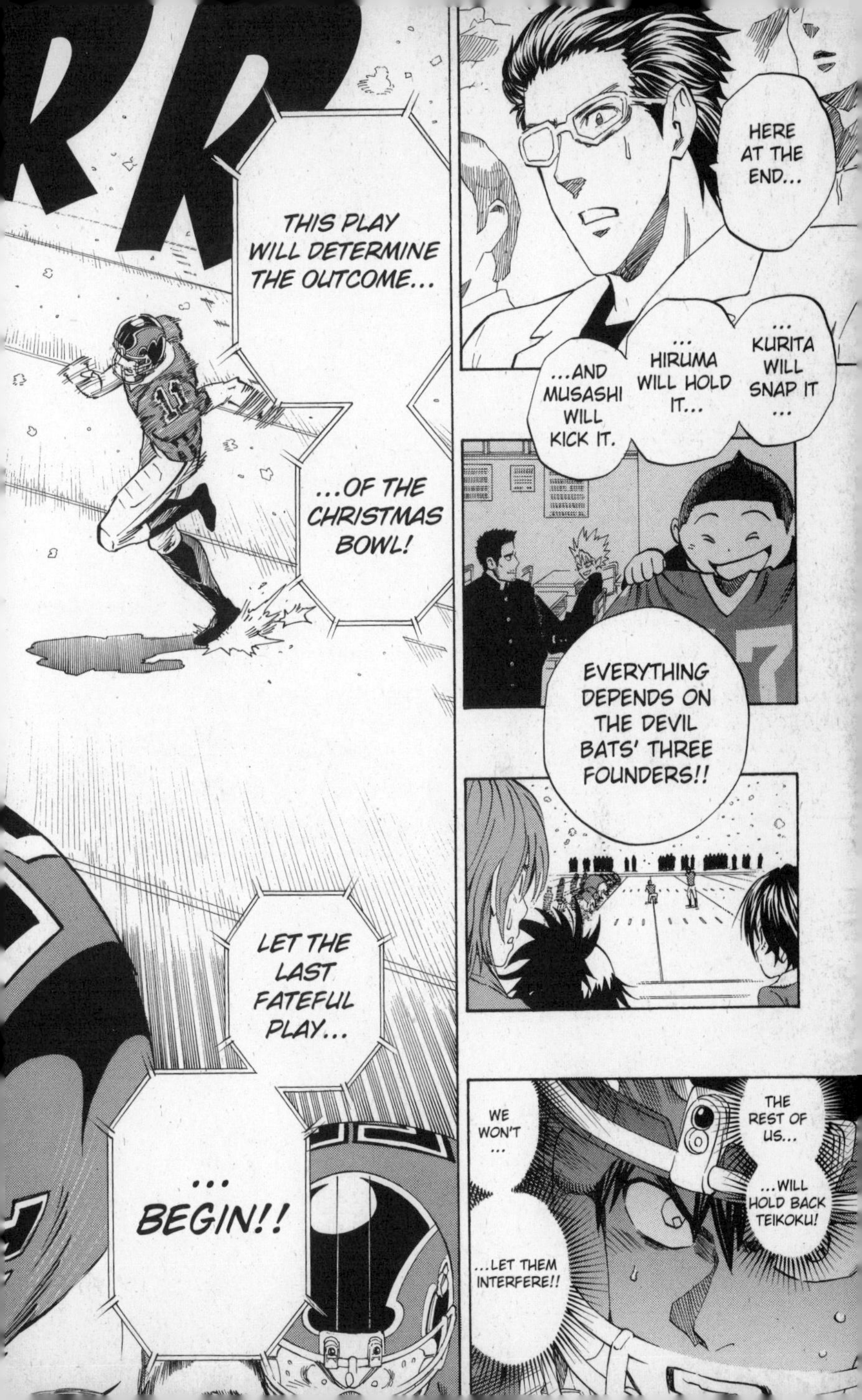
HERE AT THE END...
... KURITA WILL SNAP IT ...
... HIRUMA WILL HOLD IT...
...AND MUSASHI WILL KICK IT.
EVERYTHING DEPENDS ON THE DEVIL BATS' THREE FOUNDERS!!
THE REST OF US...
...WILL HOLD BACK TEIKOKU!
WE WON'T ...
...LET THEM INTERFERE!!
THIS PLAY WILL DETERMINE THE OUTCOME...
...OF THE CHRISTMAS BOWL!
LET THE LAST FATEFUL PLAY...
... BEGIN!!

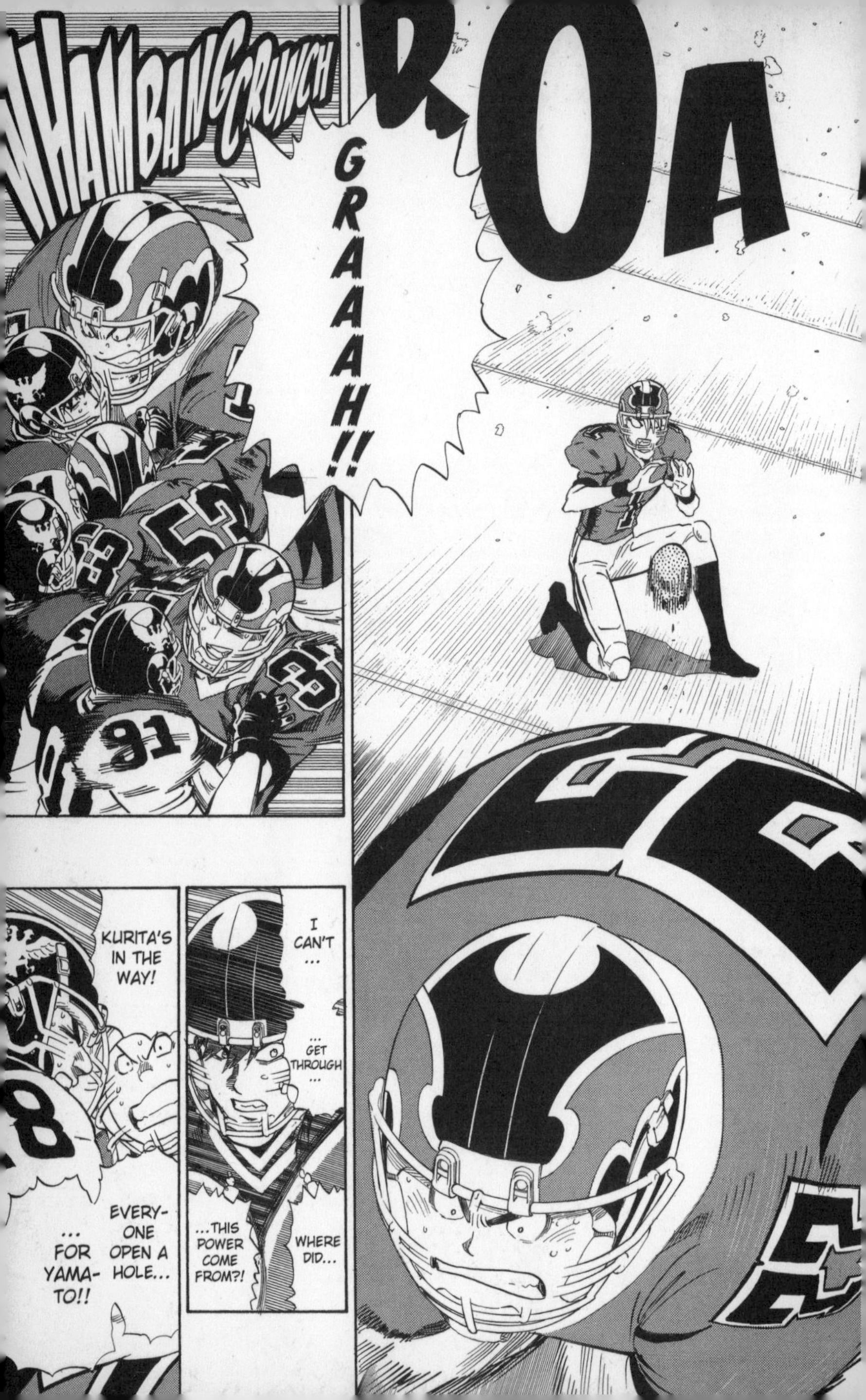
ROA
GRAAAAH!!
WHAMBANGCRUNCH
I CAN'T ...
... GET THROUGH ...
WHERE DID...
...THIS POWER COME FROM?!
KURITA'S IN THE WAY!
EVERY-ONE OPEN A HOLE...
... FOR YAMA-TO!!

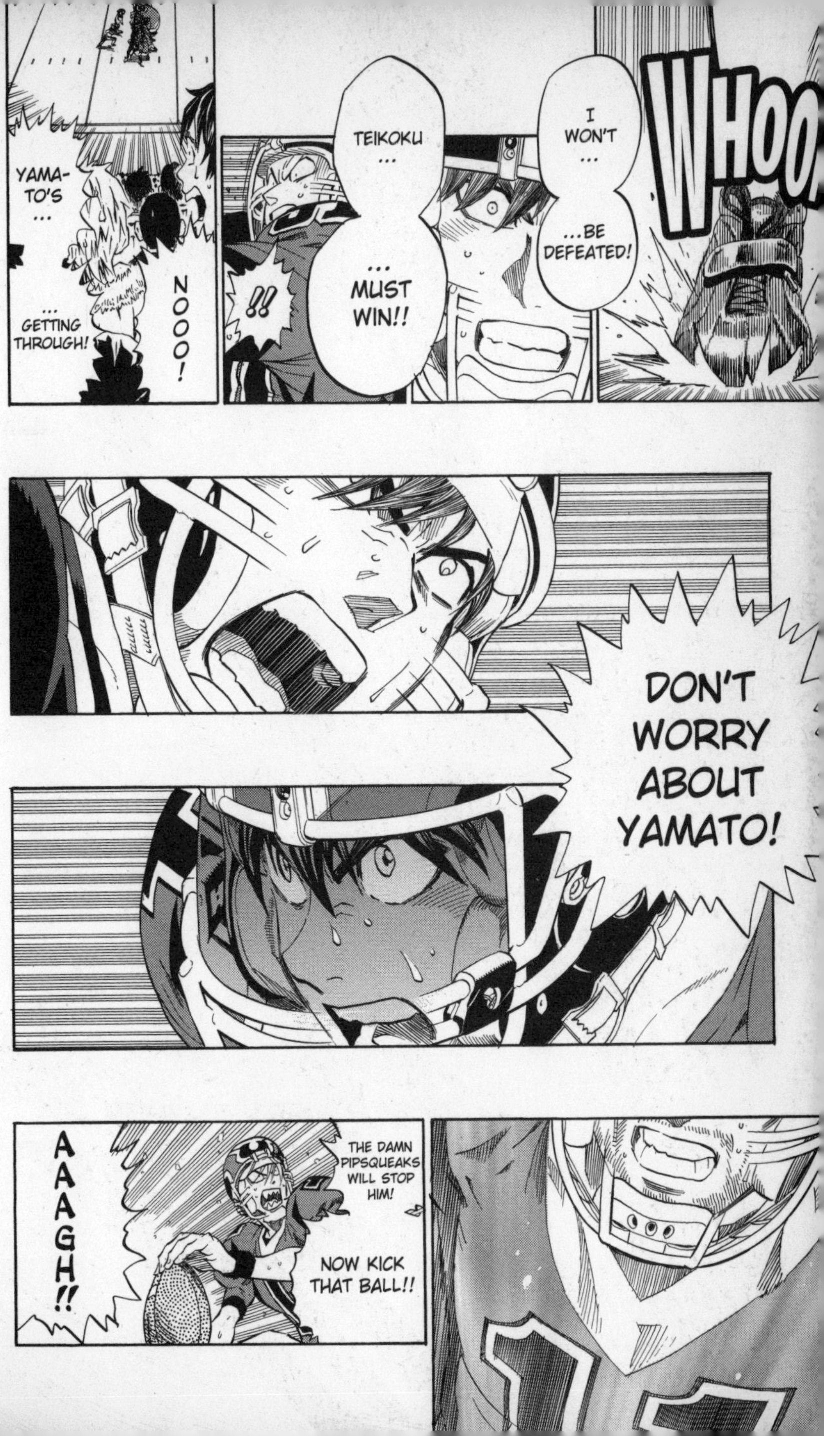
WHOO
I WON'T ...
...BE DEFEATED!
TEIKOKU ...
... MUST WIN!!
!!
YAMA-TO'S ...
NOOO!
... GETTING THROUGH!
DON'T WORRY ABOUT YAMATO!
THE DAMN PIPSQUEAKS WILL STOP HIM!
NOW KICK THAT BALL!!
AAAGH!!

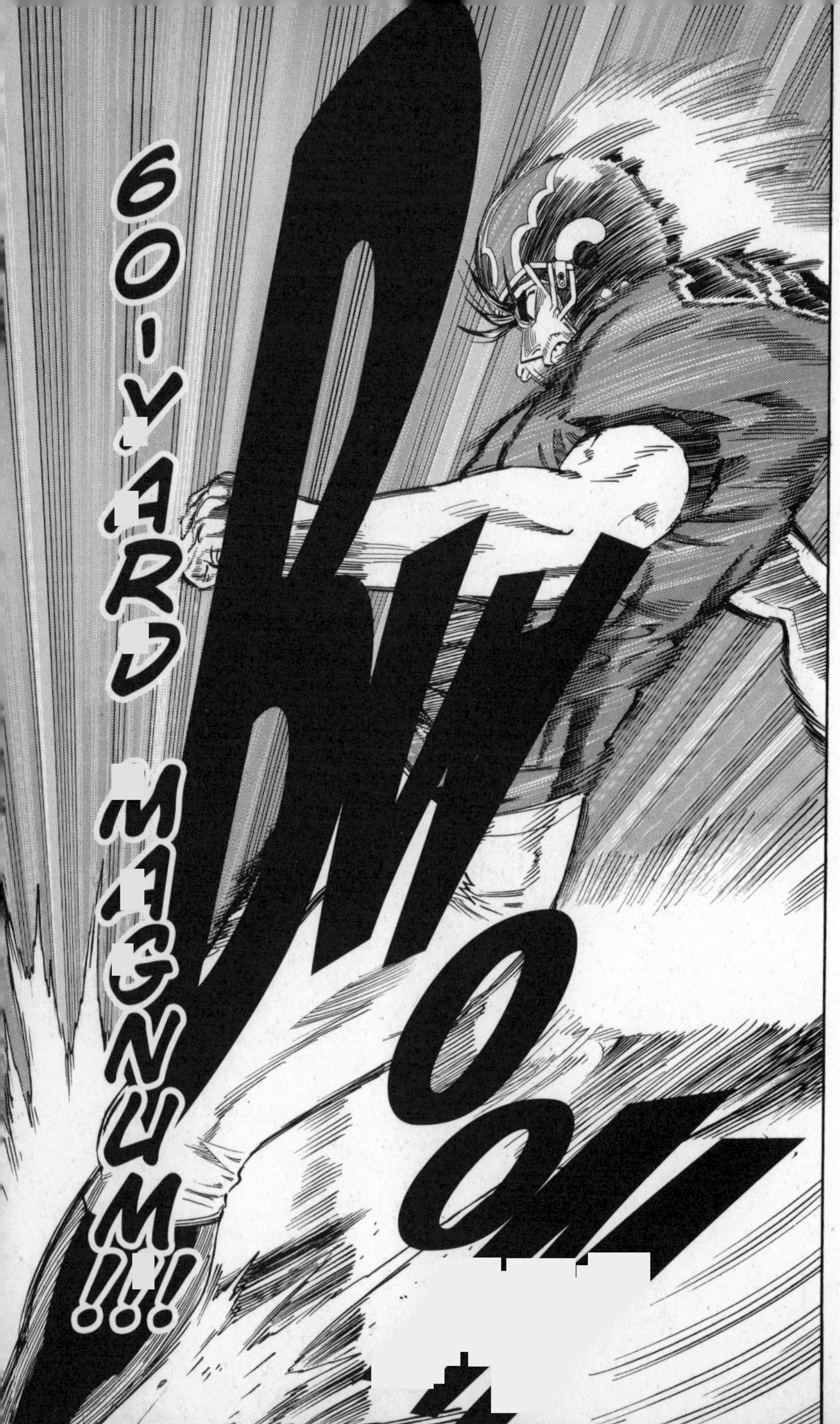
60-YARD MAGNUM!!!

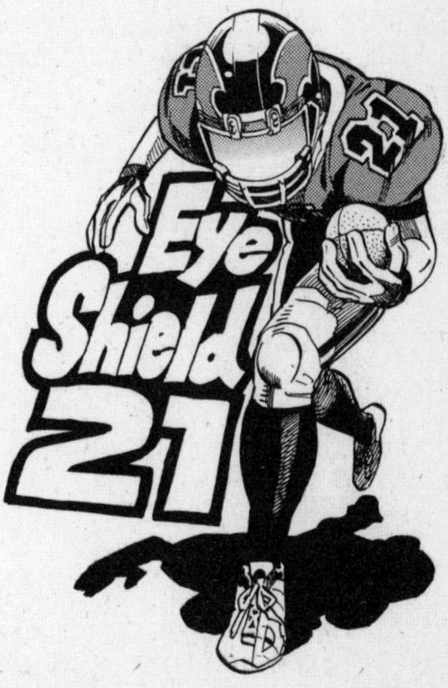
Eye Shield 21

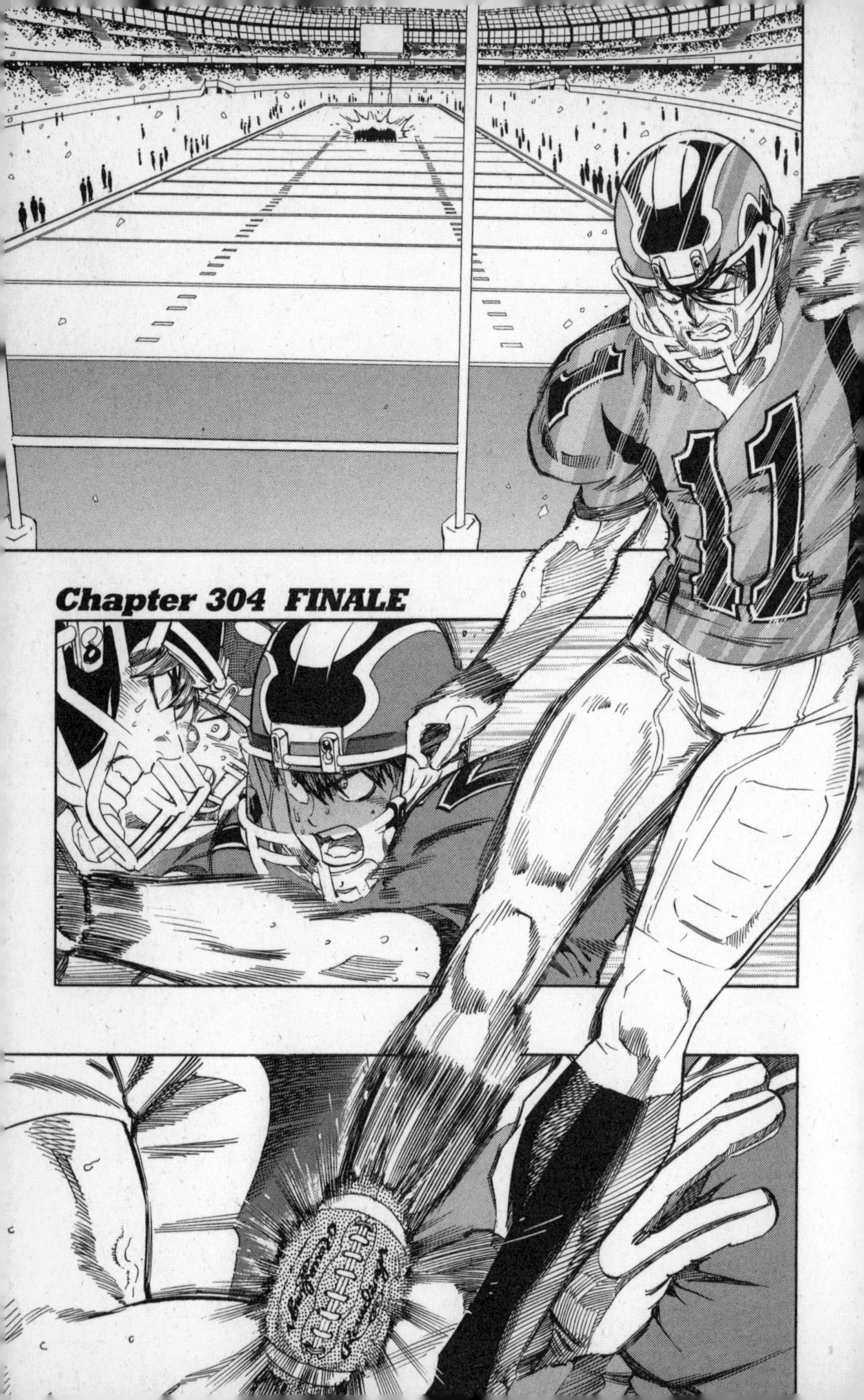
Chapter 304 FINALE

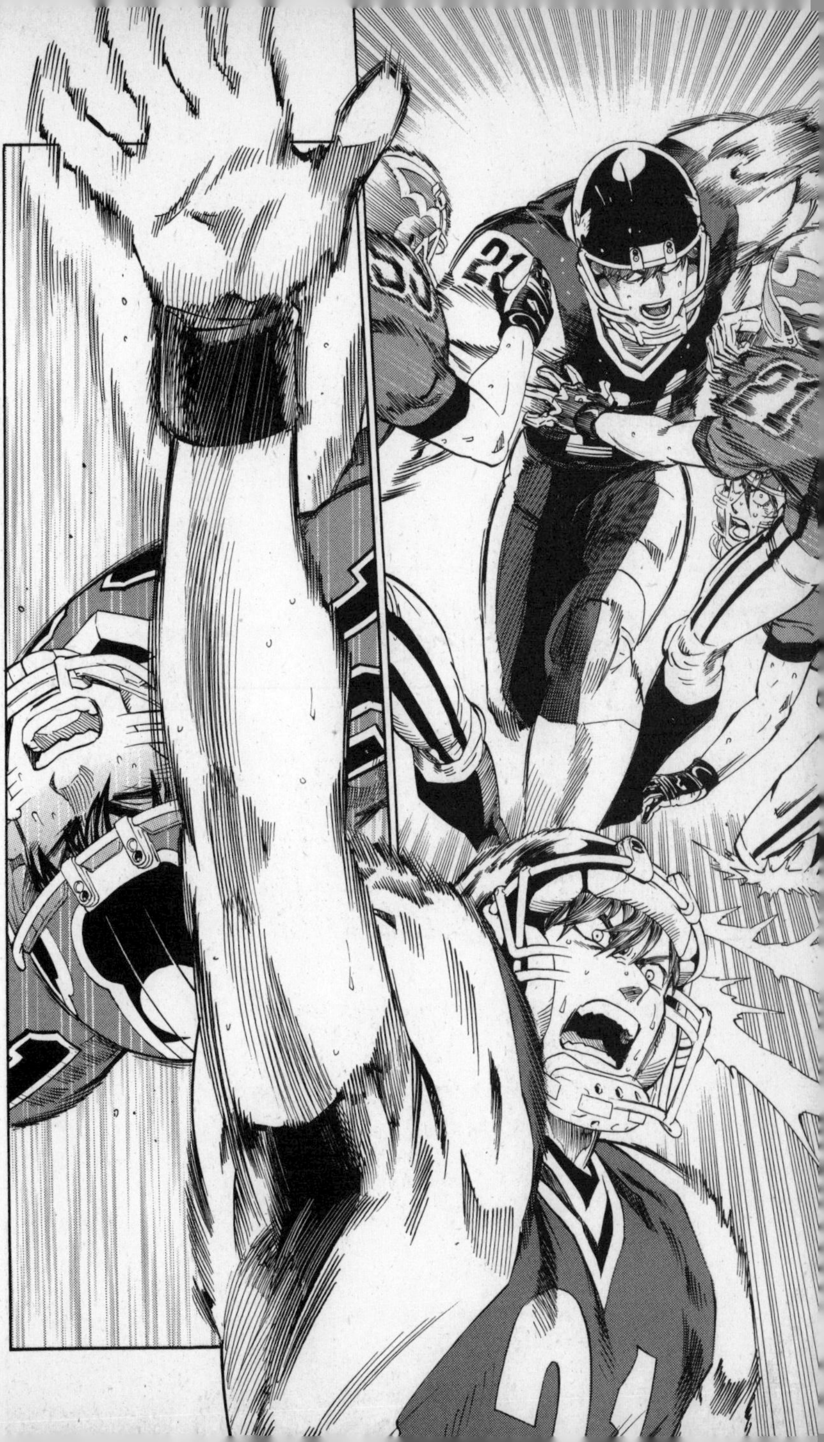

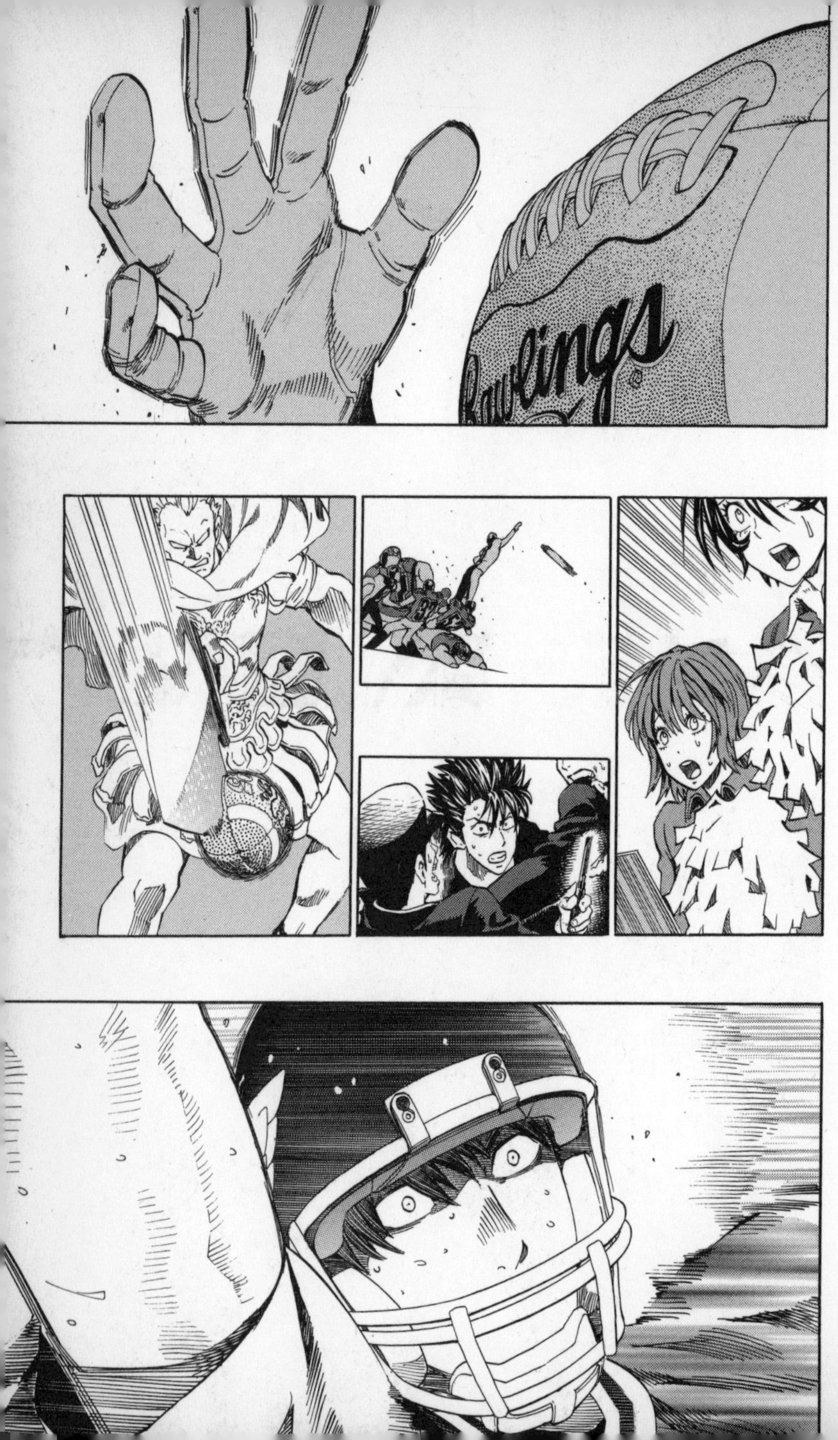
Rawlings

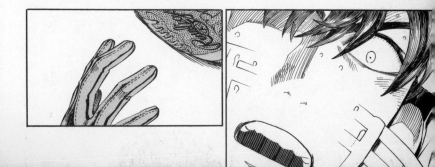

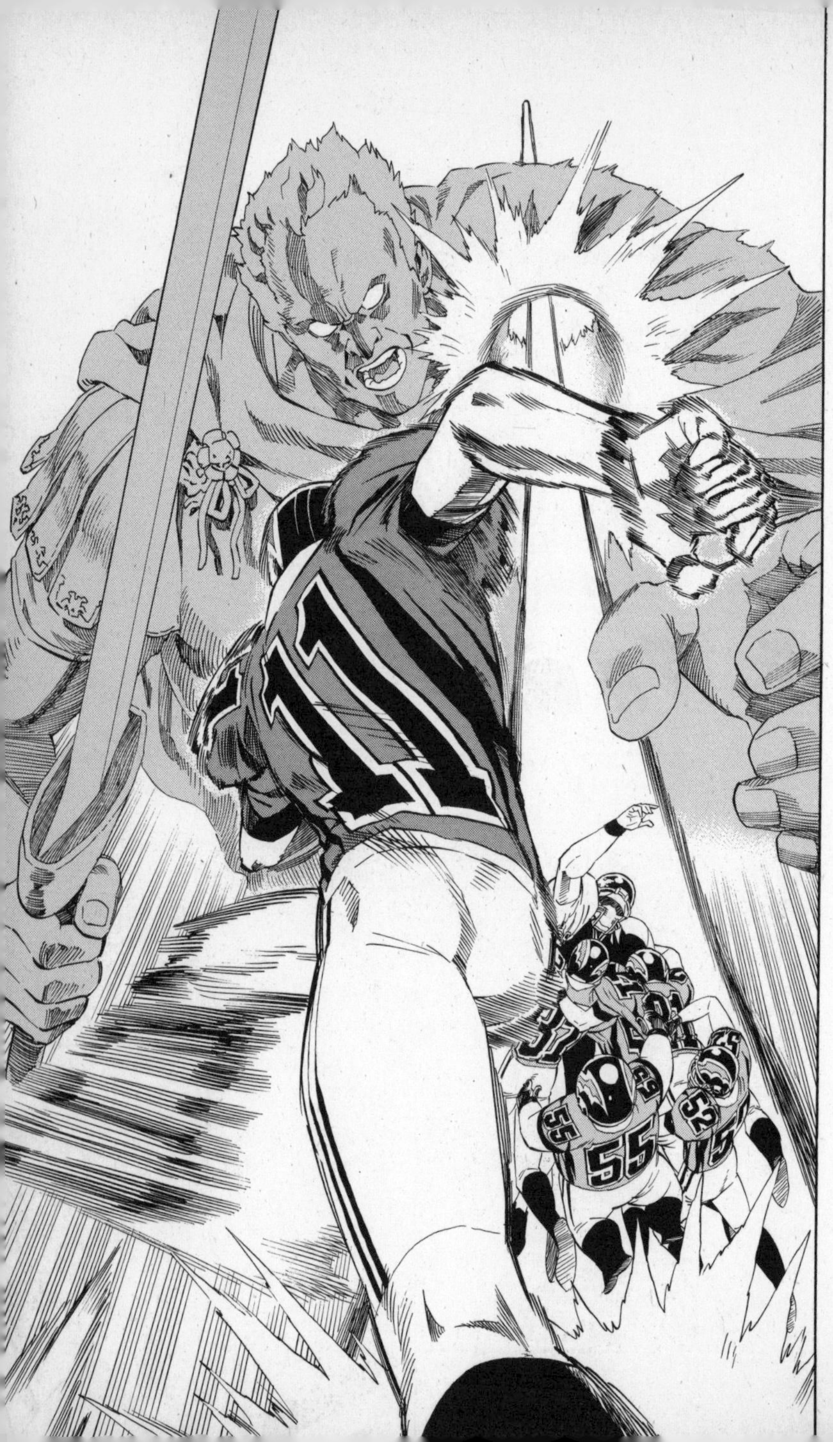

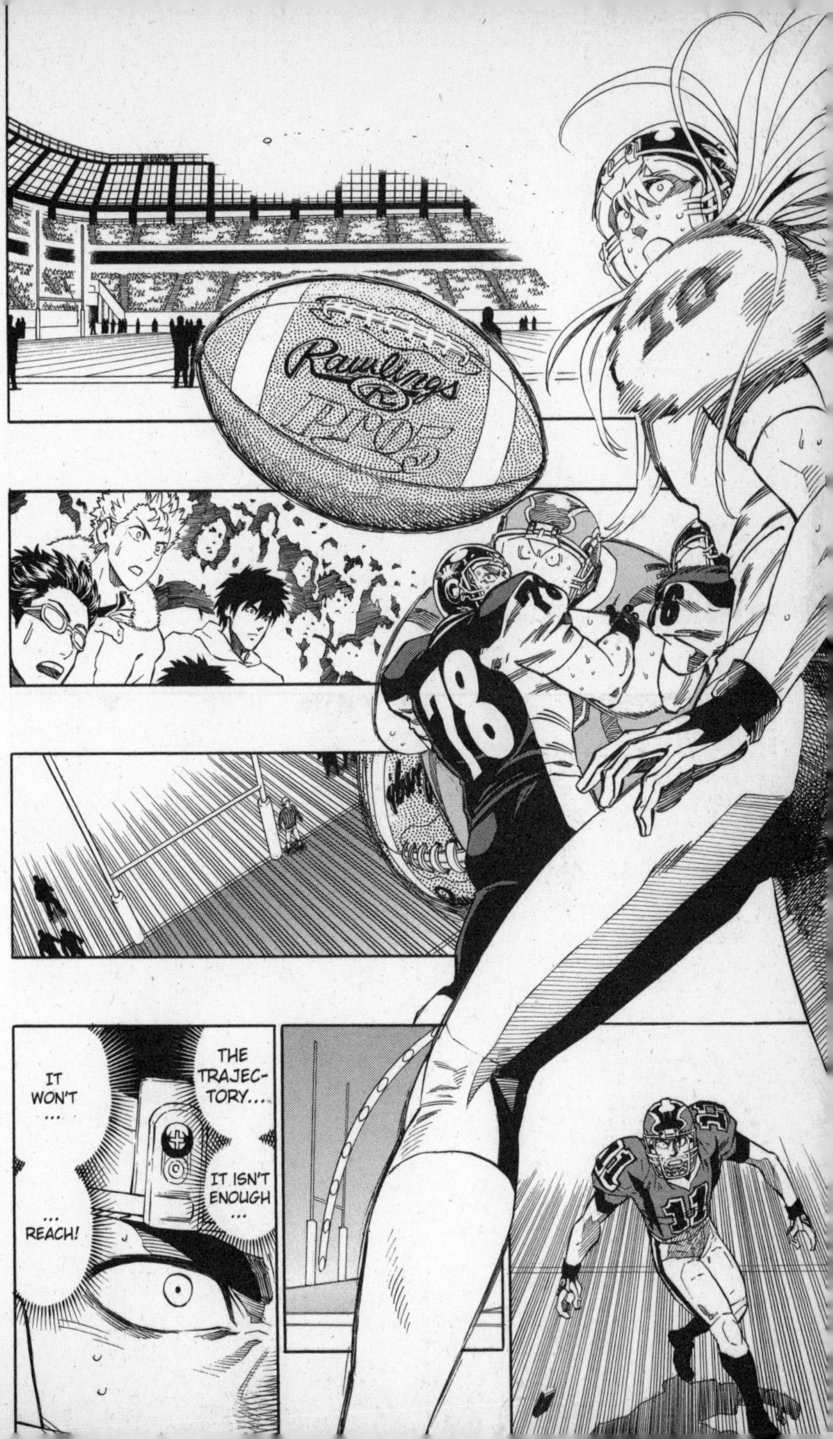
THE TRAJECTORY...
IT WON'T ...
IT ISN'T ENOUGH ...
... REACH!

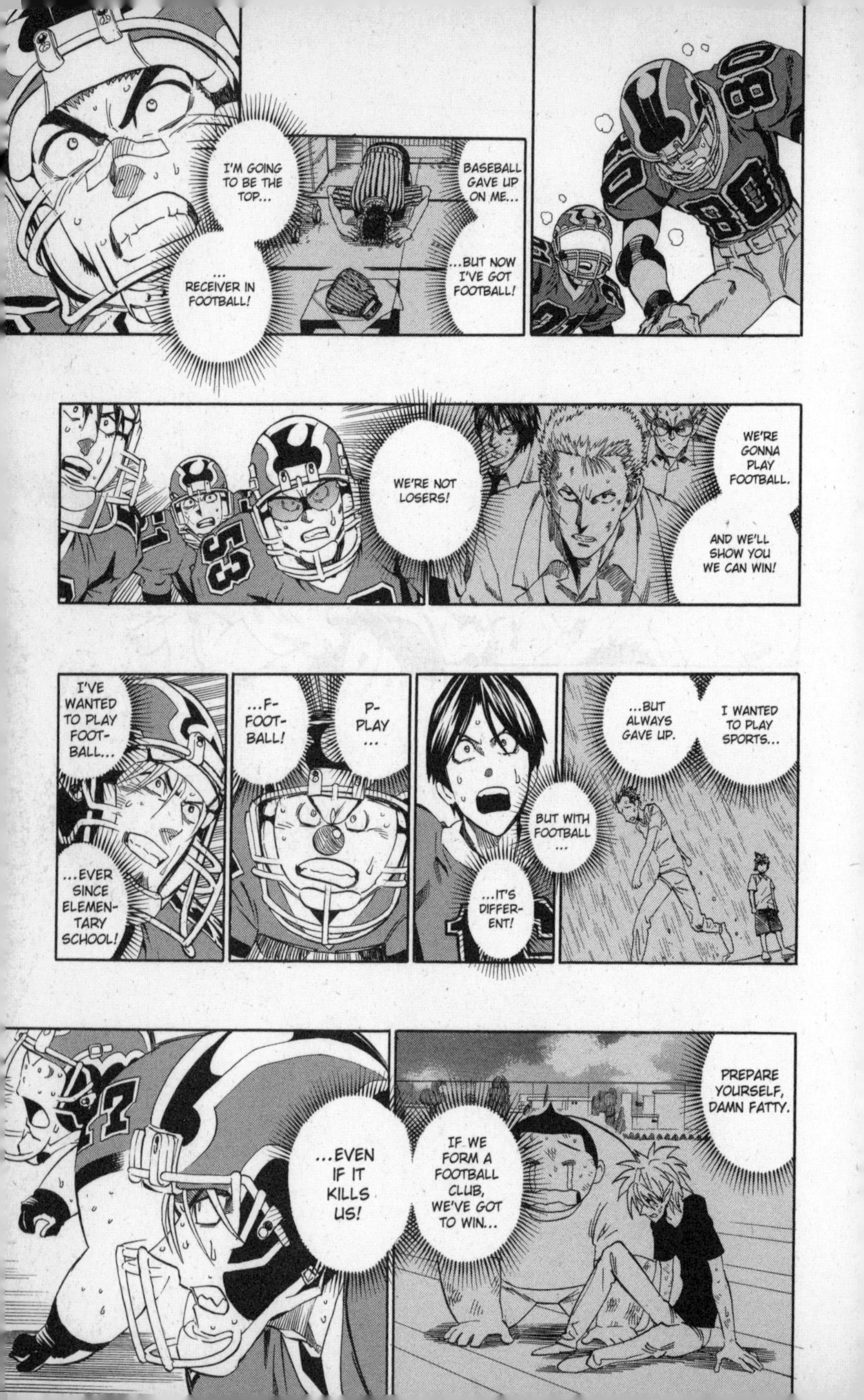
BASEBALL GAVE UP ON ME...
...BUT NOW I'VE GOT FOOTBALL!
I'M GOING TO BE THE TOP...
...RECEIVER IN FOOTBALL!
WE'RE GONNA PLAY FOOTBALL.
AND WE'LL SHOW YOU WE CAN WIN!
WE'RE NOT LOSERS!
I WANTED TO PLAY SPORTS...
...BUT ALWAYS GAVE UP.
BUT WITH FOOTBALL...
...IT'S DIFFERENT!
P-PLAY...
...F-FOOT-BALL!
I'VE WANTED TO PLAY FOOT-BALL...
...EVER SINCE ELEMENTARY SCHOOL!
PREPARE YOURSELF, DAMN FATTY.
IF WE FORM A FOOTBALL CLUB, WE'VE GOT TO WIN...
...EVEN IF IT KILLS US!

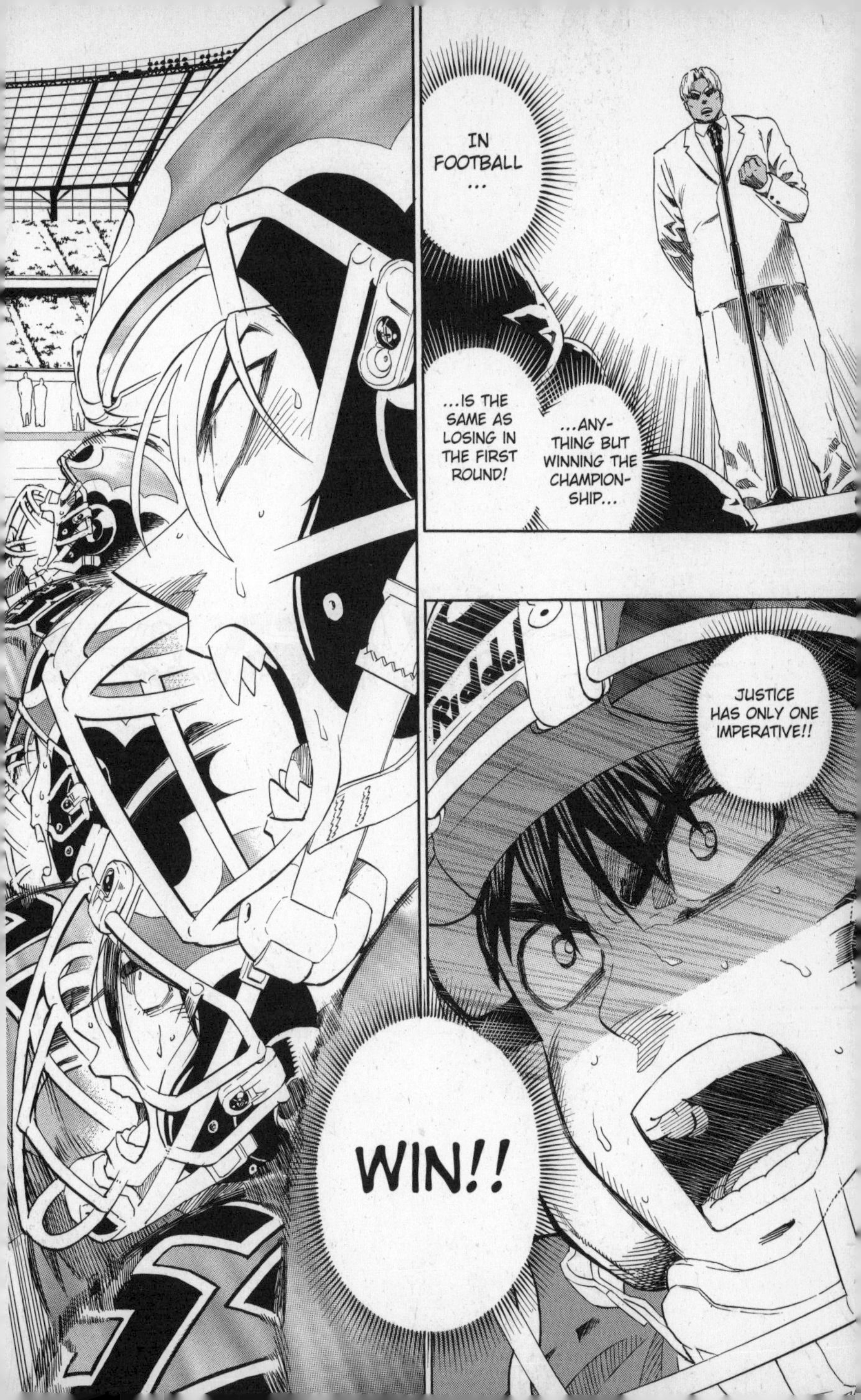
IN FOOTBALL ...
...ANYTHING BUT WINNING THE CHAMPIONSHIP...
...IS THE SAME AS LOSING IN THE FIRST ROUND!
JUSTICE HAS ONLY ONE IMPERATIVE!!
WIN!!

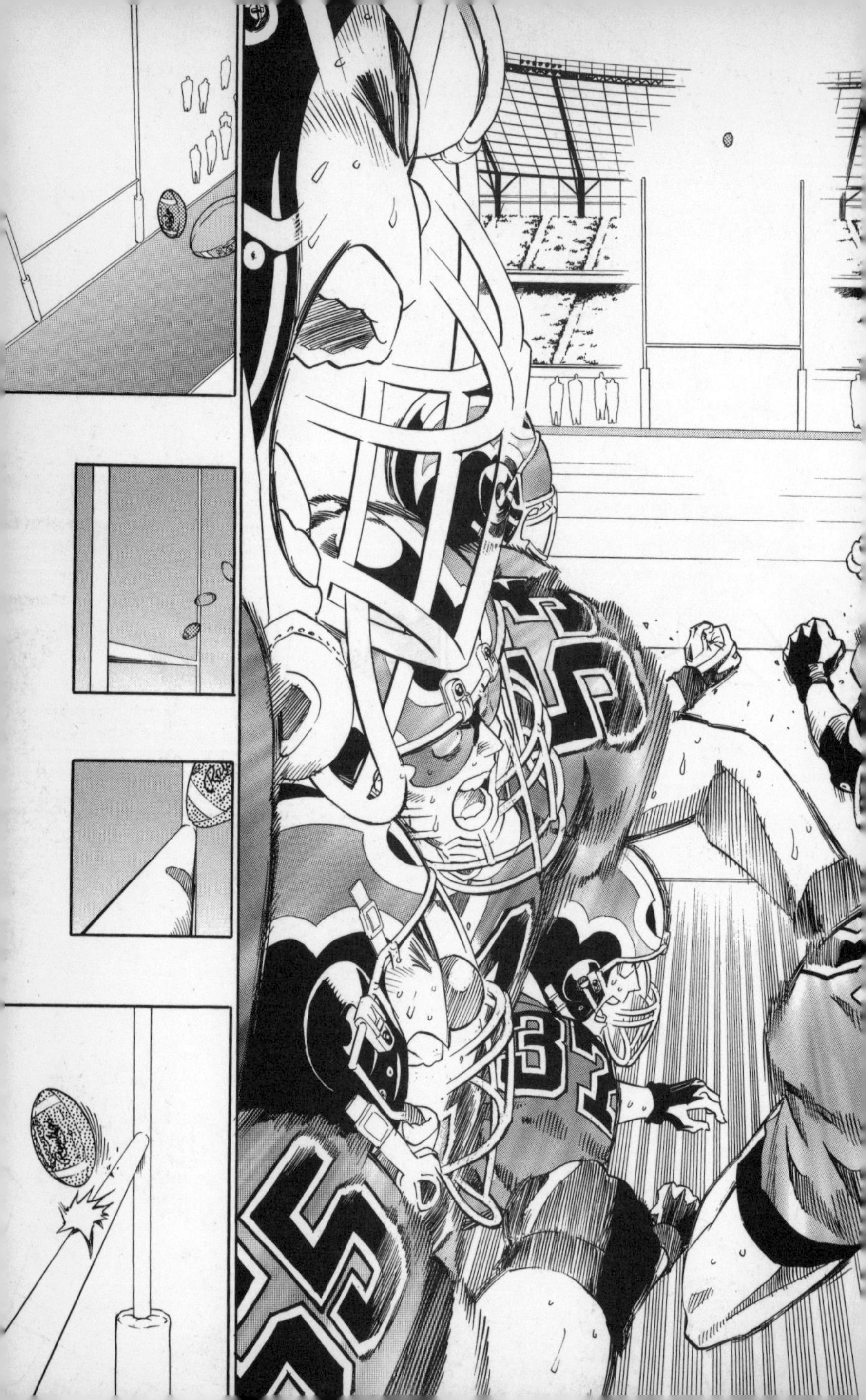

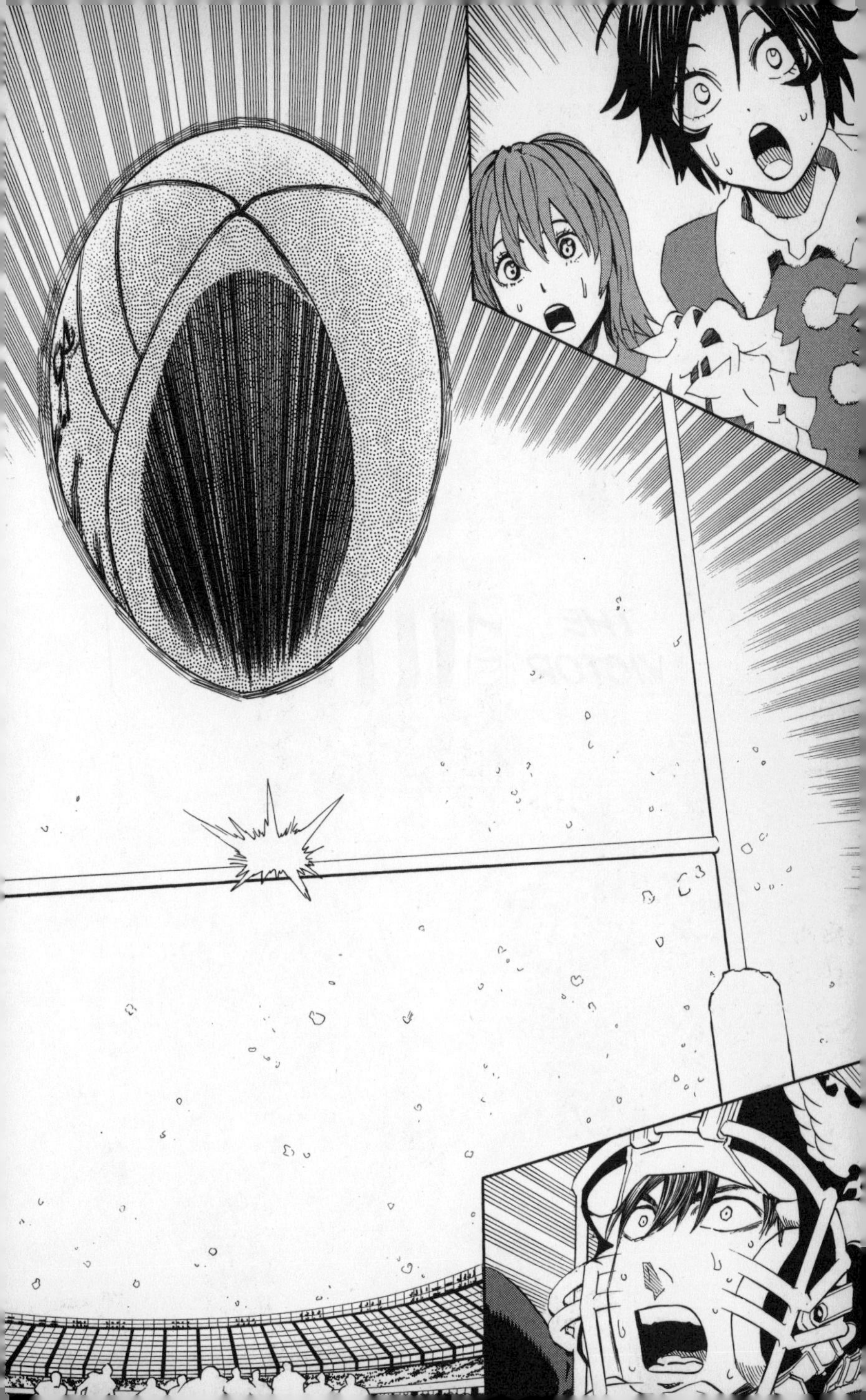

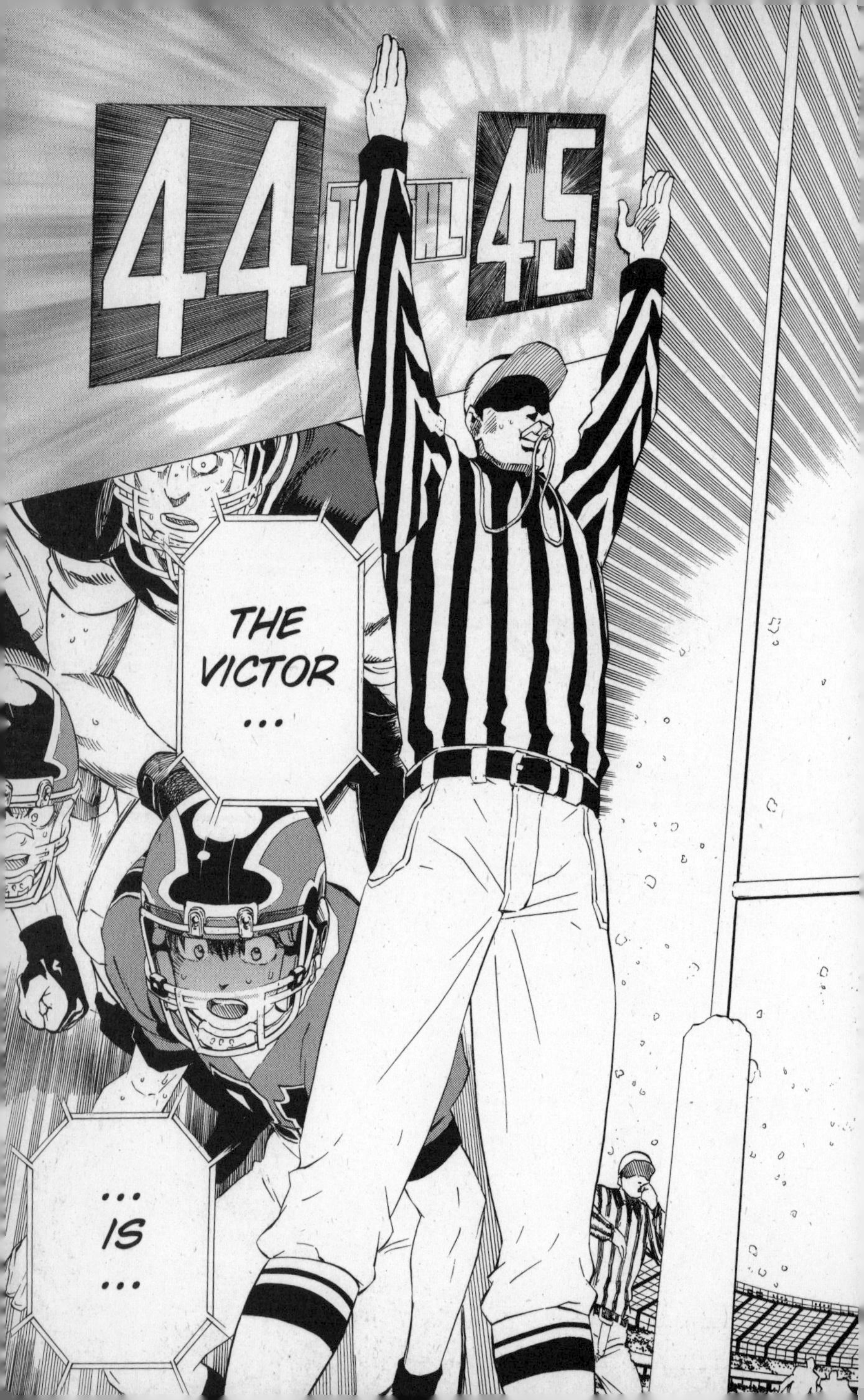
44
45
THE VICTOR ...
... IS ...

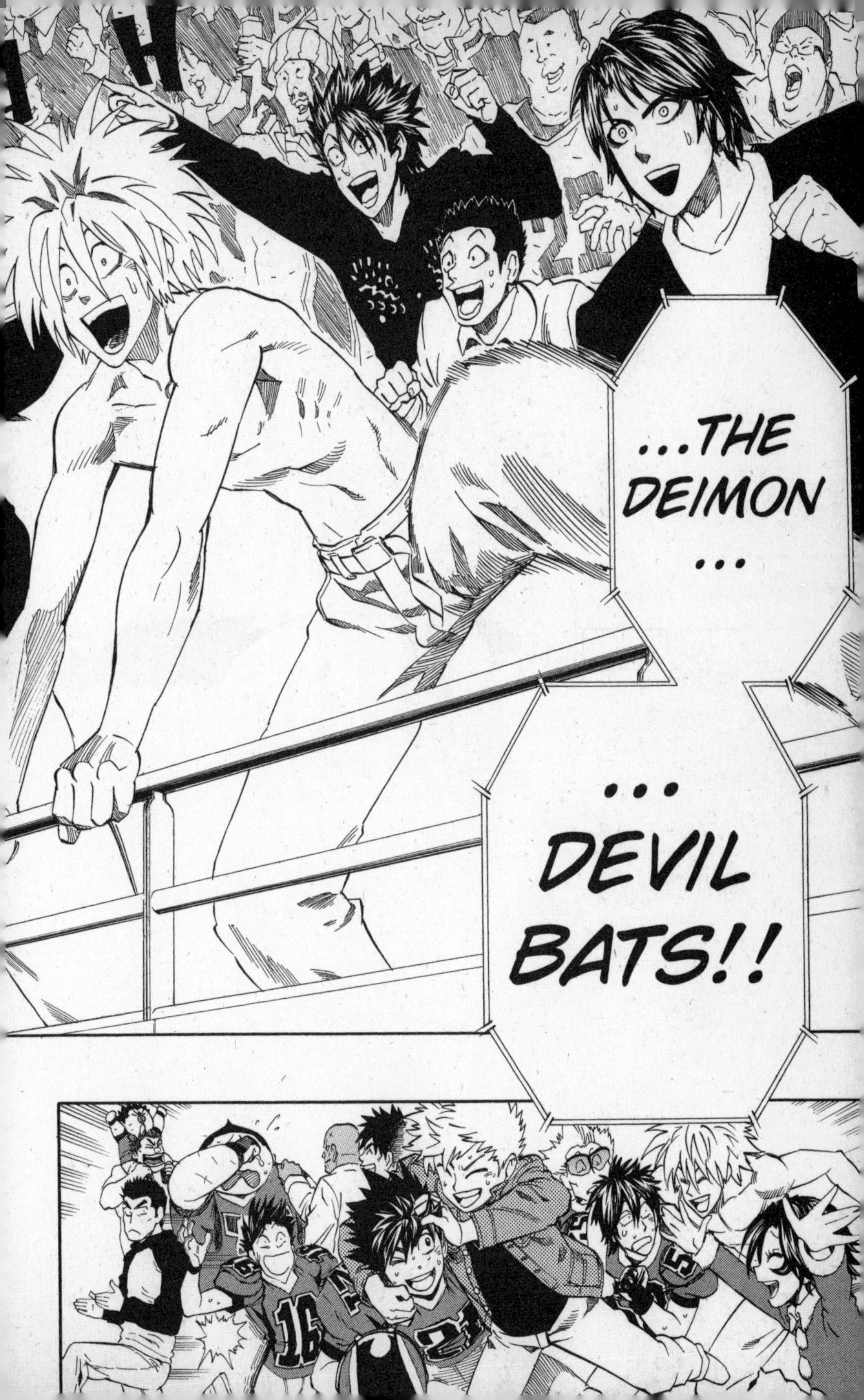
H
...THE DEIMON ...
... DEVIL BATS!!

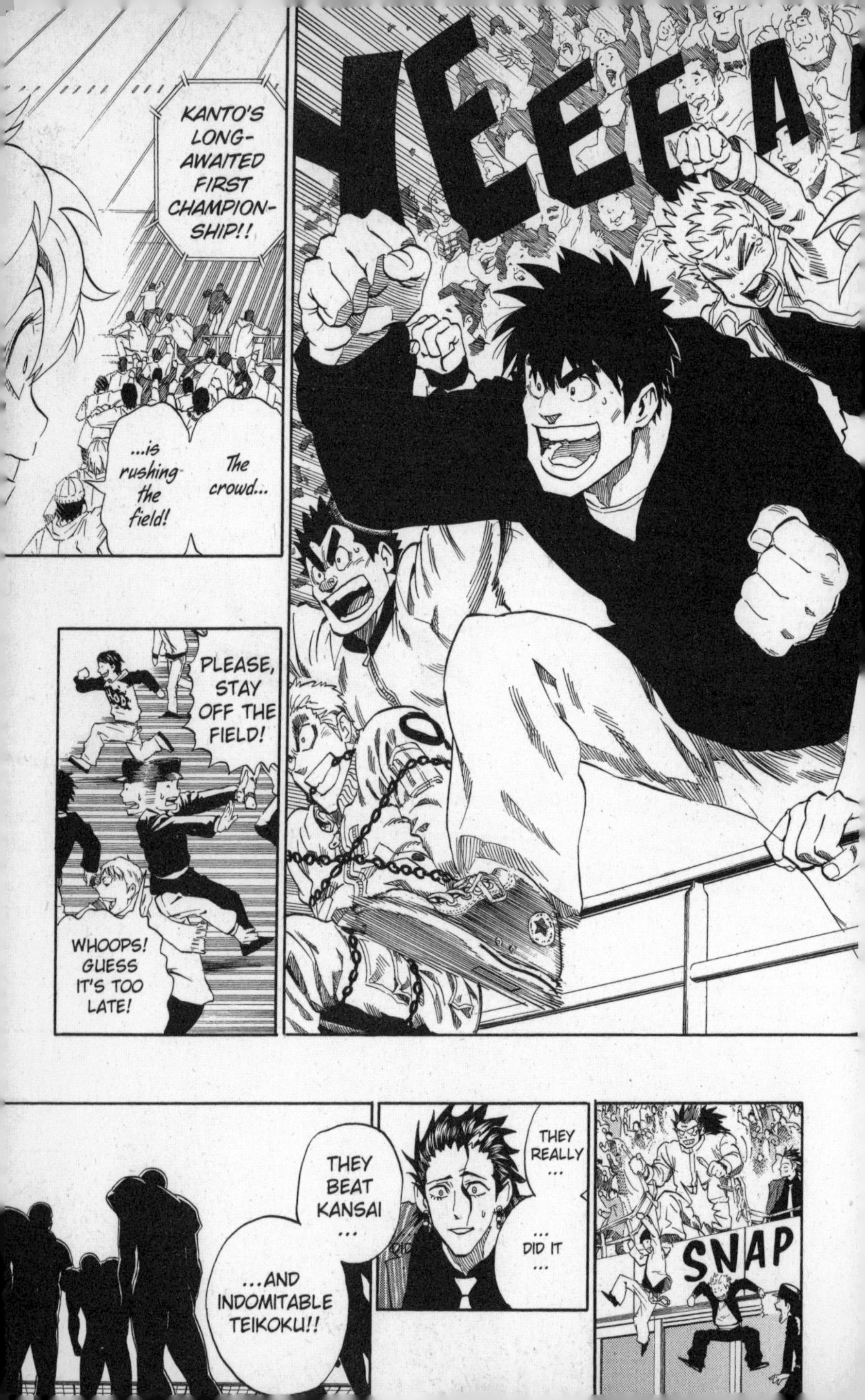
YEEA
KANTO'S LONG-AWAITED FIRST CHAMPIONSHIP!!
The crowd...
...is rushing the field!
PLEASE, STAY OFF THE FIELD!
WHOOPS! GUESS IT'S TOO LATE!
SNAP
THEY REALLY ...
... DID IT ...
THEY BEAT KANSAI ...
...AND INDOMITABLE TEIKOKU!!

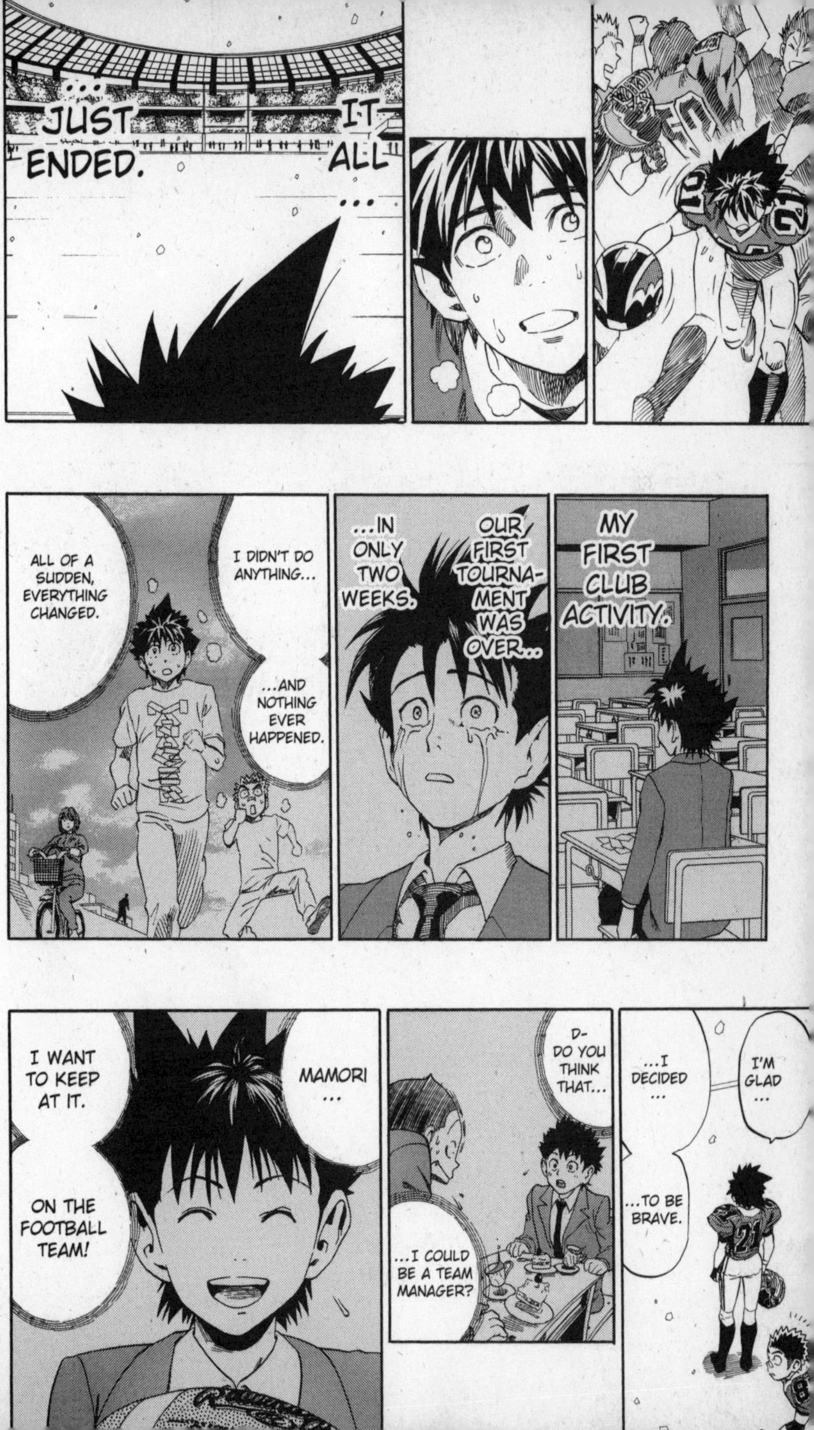
IT ALL...
...JUST ENDED.
MY FIRST CLUB ACTIVITY.
OUR FIRST TOURNAMENT WAS OVER...
...IN ONLY TWO WEEKS.
I DIDN'T DO ANYTHING...
...AND NOTHING EVER HAPPENED.
ALL OF A SUDDEN, EVERYTHING CHANGED.
I'M GLAD...
...I DECIDED...
...TO BE BRAVE.
D-DO YOU THINK THAT...
...I COULD BE A TEAM MANAGER?
MAMORI...
I WANT TO KEEP AT IT.
ON THE FOOTBALL TEAM!

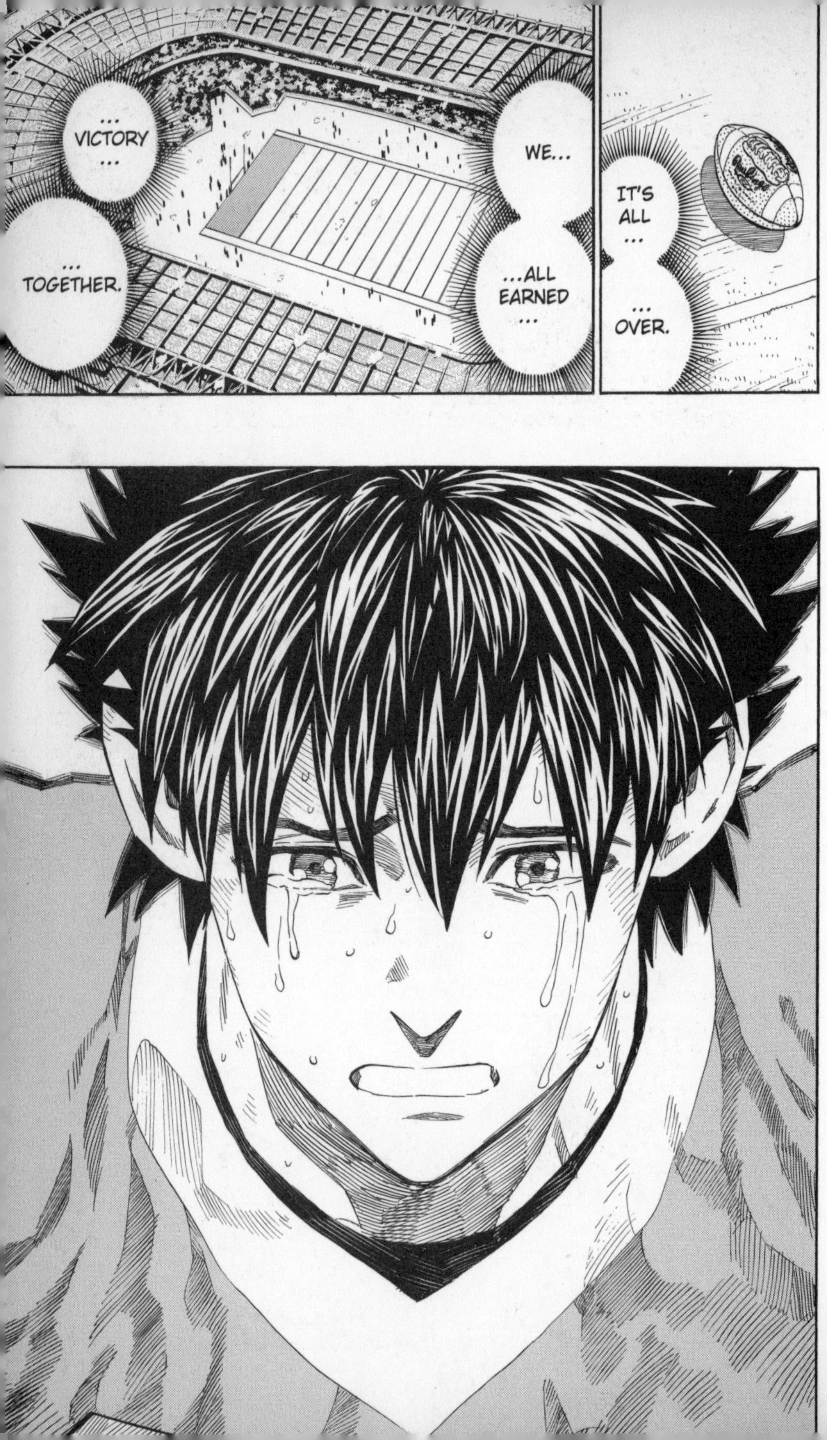
IT'S ALL ...
... OVER.
WE...
...ALL EARNED ...
... VICTORY ...
... TOGETHER.

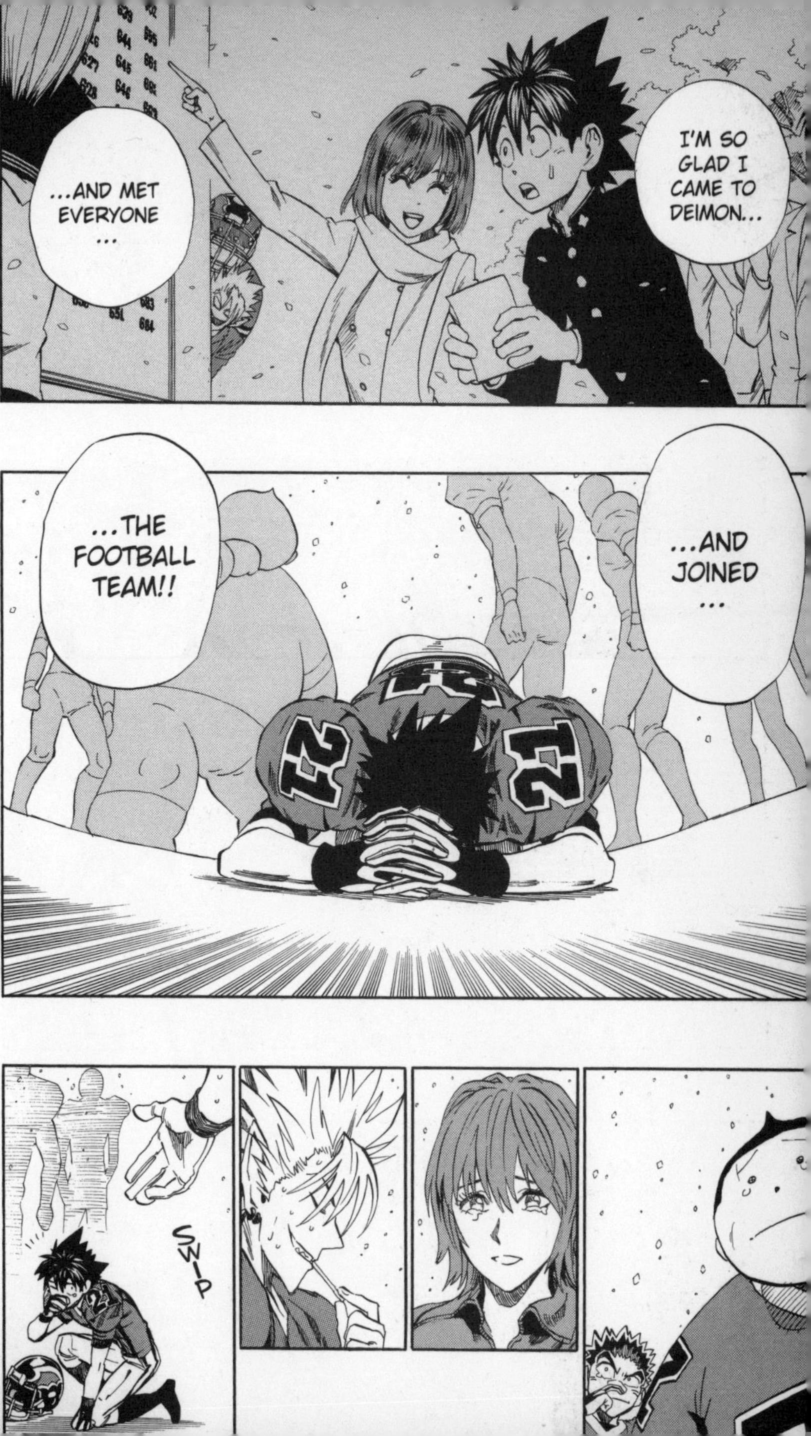
I'M SO GLAD I CAME TO DEIMON...
...AND MET EVERYONE ...
...AND JOINED ...
...THE FOOTBALL TEAM!!
SWIP

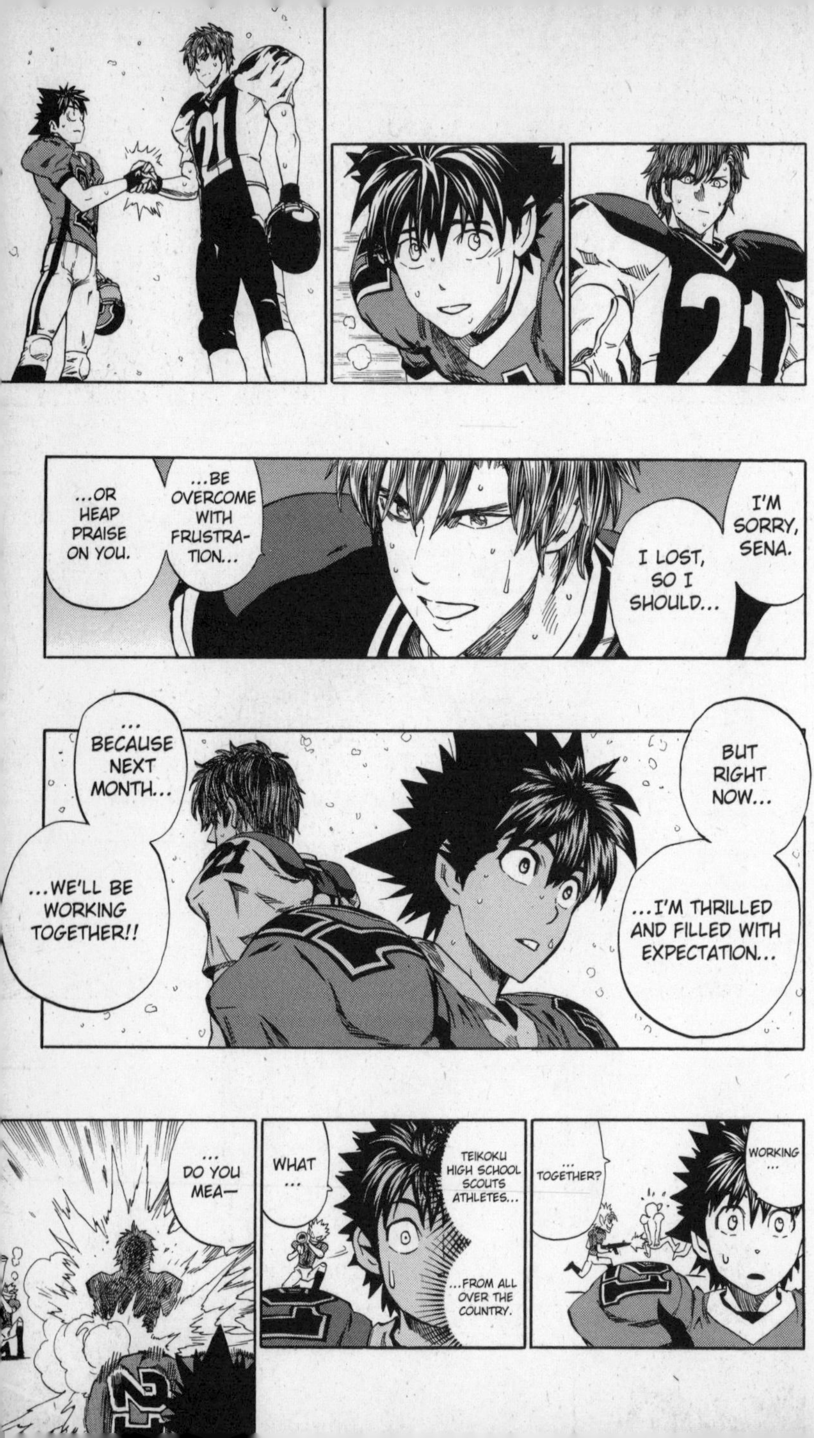
I'M SORRY, SENA.
I LOST, SO I SHOULD...
...BE OVERCOME WITH FRUSTRATION...
...OR HEAP PRAISE ON YOU.
BUT RIGHT NOW...
...I'M THRILLED AND FILLED WITH EXPECTATION...
...BECAUSE NEXT MONTH...
...WE'LL BE WORKING TOGETHER!!
WORKING...
...TOGETHER?
TEIKOKU HIGH SCHOOL SCOUTS ATHLETES...
...FROM ALL OVER THE COUNTRY.
WHAT...
...DO YOU MEA—

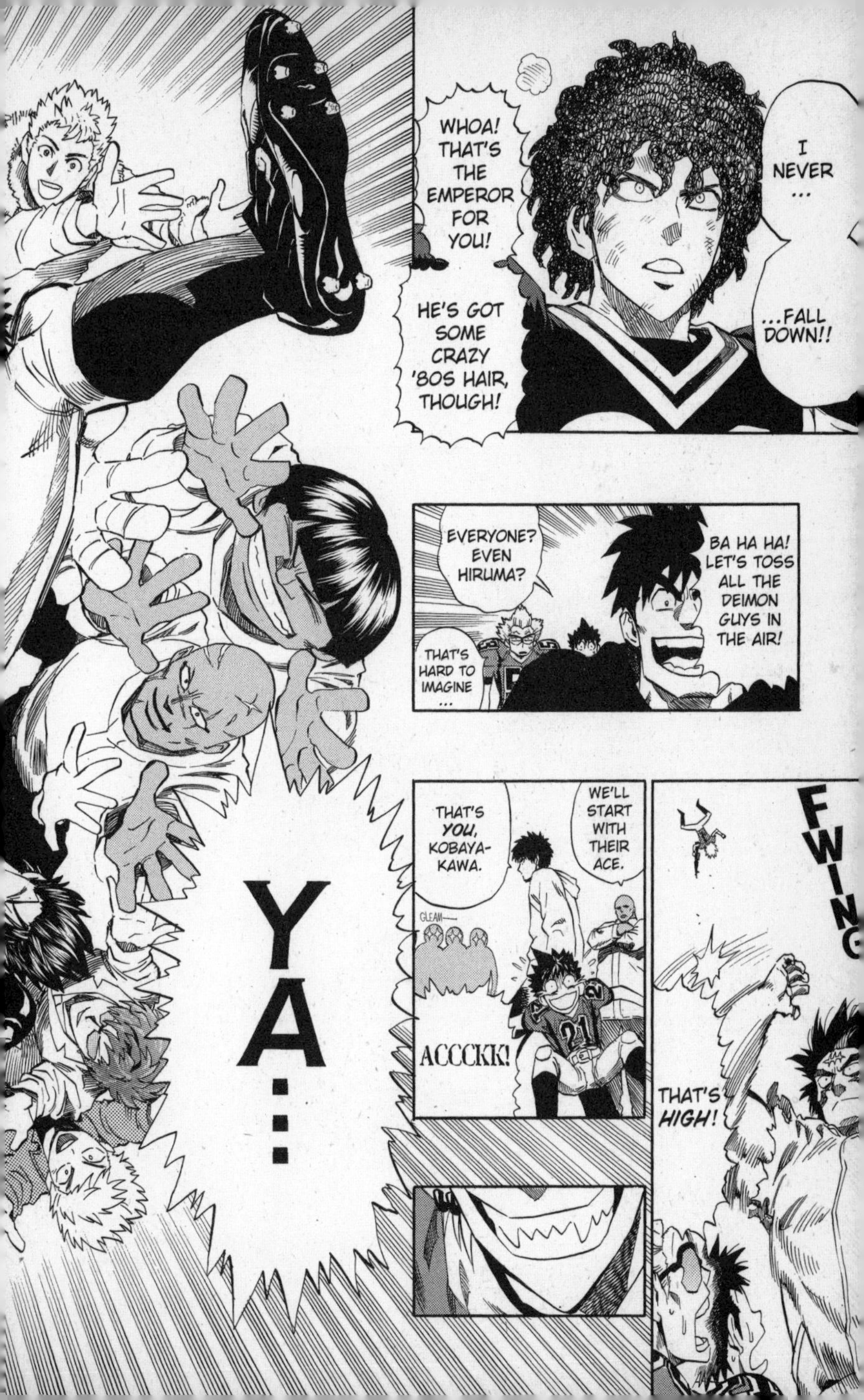
I NEVER ...
...FALL DOWN!!
WHOA! THAT'S THE EMPEROR FOR YOU!
HE'S GOT SOME CRAZY '80S HAIR, THOUGH!
BA HA HA! LET'S TOSS ALL THE DEIMON GUYS IN THE AIR!
EVERYONE? EVEN HIRUMA?
THAT'S HARD TO IMAGINE ...
FWING
THAT'S *HIGH*!
WE'LL START WITH THEIR ACE.
THAT'S *YOU*, KOBAYA-KAWA.
GLEAM—
ACCCKK!
YA...

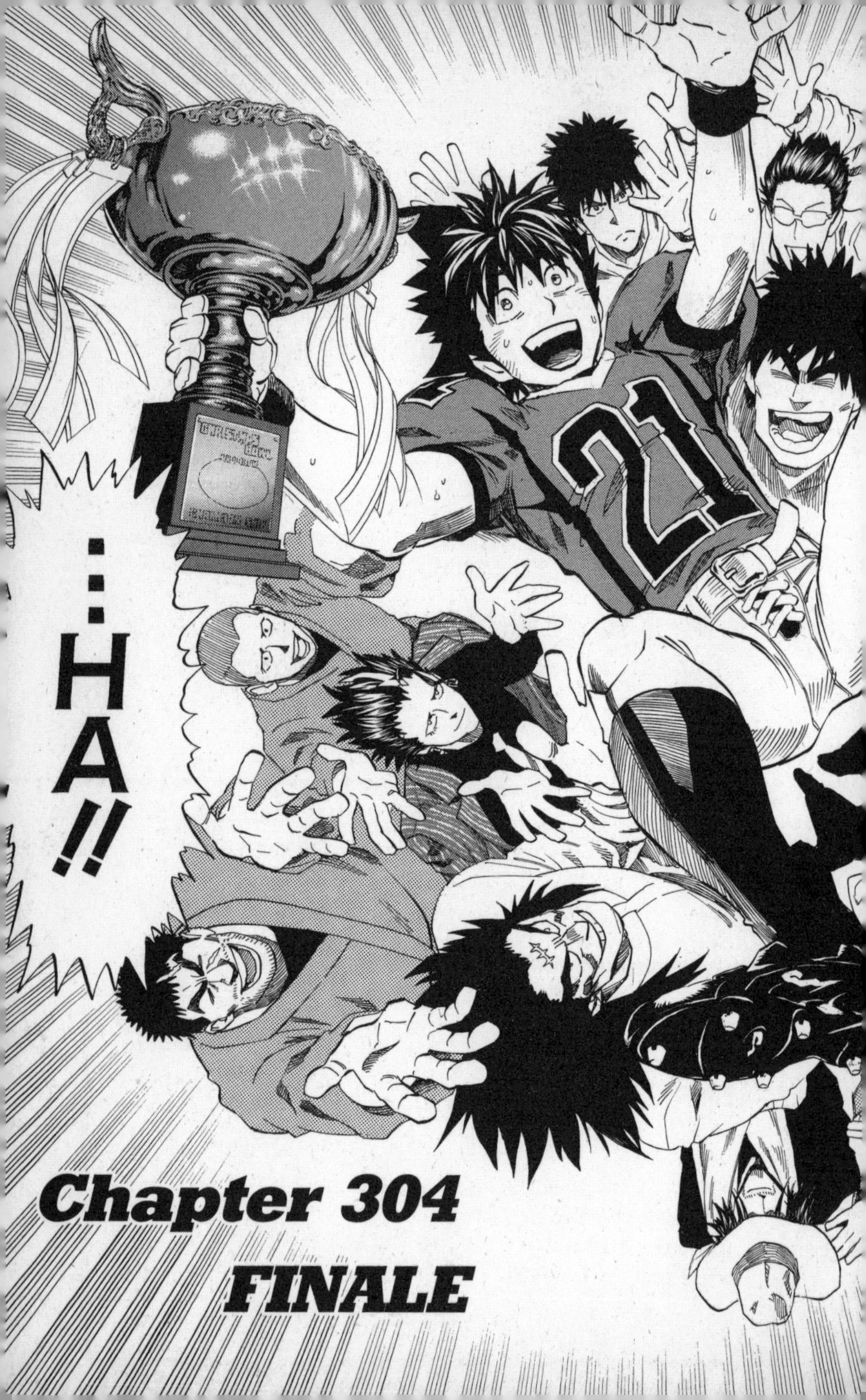
...HA!!

Chapter 304
FINALE

Investigation File #147

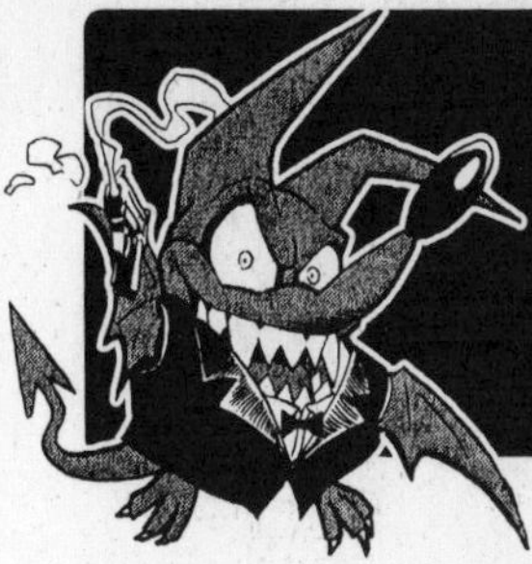

Why are Musashi and Mizumachi always digging in their ears? Have they got too much ear wax?

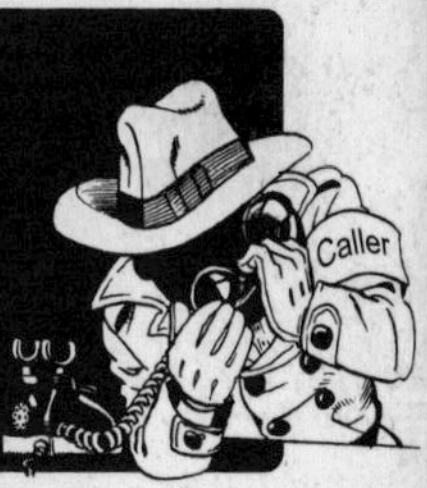
Caller

Caller name: Eyeshieldo in Okayama Prefecture

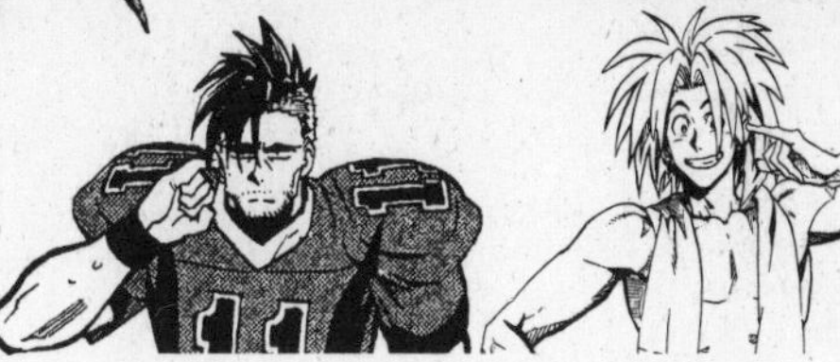

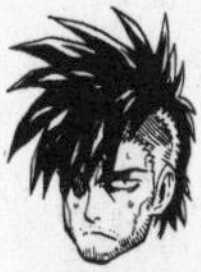

IT'S JUST A HABIT.

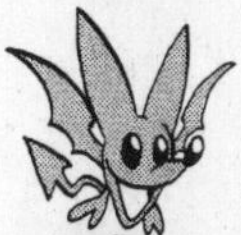

BOSS! I DID A PRECISE SCAN OF THEIR EAR CANALS, AND THEY DIDN'T REALLY HAVE MUCH EAR WAX BUILT UP!

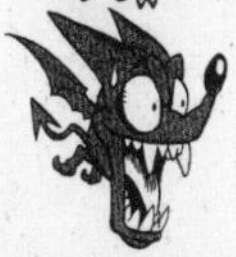

UM...THAT WASN'T REALLY NECESSARY...

Send your queries for Devil Bat 021 here!!

Devil Bat 021
Shonen Jump Advanced/Eyeshield 21
c/o VIZ Media, LLC
P.O. Box 77010
San Francisco, CA 94107

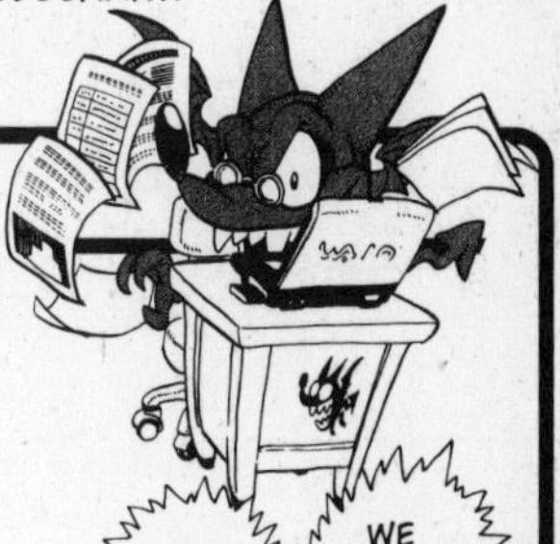

PLEASE BE PATIENT !!

WE CAN'T ANSWER EVERY QUERY ...

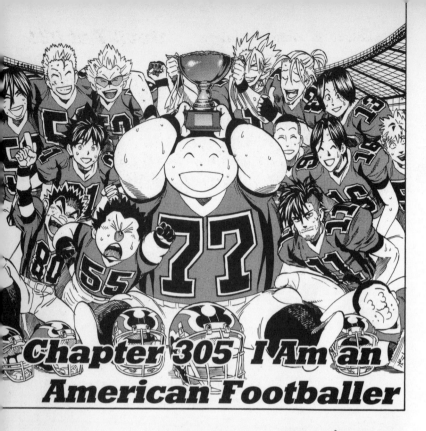

Chapter 305 I Am an American Footballer

ROAR

...

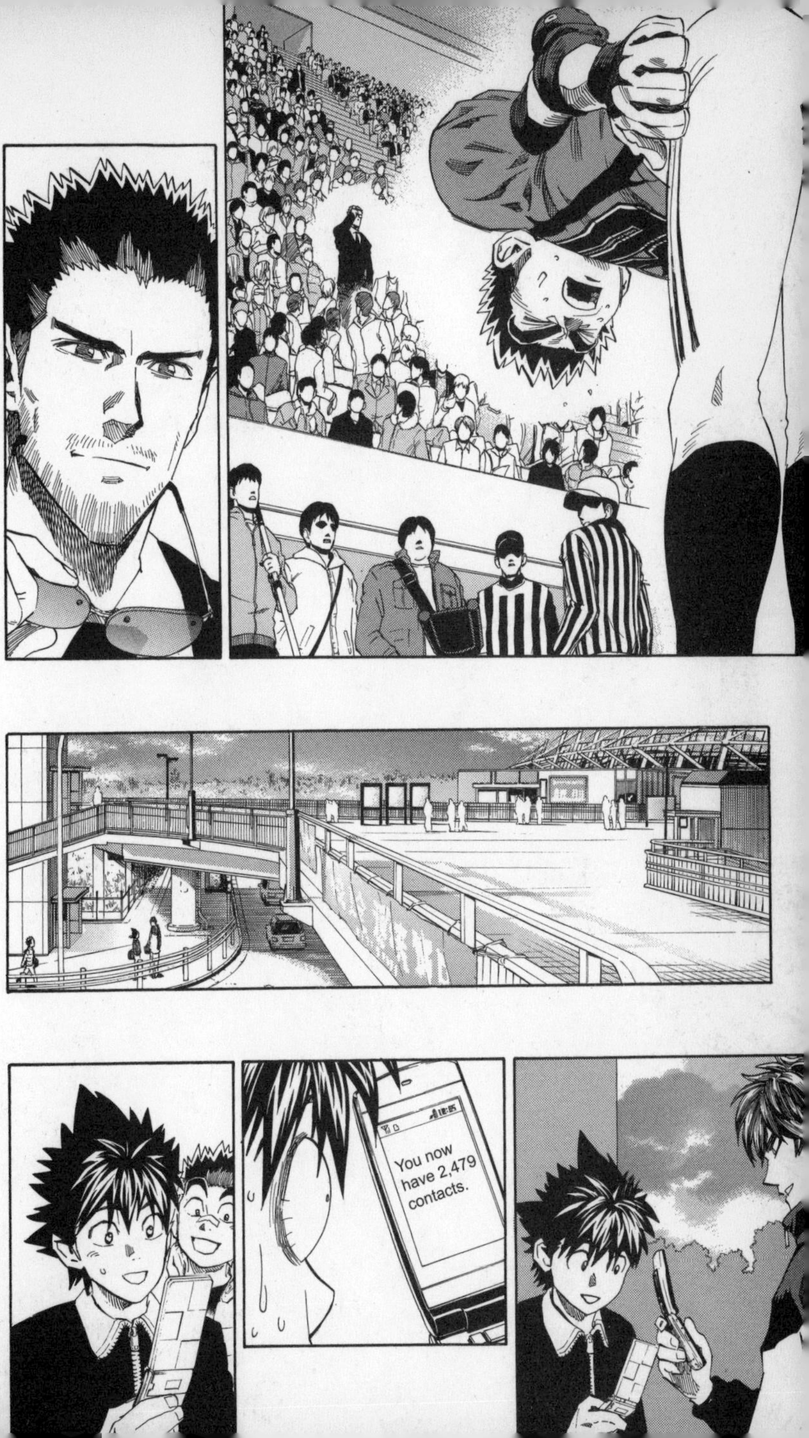
You now have 2,479 contacts.

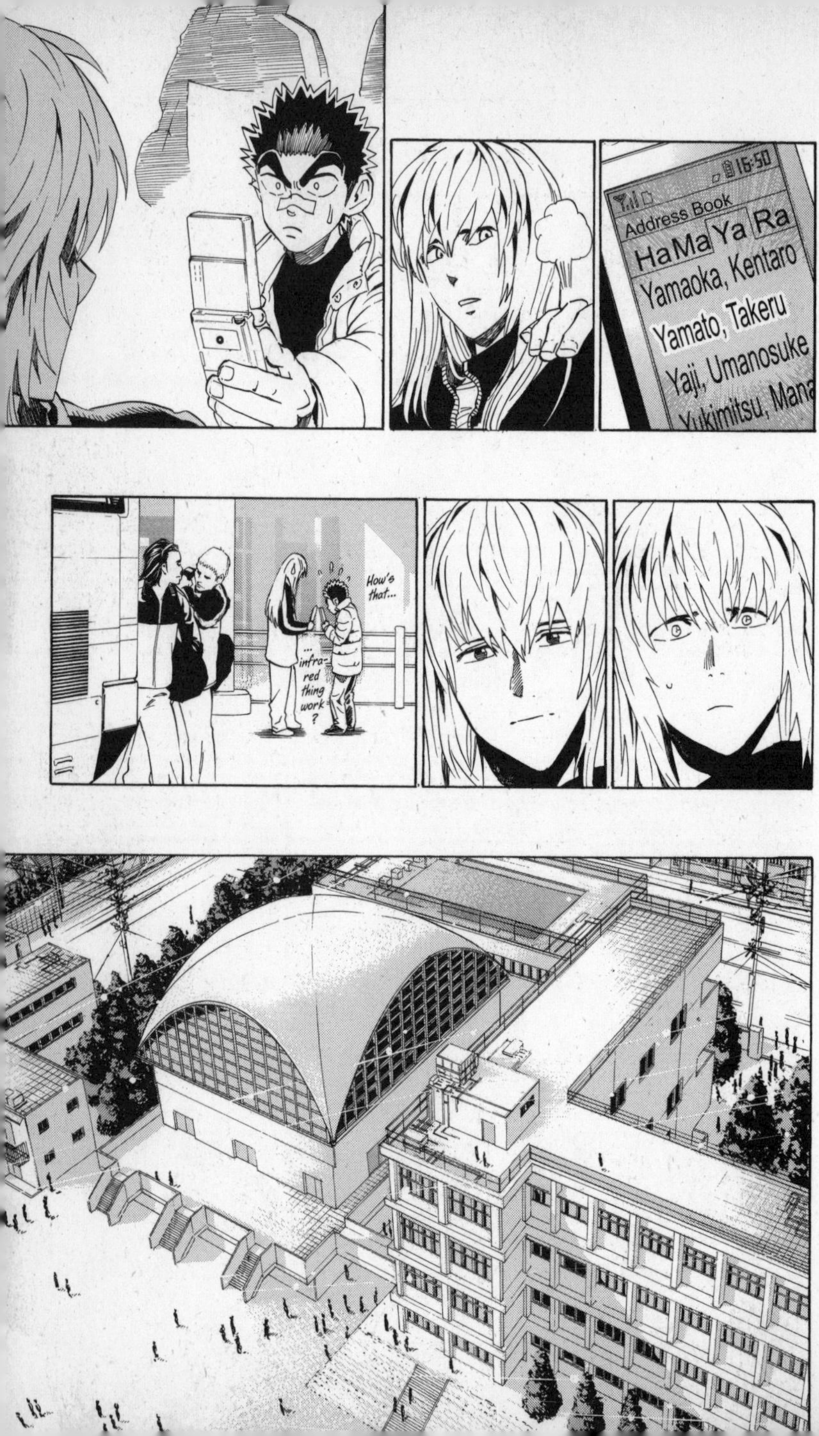
16:50
Address Book
HaMa Ya Ra
Yamaoka, Kentaro
Yamato, Takeru
Yaji, Umanosuke
Yukimitsu, Mana
How's that...
...infra-red thing work?

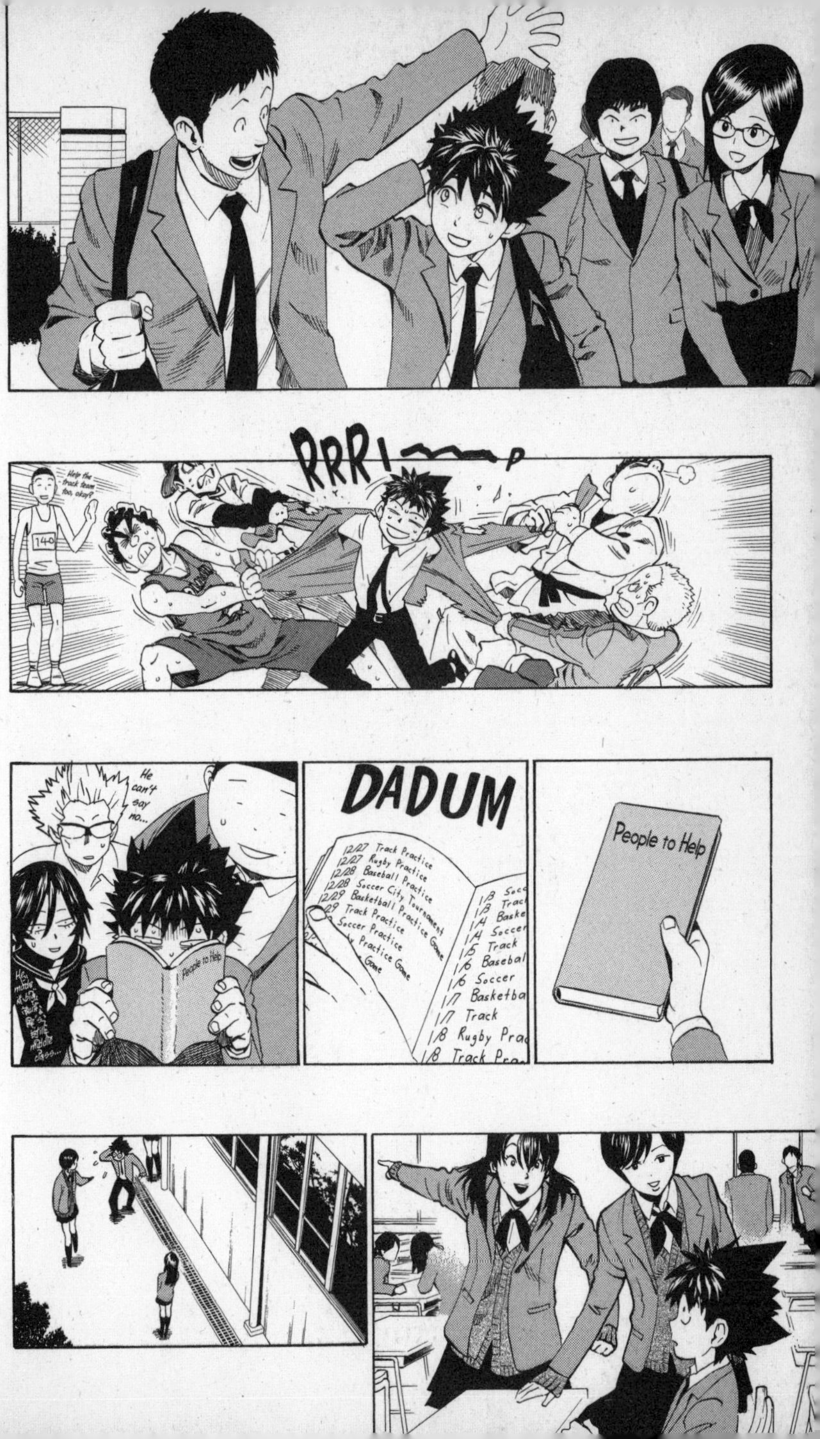

RRRI~~~P
Help the track team too, okay?
People to Help
DADUM
12/27 Track Practice
12/27 Rugby Practice
12/28 Baseball Practice
12/28 Soccer City Tournament
12/29 Basketball Practice Game
12/29 Track Practice
Soccer Practice
Practice Game
Game
1/3 Socc
1/3 Track
1/4 Baske
1/4 Soccer
1/5 Track
1/6 Basebal
1/6 Soccer
1/7 Basketba
1/7 Track
1/8 Rugby Prac
1/8 Track Pra
He can't say no...
People to Help

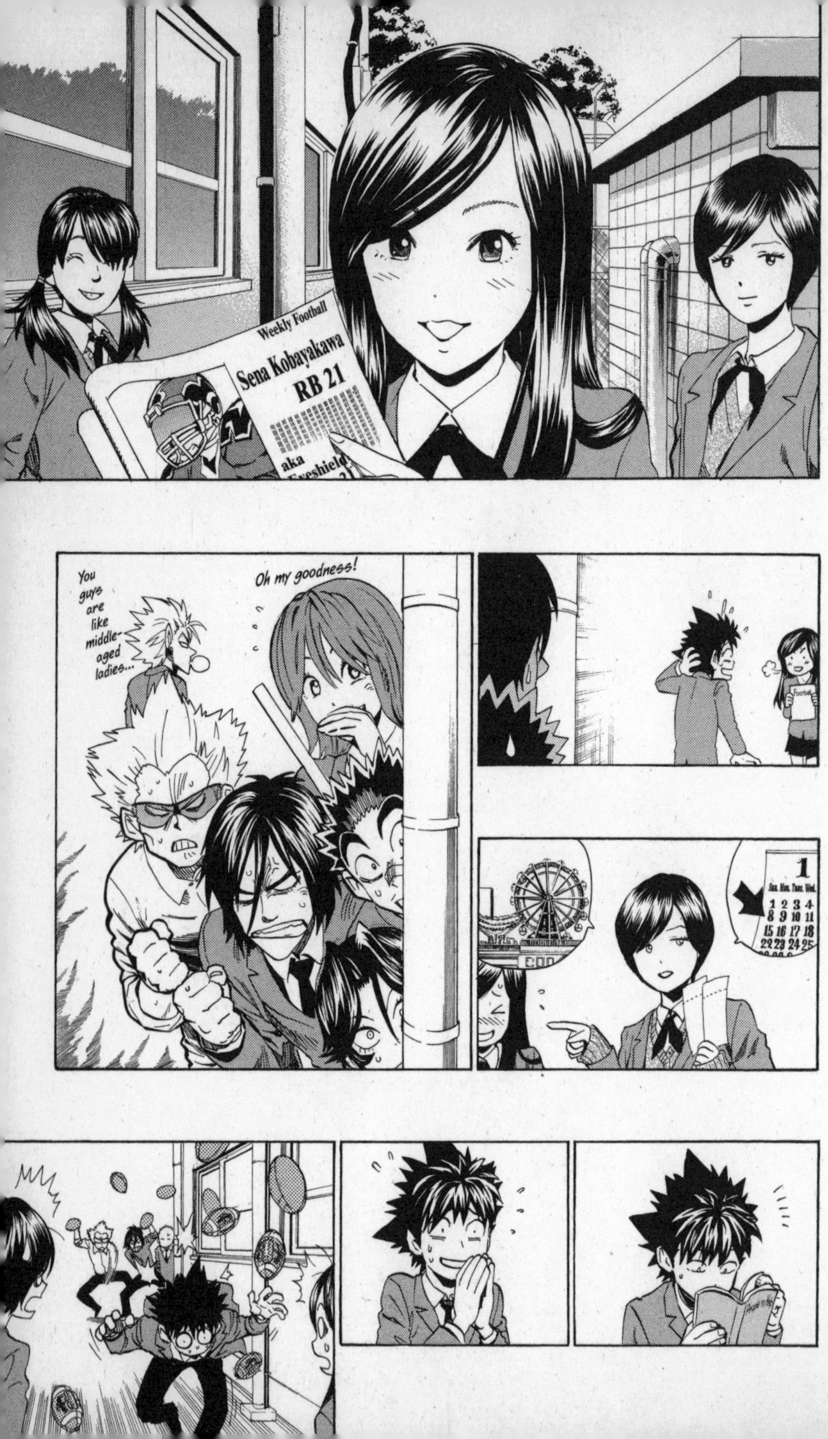
Weekly Football
Sena Kobayakawa
RB 21
aka
Football
1
Sun. Mon. Tues. Wed.
1 2 3 4
8 9 10 11
15 16 17 18
22 23 24 25
Oh my goodness!
You guys are like middle-aged ladies...

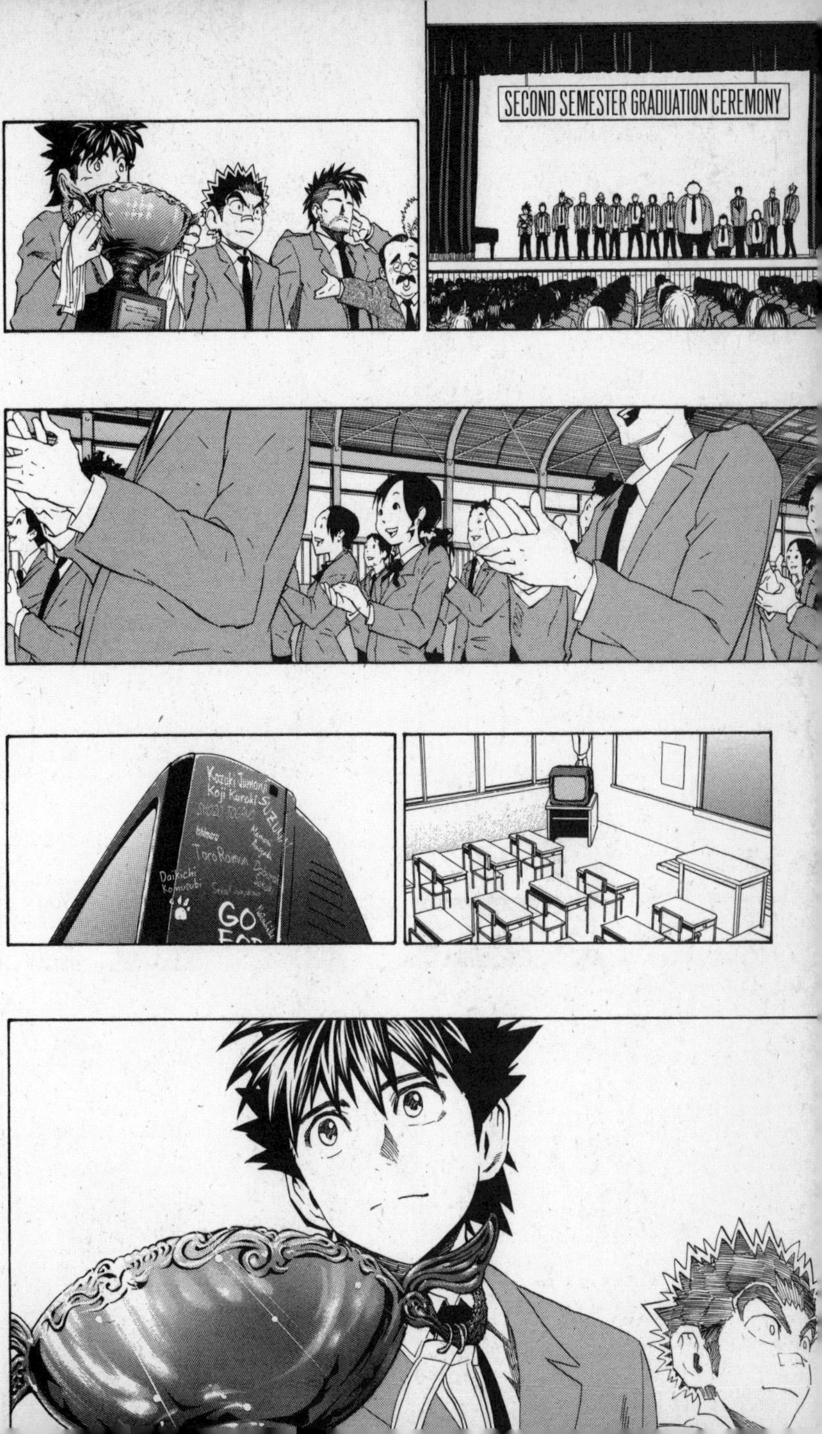
SECOND SEMESTER GRADUATION CEREMONY
Kazuki Jumonji
Koji Kuroki
SUZUNA
Taro Raimon
Daikichi Komusubi
GO

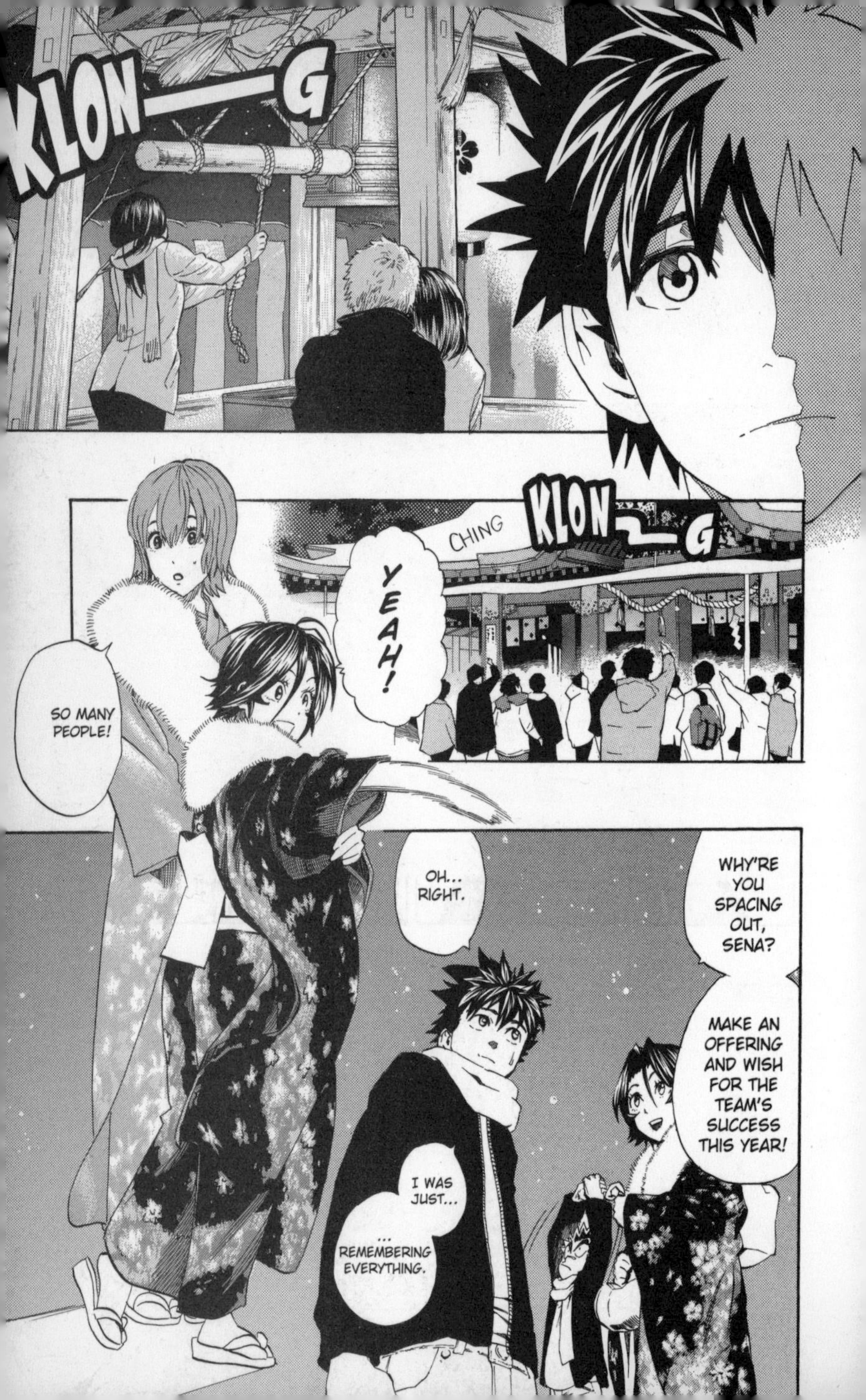
KLON——G
KLON~G
CHING
YEAH!
SO MANY PEOPLE!
WHY'RE YOU SPACING OUT, SENA?
MAKE AN OFFERING AND WISH FOR THE TEAM'S SUCCESS THIS YEAR!
OH... RIGHT.
I WAS JUST...
...REMEMBERING EVERYTHING.

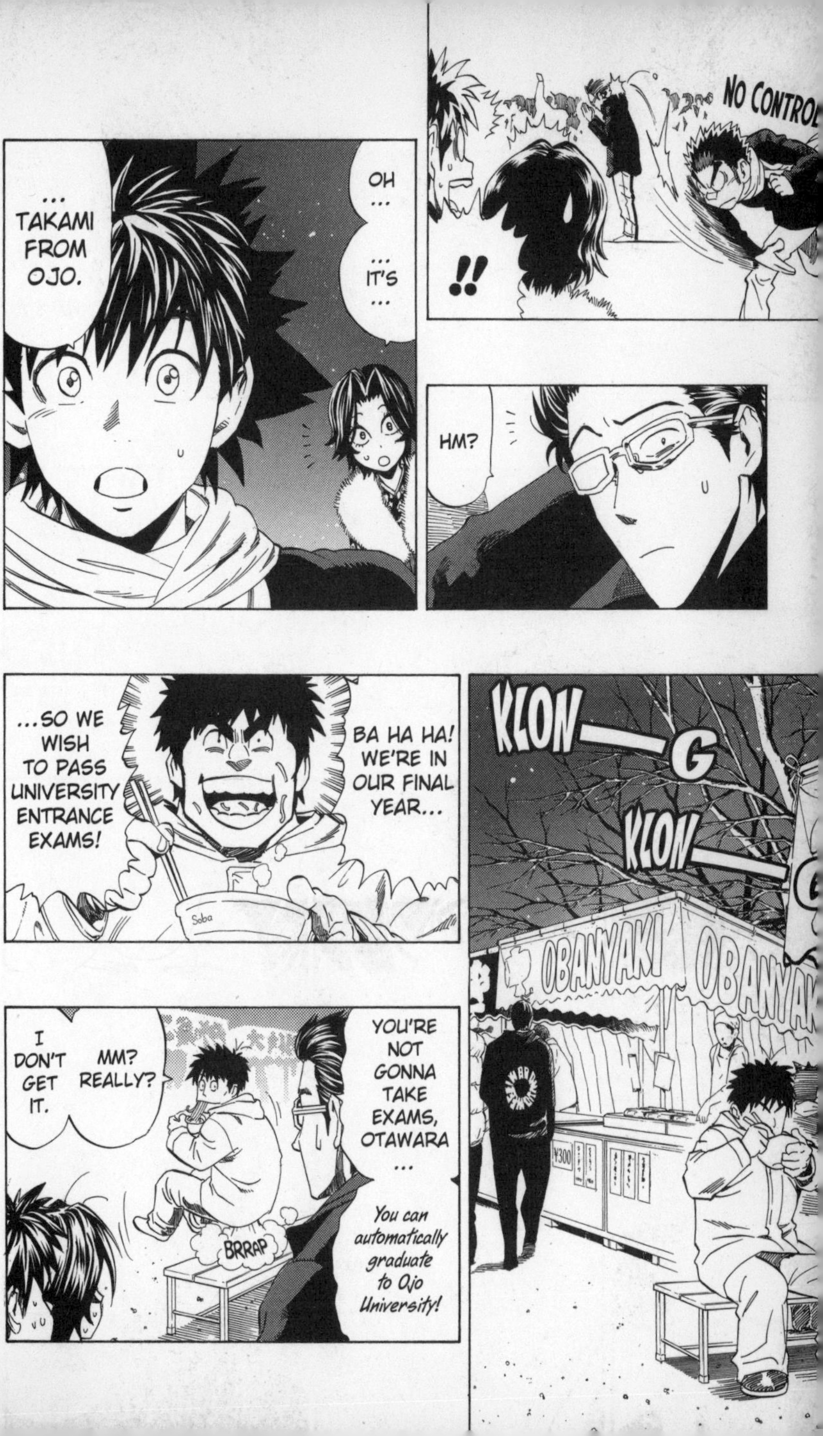
NO CONTROL
!!
HM?
OH ...
... IT'S ...
... TAKAMI FROM OJO.
KLON—G
KLON—G
OBANYAKI
OBANYAKI
¥300
BA HA HA! WE'RE IN OUR FINAL YEAR...
...SO WE WISH TO PASS UNIVERSITY ENTRANCE EXAMS!
Soba
YOU'RE NOT GONNA TAKE EXAMS, OTAWARA ...
You can automatically graduate to Ojo University!
MM? REALLY?
I DON'T GET IT.
BRRAP

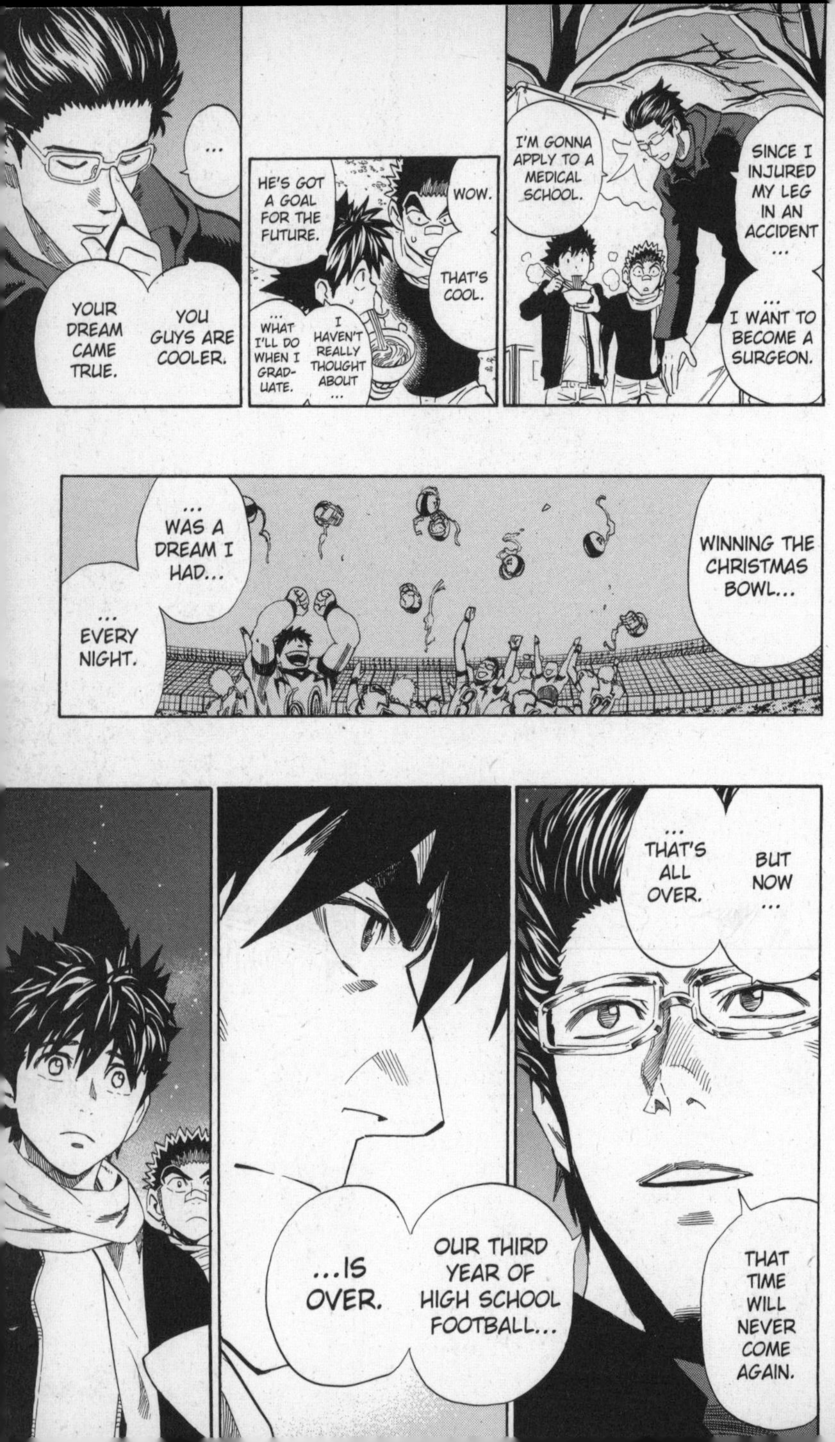
SINCE I INJURED MY LEG IN AN ACCIDENT...
...I WANT TO BECOME A SURGEON.
I'M GONNA APPLY TO A MEDICAL SCHOOL.
WOW.
THAT'S COOL.
HE'S GOT A GOAL FOR THE FUTURE.
I HAVEN'T REALLY THOUGHT ABOUT...
...WHAT I'LL DO WHEN I GRADUATE.
...
YOU GUYS ARE COOLER.
YOUR DREAM CAME TRUE.
WINNING THE CHRISTMAS BOWL...
...WAS A DREAM I HAD...
...EVERY NIGHT.
BUT NOW...
...THAT'S ALL OVER.
THAT TIME WILL NEVER COME AGAIN.
OUR THIRD YEAR OF HIGH SCHOOL FOOTBALL...
...IS OVER.

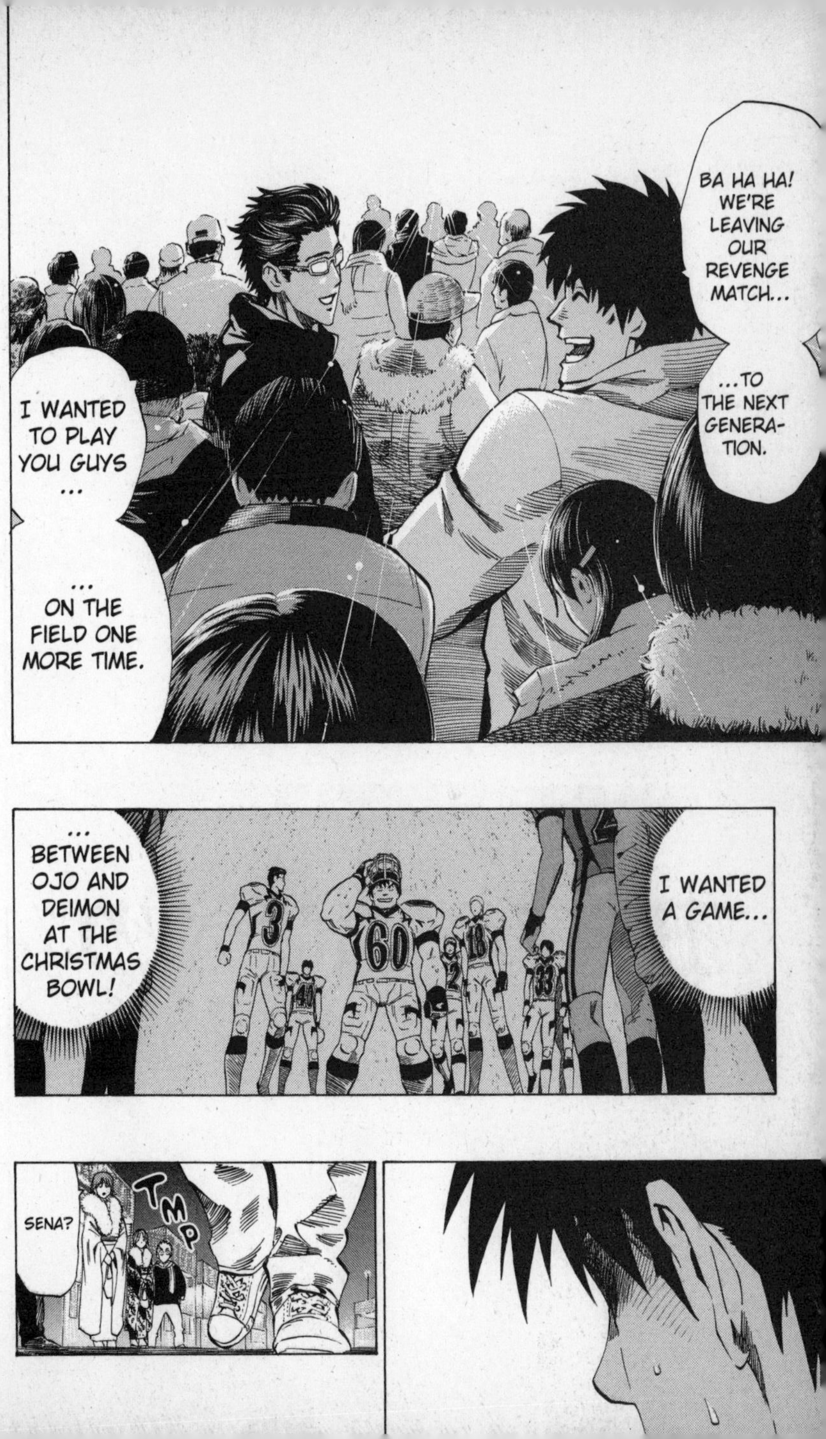
BA HA HA! WE'RE LEAVING OUR REVENGE MATCH...
...TO THE NEXT GENERATION.
I WANTED TO PLAY YOU GUYS ...
... ON THE FIELD ONE MORE TIME.
I WANTED A GAME...
... BETWEEN OJO AND DEIMON AT THE CHRISTMAS BOWL!
TMP
SENA?

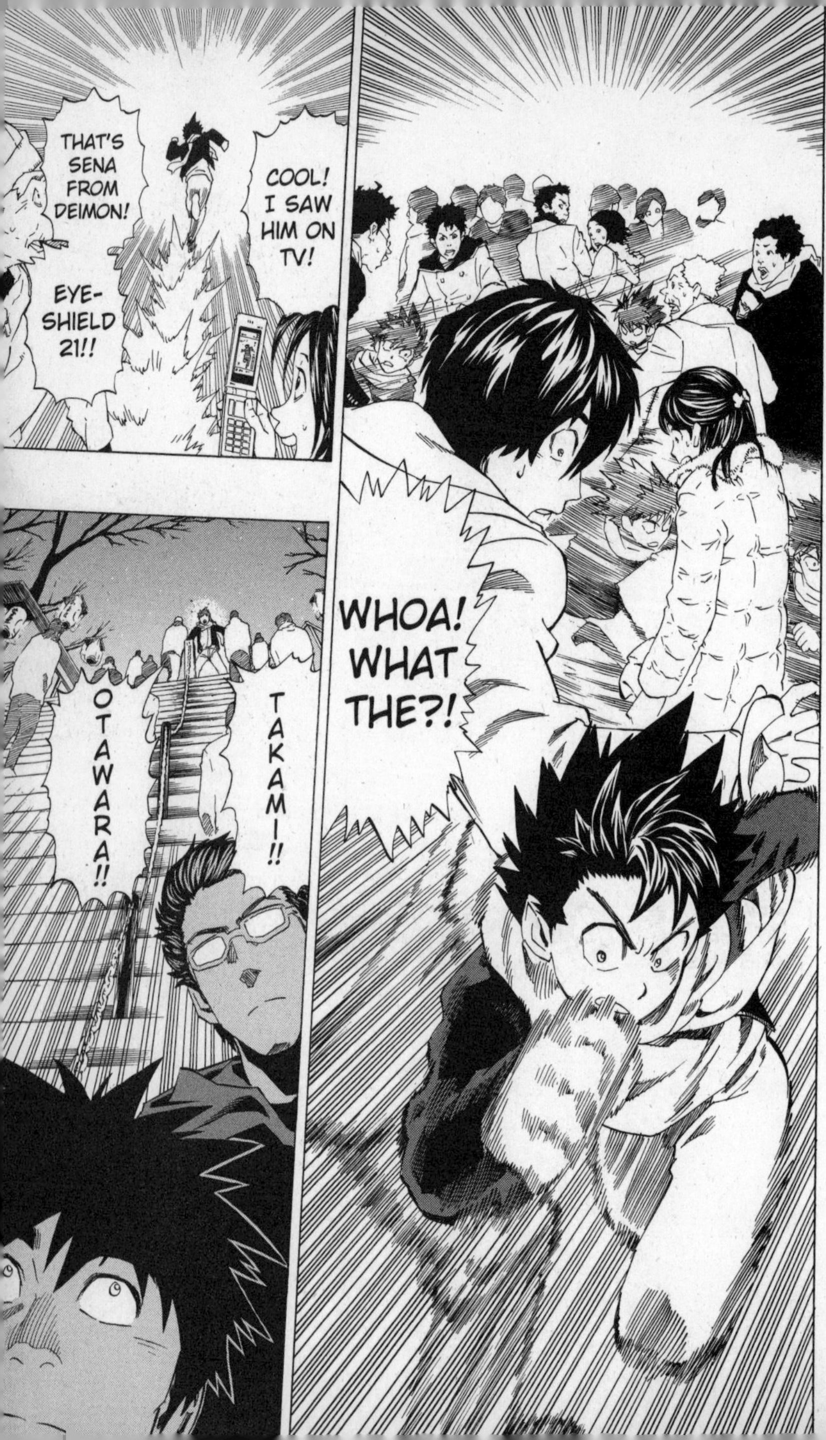
WHOA! WHAT THE?!
COOL! I SAW HIM ON TV!
THAT'S SENA FROM DEIMON!
EYE-SHIELD 21!!
TAKAMI!!
OTAWARA!!

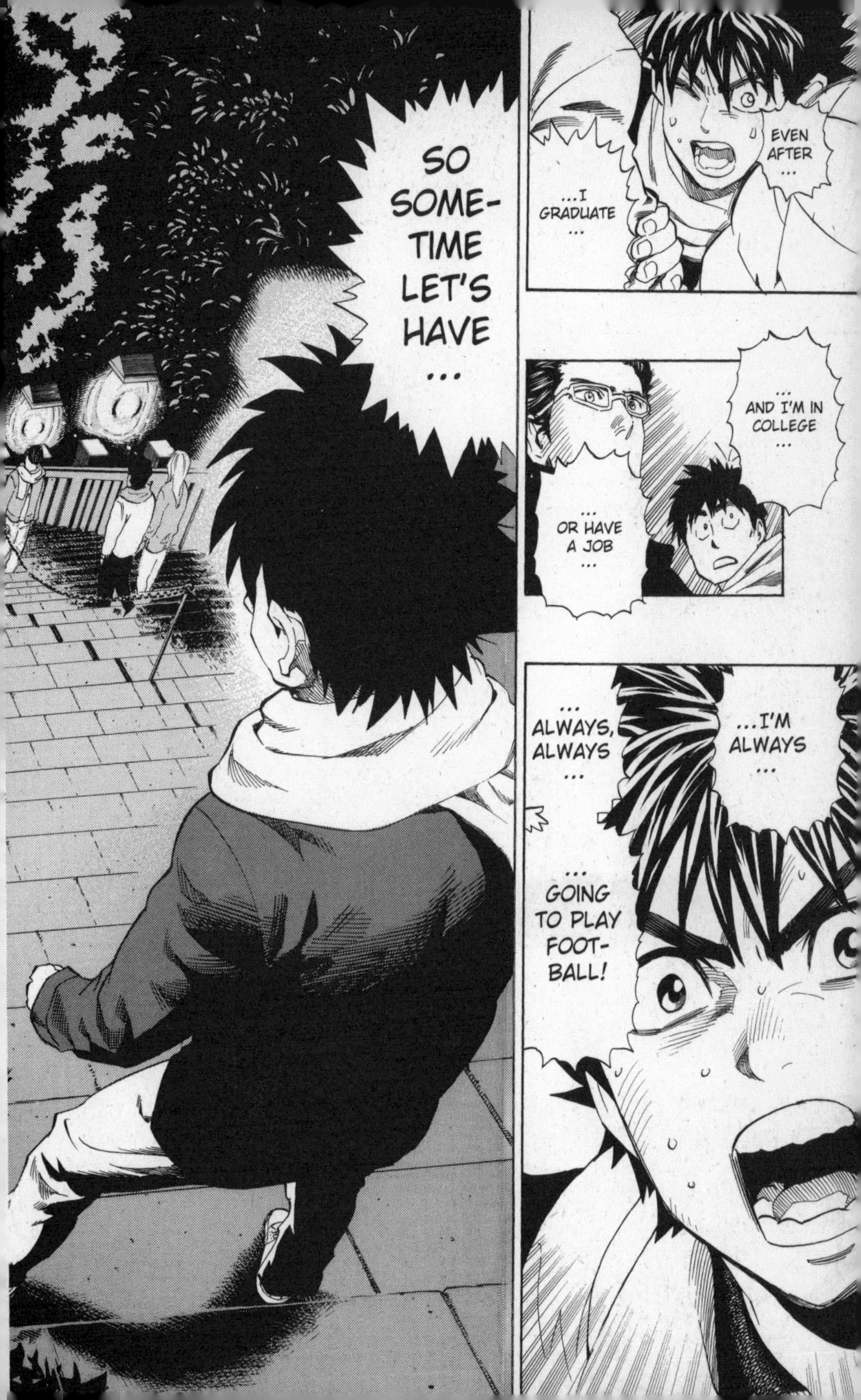
EVEN AFTER ...
...I GRADUATE ...
... AND I'M IN COLLEGE ...
... OR HAVE A JOB ...
...I'M ALWAYS ...
... ALWAYS, ALWAYS ...
... GOING TO PLAY FOOT-BALL!
SO SOME-TIME LET'S HAVE ...

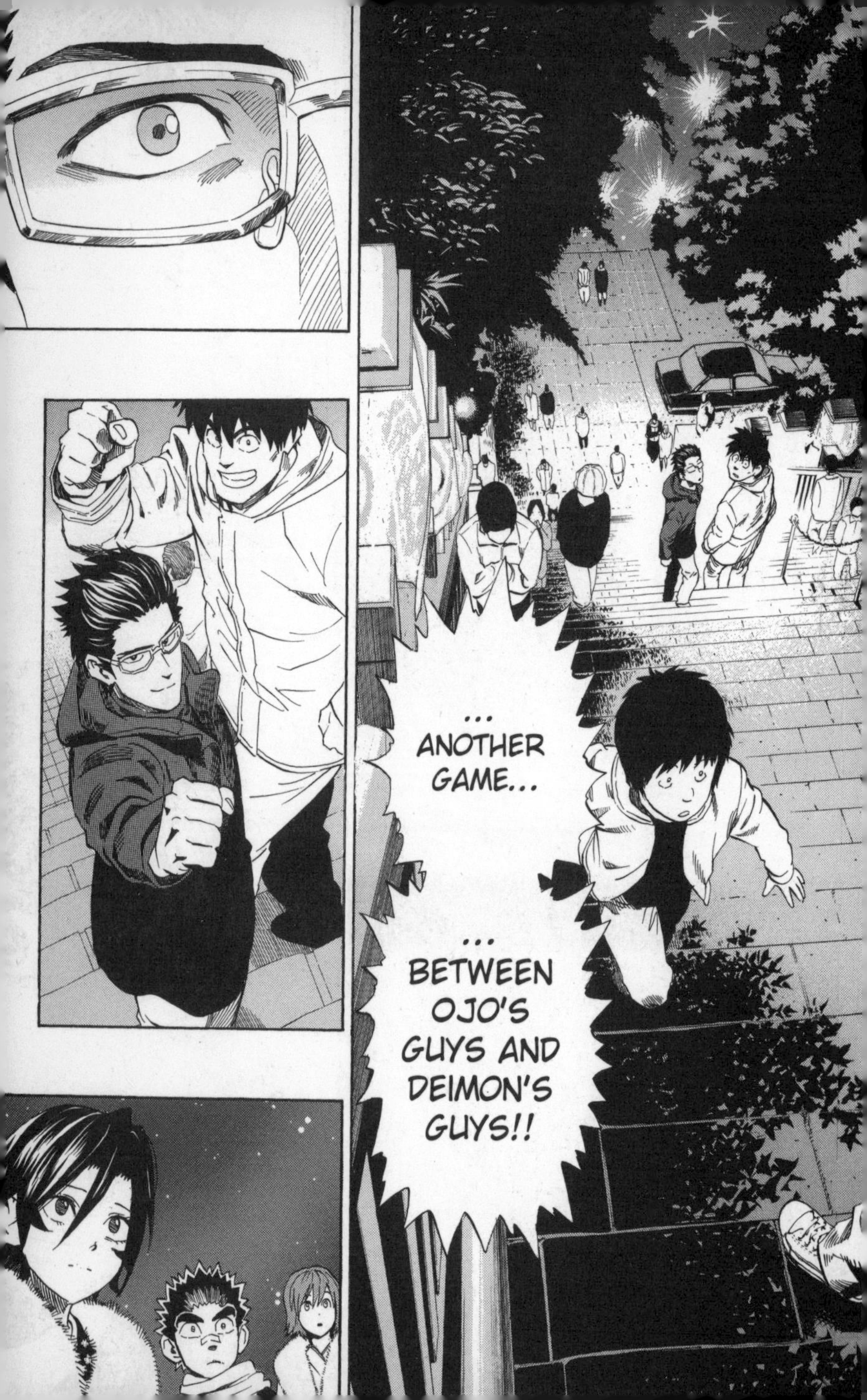
... ANOTHER GAME...
... BETWEEN OJO'S GUYS AND DEIMON'S GUYS!!

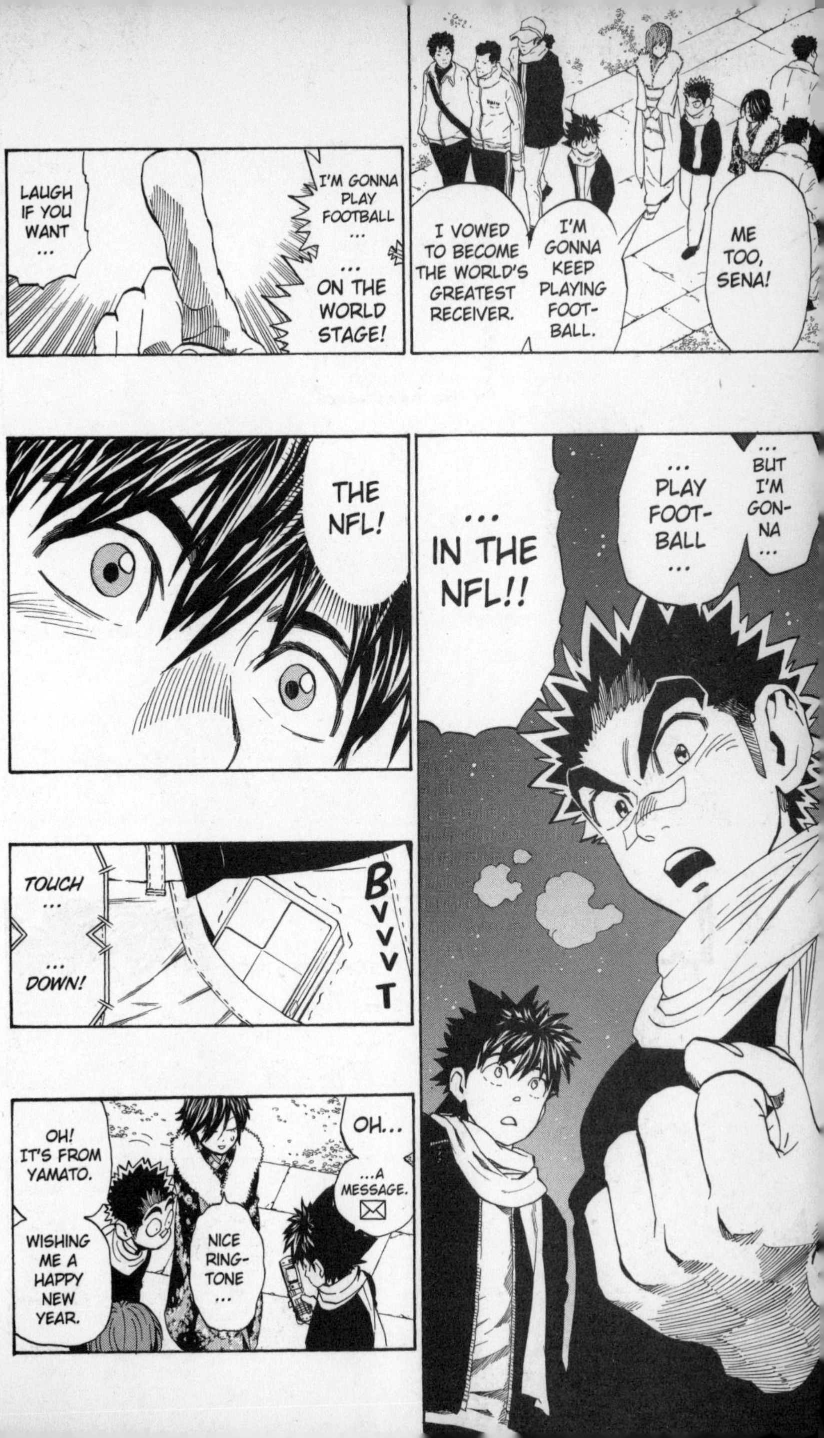
ME TOO, SENA!
I'M GONNA KEEP PLAYING FOOT-BALL.
I VOWED TO BECOME THE WORLD'S GREATEST RECEIVER.
I'M GONNA PLAY FOOTBALL ...
... ON THE WORLD STAGE!
LAUGH IF YOU WANT ...
... BUT I'M GON-NA ...
... PLAY FOOT-BALL ...
... IN THE NFL!!
THE NFL!
BVVVT
TOUCH ...
... DOWN!
OH...
...A MESSAGE.
NICE RING-TONE ...
OH! IT'S FROM YAMATO.
WISHING ME A HAPPY NEW YEAR.

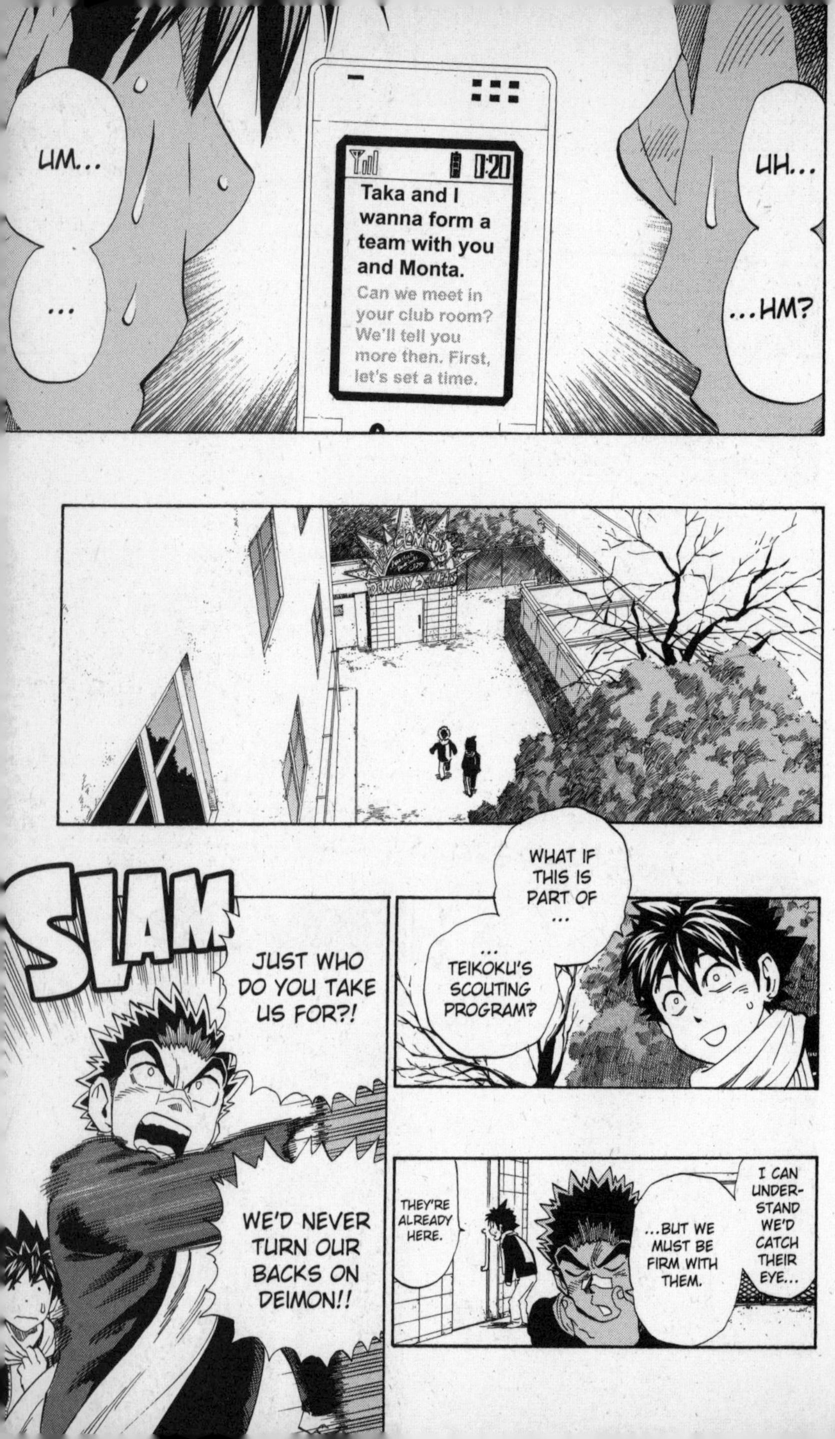
UH...
...HM?
Taka and I wanna form a team with you and Monta.
Can we meet in your club room? We'll tell you more then. First, let's set a time.
0:20
UM...
...
WHAT IF THIS IS PART OF ...
... TEIKOKU'S SCOUTING PROGRAM?
I CAN UNDERSTAND WE'D CATCH THEIR EYE...
...BUT WE MUST BE FIRM WITH THEM.
THEY'RE ALREADY HERE.
SLAM
JUST WHO DO YOU TAKE US FOR?!
WE'D NEVER TURN OUR BACKS ON DEIMON!!

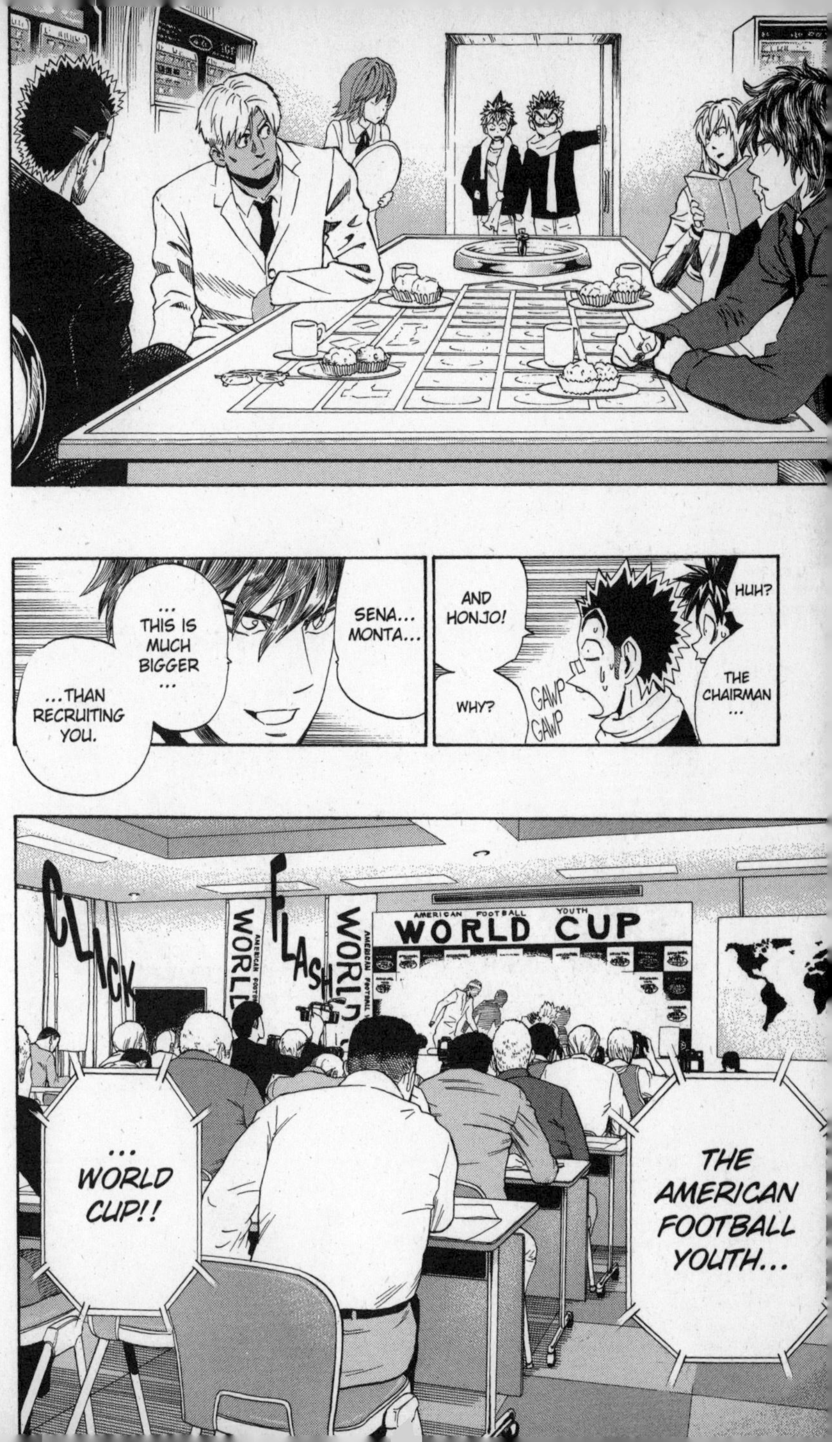
HUH?
THE CHAIRMAN...
AND HONJO!
WHY?
GAWP GAWP
SENA... MONTA...
... THIS IS MUCH BIGGER ...
...THAN RECRUITING YOU.
AMERICAN FOOTBALL YOUTH
WORLD CUP
CLICK
FLASH
THE AMERICAN FOOTBALL YOUTH...
... WORLD CUP!!

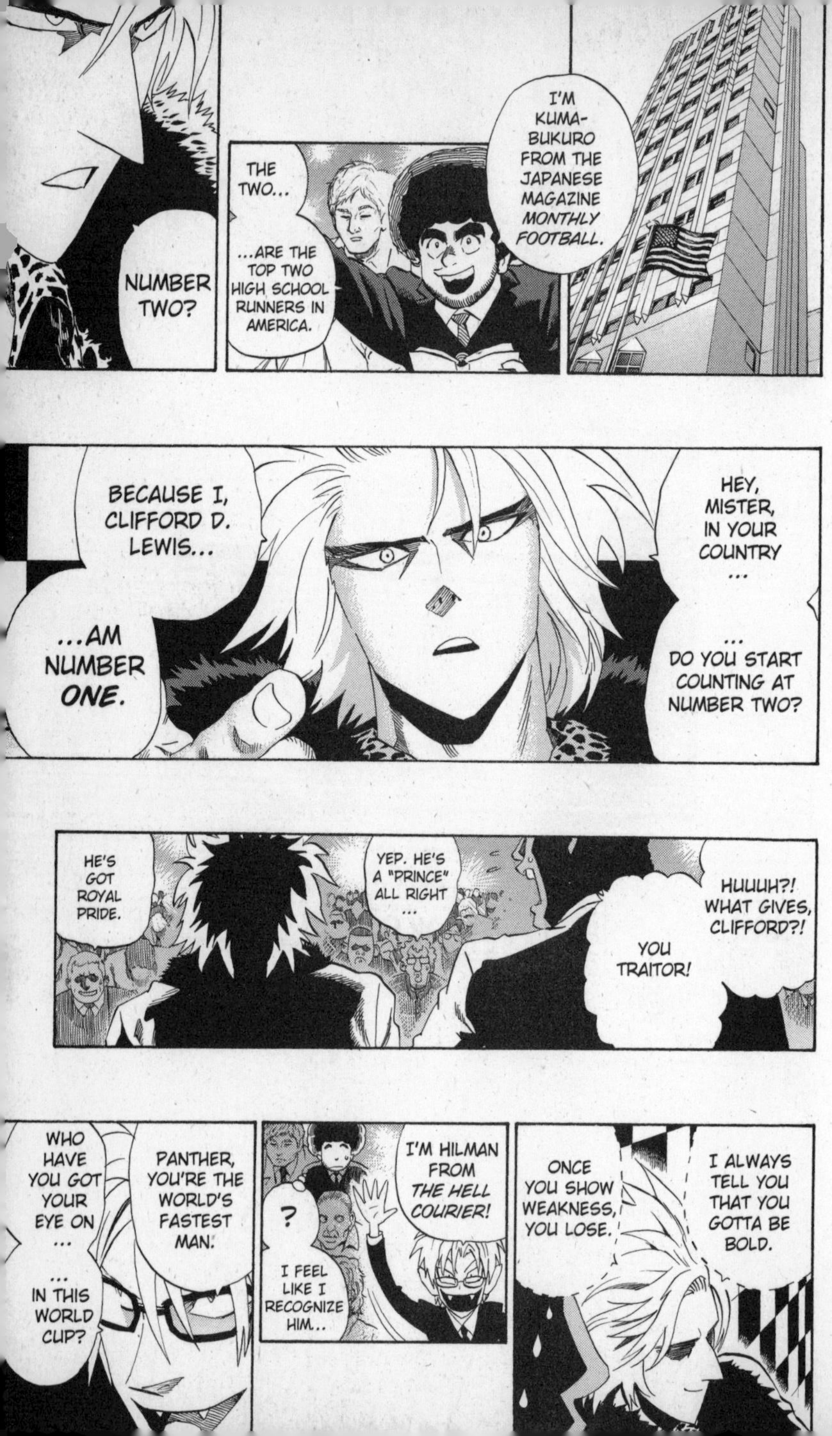
I'M KUMA-BUKURO FROM THE JAPANESE MAGAZINE MONTHLY FOOTBALL.
THE TWO...
...ARE THE TOP TWO HIGH SCHOOL RUNNERS IN AMERICA.
NUMBER TWO?
HEY, MISTER, IN YOUR COUNTRY ...
... DO YOU START COUNTING AT NUMBER TWO?
BECAUSE I, CLIFFORD D. LEWIS...
...AM NUMBER ONE.
HUUUH?! WHAT GIVES, CLIFFORD?!
YOU TRAITOR!
YEP. HE'S A "PRINCE" ALL RIGHT ...
HE'S GOT ROYAL PRIDE.
I ALWAYS TELL YOU THAT YOU GOTTA BE BOLD.
ONCE YOU SHOW WEAKNESS, YOU LOSE.
I'M HILMAN FROM THE HELL COURIER!
?
I FEEL LIKE I RECOGNIZE HIM...
PANTHER, YOU'RE THE WORLD'S FASTEST MAN.
WHO HAVE YOU GOT YOUR EYE ON ...
... IN THIS WORLD CUP?

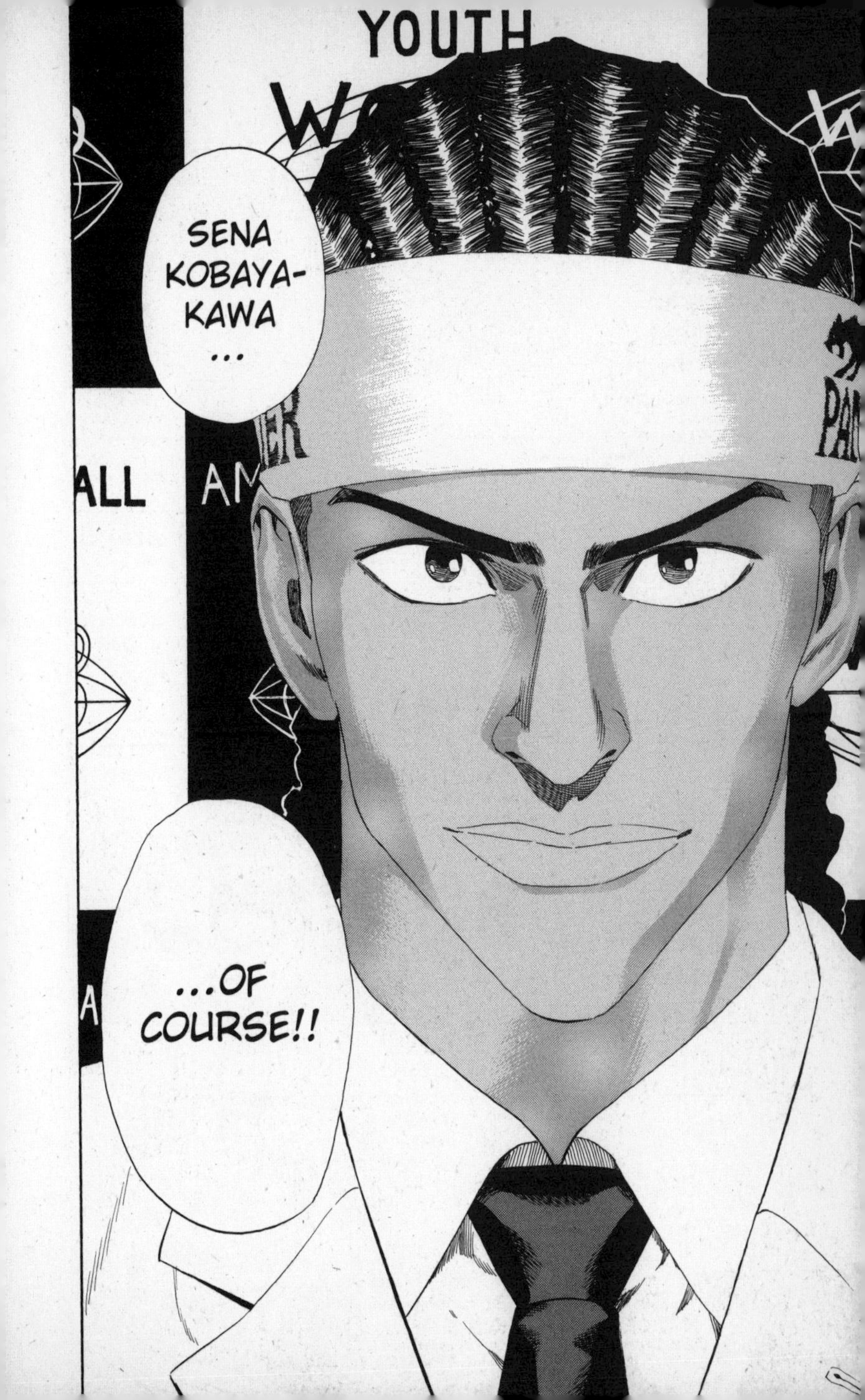
YOUTH
SENA KOBAYA-KAWA ...
ALL
...OF COURSE!!

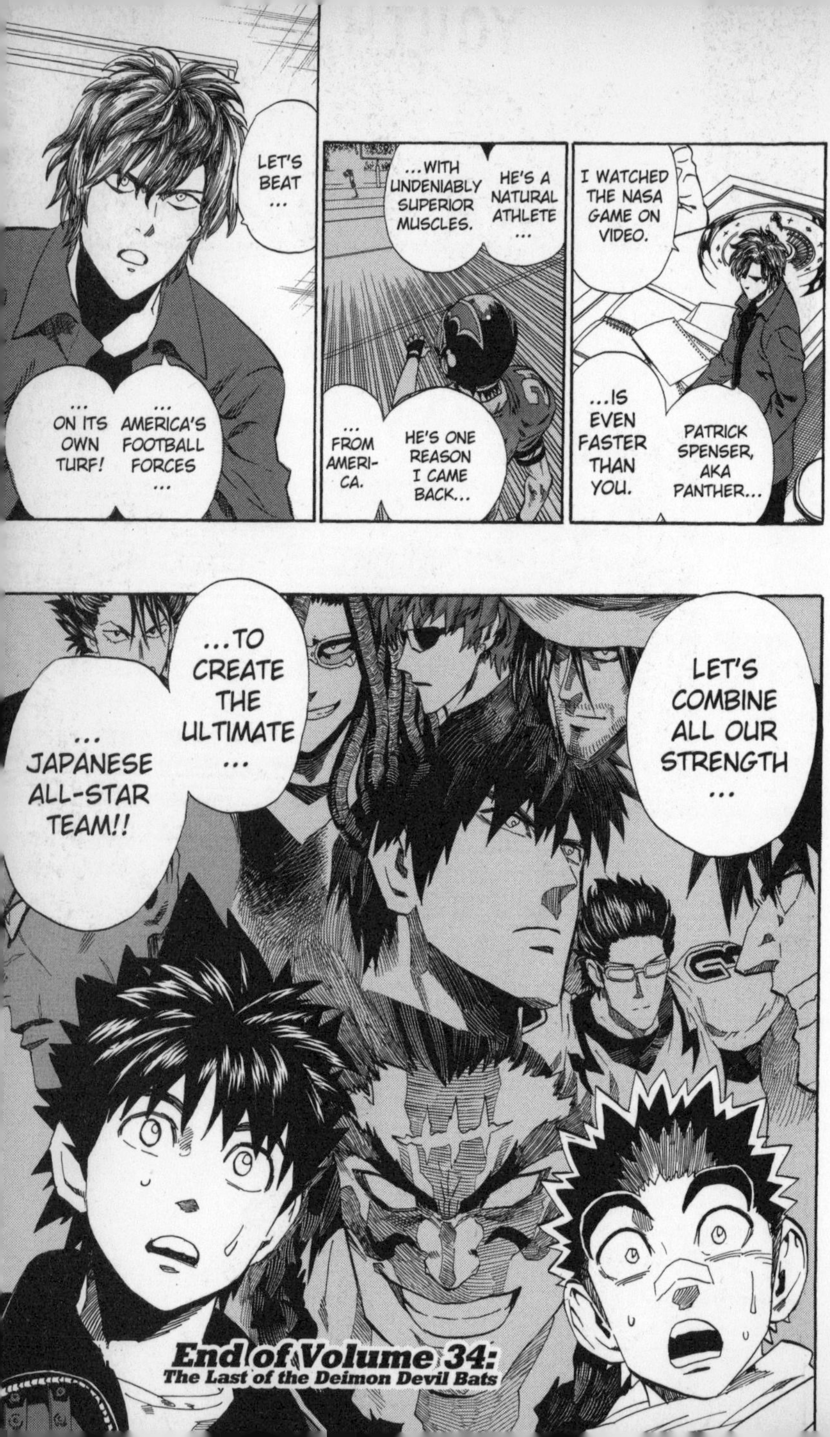
I WATCHED THE NASA GAME ON VIDEO.
PATRICK SPENSER, AKA PANTHER...
...IS EVEN FASTER THAN YOU.
HE'S A NATURAL ATHLETE ...
...WITH UNDENIABLY SUPERIOR MUSCLES.
HE'S ONE REASON I CAME BACK...
... FROM AMERI-CA.
LET'S BEAT ...
... AMERICA'S FOOTBALL FORCES ...
... ON ITS OWN TURF!
LET'S COMBINE ALL OUR STRENGTH ...
...TO CREATE THE ULTIMATE ...
... JAPANESE ALL-STAR TEAM!!

End of Volume 34:
The Last of the Deimon Devil Bats

Sena Kobayakawa
Super Hard Sports Club Helper Record

BASEBALL

GOOD

He jumped over the catcher with the *Devil Bat Dive* and scored!

BAD

He focused on bunting so he could make use of his speed and rush to first base, but he was too scared of the ball and *struck out*.

ATHLETICS

GOOD

As the runner taking over for Ishimaru in a relay, he overtook two other runners!

BAD

Used to dodging defenders, he broke past the next person on his own team with a splendid Devil Light Hurricane!

BASKETBALL

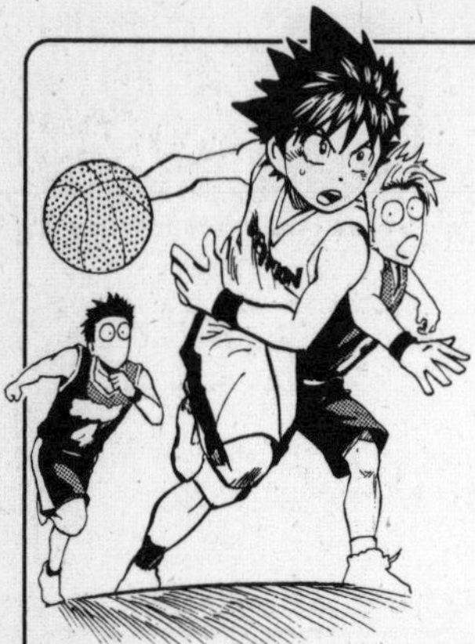

GOOD

He drove to the basket at lightspeed and no one could catch up!

BAD

He can't dribble, so he always got called for traveling. (If you don't know what traveling is, ask your dad or a friend who is in basketball club!)

Soccer

GOOD

He drove to the goal at lightspeed and no one could catch up!

BAD

No one could catch him, so he always got called offside. (If you don't know what being offside is, ask your dad or a friend who is in soccer club!)

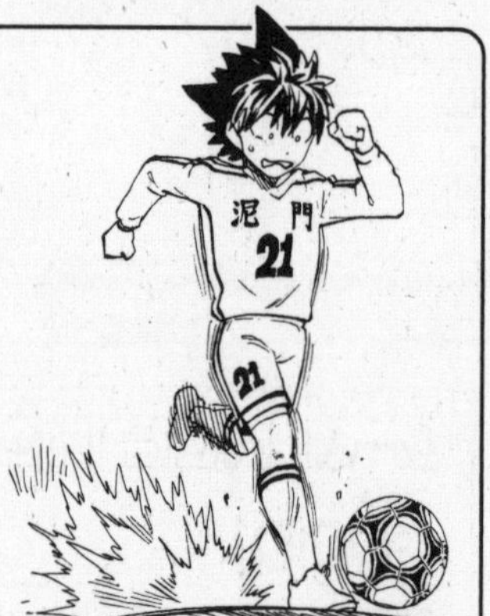
泥門
21
21

JERSEY: DEIMON

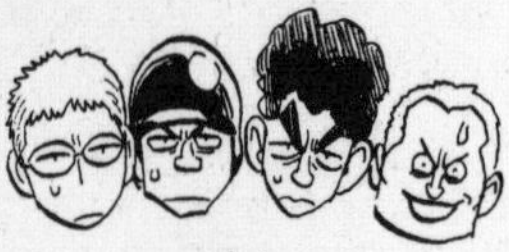

WE LEARNED THAT OUTSIDE OF FOOTBALL HE'S SURPRISINGLY UNHELPFUL...

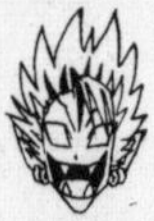

HEH HEH HEH! GOOD THING THEY LET YOU OFF THE HOOK, HUH, DAMN PIPSQUEAK?

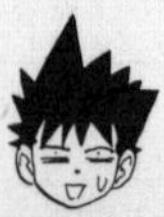

I'M TIRED...

New Year's Offerings and Wishes

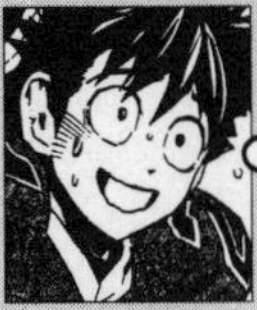

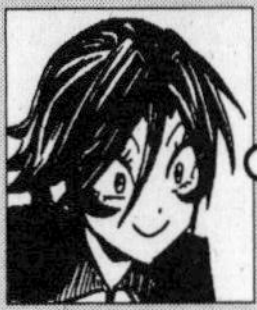

¥10

PLEASE LET THE DEIMON DEVIL BATS
WIN THE CHAMPIONSHIP AGAIN THIS YEAR!

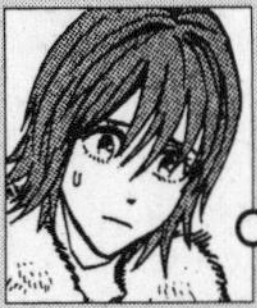

¥100

IF A CERTAIN SOMEONE SAYS,
"WE CAN WIN IT ALL AGAIN! TIME FOR MORE HELLISH TRAINING! HEH HEH HEH!"
I WON'T LET HIM GET AWAY WITH
UNREASONABLE TRAINING!

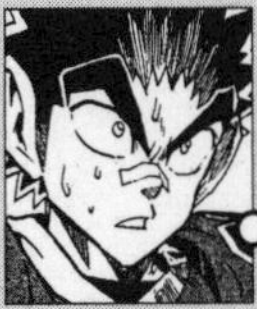

¥5

PLEASE LET ME BECOME THE BEST RECEIVER
IN THE WORLD!
NO, I WON'T RELY ON THE GODS FOR THAT!
I'LL EARN IT MYSELF!
BUT I DO HOPE THAT MAMORI AND I...

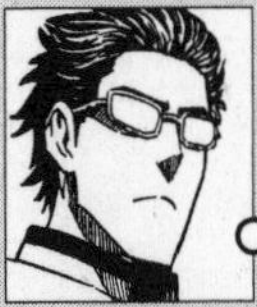

¥500

I PRAY THAT I PASS MY UNIVERSITY ENTRANCE
EXAMS. AND FOR OJO'S SUCCESS AFTER WE
GRADUATE.

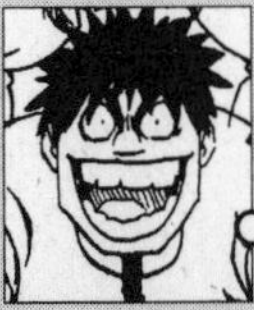

¥1

I JUST HOPE LOTSA GOOD STUFF HAPPENS.

FIRST DREAM OF THE NEW YEAR

One Fuji! Two Takas! Three Eggplants! What a lucky dream!

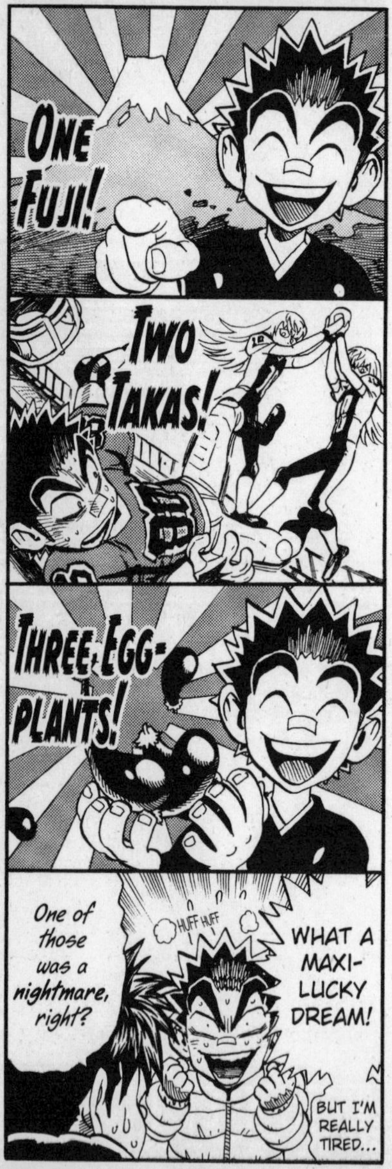

ONE FUJI!
TWO TAKAS!
THREE EGG-PLANTS!
HUFF HUFF
WHAT A MAXI-LUCKY DREAM!
One of those was a nightmare, right?
BUT I'M REALLY TIRED...

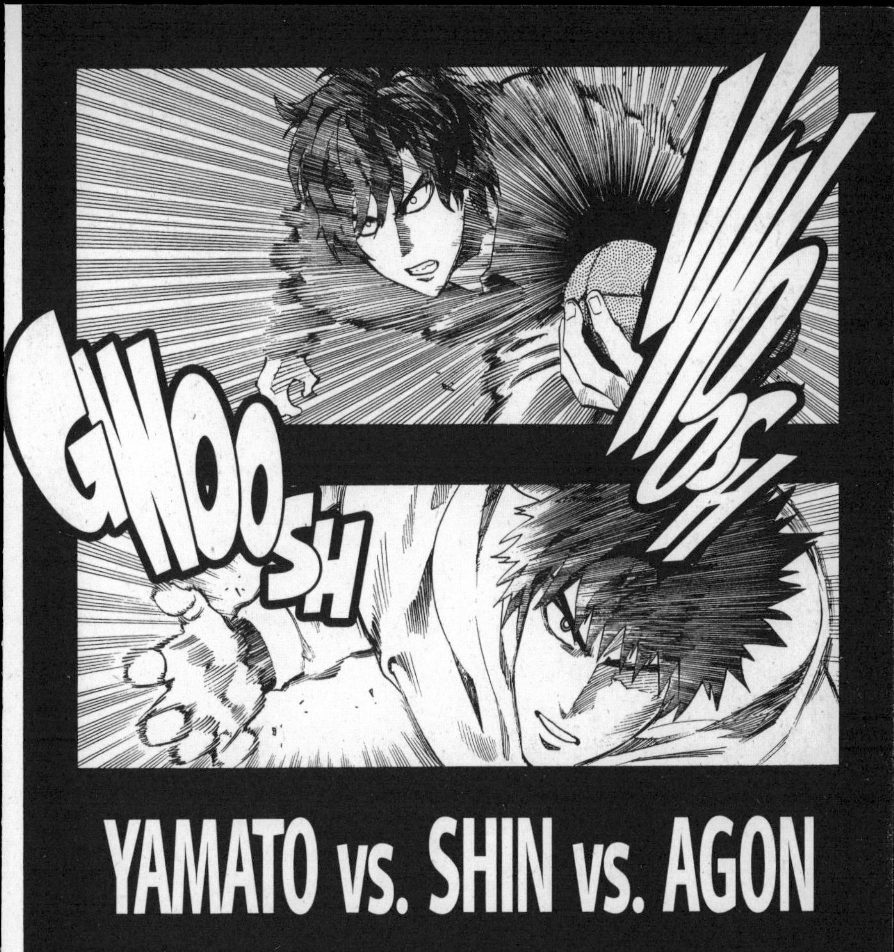
WHOOSH!!
GWOOSH

YAMATO vs. SHIN vs. AGON

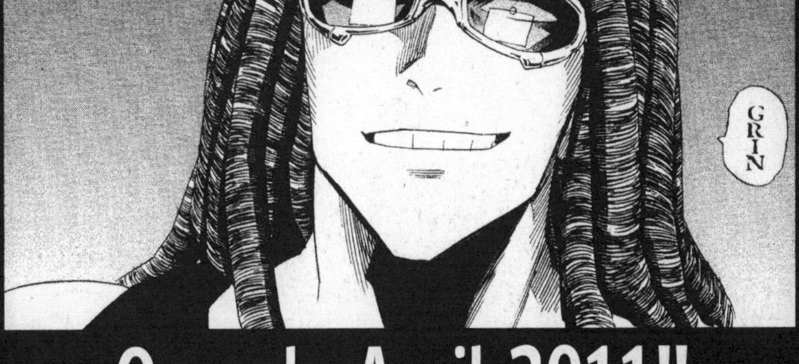
GRIN

On sale April 2011!!

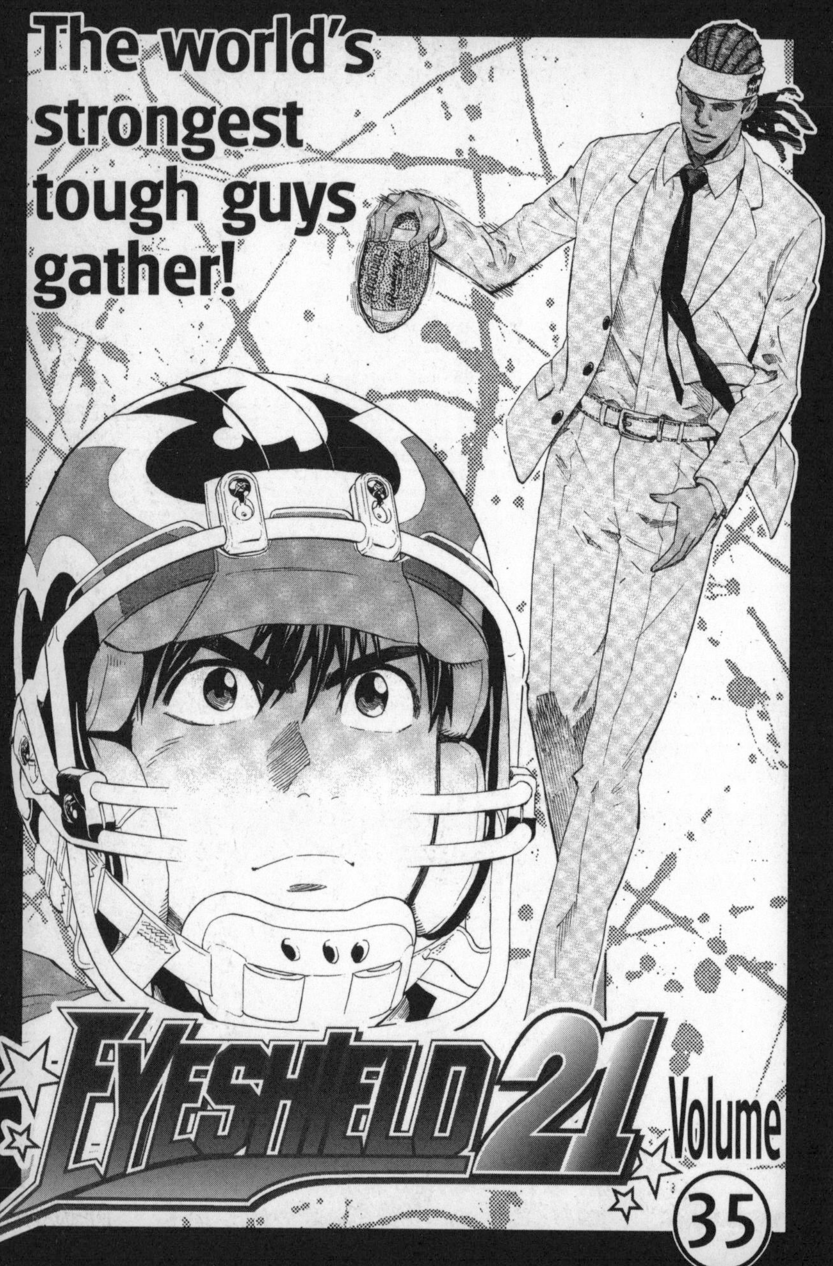
The world's strongest tough guys gather!
EYESHIELD 21
Volume
35

Eyeshield 21 Vol. 34 Staff

Original story by Riichiro Inagaki
Art by Yusuke Murata

Village Studio

Yuichi Itakura
Yukinori Kawaguchi
Yuya Abe
Kei Nishiyama
Kentaro Kurimoto
Sho Miyokawa
Kinichi Yamada
Shoji Morimoto
Daisuke Oikawa
Shunpei Soyama
Yuya Ogura

Kome Studio

Yusuke Kuji